EMBED

The blast strips the illusion of peace from the fields in an instant and automatic gunfire starts to crackle around the reporter. He's 40 but vaults like a teenage gymnast into an irrigation ditch and presses himself to the earth as the Danish troops pinpoint the source of the attack. Someone shouts 'suicide bomber', then insurgents hidden in three compounds open up at the patrol, drawing heavy suppressing fire from the armoured cars on the cliff top above.

He looks down at himself and is seized by the horror of discovery, not of a bullet hole or shrapnel wound but of thick tracks of human excrement smeared up his boots, legs and waist. His first time under fire and he lands in the Taliban's toilet, a small victory for the assailants before they die in precision bombardments. Fighting off revulsion rather than fear, he wonders if this gruesome landing hasn't saved him the trouble of fouling himself.

Zabi the Afghan interpreter is crouched on the other side of the ditch looking almost bored. His eyes light up with interest as he studies the daubed journalist.

'Shit happens,' he says with a grin.

NICK ALLEN

EMBED

WITH THE WORLD'S ARMIES
IN AFGHANISTAN

SPELLMOUNT

Every gun that is made, every warship launched, every rocket fired, signifies, in the final sense, a theft from those who hunger and are not fed, those who are cold and not clothed.

Dwight D. Eisenhower

First published 2010 by
Spellmount, an imprint of
The History Press
The Mill, Brimscombe Port
Stroud, Gloucestershire, GL5 2QG
www.thehistorypress.co.uk

British Library Cataloguing in Publication Data.
A catalogue record for this book is available from the British Library.

ISBN 978 0 7524 5889 2

Typesetting and origination by The History Press
Printed in Great Britain
Manufacturing managed by Jellyfish Print Solutions Ltd

CONTENTS

FOREWORD

I can't say exactly when I decided to throw in a well-paid, secure job with my employer of eight years, the German Press Agency dpa, and go to Afghanistan to research this book; most likely after I blew a gasket trying to get out of Kabul in July 2007 to cover the storming by commandos of Islamabad's militant Red Mosque.

The foreign press corps based in the Pakistani capital had been tracking the confrontation for months and we knew the authorities would eventually move to crush these shoots of 'Talibanization' in the heart of the city. That summer a few of us left the country to follow other stories or risked a vacation, or like me were traipsing round the Taliban's original homeland when the final chapter of the mosque drama unfolded. When a faulty altimeter prompted PIA to cancel my flight back to Islamabad the day before the storming operation, it was too late to drive via the Khyber Pass. I arrived on a UN plane the next afternoon when the assault was winding down and the government lies about numbers of bodies had begun. There was still plenty of work to do but as any news reporter will tell you, missing the main event after a long build-up stings to the core.

The decision to quit was also part-born of fatigue and frustration at sitting at a computer for long months cranking out hundreds of news wire stories about Pakistan's murky political intrigues and the confrontation between then President Pervez Musharraf and the judiciary. And I remember regretting that so much material from the weeks I spent embedded with US forces in Afghanistan since December 2006 would go unused after my agency stories were filed, and would languish in faded notebooks in a box somewhere; or like my financial records for the previous ten years, be consumed by invading legions of termites in a dark cupboard in my home in Islamabad.

Perhaps the decision to delve deeper into the soldiering life had been unconsciously sealed in a flash from the night sky over Afghanistan's Zabul province that June. I was lying on my cot at a tiny Romanian outpost, gawping at the night sky and thinking the words 'this trip will change your life' when a shooting star arced brightly overhead. An over-scripted movie moment maybe, but true nonetheless. A month later, after the mosque story had run its course I handed in my notice and mentally if not physically embarked on this project. It took me until November to fully extricate myself from the agency job and the Pakistan story, but it eventually happened and that winter I embedded again with US and Polish forces in eastern Afghanistan.

By the time I wound up the active research 19 months later I had been what the media calls 'embedded' with 13 foreign contingents for longer or shorter periods, a day in the case of the Swedes, to five months with various US units over nine embeds. The number of separate embeds altogether was over 20, with a few running into others and morphing into something different, so it's hard to say how many I did and not so important. I know people who spent far more time in the system, including an American film maker who did an entire 15-month tour with one infantry company and then more time with the Special Forces. The idea was never to embed longer and with more armies than anyone for the sake of 'credibility'. To do so would have been meaningless.

The idea was always to show something of the soldiers' deployed lives, but I had many notions about what would result from my visits mainly to the southern and eastern provinces and also a few places in the central and northern regions. Regrettably, I never got to the west and I missed some chief troop contributors to the International Security Assistance Force (ISAF), notably the German contingent. (But I did get to enjoy their well-stocked bar in Mazar-e-Sharif).

Various project impulses included a fleeting idea of an irreverent travelogue penned from inside the US military machine until I got booted out (working title 'A Year in Uncle Sam's Back Passage'), and trying to draft a comprehensive account of military operations in recent years from the ordinary soldier's point of view. Eventually I came full circle to where it was always heading: a front row seat in the front lines and backwaters of Kandahar, Helmand, Kunar, Khost and other provinces, living among ordinary servicemen and women who were doing remarkable things far from home. And I was faced with much of the drama, boredom, tragedy and farce that seem to characterize every war ever fought here or anywhere else.

My thanks go to the public affairs and ministry officials with whom my requests to visit their contingents found resonance and who helped make it happen. As it turned out, those who proved least receptive were my own countrymen in Whitehall and Lashkar Gah. After jumping through hoops and passing vetting rounds to be approved as a reporter and/or book author, my efforts to embed with UK forces in Helmand over two years to tell something of their story came to nought. The only explanation I received from the MoD was that some people on the media selection panel were uncomfortable with book authors after publication of British journalist Stephen Grey's *Operation Snakebite*. But I was fortunately still able to embed with the Royal Gurkha Rifles for six weeks in Kandahar and mingle with the Brits in Helmand while embedded with the Danes, Estonians and US Marines. I thank every member of the military who tolerated my presence.

I don't presume to have captured the functional essence of the armies I visited but with some events and experiences that individual units went through I feel pretty close to the mark. I still get mails from soldiers I met with mostly kind words about extracts they read or video clips and photos they saw. That is almost worth the effort in itself, since embedded reporters are hardly a desired appendage to a platoon; we are generally regarded as excess baggage and a liability. Alongside everything else that happens in these pages, there is hopefully a taste of what it is like to be that initially faceless media man who is thrust upon the troops from above. To some soldiers our presence is uncomfortable and unwelcome – knowing what some journalists look for I would feel the same in their place. But I was always aware of the trust this afforded me and resolved not to abuse it. I have been party to conversations that would be incorrectly understood and look outrageous in print, without hearing the audible irony of their deliverance or sharing the confusion or anger at events that sparked them. I have nonetheless used elements of such exchanges anonymously since they are important in their own right and should simply be heard. In some places names have been changed to protect individuals, while others have been left as they are, at the risk of my receiving some prickly mail when all is said, read and done.

Thanks go to all those who helped in various indispensable ways: Farhad in Afghanistan for logistical and moral support, Martijn Lodewijkx in Holland, Anastasia Lebsack in Russia and Annika Lahesalu in Estonia for research and translation; the Orkater theatre company for assist-ance with *Kamp Holland*; Nadeem, Yasir and Zahoor for so much in Pakistan; Luke, Mark and Joe at Dust and Scratches Films for fine work on the video edits and website; my agent Leslie Gardner; dpa for formally backing me as a freelancer; and to all friends, family and colleagues in London, Islamabad and elsewhere who encouraged and supported me and dealt admirably with my preoccupation and continued absence.

Finally, this project is dedicated to the memory of Captain Mark Garner, Petty Officer Tony Randolph, Lt. Col. Rupert Thorneloe MBE, Master Sergeant Allain Tikko and Private First Class Claudiu Marius Covrig (posthumous 2nd Lt). And to my son Andrew, who was in my thoughts through all of this.

Nick Allen, Essex, England

ACRONYMS

ABP	Afghan Border Police
AK	(Russian) Kalashnikov Automatic Rifle
ANA	Afghan National Army
ANCOP	Afghan Civil Order Police
ANP	Afghan National Police
ANSF	Afghan National Security Forces
APC	Armoured Personnel Carrier
AO	Area of Operations
BAF	Bagram Airfield
CIB	Combat Infantry Badge
CO	Commanding Officer
COIN	Counter-Insurgency
COP	Combat Outpost
CP	Command Post
CIMIC	Civil and Military Cooperation
DFAC	Dining Facility
DShK	(Russian) Degtyarov-Shpagin Heavy Machine-gun
ETT	Embedded Training Team
FOB	Forward Operating Base
FSG	Fire Support Group
FST	Fire Support Team
HQ	Headquarters
EOD	Explosive Ordnance Disposal
FOO	Field Ordering Officer
HA	Humanitarian Aid
HLZ	Helicopter Landing Zone
HTT	Human Terrain Team
IED	Improvised Explosive Device
ISAF	International Security Assistance Force
ISI	Inter-Services Intelligence (Pakistani intelligence agency)
IO	Influence Officer/Operations Information Operations
JTAC	Joint Terminal Attack Controller

KAF	Kandahar Airfield
KIA	Killed in Action
LAV	Light Armoured Vehicle
MRAP	Mine-Resistant Ambush-Protected
MEU	Marine Expeditionary Unit
MEWT	Mobile Electronic Warfare Team
MRE	Meal Ready to Eat
NCO	Non-Commissioned Officer
ND	Negligent Discharge
NDS	National Directorate of Security (Afghanistan)
ODA	Operational Detachment Alpha (US Special Forces)
OMLT	Operational Mentor and Liaison Team
OP	Observation Post
PAX	Passengers
PID	Positive Identification (armed)
PKM	(Russian) Kalashnikov Machine-gun ('Pulemyot Kalashnikova')
PRT	Provincial Reconstruction Team
PTSD	Post-Traumatic Stress Disorder
RPG	Rocket-Propelled Grenade
RPK	(Russian) Kalashnikov Handheld Machine-gun
SAS	Special Air Service
SAW	Squad Automatic Weapon (M249 5.56mm light machine-gun)
SF	Special Forces
TIC	Troops in Contact
TOC	Tactical Operations Centre
UAV	Unmanned Aerial Vehicle
UN	United Nations
VBIED	Vehicle-Borne Improvised Explosive Device
WIA	Wounded In Action
WMIK	Weapons Mounted Installation Kit

one

HURRY UP AND WAIT

'Welcome to Bagram PAX Terminal – Gateway to Afghanistan' reads the sign on the wall. Sports coverage on the TV in the brightly lit hall vies with the rip-roar of accelerating F-15 fighters and beating Chinook helicopter rotors outside. Servicemen and women from half a dozen nations sit bunched with contractors, interpreters, journalists and other civilians on bolted rows of plastic seats, idling away the hours as they move south to Khost or Kandahar, west to Bamyan and Herat, north to Mazar-e-Sharif, east to Jalalabad or out of theatre to Kuwait or Qatar.

It's December 2007 and bad weather in the pre-Christmas period has fouled up transport at the huge US-run Bagram Airfield (BAF) and a spate of cancelled flights has formed a clot of passengers in this 'gateway'. Packs, helmets and body armour are piled under a shelter in the drizzle, weapons stay with their owners, propped between knees or lying on the floor. Staff wearing fluffy antlers and Santa hats call out manifests of those who will fly on the next aircraft; the rest must wait until a space becomes available on a later flight and hope no one with higher priority bumps them off the roster.

Tensions are surprisingly absent despite the delays but this is the way of the military, any military – you go when you go, and if you don't, you wait. A British captain tells me 'war is extremely long periods of boredom interspersed by short periods of extreme violence.' An American sergeant who also served in the First Gulf War defines it as '90 per cent boredom, 8 per cent excitement, and 2 per cent sheer terror'.

So we wait, nodding to iPods, grappling with Sudoku puzzles, reading paperbacks, dozing or staring at chat shows and football on Armed Forces Network television. And in my case, noting interesting uniform nametags for my 'dream platoon', which grew over months to include Love, Smiley, Coward, Fears, Pagan, Sweet, Salvo, Ten Barges and Nutter, under the capable command of Captain Hook and Major Dick.

Some travellers bring boxed take-outs from the Pizza Hut located in a trailer further down Bagram's main thoroughfare, Disney Drive, which is named after a fallen soldier rather than Walt. In the Secure Area, the adjoining hall you move to once confirmed on your flight, a large mural of the Statue of Liberty against the Stars and Stripes declares: 'Land of the free because of the brave'. The walls are decked with tinsel and stockings and messages from American schools, police departments and Vietnam War veterans urging the troops to 'Be good, be lucky, be home' and 'Kick Ass'.

I'm due to fly 30 minutes from Bagram to Camp Salerno in Khost, a province on the eastern border with Pakistan. Three dozen passengers, mainly US troops, check bags onto cargo pallets before filing in the damp grey onto a C-130 transport plane that stands waiting, its four 4,300-horsepower propeller engines howling across the runway. There are a few portholes behind the lines of canvas seats but the weather has misted the glass and the sky today is one dank cloud anyway. After take-off we can only guess at our movements from the sharp climbing and banking and the pitch of the engines.

Named after the WWII coastal landing site in Italy, Salerno is informally known as Rocket City because of the amount of projectiles the Taliban lob at it from the nearby hills. To avoid drawing fire, the arriving planes keep their engines running after they land and leave as soon as the cargo and passengers are unloaded. Eight minutes on the ground was the record for his aircraft, a crewman tells us as we buckle up. Instead of 30 minutes, the aircraft flies for one hour before it touches down – at Bagram. The approach to Salerno proved too risky in the conditions and we came back. 'We wanted to find a little hole in the cloud to spiral down through,' the co-pilot tells us. 'We tried, but this is better than hitting a mountain at 60 degrees at 200 miles per hour.'

Next day the skies are still choked with rain clouds and the PAX terminal is the same cluttered scene with many of yesterday's faces. Another flight postponement means I can leave the building and cross the road to the Pat Tillman Centre for a bite.

This is a cosy retreat for an hour, a kind of military Central Perk with its armchairs and carpets, wireless connection and *Meet the Fockers* showing on a big television as guests tuck into free pizza and coffee. The facility was opened in 2005 to commemorate the American pro-football player who after the US-led invasion of Afghanistan in 2001 quit sport to enlist in the Rangers. Tillman was killed by friendly fire during an ambush in 2004 about 40 kilometres southwest of Khost city. One of his football shirts hangs on the wall in a glass case.

As I return to the terminal to undergo flight registration yet again my iPod summons the British electro-pop band Hot Chip, who sing 'Over and over and over and over, like a monkey with a miniature cymbal … The smell of repetition is really upon you.' Amen. I take a seat next to Captain Wegmann, another passenger from yesterday's abortive flight. 'The longest it ever took me to get back to my base from Bagram was six days,' says the American. 'It's like they say in the army, hurry up and wait.'

Wegmann is a medical officer at Forward Operating Base (FOB) Bermel in Paktika province, which also borders on Pakistan. It's another place where rockets rain down on bad days and where I spent a freezing week with the US 10th Mountain Division a year earlier. I'm told it's calmer there since they set up a ring of combat outposts towards the frontier, 'soaks', which draw the Taliban's attention away from the FOB.

'There are a lot of IEDs there now,' says the Captain, referring to the improvised explosive devices, or homemade bombs, that the insurgents are increasingly skilled at building and planting.

He has just brought an Afghan civilian contractor to Bagram for hospital treatment after one of these hit a road-building team. The man would have escaped unharmed were it not for a tiny shard of metal that pierced his eyeball and blinded him.

Suicide bombers are also a problem now the insurgents have realised direct engagements with troops cost them too many fighters for too little gain. In August and October 2007 two men blew themselves up near the base. One attack was at the local market and killed eight people, including three kids, according to the officer.

The other time, the bomber was dressed as a member of the Afghan National Police (ANP) and was let through a Police checkpoint as he made for the base, only blowing himself up when Afghan National Army (ANA) troops got in his way.

'All that was left of him was his lower left leg, the rest disintegrated. The four ANA guys who were killed looked like they'd been through a meat grinder, it was horrible, horrible…' Wegmann remembers. Other ANA soldiers then began to beat up the Police who let the bomber through, and when US soldiers tried to break it up weapons were pointed at them. You get used to hearing stories like this. (So many more have died since I waited for my flight back then, the IED losses growing. June 2010 was the deadliest month of the whole war for Coalition and US troops. Of the 102 killed, 60 were Americans.)

Time weighs heavily now so I flip through a copy of *Freedom Watch*, a magazine published in Afghanistan by the US military. As usual, IEDs are a prominent theme. But Colonel Jang Soo Jeong, Commander of the Republic of Korea Forces Support Group, is optimistic that the bomb disposal robots his men brought will help reduce the threat.

'We hope that our efforts can work like a fertilizer to help the noble sacrifices of the US forces,' he enthuses.

I go and take a bottle of water from the fridge and notice another familiar face, a plump middle-aged woman with frizzy dyed blonde hair and too much make-up, high cheekbones and a kindly look. She must be Russian – a decade working in Moscow serves me well in such matters of recognition.

I strike up a conversation with Zhenya, who is an ethnic Russian from the republic of Kyrgyzstan. I now remember seeing her before in the main shop (the 'PX') selling Red Army paraphernalia and souvenirs with Lenin's image, badges, old rouble banknotes and the *ushanka* fur hats with the earflaps. The foreign soldiers like to buy the gear the Soviet soldiers used here 20 years ago like the leather belts with the hammer and sickle buckle that Zhenya sells for $15. She has to drop a load of new stock at her company's stall in Salerno and get back to Bagram and home to Bishkek in time for New Year. It's her fourth attempt to fly to Khost.

'I come here every day and get pushed to the bottom of the list by military personnel, they are doing a troop rotation now and it's a big problem,' she says, already resigned to further delays. I passed through Salerno once before but didn't see much, so I ask her what it's like and whether the rocketing scares her. 'I'm used to it now but I still try not to think about it,' she replies.

Then a member of staff calls something about a change to a Kandahar flight because of the arrival of Robin Williams to do a Christmas show. Another batch of soldiers gets up and leaves, bumped from their ride in the name of comedy.

'That will be my war memories, that Robin Williams stole my plane,' an Australian reporter grumbles on his way out.

Together with 70 other passengers, the Captain, Zhenya and I eventually board our C-130 in the rain and make the 200-kilometre flight to Salerno. Inkeeping with Afghanistan's freak weather patterns we arrive in clear blue skies. One soldier gets off the plane carrying a boxed pizza for friends on the base, surely the longest delivery in South Asia that day.

As a reporter visiting different units in Regional Command-East I have a few more flights to catch before I get back to Bagram ten days later. Movement is also slowed by missed, cancelled and delayed planes and helicopters. As maddening as it can be, it's just something you have to swallow in this and presumably all other theatres of war. On the helicopter landing zone at FOB Sharana in Paktika, a soldier from Idaho shoots the stock line with a friend when our ride fails to show: 'Hurry up and wait, don't you know that's the army's motto?' The same philosophy applies in the armed forces of Romania, Estonia, Finland and other contingents I later visit.

Beside me a Polish captain checks his watch again and is informed that the Chinook pilot turned round to refuel and may not be back today. 'Spiesz sie i czekaj,' he tells me. And I do.

two

VERY GREEN

It starts for me a year earlier, in December 2006. An icy wind rakes through the Chinook's forward gun ports and out the open tailgate where another helmeted gunner sits at the edge with his legs dangling. It's dark but I can make out snow-covered peaks passing outside the porthole. I don't remember being this cold ever, not in 11 years working in Russia. I do resemble a *babushka* now, with a woollen scarf wrapped over my head against the bitter rush of air through the cabin.

I was never processed as quickly as this first time after my taxi dropped me at Bagram, which is an 80-minute drive north of Kabul. The public affairs office whisked me through, issued my media badge and took me to the rotary terminal for the flight to my host unit in RC-East.

I have brand new body armour (ex-Dutch military issue purchased three days earlier in a camping shop in Rawalpindi, Pakistan) but no kevlar helmet and therefore should not have been allowed to fly. But I take my place unnoticed among the melee of people and cargo, crammed in with large kicker boxes, backpacks and two dozen infantrymen and contractors heading to Paktika province. The pilot flies with night vision goggles and we sit shivering for almost two hours as the bird sets down at a series of silhouetted bases on the Ring Route, always climbing higher towards Orgun-e, a US stronghold located 2,460 metres above sea level.

The next day my hosts of the 10th Mountain Division root out a battered kevlar, repair it with a couple of bolts and impress upon me that I must return it when I leave. It's too damned small and perches ridiculously on my head, but that's what I get. My body armour is also a tad undersized, so occasionally when I'm wearing all my winter gear I need some-

US infantry medic of the 10th Mountain division extracts a large ball of wax from the ear of a village elder. The man is later detained with three others in a car with a high explosive reading, Margah, Paktika province, December 2006.

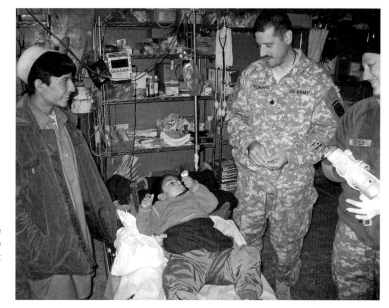

US army medics give Afghan boy a lollipop after removing a cast from his broken pelvis, Paktika province, December 2006.

one to pull the Velcro side flaps tight for me. I'm wearing green corduroys and have brand new US Army issue desert boots, acquired at the same Pakistani shop for $30. The outfit is completed by an olive drab jacket, which in a photo of me taken on the first day of my embed still has the price tag hanging off it. In short I look pretty daft and even greener than my equipment – yet oddly sturdy by dint of my sizeable frame and the snugness of my kit, producing a cross between Universal Soldier and Stan Laurel.

These ten days take me from Orgun-e to FOB Bermel to Salerno, with patrols in the mountains and a tense storming rush up a hill to find that the target compound full of Taliban doesn't exist and we are on a wild goose chase.

I watch a medic extract a large clot of wax and hair from the ear of a 70-year-old villager who all but dances a jig at the miraculous restoration of his hearing. An hour later he is detained with three others after their car is found to be so saturated with traces of explosives that the Americans' electronic detector goes off the scale. In the village of Margah I am rushed from the main street after an intel report that a suicide bomber is preparing to blow himself up among the foreigners. I ride for two days in a Humvee with three US Military Policemen of Italian and Mexican

origin, shaking with cold and laughter at their incessant banter, ('Just because the first shot you ever heard was when you crossed the US border!'). And I liked this lifestyle, despite having only seen winter dynamics of the conflict, frozen streams, sleepy villages, brooding skies, whispers of insurgents but no contact. Even FOB Bermel had fallen quiet, despite having had over 400 rockets fired at it that year, including a shower which fell during CNN's September 11 live report from the base.

The summer and autumn I knew had been bad in large areas of the country, with fierce clashes in the east with groups of Taliban crossing from safe havens in Pakistan, and Helmand and Kandahar erupting as the insurgents took the fight to the British and Canadians in the south. The next year promised a further escalation of the violence but I still wanted to experience more. The following June I spent three weeks with US and British infantry in Zabul province, and after handing in my notice at my agency, visited the Poles in western Paktika that December, spending Christmas Day on patrol in the plains.

Then, while I was grabbing a week's vacation in Thailand in January 2008, ISAF e-mailed me with an offer to embed the following week with the Gurkhas in Kandahar for one month. The invite fell to me, I learned later, 'because no one else was available'.

three

SOUTHERN SCORPION (OR TALI-WHO?)

So ended the great war of 1878-80. At its close we had over 70,000 men in Afghanistan, or on the borders in reserve, and even then we really only held the territory within range of our guns.

General Sir John Miller Adye (1819-1900)

January 18, 2008

I huddle by the wood stove in a Kabul restaurant as the only guest while I wait for my food. It's bitter out but the emptiness here is more because the foreign community is lying low after a Taliban raid on the Serena Hotel four days earlier. A group of seven insurgents, some dressed as Police officers, broke into the complex and used small arms, grenades and suicide bomb vests to kill six people and injure six more, including staff and foreign guests working out in the gym.

I'm handed a notice about the restaurant's new security arrangements, including armed guards posted in the garden and permission for visitors' bodyguards to carry concealed sidearms, provided they don't drink alcohol.

'The emergency exit is through the kitchen, up the stairs to the top, out on the roof, and then if necessary descent by ladders into the street,' it informs.

The guest house where I stay for two nights is on similar alert following the attack, which was bold by any standards and intended to send the message that nowhere may be considered safe by enemies of the Taliban.

'If they could get into the Serena they could get in anywhere,' someone dining at the next table remarks to his friend. (This establishment, the Park Residence, was bombed out with 18 dead in February 2010.)

In such a chill atmosphere and weather I'm happy to hole up until I go to join the Gurkhas in Kandahar, do some work, sleep and watch a Chinese bootleg disc of Hollywood movies that is curiously labelled 'The Super Irritable Movie Selection'. I also grab 'Top Impetuosity War Film' and 'Bloody Brutal War I' but forego the martial arts and boxing collection 'Round the World Fistworld Struggle for Hegemony'.

Finally I report at ISAF Headquarters, a massive walled and towered compound in the city centre surrounded by Police checkpoints. Together with another British journalist and some Spanish soldiers I am then driven in an armoured Land Rover to Kabul Airport for a C-130 military flight south.

I arrive at Kandahar Airfield (KAF) too late to hook up with A Company of the 1st Battalion of the Royal Gurkha Rifles and will now catch up with them in two days as they head north on a four-week operation. Meanwhile, I am received by Lt. Col. Jonny Bourne, the tall, eloquent and urbane 42-year-old commander of 1RGR who takes me through a Power Point presentation on Operation Sohil Laram, or 'Southern Scorpion'.

This unprecedented thrust into enemy sanctuary and staging grounds is double-pronged, pushing two companies with columns of vehicles and more than 400 troops into the Taliban's backyard in the north of Kandahar province. The Area of Operations (AO) covers 3,000 square kilometres of plains, bare earth desert and hills, is a known transit and rest area for the insurgents and has so far been relatively untouched by Coalition forces. The stated objectives are to help build local confi-

Gurkha WMIK Land Rover crossing northern Kandahar province on Operation Southern Scorpion, January 2008.

dence in the Afghan government and security forces, expand the ISAF presence and 'reduce insurgent capacity to regenerate for spring and prevent them from resting, recuperating, re-arming and refurbishing'. Geographically, the end goal is an insurgent stronghold called Lam, which is located in the far northwest corner of the AO, and is where the companies are due to air assault into by helicopter as a grand finale.

'We're not hell-bent on fighting, we are aiming to disrupt freedom of movement,' Bourne stresses. 'The aim in the longer term is to extend our influence in this area, to dem-onstrate to people that we are here and are a credible force and that they will see more of us.'

The advance party of 1RGR arrived in Kandahar on September 1, the same day that the forefathers of these Nepalese troops stormed the city and took its guns in 1880 during the Second Afghan War. Of the 650 soldiers, 140 were sent to reinforce British units in Helmand, one platoon was assigned to protect Regional Command-South Headquarters, and the remainder became a mobile asset available for deployment any-where in the southern sector as needed.

Before Sohil Laram, the Gurkhas staged several operations in Helmand, Kandahar and Uruzgan provinces, engaging the enemy within seven days of deploying. Actions included the defence in December 2007 of the strategic Helmand town of Sangin from a determined Taliban assault, which was hailed as a great achievement and resulted in the decoration of a number of Gurkha soldiers and officers. One man was killed in action, Major Alexis Roberts, who died in an IED strike west of KAF on October 4 as his unit was returning to the base after an operation. Another 12 men had been injured so far on the tour when I joined them, rising to 15 in the next two days.

'Many of them could have been killed,' Bourne tells me. 'We had a guy shot through the chest without hitting any major organs. He was leaning over, the bullet went in above the breast plate but popped out above the back plate. We also had one guy shot through the face as he was shouting and the bullet came out of his mouth – by rights he should be dead.'

But the loss of Major Roberts shook up the company and those back home.

'Suddenly there was a realisation that this was real,' says the Colonel, who in a tribute to the fallen soldier wrote:

> 1st Battalion The Royal Gurkha Rifles will never be quite the same again. Losing Lex is hurting us all, but we are not bowed and we are certainly not broken. We will work through our grief because Lex's loss has made us that much more determined to make a genuine impact while we are here in Afghanistan. That is Lex's legacy and we will honour it. Lex died amongst the Gurkhas he so loved. They will ensure that his sacrifice is not in vain.[1]

More operations followed the loss, building up to this, the longest of the deployment. In the bigger picture, Southern Scorpion punches into what is known in intelligence circles as the Jet Stream, or even the 'Banana of Terror' by some Canadians. This greater than 350-kilometre arc of intertwined transit lanes and safe houses is used by the Taliban to move men and supplies from bases in Pakistan through Paktika and Zabul provinces and northern Kandahar to fight the British in Helmand, with spur routes north to engage the Dutch and Australians in Uruzgan, and south to harry the Canadians around Kandahar City. The same routes are said to have been used in the war against the Soviets two decades before.

'I very much see the Jet Stream as something like a super highway,' a Gurkha intelligence officer says. 'It's not just one or two routes; it's generally a lot of movement in a crescent shape around Kandahar. The name conjures up images of thousands of people pouring through these passes but it's more like scores – the Taliban couldn't support large groups, they need to move in groups of four or five. But the bulk of the actual fighters are probably indigenous to this area of Afghanistan.'

Overall, my briefing indicates that I'm in for plenty of what Bourne terms 'good gritty soldiering' and hard use of 'the infantry boot' in the wintry hills and mountains, coupled with the worst aspect of operating in this country.

'We anticipate quite a lot of IEDs in this area, that's traditionally the case,' he warns me.

It happens on Day 2 of Sohil Laram. Triggered by a hidden watcher, a powerful remote-controlled IED rips apart the front of a jeep carrying A Company's reconnaissance commander, flipping the vehicle and its three occupants into the air. Suffering shattered limbs, concussion and one caved-in face that takes ten hours of surgery to reconstruct, they are lucky to have survived.

'It was horrible, horrible, the Major was just lying on the ground twitching, I thought he was dead,' a British NCO attached to the Gurkha operation tells me later. 'The Taliban call themselves brave warriors, are they fuck, they bury these things under the road, they're just cowards.'

But insidious as the IED usage is, I imagine the insurgents call it quits for the devastating air and artillery power of the Coalition Forces.

I catch up with A Company on the third day of the operation, having ridden 40 kilometres northwest from KAF with a column of Viking tracked personnel carriers crewed by the Royal Marines. I'm crammed inside the armoured trailer compartment with piles of kit and weapons, three Gurkhas and a Scottish doctor, Major Doug Reid. I manage to doze off with my right leg outstretched between the doc and a 66mm anti-armour rocket, but am wrenched back to agonized consciousness as an SA80 rifle fitted with an underbarrel grenade launcher tips over and cracks me across the shin.

I chat a little with my neighbour. It turns out that Reid was in the back of the Pinzgauer Vector truck when Major Roberts was mortally injured by the IED. The driver was also hurt but the doctor and four others clambered out unscathed.

'There are a lot of lucky boys walking around here,' the doctor says.

The company's harbour area is in the middle of a wide, earthy plain with a few mud compounds and craggy hills in the distance. More than 50 vehicles are parked up in defensive formation, Vectors, WMIK Land Rovers bristling with weapons, flatbeds with containers, a Foden recovery vehicle and JCB excavator, and the Humvee and 23-ton Cougar mine-resistant truck of an American explosive ordnance disposal (EOD) team.

I find the officer in command, Major Paul 'Pitch' Pitchfork, talking to a US Special Forces officer by a large map of the AO. Aged

British troops battle the cold, Operation Southern Scorpion, February 2008.

36, of lean build and with the look of a lady's man, Pitchfork has an easy, humorous manner I never saw flag despite problems that sprouted like hydra heads that month, and the endless planning between driving and footslogging. In fact, as arduous as it got, he and several of the officers repeatedly spoke of the sense of freedom and release they felt in this environment compared with the administration-heavy work back on base.

'It's ironic that you have to come out into the middle of enemy territory to get a break from your computer,' an artillery Major observes, while Bourne says one morning with the unencumbered air of a man on a hike in the Cotswolds, 'It's refreshingly simple here, you get up, you have your breakfast, burn your trash in the pit, you know the form.'

Pitchfork, who was later awarded the Military Cross for his leadership in the defence of Sangin, talks me through the operation while standing at the map. It is dotted with red markers denoting three dozen recent finds and explosions of various IEDs, including two since the start of the operation. The day before the jeep was wrecked, the engineers discovered a device consisting of two 155mm shells and an Italian anti-personnel mine buried on high ground where they stopped to survey the land.

'One was found, one went off, that's two in two days, so they're out there,' Pitchfork says. 'IEDs are my biggest worry by far – they can shoot at us until the cows come home, we'll just shoot back.'

So great is the danger that the column can only travel cross-country now: 'We have to take the hard route because if we take the easy one they'll blow us up.' The following day several men on motorbikes are spotted circling the column at a distance and zipping in and out of villages. There is no way this number of military vehicles can move undetected so there ensues a constant two-way game of cat and mouse as ISAF hunts the Taliban and they try to guess the column's route and presumably plant devices in places where it might pass. To counter this, the JCB excavator is used to dig alternate entry and exit points in the banks of the wadis, or dry river beds, that we cross.

Occasionally, French Mirages or F-15 and F-16 jets flown by US, British and Dutch pilots sight suspicious activity on hilltops. White phosphorous artillery and mortar rounds are sometimes dropped to deter prying eyes, but we are always being watched.

'The enemy have got eyes on us all of the time,' says Major Greg 'Psycho' Castagner, our Canadian JTAC (Joint Terminal Attack Controller) whose job it is to coordinate air cover and strikes during the operation. 'They've got good EWS – early warning system – usually a guy sitting on a hilltop with a cell phone.'

For the next four weeks he and I ride in the back of a Vector with two men from the Royal Horse Artillery who with Castagner form the Fire Support Team, calling in air and artillery strikes and aerial reconnaissance as required. We are squashed in the tiny truck with two other soldiers, their rifles and a 7.62mm machine-gun, boxes of ammunition, jerry cans, piles of rations, water, radios, an axe, pick-axe and spade. Our packs are hung on the outside of the truck together with a large waterproof sheet that we unroll and peg to the ground as our 'tent' at night.

The Vector is a home of sorts, but one that jars our teeth on every rut, batters our helmeted heads against the hatches and constantly refrigerates us, to the point where we can no longer feel our feet as we trundle across the province. The armour is too light to fend off much in the way of an attack but it still beats walking, of which the troops do plenty from the outset.

The vehicles harbour up again the next day at 1630 as dusks falls and the mutual stalking takes another turn. That night 100 Gurkhas and their officers are to do a 16-kilometre 'tab', or march, over the hills into the villages of Naser and Bagak where numerous Taliban are thought to be staying.

The troops leave at 2100 and start the trek across a gaunt landscape of hills and ravines bathed by a full moon in a huge canopy of stars. After two hours the ridges open towards distant snowy peaks to the north and we descend onto a plain that is followed by more slopes and troughs. The column pauses and rests every 25 minutes until after six hours on the move everyone draws into one protected spot. The troops have covered too much ground already if they are to reach the objective at first light so we freeze silently for 40 minutes, listening to the faint buzz of a Predator drone that scans the route ahead for movement. I am intrigued to hear that the aircraft is remotely operated from a US military base located outside Las Vegas.

As the sun peeks over the horizon the Gurkhas move simultaneously into Naser and Bagak, which are miserable clusters of compounds and piles of garbage and human shit. The dozen Afghan soldiers with this combined task force perform a haphazard search of the first compound, prodding randomly under blankets and in boxes. It's dark and dusty in the houses, which are heated with wood-burning stoves under arched mud brick ceilings. The owner stands back as the ANA poke around, while the women and children are as usual kept somewhere out of sight.

The Gurkhas wait outside near a roofless toilet that is heaped with excrement. Litter is scattered all round the yard and through the bare pomegranate and apple tree orchards. The streams and soil are frozen solid and all life appears to have ground to a halt under winter's yoke, apart from the occasional motorbike or tractor chugging through the bare fields.

I ask the 70-year-old owner of one compound if he understands why the soldiers have to look in the houses. He tells the interpreter he does and professes to have no love for the insurgents, who he says killed one of his sons with an IED and maimed another.

'The Taliban are all over this area, all the time they come they take something from us, chickens or bread,' he says with the standard subdued resignation that is born of…well, being born here.

That night the platoons occupy three empty compounds in Naser and post sentries while the Gurkhas get to work on supper. They buy and slaughter 17 chickens and a sheep from the locals and turn them into a giant curry that I

Gurkhas of 1RGR prepare for what became known as the 'Lam Death March', Operation Southern Scorpion, February 2008.

unfortunately sleep through after the exertions of the previous 24 hours.

'I don't want this to become the main event of the day, we must remember that we are in an area where ISAF only comes rarely and in dribs and drabs, and the Taliban are around here,' Pitchfork impresses on the men amid general excitement at the prospect of hot food and rest.

The next morning there is a mini *shura* meeting between half a dozen villagers and Lieutenant Robert Grant, the Gurkhas' 'influence officer' who is tasked with learning as much as possible about and from the locals wherever we go. They tell us what we hear in many places, that there is a problem with water supply and irrigation, no money for corn and that they need money from ISAF for seeds and a well. The villagers' apparent spokesman claims security is fine in Naser and that the last appearance by the Taliban was four months ago. But another man says a group of Afghan and Pakistani fighters came through in the last fortnight. As the troops leave the village they receive a radio warning of a high IED threat on the paths.

'In Helmand what they would do is watch us move and then slip a few IEDs on the tracks to catch us on the way in or out,' Lieutenant Aloysius Connolly says as he shoos his men off the tracks and onto the fields. 'We'd take care of business in a village and they'd place pressure plates and try and get us during our extraction.'

At 1600 the force rejoins the vehicles at a new harbour, a welcome sight after covering 25 kilometres in the past 43 hours. Intelligence sources then report that the soldiers have in fact been unwittingly mingling with the enemy in the two villages.

Lt. Col Jonny Bourne of 1RGR appeals to
elders of Lam to reject the Taliban, Operation
Southern Scorpion, February 2008.

'Reliable sources told us that a senior Taliban leader and 22 fighters were in Naser that night we stayed,' says the Gurkha's G2 (intelligence) officer, Lalit Gurung. 'They just hid their weapons and blended in with the local population and were even walking on the streets while we were there. We only searched some of the compounds, not all.' In addition, ten more fighters were reported to be hiding in the madrassa in the first village we passed through.

We are not alone.

On Saturday January 26 the column sets off across the desert toward the district town of Khakrez, a tiny island of partial security in these parts, populated by 2,000 people and manned by 80 Afghan National Police who just about manage to keep the place in government hands.

'Show of presence coming up, it's going to be low and loud,' JTAC Castagner warns before two Dutch F-16s roar overhead and drop flares as they scan the ground. 'The pilots look for large groups of people and they are smart enough to know what an ambush looks like. In one orbit they can cover the entire route we will travel on this mission.'

Low flyovers are handy for impressing locals and intimidating would-be assailants, but 4,500 metres is the optimum height for a jet and 3,000 metres for a Predator to make reconnaissance runs. With the visual equipment on board the pilots can distinguish a high level of detail, and the aerial surveillance is simply reassuring for ground forces.

Throughout the morning there are sightings of motorcycles and lone cars moving around the column but by mid-afternoon we reach Khakrez without incident after a seven-hour journey from the last harbour. As the vehicles groan across a cornfield being sown, someone hops out and gives the farmer $20 in afghanis for the disturbance and damage to his crop.

Others have also been busy planting on this southern approach to Khakrez. The previous day a local man lost a leg to an anti-personnel mine that was likely laid for the British. Then again, the area is still blighted by Soviet 'legacy minefields', so it's hard to be sure.

Buttressed by a large plain of farmed fields to the south, Khakrez nestles along a bank of low, steep hills to the north from where the Afghans fought the Soviets during the jihad and where the Taliban are now said to shelter in caves and refuges. Thinly stretched over three kilometres, the town is guarded by two Police checkpoints on the approaches and has a central redoubt in the District Commissioner's heavily fortified compound.

The ISAF vehicles have to stop on the way in to scan the route. To pass the time, Lance Corporal Joe Atkinson from North Yorkshire entertains the local kids with an impromptu JCB show, nodding and twirling the arm and scoop and dancing the vehicle from side to side on its stabilizers.

The column then pulls up at some dilapidated guesthouses built to accommodate Afghan tourists who would come in happier times to picnic and see the Khakrez shrine, a blue and white domed structure that was refurbished by the former Kandahar Governor Gul Agha Sherzai after US bombing in 2001. We are greeted by a group of policemen with red-painted nails, eyes rimmed with black kohl, and rifles decorated with purple and orange pom-poms. The troops are bemused by their effeminate appearance and one Brit promptly dubs them the 'mascara bum-boy militia'.

Some of the soldiers have to sleep outside under suspended groundsheets but a lucky few including the Fire Support Team and the reporter get a floor spot in a room with a flaky ceiling and broken windows, a palatial improvement on the previous days spent in the open.

The Gurkhas unroll razor-edged concertina wire on vulnerable stretches of the perimeter and pull two Vectors across the gateway to stop anyone charging up the path and blowing himself up in our midst. Intel reports say two senior Pakistani Taliban leaders are currently meeting in the area with their Afghan allies to discuss suicide and IED attacks, while the update on our ultimate objective of Lam says about 80 fighters, including some Pakistanis and Chechens, are hunkered down there.

The next morning Pitchfork sends out a patrol which draws immediate enemy i-com chatter as it leaves the compound and heads down the hill. I wonder what I have to do with anything as a smirking ANA soldier says something to the interpreter and makes a throat-cutting motion in my direction.

'He says if the Taliban capture you they won't know you are a journalist and will cut your head off,' the interpreter says, pointing at my Dutch military body armour, US Army boots and kevlar helmet.

Maybe he has a point, but I had decided months before that I prefer not to stand out as someone 'special' by wearing a blue vest and helmet like many of my colleagues. Use of military clothing and equipment by the media is generally discouraged under embedding rules to avoid confusion. But to me it seemed the more I blended in the better, since differently dressed people get taken for high value targets like State Department officials, contractors or Special Forces – almost anyone but journalists.

The patrol of Gurkhas and ANA winds its way past compounds, trash-filled ditches and the open depths of the karez wells that connect underground and were used by the mujahedin in their fight against the Soviets. After a couple of kilometres we stop in a small sub-village called Sturgadan where a bearded, turbaned man wrapped in a blanket serves some of us tea and raisins outside the mud walls of his house.

'When you come to the villages the Taliban leave, and when you leave, they come back,' he tells us. 'If we go near them they try to force us to go and fight the Coalition Forces and the ANA. People are really afraid of them around here.'

Introducing himself as a landowner and farmer, the man names Naser and Lam as insurgent centres and says a lot of young men in the villages join the Taliban for the summer fight and rest here in winter.

'You have no idea who you are fighting, who you are supposed to capture – they all look just like me,' he tells the soldiers almost pityingly, and adds that we were lucky not to hit any IEDs on the way into Khakrez. The man might be who he says he is but Lieutenant Grant is wary of these social encounters that he, as influence officer, must cultivate.

Officers of 1RGR at the end of
Operation Southern Scorpion
(Major Paul Pitchfork is centre front).

'They'll drink tea with you by day and fire rocket-propelled grenades at you at night. We know for a fact that some of the people we had shuras with in Helmand were Taliban, they just want to check you out, form an opinion of you. And the hills have eyes,' he says, nodding at the low crests behind us. 'They could have observers in any of those watching us and we wouldn't have a clue.'

We get back to hear that the planned air assault into Lam is now jeopardized after the Taliban tracked and attacked the column's roaming Fire Support Group near the village. Three men fired a rocket-propelled grenade (RPG) and Kalashnikov rifles at the British scouts and then jumped into a car and drove back to Lam. A Harrier jet disabled the vehicle

with a missile but all three climbed from the wreck and took shelter in one of the houses. Intelligence reports say two trucks full of weapons were promptly moved out and that senior insurgent leaders in the village headed north while small groups of fighters dispersed in different directions.

But Lam is still the objective, and in order to divert attention it is decided to send A Company northeast for a few days until that village settles down. Then C Company will fly there by helicopter while A Company tabs in over the hills.

'It's not a disaster if we don't capture any Tier-1 leaders, our main goal is to disrupt the Taliban and prevent them getting their act together before the weather improves,'

Pitchfork reminds platoon and section leaders at the evening's Orders Group meeting.

The next morning Khakrez is smothered in a ten-centimetre white layer and the Gurkhas take photos and throw snowballs. I go with Lieutenant Connolly to the adjacent compound to meet the deputy Police Chief Gulbuddin, a shy 30-year-old with a neatly trimmed beard, no formal rank and no socks under his shoes on this wintry day.

He says the ANP force of 80 maintains the two checkpoints with 15 men in each but they don't do any patrolling at this time of year and generally don't go any further than five kilometres out of town. The last time they tried to broaden their patrol reach one of their Ranger pick-ups ran over an IED by Naser and five policemen were injured. Further explaining their reluctance to go far, we learn that 40 ANP were ambushed and slaughtered on the road from Kandahar eight months earlier while escorting a delivery of weapons to Khakrez.

An hour later I return to the Police compound with Pitchfork who asks the deputy chief more about the area. The rest of the ANP stand around in their blue woollen uniforms and a mix of shoes and ISAF issue boots, smoking and studying us with black-lined eyes. One youth says that apart from manning the checkpoints their current duties are to 'eat, sleep and sit in the police station and do sentry duty on the roof'. It's perhaps flogging a dead horse but Pitchfork tells the deputy that it instils confidence in the locals to see the Police out and about, so they agree that the Gurkhas will take half a dozen of his men on patrol. There's still no sign of the Khakrez District Commissioner which perplexes the Major: 'I'm surprised he doesn't want to meet the commander of the ISAF forces who are living in his town.'

During the four-hour joint patrol the British try to impart some basic skills like how to place men at strategic points, but none of the ANP have had more than a month of formal training and they seem to take nothing in. Meanwhile, people we meet on the way say there is no proper school in Khakrez but the town does have a small clinic with half a dozen staff, and the bazaar serves the entire region. On the way back to base the Gurkhas take the opportunity to buy live chickens there for supper and spirit them away in their packs. That evening we hear blasts and shots to the northeast, which prove to be another RPG attack on the Fire Support Group ten kilometres away.

The next morning a platoon walks four kilometres southeast of Khakrez under cover of two US F-16s and then a pair of French Mirages. The snow has all but melted now and the soldiers cross the bare fields to the village of Sherghah.

Grant and a Gurkha Captain sit around a large crater-like hole with a village 'elder' called Mohammed who is only 35 but whose face, feet and hands have been dried and tautened by the sun and frost. Afghans age very fast. As they talk, a bunch of kids toss stones at a turd in the bottom of the hole, which contains both ice and dust.

Unlike other areas in the south, there is no evidence of widespread poppy cultivation here. According to Mohammed, the farmers grow wheat, corn, grapes and pomegranates in spring and summer and if they can afford it, seed wheat in winter as well in case there's enough precipitation to squeeze out an extra harvest like now. In the coming days the region receives more heavy snowfall during what is described as its harshest winter in 30 years. But the farmers are actually pretty happy at the extra flour this will yield, even if the gain is partially offset by the need to buy more firewood. We hear from several sources that the District Centre took deliveries of United Nations flour three times last year but that hardly any made it out to the villages.

'Even if the UN brings us wheat the Taliban will come later and ask us why we accepted it, so we are always in trouble, always at risk,' Mohammed says. 'We like democracy and this government but we have lost faith in the district government, no one will listen to our problems there.' He then claims that the Khakrez Police are as bad as the insurgents, and that one month ago some ANP came and beat the imam, or prayer leader, who was from Tambil, a famous Taliban stronghold to the north. They allegedly took him and two others to the district centre and later released the man's dead body, which he says had nails driven into the legs.

'We are equally scared of the ANP and the Taliban,' Mohammed tells us, adding that as soon as the soldiers leave someone will phone the insurgents and inform them of this talk.

The atmosphere in the next village is far more defensive. This is where Taliban came and burned all the school furniture three months earlier and threatened any families that continued to use the building. Locals say some fighters came through recently and had a meal with the elders outside the mosque.

At the next village a man beckons to us to sit down and he brings tea and food. He says he's never seen ISAF soldiers before but that the Taliban move through here a lot and were last seen a month ago: 'Half are Afghans, half are Pakistanis. If we don't give them food they beat us.'

He is interrupted by the appearance of his 70-year-old father, who becomes agitated at the soldiers' presence by the family home.

'Why are you giving them bread and raisins? If the Taliban find out they'll kill us,' he yowls and then relaxes a little and reminisces about how he and his sons lived in mountain caves in the area when they fought the Russians.

His nephew Abdul joins the group, introduces himself as a member of the ANP in Khakrez and tells us that the arrival of ISAF meant he could pop home for a quick visit. He pulls up his shirt to show huge scars across his chest that he says were caused by a burst of insurgent machine-gun fire but have not dampened his fighting spirit.

'If you bring 50 ANA here then 50 villagers will join them, and if the Coalition Forces give us weapons and ammunition we can easily defeat the Taliban,' he declares. 'Once there is security here you can build schools, clinics, whatever you like.'

The patrol gets back to Khakrez after ten hours and 16 kilometres to find that Lt. Col. Bourne has arrived. He insists that Lam is still very much the prize and emphasises the value of these past days.

'Don't underestimate the effect we've had. If we can get ISAF troops into a place the Taliban regard as their own sanctuary then that's an achievement. Even if we don't go home with dead Taliban we have had an impact. I'd like to see them pull back into the mountains for a few days, get cold and not know if they can come back.'

The next morning I go down to the District Centre with the Colonel and the Major, Lalit the G2 intel man and an interpreter. The DC is a heavily fortified compound that withstood two major insurgent assaults in the previous eight months. Its walls are dashed with bullet marks and holes punched by RPGs, a reminder of the tenuous hold the central government has over this and other remote settlements.

Inside the courtyard, wooden ladders lead to sand-bagged machine-gun posts on the roof and walls, while a rose garden withers beside a wooden stable where a big dog with clipped ears is tethered next to some goats. In the centre stands a two-storey brick and plaster building flanked by sofas and armchairs where turbaned visitors recline and watch us.

The soldiers leave their weapons, helmets and body armour under guard in the hall and we are shown into a ground-floor room with a large red patterned carpet, a gas heater and two cages with chirping birds. There are three beds but District Commissioner Haji Abdul Wahab sits on a mattress on the floor, chewing tobacco and dribbling brown gunge into a stained spittoon as he talks to us through beams of sunlight and dust.

Dressed in an Afghan *payran tumban* long cotton shirt and pants and a waistcoat, the 53-year-old official has a full, black-dyed beard, a shaven head under his little *rakhchina* pork pie hat, a bulbous nose in soft features, twinkly brown eyes and sprouts of hair coming out of his ears. Of medium height and portly, he would seem quite the gentle uncle were it not for stories we've heard, if not about him directly then about his security force. He wears large gold rings and a chunky gold watch, while on the floor before him a Samsung cell phone adds to the chorus from the cages with a birdsong ring tone that interrupts talk every couple of minutes. In provincial Afghanistan you are measured by your bling, and a call on your mobile takes precedence over guests.

'The Taliban don't have a specific location where we can arrest them,' he says, identifying Tambil and Lam as key villages on the enemy rat lines between Sangin in Helmand to Shah Wali Kot to our east, where C Company has been working. There is a plan to hold a shura of elders from the whole district in Khakrez in the coming days and the commissioner wants assurances to be given at the event that ISAF are not just here for a couple of weeks.

'Many civilians here are afraid of the Taliban – 80 Police aren't enough to provide security for everyone here,' he tells the Colonel, and complains that the Kandahar provincial government promised to reconstruct the checkpoints at Khakrez but that nothing has been done.

'The enemy are busy watching us now,' he says, 'and they kill civilians for talking to the ANA and ANP.'

He says the town needs a better clinic and a proper school. But as his compound's battered walls tell, it's the constant enemy encroachment on Khakrez that threatens to overturn all other progress in the district.

'I don't have enough men to defend this whole area, I feel we are surrounded,' the official says glumly.

After the meeting the column drives 15 kilometres northeast towards Tambil but stops short so as not to reveal the exact destination.

'The more we signal our intent the greater the chance for someone to jump on a motorbike and stick an IED in our way,' Pitchfork says, but as usual the troops have enemy eyes on them all the way. Three kilometres out from Khakrez someone gives a two-minute signal with black smoke and there are winking lights and mirror flashes in the hills around us as we drive. At the same time, intelligence reports say the approaches to Lam are being fortified with IEDs, anti-personnel mines and mortars.

We sleep out that night, burrowed deeply into our sleeping bags under the sky's icy palette. Undisturbed by any light pollution, a dense speckled mass of stars curves down like a giant dome to the very edges of the horizon, creating a planetarium effect. I'm staring up in awe when my phone bleeps with a text message from a musician friend in London: 'On Euston Road drinking fine Shepherd Neame ale, got a gig in Bethnal Green.'

The next day the column continues towards Tambil as part of the deception feint away from Lam. On the way the scouts discover several systems of underground shelters and crawl in clutching torches and pistols like US tunnel rats in the Vietnam War. There is no sign of life but these are either shelters for shepherds or militants as they cross the plains from Lam to Naser. All face north and some appear to have firing slits.

In one spot, four deep entrance ways cut into a hillock lead into neat, windowless chambers hewn out of the earth with a pickaxe. The EOD team finds two US-issue hand grenades buried in two of the entrances. Pitchfork considers blowing up the shelters with bar mines or an air bomb but the Khakrez commissioner later tells him that they are for shepherds and shouldn't be destroyed. Shepherds with grenades, apparently.

The column sets up a harbour two kilometres from Tambil, where the Taliban trail proves to be the strongest yet. Lam lies 15 kilometres to the west but for now the platoons must concentrate all activity here and foster the deception. Tambil is the usual rambling mishmash of compounds, walls, wells and crop fields, all set beneath a small rocky hill. I-com chatter indicates the enemy will lay mines 800 metres away from the harbour and use rockets if possible but these intercepted messages are often red herrings to draw the ISAF troops in a certain direction or simply to make them nervous. Then again, the messages have been pretty reliable so far – the RPG attack on the Fire Support Group was first communicated by radio.

Complicating matters, the British get their first case of diarrhoea and vomiting as one of the Royal Horse Artillery guys in my truck fills his pants. Pitchfork orders strict hygiene control measures to stem an outbreak, which if unchecked can potentially disable the whole company. For the next two days the platoons do patrols through the village, where the Taliban presence is almost tangible.

'They are playing hide and seek with us,' a Gurkha Corporal says. 'They are not so stupid that they will stay and fight lots of soldiers.'

There are about 130 compounds in Tambil but only about 30 are inhabited in the winter as most of the 800 inhabitants packed up and went to Kandahar until spring. Intel officer Lalit, an interpreter and I sit down with one of the elders in a small mud room warmed by a stove with a chimney pipe fed through the roof of wooden boughs.

'We are poor people, we don't know anything about the Taliban,' the man says as we eat

Gurkhas brew up in
Khakrez.

Fancy a cuppa? Men
of 1RGR look after their
reporter after a 16-
kilometre night 'tab' over
mountains in Kandahar,
Operation Southern
Scorpion, January 2008.

One for the pot.
Returning from patrol in
Khakrez.

gritty naan bread with raisins and drink sugared tea. 'We haven't seen any Taliban recently but sometimes they come through here on motorbikes heading to Lam or Shah Wali Kot.'

Insurgents burned down the school more than a year ago and they have no doctor or teacher any more, he tells us.

'If ISAF build a school here the Taliban will burn it down, they don't want us to have a school. How can you say this is a peaceful place – the Afghan government hasn't got access here and can't give us security.'

This is probably the most authentic statement we hear in Tambil. The next three men we meet tell us almost verbatim and clearly prompted by someone: 'The Taliban travel through the village but don't stay for more than 24 hours.'

Another assures the soldiers, 'I am 100 per cent sure there are no Taliban here, just civilians, everyone here is just innocent, honest people,' while others say they last saw militants here four or six months ago. It's anyone's guess whether the local men are pro-Taliban, insurgents themselves, or just caught in the middle and terrified.

'The Taliban have been here for a long time, we are here today and gone in a week,' Lalit says. 'The locals know that and know they have to support the Taliban.'

As the patrol starts to move out of the village the interpreter overhears a radio instruction to prepare ten men to fight ISAF, while someone else asks over the air whether the soldiers 'searched the compound'.

'They are right here watching us and I don't think from the high ground but mixed in with the locals,' Pitchfork says as we work our way back through the snow-piled alleys.

'The atmosphere talking to the locals is completely different, this place is teeming with Taliban,' Grant agrees.

It's tense as we pass along the fields with the call to prayer wailing overhead from the mosque, expecting shots to ring out at any moment. Within five minutes of our leaving the village a hidden watcher reports that 'ISAF forces are heading towards their vehicles.'

Attention is focussed on Tambil for two days as we wait for the move on Lam, a daunting 18-kilometre night march over snowy hills and wadis in sub-zero temperatures. A total of 110 Gurkhas and Royal Engineers will do the mission but the ANA Lieutenant refuses outright, saying his dozen men will mutiny if they are made to hike this far. A sense of foreboding grows perceptibly over those two days. We've been on the move for more than a fortnight and the elements and outdoor life and general lack of hygiene are starting to take their toll, causing cracked hands, frost-nipped feet, diarrhoea, constantly running noses, we all stink to high hell – and now the Lam tab.

'It will be pitch black, we'll be moving over rough terrain, we don't know what the weather will be doing – it's going to be a monster,' Pitchfork warns the section leaders. 'This is going to be a grit-your-teeth-and-get-the-fuck-on-with-it operation, 48 hours of pain and we'll be back here and can get our heads down for a day.'

Various factors can hobble this mission, from IEDs, ambushes and blizzards to accidents. But the Gurkha Command and ISAF have made up their minds that the Lam tab will go ahead, and A Company's doctor, Major Simon Johnson, is worried.

'This is not an exercise, it's big boys' rules, people can die in those mountains or at least we can have a couple of broken legs and then this thing becomes a rescue mission,' he tells me the day before we set off. That night I find the doc in the communications tent penning a letter to his local pub in Yorkshire while he has a stint of radio 'stag' duty.

I'm in the back of an armoured minibus with a machine-gun on top as we chug our way across the deserts and wadis looking for those less than pleasant Taliban chaps and try to take their stranglehold off the villages and towns they use to sustain themselves and shelter in whilst preparing for their spring offensive. We're pretty self-sufficient but I think I need a bit of a scrub down and shave before popping in for a pint. We've not seen a shower or a bit of porcelain in over a fortnight and the beard itches like hell. On occasion we've bought a goat or a sheep from the local farmers and knocked up an 'all-in' Gurkha curry. I braved it and really did like it – just best not to ask what the chewy bits are and be glad we are normally eating in the dark.

A scandal flares when it emerges that the ANA have been making hundreds of dollars by charging the Gurkhas $20 for chickens they buy from village bazaars for only $5 to $10. And if there is one sure way to irk a Gurkha apart from offending his honour, it's to mess with his cooking supplies. I have now become used to their culinary rituals, how the Nepalese soldiers buy livestock at the markets and cook up with jars of spices and big pots over open fires.

'When Gurkhas come back from a mission their packs are heavier than when they go out because they are full of chickens, rice and bread,' says Deepak Gurung, a signaller Corporal I share a tent with. The Gurkhas have formally served in the British Army since the 1840s, when the Nepalese were designated a 'martial race', meaning they were viewed as being naturally warlike and aggressive in battle and possessing such qualities as courage, loyalty, physical strength, tenacity and orderliness. To become one of the 3,600 members of the Brigade of Gurkhas today is a hugely prestigious and financially sound achievement in Nepal. Competition is so tough that only one in 300 applicants makes it through selection, but few expect to draw their famous curved *kukri* knives in anger any more.

'There are no close-quarter fights these days with all of the long-range sophisticated weapons, so we normally use them for cooking and cutting firewood,' Lance Corporal Nam Bahadur Gurung says, unsheathing the shorter kukri that some soldiers wear on their belts. In Helmand their eating habits were not lost on the Taliban, who set up roadblocks around the British base in Garmsir to prevent locals from bringing in livestock for the troops. 'Only a Gurkha unit could have that sort of effect on the enemy,' Lt. Col. Bourne later wrote in a regimental newsletter. During a subsequent visit to this base, FOB Delhi, I found this proud piece of graffiti in a watchtower overlooking the River Helmand.

> Gurkhas spent many months here where nothing was. Within months we established peace. Now we have kitchen. Once upon a time here we got 30 TICS (Troops in Contact) in one day, but now it's peace. A great achievement. We ate more than

300 goats, 1000s chickens here (fresh ones). Imagine it. Can you do it guys? No one said well done, but we know we did it well. Now you can see people, children playing around, isn't this our achievement, who counts it? No one. Then suck my dick. We had cleared the way of you guys, now it's your turn to do something within your tour of duty.

Under which a disgruntled Jock on a later, quieter tour has added 'You c★nts talk pish', and another, 'There's more action in ma gran's fanny than this place.'

On Monday February 4, the day before what becomes known as the 'Lam Death March', French Mirages give a show of force, roaring through at less than 100 metres over Tambil and deafening friend and foe alike. The dawn is freezing but then the sun comes out and creates a quagmire of melting snow across the plain and in the large tent I share with 15 others. One is the Welsh medic who was with the FSG when they got shot at above Lam a few days earlier.

'We got to the top of the mountain and the lads had eyes on the village. I was on sentry duty and had five minutes to go. It started snowing and I thought it couldn't get any worse, then next thing I heard the whistle of an RPG that landed in front of us,' he says, smoking forlornly on a stretcher and suffering from acute groin strain as he waits to be flown out by helicopter.

'They tracked us; we were in the middle of the Taliban firing positions around Lam. If they'd stopped and thought about it they could have outflanked us and we'd have been screwed. There were literally 24 blokes walking along and slipping over, it would have been perfect for them to ambush us.'

Even after the disturbance and evacuation of some Taliban leaders, intel reports say there may still be around 40 fighters in Lam. The mud is now slowing everything and creating World War One trench conditions in the tent where the soldiers lay duckboards made from wooden pallets and try to dry their boots over flickering hexi stoves. The only warm place is by the burns pit where the flames from the camp debris draw a steady crowd of huddled, frost-breathed soldiers. Inside the

Gurkha patrol approaches Taliban village of Tambil, Operation Southern Scorpion, February 2008.

tent the young men trade the usual stories of blood, guts and nooky. The dog handler from Yorkshire tells of a soldier in Helmand who trod on an IED and promptly disintegrated in the blast, which deposited his flak-jacketed torso onto the roof of the nearest house.

'Afterwards they found his rifle leaning neatly against the wall like he'd propped it there,' he says before the conversation tacks to 'Team America' and how even the Afghan interpreters are quoting 'dirka dirka' lines from the cult 'War on Terror' puppet movie. There follows a grave discussion about the worst position to catch your girlfriend in while having sex with another man.

'I reckon it's got to be with her on top, because she's in charge and clearly enjoying it,' one concludes.

'How about her in Reverse Cowgirl?' someone else counters. 'Because she's not only on top and in charge, but it's also her looking back at him and saying "hey, check this out".'

That day I learn that my signaller neighbour across the quagmire, Corporal Deepak, is a pop star back in his homeland and that his debut album 'Why I dream of You' was Number 1 in the Nepalese charts for three weeks.

'I'm going to release the follow-up when I'm on leave after the tour,' the 27-year-old says contentedly as he sits on a jerry can in a bog, scooping snow out of a bin bag to melt in his mess tin for tea. Deepak is from western Nepal and has been in the Army for seven of the 15 years he plans on serving.

'Singing is just a hobby. I'm trying to write a song about what it feels like while I'm in the field on operations, missing my family.'

He is also working on a song about signals jargon, so stay tuned folks and prepare to see his Vector traded for a pink stretch limo with chrome portholes as he cruises through downtown Kathmandu.

The troops form up after dark on February 5 and move out at 1900, trudging through the crisp snow in single file. There is no moonlight but the long column of figures stands out sharply on the white landscape as it passes across an open expanse between clusters of compounds. Dogs bay madly at our approach and it would not take much for someone to pass the word and for an ambush to be prepared. We are already feeling uncomfortably exposed when illumination shells go up and practically spotlight us. These mortar rounds are meant to guide the incoming medevac helicopter but the timing is lousy. The escort chopper circles endlessly and then fires an infrared flare with a bang that to us seems like an RPG coming our way from Tambil.

The temperature is minus 11, driven by a biting wind through our layers and into our bones. The troops labour through the snow-drifts under packs, weapons and ammo and when they stop to rest, the sweaty heat of exertion is quickly replaced by an icy chill. The column has covered less than three kilometres when one of the engineers falls ill with exhaustion. They try to walk him through it for another kilometre but more soldiers are already succumbing.

Pitchfork detaches a section of Second Platoon to take the eight casualties back to the vehicle harbour. The cold weather is interfering with radio communications so messages have to be relayed by runners over a few hundred yards, which slows things down even more. We stand for 40 minutes and then hear shouting from up the line as one of the Nepalese soldiers falls comatose with hypothermia. Major Johnson comes to attend to the man, who is being propped up inside a tight circle of his mates for warmth. They get him to eat a Snickers bar to generate body heat; meanwhile another soldier falls into the same state and it's clear the mission is breaking apart.

'We've got to get moving now or someone's going to fucking die,' someone says as Pitchfork seeks permission to terminate. It's thankfully granted and the column sets off back towards the harbour. Four Royal Marine Viking vehicles meet us half way and collect the casualties, probably saving their lives.

'We had no air support, the guys would have had to stretcher the sick back or go firm in the snow,' the doc tells me later. 'People would have died, regardless of what I had in my bag I didn't have a solution to what would have killed those guys. "You must walk or you will die" – I actually said that in a medical consultation.'

The Marines are amazed the march was even attempted by what are essentially troops trained for jungle and not winter warfare.

'You were close to Arctic conditions, you need your kit and you need your safety, and you were pushing the limits,' their commander later commented to Lt. Col. Bourne with clear disapproval of the venture.

We get back to the harbour around 0100, have a brew and collapse into sleep. It's short-lived relief as we are now rescheduled to drive to Lam in the Vikings at 0500. I wake after two hours, condensation has frozen inside my sleeping bag, my upper body is frosty and damp and my throat is painfully swollen. The laces have frozen solid in the metal loops in my boots which I forgot to leave opened up and ready to put on, and I can't work with them for ten minutes because my fingers are split and swollen. It's a shit day already. I ride in a Viking with eight Gurkhas and we are not pleasant cargo at this stage of the operation.

'Wherever the Army goes the pong goes with them,' one of the Marines complains as we are loaded for the three-hour drive over the hills to the village of Atalay on the far outskirts of Lam. C Company already landed in Chinook helicopters and is busy searching compounds. No one we meet knows anything about the Taliban and it's quickly clear that after the long build-up this will be a day of denial and deception.

The most interesting episode is the search of the home of a man who says he's a doctor. He has a room piled with large stocks of pharmacy drugs like antibiotics and treatments for stomach ailments, but people living two kilometres away aren't aware of him at all. The man has a repetitive conversation with Pitchfork and Johnson, insisting that he bought the medicine in Kandahar, doesn't really know what it's for, and that he is just an 'honorary' doctor, having taken over the business from his father. An engineer poking around with a metal detector finds a 9mm bullet in the man's house, but the 'doctor' says he has no idea where it came from.

'This is a Taliban village, maybe someone dropped it while passing through and my kids found it and brought it in,' he says, telling the British that there were over 100 insurgents here but that they left two days ago.

In his garage he keeps a large radio antenna that he says is for listening to Kabul radio, and piles of car stereos, which, although not contraband themselves, can be used to furnish components for IEDs. One radio is just an empty housing and he gives the implausible explanation that it was broken and he 'took out all the workings and sent them to Kandahar for repair'. They also find two mobile phones converted for use as walkie-talkies.

'He's not your ordinary Afghan living in a village, there are just too many factors. He's obviously got some money, a tractor, a car, an antenna,' Pitchfork says, but decides against taking him in after a chemical test for explosives on his fingers reveals nothing. He's highly fishy but the evidence is still circumstantial, if strongly so.

Other people say the Taliban who come here are not Afghans, openly carry weapons and were still present the previous day. Someone even says the last insurgents fled when they heard the helicopters approach this morning.

That night A Company occupies a large, disused compound and although the Vikings are parked all around, security is precarious – there is too much high ground and the troops are compacted in one spot. The next morning we drive into Lam and join Bourne and the officers from C Company in a high-ceilinged compound room heated with a large metal stove. Thirteen invited elders file in and take seats, but only three do much talking, an old man of 70, his son and one other. The rest take in every word, however, and it's a certainty that at least one Taliban representative or informant is present.

We hear once again that the insurgents don't stay here and just stop to eat while travelling elsewhere. The limits of credulity are stretched further when the elders say they are unaware of the recent Harrier missile strike, even though the car still stands disabled in the village, its bodywork ripped open and seats stained with blood. One man says the Taliban will reappear in Lam as soon as the soldiers leave, and the whole group rejects the idea of permanently stationing Afghan government forces here.

'We can't support the ANA because we are afraid of the Taliban, they live in the mountains by day and come into the village by night,' says one elder. 'If you build a checkpoint with

ANA they will come at night and kill everyone who supports them.'

Bourne asks them what they need in this community of 2,000 people and is told everything from water, local administration, roads, to a hospital and a school – only for boys of course.

'The international community has money to spend on projects to develop villages but first we need security and support from you to make sure the money is spent in the right places,' he impresses on them. 'Even if the Taliban offer you anything, it's only temporary while what we are offering is a ten-year plan.'

The elders leave and the Lam mission winds down.

'I understand that it's a worry for them that if they support us it's a threat to them. It requires a leap of faith,' the Colonel tells me and a Dutch journalist who arrived with the other company. 'It's a slow process and one has to understand that it will be. We want to give confidence in the ability to defeat the Taliban, hence the aircraft, but we don't want to leave them frightened. The villagers are so closely related that you only have to upset one individual and you've lost the village… It's a question of digging under the surface, at the moment we are just at the top layers. The important thing is to come back soon.'

The Vikings bring the soldiers back to Tambil from where the whole column starts the journey back to Khakrez, 14 kilometres as the crow flies but twice as far the way we have to drive. It takes us a day and a half with breakdowns and cutting the wadi crossings. The sun is rapidly drying out the land but the soldiers are shivering with numb feet in the vehicles. The book I'm reading in the truck quotes the words of Thomas Hobbes: 'The life of man [in a state of nature] is solitary, poor, nasty, brutish and short.' It certainly is in this neighbourhood.

After the dog handler checks out the guesthouses for booby traps we reoccupy our old digs. The news of the day is that the 'doctor' whose house was searched in Atalay is in fact a local Taliban leader and evidently a very cool customer.

The final event of Southern Scorpion will be a shura of village leaders from the entire district and will, according to the district commissioner, draw more than 100 people. To boost the image

British troops enjoy first warmth in weeks, Khakrez, Kandahar province, February 2008.

of the government, he and ANA and ANP will run the event while the British troops hang back and secure the outer fringes.

'It's very important that people see that Afghans are providing security, we will be further away, watching the roads and on the rooftops,' Pitchfork says.

Ahead of the event ISAF steps up air searches of the area and dozens of illumination rounds are fired at night to deter IED planters. It's hoped the Governor of Kandahar will attend but he then narrowly escapes assassination by a bomb hidden in a culvert as he drives to a similar event sponsored by C Company in Shah Wali Kot. Three civilians thwarted the attack, running to the spot and

waving at the approaching vehicles but then being injured themselves as the device was prematurely detonated.

'What happened in Shah Wali Kot could easily happen here,' Pitchfork says. 'If they can kill the Governor or his cronies or an ISAF official it would totally nullify what we're doing.'

The District Commissioner is confident his men would notice any strangers from out of town but says vehicle-borne suicide IEDs are the biggest threat. The Gurkhas position two snipers on rooftops and the mortars work all night before the event, firing 90 illumination rounds that thump and light up the whole area and don't give anyone much sleep.

British troops doze in a Vector. The Vector was introduced in 2007 as a better-armour-protected version of the old 'Pinz', or Pinzgauer, which had shown itself to be vulnerable to mines and IEDs. The Vector didn't turn out to be much better and was withdrawn.

On February 12, the day of the shura, the Fire Support Group are in position 10 kilometres out of Khakrez and two platoons set up roadblocks three kilometres out. It's a cool crisp morning, the blue cupola of the shrine glistens in the sun and the mood is positive as the guests start to arrive. The shura will take place at the DC compound where all morning the Police have been preparing and grilling lamb for lunch. An impressive total of 148 elders show up, including one from Lam, and they are all searched and photographed on the way in.

Then two helicopters carrying VIP officials sweep in low and land near the market, causing a commotion among the locals. The last that is heard from the Taliban that day is an i-com message from hidden observers that 'the Governor of Kandahar has arrived.' They are told to wait for further instructions and then the air waves go dead for the duration of the event.

The Governor did not arrive, however, and the group is instead led by Colonel Christian Juneau, the Canadian deputy commander of Task Force Kandahar. He is accompanied by the provincial Police Chief and a man the

British believe to be the deputy Governor. He is in fact Malim Akbar Khan Khakrezwal, an ex-mujahedin commander from this area, the former intelligence service chief for Kandahar and now a prominent tribal elder.

Before the shura begins in the courtyard there is a short meeting of the military and civil officials upstairs where Khakrezwal reproaches ISAF for waiting so long before taking action against Lam and other trouble spots.

'The situation in Lam was ignored for the past five years and the Taliban now have a lot of support, you going there and staying a few hours is not going to change anything. The Taliban know you will leave and then they come straight back and whoever is suspected of helping ISAF will get their throat cut. The only reason they support the Taliban is because they are so brutal.'

He also says the insurgents have instructed farmers around Khakrez to each plant one hectare of land with poppies or be killed.

'The Taliban tell farmers they must cultivate poppies while the Coalition says they shouldn't. Who are they to listen to, the Taliban or district leaders? Until your forces can protect these people don't pressure them too much if they do something wrong. When you have a presence here then you can arrest them, but it's wrong to jail people for aiding the Taliban in an area where there are no government forces because they have no choice.'

Khakrezwal's phone then rings and he fields a wrong number call that he says was a Taliban member trying to inform colleagues that an attack is under way in Shah Wali Kot and that they need reinforcements. He plays along and asks where he should send help but the caller smells a rat and rings off.

The shura begins and there is a series of impassioned speeches, starting with a plea to the elders by Kandahar's Police Chief that they read the Koran and see that there is nothing that prohibits construction of roads, electricity lines and schools.

'They use the name of jihad for their struggle but it is an excuse for their own self-interest. Some of the scholars are corrupt because they do not speak out against this. We know those people who are on the wrong path but we have failed to tell them this, so where is our own responsibility?' he asks the silent but attentive crowd of men seated on mats in the yard.

'In other provinces people are going to school and graduating but in Kandahar every year 1,000 to 2,000 of your brothers and sons are taking up arms against others and being killed. I look forward to the day that the ANA and ANP are able to defend Afghanistan and we can say "Thank you very much" to our international partners and they can go home.'

The Canadian Colonel takes the floor and tells them that their villages are gradually falling within the reach of military protection but that they must be patient.

'We would like to provide security everywhere but can't. We are moving that security and development bubble and getting very close to Khakrez and that's why we are here today. But even with the Afghan security forces it's not enough, we need you to get busy and help provide security in Khakrez.'

A few of the elders speak as well, reinforcing the message of impotence and fear we have heard so often in the past weeks.

'When you come here you patrol and as soon as you leave the situation gets worse,' one man says, and motions to the rows of tribesmen beside him. 'These people will get a visit from the Taliban this very night, we cannot even tell others that we were at the district centre today. We need law enforcement so we can trust the government. When we have security the children can go to school, people can work. If the international community wants to help us then now is the time to do it.'

Khakrezwal then speaks critically about ISAF and the Governor for not improving things sooner and it becomes clear that he has his own agenda. Later he tells me what I had heard elsewhere, that his tribe, the Alokozai, has been excluded from decision making and power sharing in Kandahar and its people are now turning to the Taliban.

'We are torn between two forces and we don't know which way to go. We are not just the biggest tribe in Khakrez but also in Kandahar province, and we are being left out. My tribe doesn't trust the government, which has now lost our loyalty. That's why people are being drawn towards the Taliban. Khakrez is just one example, it's a hanging town,' he says, claiming that the Kabul government pays off key players in a big dirty game with huge sums of money: 'If you knew everything that goes on in Kandahar you would have no black hair left in your beard,' he says darkly.

Mr Khakrezwal was one of the sharpest Afghans I met on my travels; mentally adroit, forthright and eloquent, and well able to hold his own against the arguments of the foreigners. He was shot dead in the street outside Kandahar City four months later.

No-one disrupts the shura and it is deemed a moderate success for this reason alone, even though Bourne and Pitchfork are nonplussed by the unexpected railing against ISAF by the former intelligence chief. The next two days are spent driving across the desert back to Kandahar. Again, we are watched all the way and the ambush prospects grow as we enter some tight passes through the hills, but the column's air cover is effective.

On February 13, two OH-58 Kiowa Warrior scout helicopters of the 101st Airborne 'Eagle Assault' swoop in unannounced and scan the route. One comes under fire from a hilltop and the female pilot promptly rockets a group of six insurgents carrying weapons and radios.

'At least we killed some Taliban in four weeks,' Pitchfork observes dryly as we travel the last kilometres back to Kandahar City.

The day after we reach KAF the company assembles at the Gurkhas' base at Camp Roberts. The unkempt, stinking mass of soldiers I travelled with that month has been replaced by smart ranks of scrubbed, shaven men in clean uniforms, hair freshly trimmed and wearing an array of coloured berets of the various regiments that contributed to Sohil Laram.

'We can be proud of what we did in those four weeks,' Pitchfork tells them. 'Our presence in an area they usually feel safe in has demoralised the Taliban as they prepare for their spring offensive. A number of key leaders who were in the area of Lam had to move, they were identified and two or three were killed by US Special Forces. One IED facilitator was killed, we didn't kill him but our presence brought him into action and he killed himself and that's good enough for me. Yes it's good

to get into a fight, kill some Taliban, it's something we enjoy, but that's just a small part of the jigsaw. What we have been doing is causing disruption in the wider area.'

Episodes like the averted assassination of the Kandahar Governor are welcomed as indicators of progress among the local population. As Bourne said, 'In a short space of time we gained the confidence of those people enough that they were prepared to risk their lives for something important.'

Then again, for many of the communities living out on the fringes the occasional visit from ISAF and the ANSF only increases the danger of them being hurt. Until they have Police or Army units near their village that protect them and don't bring additional crime and oppression, life for most will sadly remain, as Hobbes puts it, solitary, poor, nasty, brutish and short.

According to the Canadian Colonel Juneau, a quarter of the province's population of one million still lives outside the 'security bubble', measured by the range of the guns on the ISAF bases. In the case of Khakrez in January 2008, this was FOB Frontenac, situated 40 kilometres away and, in an echo of General Adye's words more than a century ago, too far for its artillery to be of any use.

In reality, the reach of the ISAF forces on the periphery is occasional and short-lived at best, while Afghan government forces can subsist in places like Khakrez but remain woefully unable or unwilling to tame such insurgent-prone areas by themselves. What remains is a vast expanse of territory and villages that cannot be protected and is therefore vulnerable to intimidation and control by any insurgent and criminal forces that choose to operate there.

While the situation with its shades of protection and security bubbles might sound complicated, it's not at all to most people living here. One elder I talked to after the Khakrez shura summed it up with Afghan survivalist logic born of decades of war, fear and persecution: 'If we don't support the government then the Taliban won't hurt us.'

four

NOTHING PERSONAL

There's a pretty fine line between being embedded and being entombed.

Dan Rather, CBS News Anchor – 2003

If we'd had today's media in World War Two we'd never have won.

US soldier, Helmand, 2008

Even when a good rapport is established with the host unit, the embedded reporter must always remember that they are an outside visitor, and not a particularly desired one at that. As a US Major told me when I arrived in his AO, 'We are still from two opposite poles, trying to get along nicely.'

For all the goodwill the sides can show while working together, the underlying them-and-us situation became clear to me at the end of Southern Scorpion. As our column drew close to Kandahar the artillerymen I had travelled with in the back of the truck for four weeks put me in the front passenger seat with no explanation apart from the words 'It's nothing personal.' It dawned on me as we entered the city that it had been decided that if anyone was to be mangled in the cabin by a bomb blast, it should be the reporter.

★ ★ ★

Scribes of one kind or other have accompanied armies to battle for centuries. But not since World War II have so many media workers trodden the combat trail as during the 2003 invasion of Iraq. The previous year, despite resistance by President George W. Bush and Vice President Dick Cheney, Secretary of Defense Donald Rumsfeld approved a plan to attach large numbers of domestic and international reporters to US military forces during Operation Iraqi Freedom.

With his support, the Department of Defense's public affairs team developed an aggressive media embed programme with five primary stated objectives: to build and maintain American public support for US policy on Iraq; to counter Iraqi misinformation, disinformation and propaganda; to generate and maintain international support; to take offensive action to achieve information dominance; and to demonstrate the professionalism of the US military.

At the peak of combat operations, more than 700 American and international reporters, photographers and cameramen were embedded with US forces in Iraq. Sceptics felt this proximity to the troops would strip reporters of their objectivity, while military officials feared they would compromise missions and endanger US forces by revealing sensitive information. Five months after the invasion, when the move seemed to have paid off for its architects, Rumsfeld acknowledged, 'It was a roll of the dice. It had never been done before like that.'[2]

In a 2008 study of 742 news articles written by 156 English-language print reporters in Iraq during the first six weeks of the war, Penn State University sociologist Andrew Lindner found that journalists embedded with American troops emphasised military successes more often than they covered consequences for Iraqi citizens.

'The embedded program proved to be a Pentagon victory because it kept reporters focused on the horrors facing the troops, not the horrors of the civilian war experience,' Lindner wrote. 'With the vast majority of embedded coverage citing US military sources, as long as the soldiers stayed positive, the story stayed positive.'[3]

The practice has since been adopted by many countries with forces deployed in Iraq and Afghanistan. A media embed can last from a day to weeks and even months, with journalists working close to command structures on main bases or living with troops at small outposts, accompanying host units on patrols and outreach missions, and if requested, on combat operations. As the original 2003 Department of Defense media embedding guidelines note, 'The personal safety of correspondents is not a reason to exclude them from combat areas.'

But as common as the practice has become, the pros and cons of this relationship are still debated. Censorship as such may be absent, but there is still the compulsory and controversial vetting of reporters' stories by the British military for 'Operational Security' issues, i.e. aspects that could reasonably endanger the safety of troops or reveal sensitive procedures. Some reporters claim that this is the thin end of the wedge, used to apply pressure on them in other aspects of their stories, like removing facts that are merely embarrassing or politically inconvenient.

Opsec was an issue for the Dutch military when a reporter who was invited to take part in an operation got stranded in Kabul by bad weather and mentioned missing the operation in a blog. With that snippet of information in the public domain the operation had to be cancelled. But the Dutch with their liberal ways forgave him and he could return at a later date. Carelessness might be forgivable, callousness not.

'The ones I have trouble with are the young ones who are hungry to score with their editors back home and go after the scoop,' a Dutch public affairs Major told me. 'I expect them to adhere to operational security but they say screw that, "this is news".'

Some journalists refuse outright to be embedded. 'With their commitment the "embeds" oblige themselves to publicise nothing that could endanger the safety of the troops,' Arnold Karskens, war correspondent for the *De Pers* daily in Amsterdam, told Holland's *NRC Handelsblad* newspaper. 'But they also agree with the elastic concept "not to compromise the operation". So embedded journalists keep silent about interesting pieces of information, for example about the Dutch military taking part in American missions within the framework of Operation Enduring Freedom. In their coverage there was never a word about bombardments by Dutch troops, such as the one in Chora in June 2007, which even according to one ISAF commander, "was in breach of the rules of war".'[4]

Continues Karskens: 'Furthermore, the embedded media never showed a picture of a house destroyed by an ISAF bombardment in Uruzgan, and not once did any journalist actively research a case of human rights violations. In short, embeds throw away the Code of Bordeaux about the journalistic mode of operation, Article 1 of which states: "Respect for truth and for the right of the public to truth is the first duty of the journalist."'

Reporters cannot by definition be wholly impartial while they are accepting food, accommodation, transport and protection from the military. Moreover, regular participants in embedding programmes know that successive negative stories and images about their hosts can harm their chances of being accepted again. An internal ISAF memo about each journalist is forwarded to public affairs officers and unit commanders before you arrive, detailing your slant and manner of reporting while embedded. I managed to see a printed copy of my memo in 2009, analysis of which was drawn from 21 stories I had previously written while embedded. Among other observations – 'lives in Pakistan' was highlighted in yellow marker pen – it was concluded from the quotes used that my coverage position was '61.9 per cent neutral, 23.8 positive, 14.3 negative'.

Not least of all, the physical and logistical constraints of an embed will affect the journalist's perspective.

'You're going to have the famous fog of war,' Phil Bronstein, editor of the *San Francisco Chronicle*, told the *Washington Post*. 'If you're in a unit, you'll get to see combat in that particular moment in that square mile of the world. But we don't have any mechanism for seeing the larger picture.'[5]

Paul Slavin, executive producer of ABC's *World News Tonight*, offered a useful metaphor describing media concerns about embedded reporting: 'We were looking at the battlefield through 600 straws. It was difficult to contextualize it.'[6]

Simon Klingert, a German photojournalist I met in Khost, added: 'The point of view you have while embedded is more often than not limited by Hesco barriers on both sides. But when you realise the amount of work you can get done when everything goes well in relation to the cost, you can't beat it.'

Apart from air fares to and from the country, and your insurance cover, there are generally no costs imposed on the journalist or media organization, so in monetary terms it's a bargain. But regardless of how senior officials may see embedding as a means of managing the media, and despite the distaste of some journalists for this form of access, the reporter is still often trapped in a peculiar bubble among the troops. This can either provide valuable fly-on-the-wall perspective, or lead to isolation from what is really going on around them. We are often an unwelcome presence amongst people who previously had their fingers burned by scoop seekers, remarks taken out of context or words twisted. Or they just fiercely disagree with the view expressed in the final story. Here I quote from British soldier Corporal Lachlan MacNeil's diary published in *The Guardian* in June 2008 from FOB Delhi in Garmsir.

While at Delhi I saw a copy of *The Guardian*. The Pakistan correspondent had come down and done a few interviews and the headline on his story was 'UK forces fighting losing battle' or some rubbish like that. The facts are simple. We are now dominating Garmsir. We have killed Taliban, taken no casualties and have now pushed and secured further south than any other British Army unit. Garmsir is now opening its hospital again. If you asked the locals they said they thought they would never see it again. As I write this, the Taliban in our area of operations are in turmoil, taking heavy casualties every time they feel brave enough to pop up. I don't see this in any way as losing any battle.

The media need to understand we didn't ask to come here; we were sent and we're doing a difficult job in extremely harsh surroundings. I drink at least nine litres of warm water a day; I have over 100 mosquito bites on my body. Nobody here

moans about it, we just get on with it. What does annoy us is being misquoted and giving the British public the perception we're losing.

It must be noted, however, that British gains in Garmsir at the time came mainly on the back of the deployment of the 24th US Marine Expeditionary Unit. Previously there were still entrenched front lines and an effective state of siege of the British by the surrounding insurgents. The main Taliban stronghold in the area, Jugroom Fort, operated until the US forces captured and destroyed it that April, despite earlier British attempts to take it.

There was a broad distrust of media in most of the armies I visited, maybe symptomatic of growing public cynicism and distaste towards journalism and the tabloid breed in particular. Too many reporters have been seen digging around for scandal and controversy in their host units and bases.

'It's bad when you've got a journalist looking for an issue so they can write the Army's this and the Army's that,' a British Corporal in Helmand said in 2009. 'We had one like that in Iraq, but they seem to be leaving people alone in Afghanistan at the moment.'

'The good thing about Iraq is that it kept the media off our backs here so we can do our job,' agreed a US infantryman in Khost.

The caution isn't just limited to being in-theatre either. At KAF I waited for a flight to Camp Bastion at the same time as 150 British troops on their way back to the UK. A film screened in the terminal, *Going Home*, warned about strangers casually probing issues like civilian casualties, stressing that 'there's always some journo looking for a story.'

Soldiers are increasingly used to reporters being among them but are naturally wary of scrutiny as they work. While I was with the Canadians in 2008, one officer said the last print reporter they had would surreptitiously switch on a dictaphone during conversations. That summer, representatives of the Canadian national press living on the Provincial Reconstruction Team (PRT) base Camp Nathan Smith in Kandahar City were barred from the gym and fire water reservoir where the soldiers would swim. Some had complained that they couldn't relax when journalists were around, knowing their comments might be logged.

While the Canadian approach is that all conversations are admissible, US embed regulations state that anything quoted in stories has to be on the record. One reporter for the *Stars and Stripes* US military newspaper was barred from embedding in Mosul in Iraq for having quoted remarks the military objected to as private between soldiers.

When you join a new unit you are pretty much ignored by the soldiers for the first few days and have to accept that behind your back and sometimes within earshot you are not the reporter but the 'fucking reporter'. Seldom are people openly hostile but there can be a brusque detachment from you. Then if you pull your weight and don't gripe, after a few patrols and missions the soldiers will start engaging, maybe ask where you are from and where you've been. What your name is, even. Unsurprisingly, obstacles can be magnified if the embed is a woman.

'You are a woman in a man's world, always talking about men's things, so as a woman you have to prove yourself,' said Dutch freelance photographer Marielle van Uitert, who spent two weeks with her country's contingent in Uruzgan in 2008.

Sometimes soldiers will take advantage of a quiet aside to voice opinions on things they don't like in their unit or their country's approach to the Afghanistan involvement, or maybe they just want to talk about home, girls, bars and music with someone from outside the platoon environment. But it's a mistake to think you are buddies even after a heart to heart. When you run into that person again among other soldiers they may seem aloof, since it is awkward to be seen as cosying up to the journalist.

The best place to talk is in the guard towers, where the soldiers are often on their own and bored. Some of the most honest and informative exchanges I had took place with a view down a machine-gun pointing over sandbags and concertina wire. But your place is still that of the outsider. This might mean that you get your own separate sleeping area. Or it may equally mean you are put in the front of the truck as you enter suicide bomber territory, or perhaps the rear right seat in the US Humvee,

which statistically is the worst place in the vehicle: the front right wheel will tend to run over a buried IED and depending on the speed of the vehicle, the charge can detonate a second or two later under the fuel tank and the back seat, folding the occupant in half and possibly roasting him.

'We usually put the interpreters and you guys in the back, not ourselves,' an American driver informed me in Zabul in 2007.

Then there is the opposite end of the scale, what one Canadian reporter described to me as 'love bombing', when you are taken so far under the wing of the members of your assigned unit that you feel bad writing anything negative about them.

But for all their wariness, many soldiers acknowledge that few people back home really understand what they do in Afghanistan or Iraq and the conditions they work in. So they are mostly glad to see moments of their lives on tour faithfully conveyed by embedded reporters, especially if they are with TV, perhaps partly because the equipment is so large that they are not perceived as being 'sneaky'.

'I've always found the troops are generally pretty happy to have a cameraman around,' said a member of a crew for a major US network. 'Everybody wants the chance for their Mom to see their son on TV.'

Sadly, the relentless tally of casualties became so commonplace that it was likely just a cause of tutting around Western breakfast tables before work. That's why stories and photos of individual soldiers and families matter, to bring those numbers to life for people far away.

This endeavour then collides with the decision by the *Associated Press* to distribute a photograph taken by staffer Julie Jacobson of mortally injured US Marine Lance Corporal Joshua Bernard. Hit in the legs by an RPG in Helmand in August 2009, the 21-year-old died shortly after he was evacuated for treatment. While the Marine's family requested that the photo be withheld it was syndicated anyway, although many larger papers chose not to run it. Jacobson herself cited the need to show what's behind the casualty figures, a line which while hard to fault on face value, can get used by reporters to better their access, attend ramp ceremonies etc and boost the circulation prospects of their photos and stories. The photographer later wrote, 'Death is a part of life and most certainly a part of war. Isn't that why we're here? To document for now and for history the events of this war?'[7]

'Bullshit,' responded one military blogger. 'She thought of the pictures she had taken and "$" came to mind immediately. "Jackpot!" her mind screamed. She got paid for that picture, and she will continue to get paid for it for some time, especially after the furor that erupts…Such selfishness and what a ridiculous attempt to couch it in ethical terms.'[8]

Prominent war photographer Don McCullin, who covered the conflict in Indochina for *The Sunday Times,* agreed with Jacobson amid a furious debate, saying, 'She probably did the right thing because otherwise why are we there?'

But compared to the spontaneous and largely unregulated work of photographers in Vietnam, media are far more managed and obligated in the modern embedding system. US rules specify that relatives of casualties must be notified before material is made public (her agency waited until after Bernard's funeral), and that the face of the casualty is not shown. It was in this photograph.

Apart from moral considerations, this could be ruinous to the fragile relationship between troops and embedded media. Many soldiers will now regard embeds to be absolutely waiting for the money shot of them gasping their last in a pool of blood. Embedding rules can be expected to change to thwart further publication of such images, especially as the military knows that distressing pictures are helpful to the enemy's cause.

As for showing what's behind the casualty figures and waking people to sacrifices made far away, I personally don't believe such an image will have any lasting positive effect. Instead of making people stop and consider the harsh reality of war, the photo in question is more likely to attract gawping fools who just want to see a dying human. McCullin went on to say in his comments to *The New York Times,* 'Have we learned any lessons from the countless pictures of pain and suffering? I don't think we've learned anything. Every year there's *more* war and suffering.'[9]

Again, what this shot may do is to indeed encourage competing photographers to push the limits and gather such images, angering both lower ranks and higher Command to the point of shutting doors that were prised open in recent years.

Through the example of Nick Meo, a reporter for Britain's *Sunday Telegraph,* I had learned earlier that the military will round on you in a moment if they suspect you of being surreptitious and disrespectful to the dead and the troops in general.

Meo was in an American MRAP truck that struck an IED at night in Kandahar in late 2008, killing the top gunner and injuring others. There was a wrathful backlash over his alleged denial that he had shot video footage of the aftermath and over what some denounced as heavy embellishment of his first-person account of the attack. Contended aspects included description of massive return fire with disregard for civilian homes, and Meo's claim that he saw a post-it note at Kandahar Airfield listing him as KIA, all of which erupted in an ugly and public exchange between him and elements of the military.

What struck me was the sheer fury that erupted in ISAF circles, manifesting itself in circulated e-mail exhortations to hound the reporter from the system and in the distribution on the grapevine of fake excerpts of a supposed diary he had written that exuded callousness and contempt for American soldiers. What was probably meant as a satirical riposte stank of vengeance and might easily have earned him a beating from some gullible, enraged soldier.

There was no formal action or complaint against him from ISAF, but members of the public affairs team and beyond drew their daggers privately and many individual soldiers and the military blogging network joined in. 'There was a lot of very personal abuse afterwards, some of it silly, much of it threatening,' Meo told me in an e-mail much later.

> I do not understand why the soldiers thought I was being disrespectful to the dead. I was not. I think they were more angry about the description of what happened after the bomb. I did not at any point deny I was shooting video – that is

allowed under the embed rules. Some of the soldiers told me to stop filming during the incident and were pretty aggressive about it. But I did not stop and told them I was allowed to.

My account was accurate and not embellished, nobody has indicated any point of embellishment except for the woman who claims I made up the KIA note. For the record – the note was there exactly as described.

My view is that you have to report accurately, and sometimes that upsets people and they abuse and threaten you. But you can't let that stop you from doing your job.

Described as the 'forgotten war' in many stories after 2001, the Afghan conflict lagged behind that in Iraq in terms of casualties, including among journalists, with 12 foreign media workers killed at the time of writing, most of them in 2001, compared to the latter's tally of two dozen. But with the intensification of the fight since 2006, the hazards for the media grew accordingly.

'Embedding three or four years ago didn't used to be that dangerous, they'd stick you at the back of a lot of soldiers and you'd be OK,' Meo told me in 2008, a few months before the IED incident. 'Now with all these bombs and mines you only have to be sitting in the vehicle that gets hit. You're at the same risk as the soldiers.'

That sense of vulnerability was present among all the journalists I met while embedded, from veterans to newcomers.

'What I did not expect is that I would go on patrol, it's very dangerous and it's my first time,' Dutch photographer van Uitert said as we sat in the Windmill Café at Kamp Holland. 'I did not expect to be in an open-topped Mercedes Benz. At first I felt very vulnerable, but then I felt very free because I had the opportunity to make pictures. I did say a prayer every day and believed in my destiny, I knew it wasn't my time to be blown up. That's the way you should think or otherwise you won't leave the camp. You have to be aware but it shouldn't control you, you have to be focussed.'

Seasoned war reporters tend to pick their path more deliberately.

'I started wondering in the past couple of years,' said Bill Neilly of Britain's ITN news channel. 'When you go into a conflict zone and you take ten helicopter rides, four convoys and six patrols, that's 20 times when you're vulnerable. I haven't decided to not do this, but to do less.'

'In my heart of hearts I believe it's a numbers game – every time you go outside the wire it's a spin of the wheel,' said Graeme Smith of Canada's *The Globe and Mail*. 'But I try to limit my exposure now, whether it's going out on patrol or into Kandahar,' he added, hazarding the odds of an IED strike at 1000-1.

Stewart Nusbaumer, a 61-year-old former US Marine turned journalist, was in 2009 still doing three-month embeds with infantry units in Afghanistan, despite wearing an artificial left leg in place of the one he lost in combat in Vietnam. And he knows the score better than most.

'I don't have a death wish. And I still get scared when the bullets are flying,' he said one evening in Bagram as we waited for flights.

The practice of some journalists of familiarising themselves with weapons for emergency self-defence is also an issue. A scandal blew up in Holland in October 2006 after Dutch documentary filmmaker and ex-soldier Vik Franke grabbed a rifle during an ambush in Uruzgan and shot back. It's not known if he killed anyone, but NATO estimated that about 20 insurgents died in the clash with a patrol of Dutch Special Forces and ANA, while several civilians were wounded.

'I once learned in military service that in a situation like that you should return fire,' media later quoted Franke as saying. 'That's why I took the Diemaco [rifle] from a soldier and shot in the direction of a cornfield where the muzzle flashes from Taliban weapons could be clearly seen.'

The NOS Dutch Public Broadcaster, the country's equivalent of the BBC, reacted sharply to the incident. Embedding of reporters was suspended until assurances were received that no gun-toting by journalists would be tolerated during their stay with the military.

'A journalist is a journalist and not sometimes a soldier. This leads to dangerous and unwanted role-play,' the broadcaster's Editor-in-Chief, Hans Laroes, wrote in a letter to the Dutch Defence Ministry.

Ultimately, a major obstacle to bridging the gap between troops and reporters is the utter tripe that sometimes gets printed and only hardens the scepticism in the military. Apart from anger at misquotation, there is derision of hacks who file dramatic lines based on hearsay or without going outside the wire. Like the British lads' mag writer who 'swapped an air conditioned office for the hot hell of Basra' to craft these magnificently awful lines.

> All military personnel on base are armed if not with a rifle then with a side-arm. It's unnerving … some of these guns have put empty spaces where Iraqi brains have been; the artillery has separated men's legs from their torsos. Our escort, an officer called Tim, tries to hand his gun to us so we can see what it feels like. We look at it with fear, like a grenade he just pulled the pin out of.

I might have inadvertently chipped a few slivers from the media disdain of one US Marine in Garmsir in 2008 during a conversation about how Prince Harry's brief service with British forces in Helmand earlier that year will have improved his public standing.

'Otherwise the media will make out that he was a coward,' he said as we trudged through clouds of moon dust after a patrol in the Green Zone.

'Well some might but certainly not all – not everyone is out to distort things.'

'All press are like that. You have to make a story sexy.'

'That's pretty unfair,' I objected. 'That's like me judging all US troops by the example set by that inbred runt and disgrace to your colours, Lyndie England.'

This mention of the Abu Ghraib jailer who posed for photos with naked, hooded and tethered Iraqi detainees could hardly have endeared me to the Sergeant. He said nothing in reply but I noticed that after this exchange he occasionally stopped for a chat and fixed me up with rides.

During this deployment, the Marines were given certain guidelines how to interact with the media and told not to 'spit, swear or adjust' (i.e. move their private parts) when talking to journalists. I found them pretty friendly on the whole, apart from one Staff Sergeant whose only words in my direction were, 'Don't talk to me, don't come near me.'

After the last reporters finished their embeds, the Marines' public affairs chief sent out a mail thanking us all for our participation and noting the effect this had among the troops: 'There are quite a few converts out there who initially wanted nothing to do with "embedded media" but you won them over.'

An embed certainly goes better if a rapport is developed, but occasionally it's easier to remain the nameless reporter, get in and out and not care what the troops make of you. Sometimes the lines are just too deeply drawn. After what seemed to be a sincere talk with a British Sergeant Major about battle stress, we shook hands, told each other to take care and parted company. As I walked away the wind carried some of his subsequent words to my ears: '…some German fucking newspaper wanting to hear that we are blowing up as many civilian compounds as possible.'

★ ★ ★

In June 2008 I miss my ride from the ANSF compound in Gereshk to my lodgings with the Danes at FOB Price. A couple of hours later a small convoy of British vehicles comes and picks me up together with a trailer full of six Javelin missiles worth $650,000 that had also been forgotten that morning.

There are no seats left in the vehicles so I sit uncomfortably exposed on top of piles of rations in the back of a WMIK. As we pull into the main street the 21-year-old infantryman at the Mark 19 grenade launcher turns and tells me, 'If we get into trouble hide behind me, that's what I'm paid for.'

He'll learn.

five

ACTION AND REACTION

The guys we lost are the ones I never would have thought of. It's a horrible thing to think but before you deploy you look at everyone and you can imagine who would get killed and injured. But people you never picture getting hit do. You realise how random it is.

18-year-old US infantryman, Kunar

For that you can probably blame decades of war and disaster movies where the hysterical guy bites the dust twenty minutes before the credits roll. In reality, soldiers become keenly aware of the arbitrary way death and injury can befall the most savvy, experienced and popular among them. Often it's a chance IED strike or pot shot, hence the age-old and still prevalent view that if a bullet has your name on it you will catch it regardless.

In Kandahar in 2008, Master Corporal Gavin Flett of Canada's 39th Combat Engineer Regiment carried a 7.62mm round engraved with his name in an ironic/superstitious bid to escape being hit by it. He vaguely recalled actor Rowan Atkinson's 'Black Adder' but said he didn't know Private Baldrick had done just that in the WWI series. Like many who served in Afghanistan or Iraq, the 33-year-old reservist said active service had radically altered the way he looked at life. And like others, he took a vivid memory of combat home with him.

I saw a guy lose both of his legs, I think about it every day. He was about 10 or 15 feet in front of me and *boom*, everybody blew up, we pulled the guy out and he didn't have any legs. We carried him out under fire 600 or 700 metres. I'll never forget his face, it was all grey and green, he had a bone sticking out of his left leg, and there was a big chunk of meat dangling off and bouncing around. I watched smoke envelop the guys, two came out without a scratch, four were pretty fucked up, one had half his face blown off. I'd never seen anything like that, it was traumatic for me.

I told my wife about some of it when I was on leave, I needed to get it off my chest, but I only gave her the general gist, not all the details. If you bottle it up it gets you later in life.

True to the movies, however, is the eagerness of the rookie soldiers to get some action, although for most the novelty quickly wears off.

'I was always pumping on about going out on patrols and making contact, then I got shot at and I was like, "I really don't care much for being shot at any more",' 20-year-old US infantryman Alex Goduti said in Kunar after his squad came through another fight but took no casualties. The soldiers with more life experience under their belt shrug off the yearning for a fight as youthful zest.

'Most of the boys are here for some action, they're adrenaline junkies,' adds a Danish armoured car gunner in Helmand. 'This is my third war, I don't care about the Taliban, I'm just here to do my job.'

'I think it's the same in any Army, it's the young guys looking for some action,' said Dennis, a Dutch infantry Sergeant serving in Uruzgan. 'After one time with dead and wounded they will never want that again.'

The randomness of tragedy in the field hit Estonia's small contingent in Helmand on August 23, 2007, when a 107mm Taliban rocket killed Sergeant Kalle Torn and Junior Sergeant Jako Karuks as they ate their lunch in the shade of an armoured car. These were the Baltic republic's first fatalities in Afghanistan, although other soldiers were seriously wounded by IEDs. When I joined the troops of Estcoy-6 nine months later there was plenty of go-get-'em enthusiasm among these NATO newcomers (the former Soviet republic joined the alliance in 2004) as they did final training at Camp Bastion in Helmand before moving to their patrol base in Now Zad.

'It was my dream; I wanted to see what's here, not like it's shown on TV but the real war. But let's see after the first contact if this is really the place I want to be,' said Ivan Tsygankov, a blue-eyed, bandana-clad ethnic Russian member of the contingent who was sheltering from the heat under a vehicle.

The 'real war' was not long in coming. Four days later, on the eve of the company's departure north, the blue, white and black national tricolour was already flying at half-mast at the Estonian encampment. The previous evening the weight of a stack of spare tyres caused a truck tailgate to crash down onto Sgt. Major Ivar Brok's head, mortally injuring him.

'We expected losses on the battlefield but not like this,' said the contingent's padre, Lieutenant Silvester Jürjö. 'But this sort of thing could happen any time, any place, including in Estonia, that's life.'

Conversations often turn to especially senseless incidents, like the death of Captain Jonathan Snyder, a Canadian who drowned under the weight of his equipment when he fell into a 20-metre-deep karez well during a night patrol in Kandahar in June 2008. Nothing is viewed as being too unlikely to happen to anyone, so even the big mouths tone it down when it comes to confronting one's mortality. The realisation helps temper inevitable squabbles that flare between members of a unit.

'Someone might say "I hate that guy" over something but they usually come back and make up – you don't even want to end a conversation like that because you never know what's going to happen,' said US infantry Sergeant Dave Lazarou.

It's all extremely humbling to hear, especially when you are sitting in a casualty's seat. In Khost province, I rode in the Humvee that a US infantry company's executive officer died in during the opening salvo of a ferocious enemy ambush at close quarters two months earlier. The intensity of the engagement shocked even the most battle-hardened

soldiers of the US 2nd Battalion 506th Regiment of the 101st Airborne Infantry Division, the modern-day incarnation of the legendary 'Band of Brothers'.

'This is my third deployment to Iraq and Afghanistan, I've been in fire fights and ambushes and this was the first time I thought we were going to make the news, a whole platoon killed,' Staff Sgt. David McNeil said.

When they finally cleared the ambush zone the platoon had lost the executive officer, a young Lieutenant who at the last moment took the rear right seat instead of an embedded Belgian photographer.

'He wanted the Combat Infantry Badge, he would come along on dangerous missions so he could get it,' another soldier recounted. 'We used to call him "the CIB chaser", when he went with us nothing happened so we joked that we should take him for good luck. The first time he came under fire he was killed within 10 seconds, an RPG round came through the rear of the truck, struck him in the back and blew him in half. He never knew what hit him.'

As for the act of killing the enemy, it is usually described very matter-of-factly, as part of the job, and if it weighs on the conscience of individual soldiers, they keep it to themselves and their friends or counsellors. But since they are explicitly trained to do this, most troops, and especially the infantry, seem keen to dispatch an enemy or two if they can. Sgt. Daniel Firkus of the 2-506th Airborne had three confirmed kills during his tour and offered this perspective, 20 months after we met in Khost and after he had left the military.

This is something I have given much thought to in the past year. From the day every infantryman enters the Army, he is made aware that his primary job is to destroy the enemy. This is made very clear to him. He is resocialized with cadences about death and exercises that require 'Kill!' to be hollered upon completion. The act of killing enemy combatants is glorified. This makes men who are eager to do their job appear blood thirsty, or as war mongers. But this is important because it creates a soldier who will act on instinct and not hesitate under stress.

USMC Cobra providing fire support to ground forces after a contact.

In my personal experience with taking the lives of others, the feeling of a job well done is only temporary. Immediately after killing I felt satisfaction that I had done my job well. This feeling of contentment is reinforced by the praise and respect of peers, subordinates and superiors. It was later that I began to think of my actions from a different perspective. Did the man have a family? Was he a good man, or was he the evil murderer he has been made out to be in military culture? I'm sure these are questions I will deal with for many years to come. In the end, I must ask myself, 'Would I do it again?' The answer is yes. Even now, being home and no longer part of the military, I still have a 'better him than me' attitude.

For those who were still on active service and had not had the benefit of passing time and prolonged reflection, the act of killing was more likely the flipside of the coin of their own potential death or injury.

'I don't mind killing people, it's seeing my buddies getting blown apart that gets to me,' a US Marine Corps Captain said.

'This is nothing like in the movies, this is not fun,' a Sergeant of the US 1st Battalion 4th Infantry Regiment told me at FOB Baylough in Zabul province in 2007. 'But I put a guy in my crosshairs and I sleep well at night because we never shoot first. I chuckle when I hear the news, none of what they or the president are saying has anything to do with what we're doing here. We're securing an area and trying to make sure no one gets shot in the face, and that's all.'

With the Taliban so adept at extracting their battle casualties, the absence of dead enemy after a fight is an annoyance for many.

'You see pink spray come off them as you hit them, we find blood spatters, but they always pick them up and move them before we get up there,' said Sgt. Luke Hearn, who also served at Baylough, one of the most frequently attacked outposts in the country at the time. 'In six and a half months I've yet to see a body but we know we've killed plenty. It's frustrating, you want some confirmation, job satisfaction.'

Adaptation to the job takes many forms. Soldiers often speak of rapid acclimatization to things that just a few weeks earlier had seemed unreal and terrifying.

'The first time you set foot in the Green Zone you think, right, I'm going to die,' a British Major said. 'Same with the first air assault we did – it turns out we were all thinking that .50-calibre rounds were going to come through the fuselage. Then you do it again and again and it's OK, you become used to it, you get more fatalistic about whether it's going to be you [that gets hit] and you just do your job.'

This makes it all the tougher to bear the chance casualties after the hard work is done. A case in point was Major Alexis Roberts of 1RGR, who died on the return journey to KAF.

'If you lose someone going in or during the operation it's unpleasant, but during extraction it's like you are coming back from work, it's just…' the same British officer said, running out of words.

On the whole, people don't immediately shy away from talking about friends who were KIA, perhaps as a means of coming to terms with it. Comments sometimes come across as so offhand they might seem callous, like 'You can sleep in the dead man's bed.' But read between the lines and you realise that the more abrupt the reference, the greater the sense of personal loss it probably hides. The repercussions of each death go through the unit and beyond, separate yet still intertwined with the grief of the bereaved family.

In a diary written during a six-month deployment in Helmand and Kandahar in 2007–08, Lieutenant Robert Grant of the Queen's Gurkha Engineers wrote:

Lex's death has hit the Brigade of Gurkhas quite hard and attending the ramp ceremony at Bastion was a poignant and sobering moment. As always it really brought home just what people are risking out here, how much they are preparing to lay on the line.

Lex had two young daughters and a wife, a family now shattered forever. I can't help but question what for in a way? It's at times like this you fully see war to be the utter waste of humanity that it is and you invariably question why. The only answer which seems to make any sense to me is Plato's adage that 'only the dead have seen the end of war'.

Susie Roberts, the Major's widow, wrote after his death:

Lex was my best friend, the most wonderful husband and deeply loving father to Alice and Freya. He died doing the job he loved and I had just received a letter from him saying how much good he felt he was doing for the people of Afghanistan and how proud he was to be part of the Royal Gurkha Rifles.[10]

The national flags of the ISAF members on the bases increasingly fly at half mast to signal losses, and now they are rarely fully hoisted in the spring and summer months. But the first casualty in a unit hits home hard. As Lt. Col. Bourne of 1RGR said after that IED strike, 'Suddenly there was a realisation among the men that this was real.'

The same realisation overtakes observers of the conflict too. In May 2008 I attended an outdoor service at Camp Bastion for British Territorial SAS Trooper James Compton, who was killed in action near Musa Qala. The service took place around a memorial cross made of brass shell cases and involved several hundred soldiers from countries with forces in Helmand – Britain, Denmark, Estonia and the United States. As the soldiers snapped to attention an Apache roared low overhead on its way in to land, then a pin-drop silence enveloped the gathering and the evening air was weighted with the traditional reading of the British Act of Remembrance.

'They shall not grow old as we who are left grow old. Age shall not weary them, nor the years condemn. At the going down of the sun and in the morning we shall remember them,' a member of Compton's squad proclaimed across the square.

A bugler then played The Last Post followed by a piece by a Scots piper, and Army chaplain Colin McLeod gave the eulogy in the second such service he had performed at Bastion since arriving. I never met Compton but remember being more moved on that still evening at Camp Bastion than at any other time in Afghanistan, and impressed with the solemnity and feeling those few words carried.

'You want to get it right for the men, so they know it's being done with dignity and respect,' McCleod said afterwards.

It doesn't necessarily require fatalities to bring home the hazards of the combat zone, a taste of indirect rocket fire will do. Many bases take salvos of projectiles fired from afar; a few cause injury and material damage but the main effect is to create a sense of vulnerability.

'I noticed that after a few rockets there was a change in people, they got a little edgy, they'd flinch when they heard things, although you don't hear them come in, they travel at the speed of sound,' said Sgt. Major John Beddows, a 48-year-old reservist serving in Kandahar with the Royal Canadian Horse Artillery.

A day earlier a 107mm rocket hit his base at Masum Ghar, dropping a one-kilo chunk of sizzling metal through the tent roof near the Commanding Officer's desk, while a small piece of flying shrapnel injured a soldier who was phoning home. Tucked into a rocky loop-shaped depression at the foot of a hill, the Canadians call Masum Ghar the 'catcher's mitt' because of the way Taliban rockets fired from the farmland below reliably explode within its perimeter.

At bases and outposts across the country you hear many stories about near misses and improbable hits. I met US medics in Paktika in 2006 who had treated a soldier with a stomach wound which when unwrapped on the operating table revealed the fins of an unexploded RPG lodged in his guts. The staff instinctively ran for cover and then came back into the theatre one by one and removed the projectile.

'He's only the second person in history to have this happen and survive,' one of the attendant nurses said.

Another American serving in the province at the time had a bullet go through the back of his helmet, penetrate his scalp, zip round the top of his head on the outside of his skull but inside the skin, before it popped neatly out of his forehead. He arrived at the aid station with a big grin on his face at his lucky survival.

'In this platoon we had five guys shot in the head and they all survived, it's crazy,' said Lt. Sean Parnell, who in that year in Paktika commanded three dozen men of Bravo Company, 2-87 Infantry, 10th Mountain Division. His medic bore a classic 'Action Man' scar across his cheek where a round grazed him, cutting deep enough to leave a permanent 'free beer for life' mark but not so as to rip off the side of his face.

Despite receiving ten Purple Heart medals for combat injuries, the company only lost one man in a tour that also saw them briefly thrown into Helmand to support the British. Corporal Jeremiah Cole died after his truck hit what they believe was a legacy landmine lying undetected in Paktika since the Soviet occupation.

Soldiers often reverently produce mangled bullets and chunks and slivers of shrapnel that they dug out of their body armour. Elsewhere, Humvee gunners have slumped dead through the hatch after a random burst of long-range enemy fire.

Particularly after bad occurrences, nervousness and fear among soldiers going on missions is masked with flippancy and forced jocularity but betrayed by pensive looks as they get moving. Waiting to go is the hardest part, when each soldier has to deal internally with the anxiety.

'I think you are an idiot if you don't have any fear,' Sgt. Major Beddows said. 'When I first got here, all of us had heard in Canada about IEDs. There was a wave that came over me, I thought "oh my God", but it wasn't fear for myself, it was what if I had a wounded soldier? I went for a three-hour walk and it came to me that I can't control who lives and who dies in Afghanistan and the fear left. But for the first three months I lied to my wife, I had to get intimate with Mother Earth a few times here, Afghanistan is a dangerous place. And war is hell – but this is only a counter-insurgency, so it's heck,' he laughed.

Loved ones and home are never far from people's thoughts as they do successive tours with the threat of possible bereavement for their families that these carry.

'Every time there is a fight like today I think afterwards, what would happen to my wife and kids if I got killed?' First Sergeant Chris Weiskittel of the US 1-4th Infantry in Zabul said after coming through a Taliban ambush.

Many say they avoid talking about the danger and the casualties when writing or phoning home and keep the description of their day brief and circumspect while steering the conversation to things they miss. Apart from anything else, Operational Security means they can't talk much anyway about what they are doing.

'I call home for an escape, I want to hear about mundane life, what so and so said to whom, who went shopping for what, it makes me happy to hear about this stuff,' another Canadian said.

Apart from not wishing to worry people, they often don't know how to describe this often brutal and spartan life, apart from with superlatives about the extreme heat and dust, cold and ice. Time and again you hear people say things like 'No one can really understand what it's like if they haven't been here.' A Scottish infantryman I met in Helmand kept it a secret from his friends at home that he was in the Army at all and had for years maintained the pretence that he was working in construction in London.

'What are you going to tell them, that you held an injured little girl in your arms because one of our unexploded bombs went off? And people always ask stupid questions like did you kill anyone?'

By contrast, he is one of those who seem to have been hooked by the exhilaration of combat and claims he only stayed in service because a mortar shell blew up in the sand three metres in front of him in Iraq.

'It was this that stopped me leaving the Army. I know it sounds strange, but the rush you get when you are in contact, it's fucking brilliant!'

For some, life at the front is just more navigable than other types of work.

'It's my second nature, I perform best when getting shot at – put me in front of a pile of papers and I'll panic,' said Sgt. Bruce Hunter of the 2-506th Airborne.

Some of the cumulative tension on tour gets worked off in fire fights and the gym, and shooting live rounds at wooden targets and vehicle wrecks on the ranges is an outlet of sorts. 'It provides a bit of stress relief from this dog shit,' a Canadian Sergeant says before launching an M72 anti-armour rocket at an old Hesco barrier.

Likewise, when British troops in Kandahar found a suspected Taliban get-away car hidden in a deserted wadi, their Major suggested to the platoon commander that they put a burst of 7.62mm fire into the engine block to disable it.

'But there are other ways so I left it to him – you've got to take the boys off the leash once in a while.' The vehicle was destroyed with an anti-tank rocket.

Regardless of whether active service feeds or frays the essence of an individual, I never met anyone who counted on going home exactly the same person. The expectation to return a changed man or woman grows from a mass of impressions and experiences of the tour, the chasm between the secure pace of home life and Afghanistan's violence, abject poverty, absence of basics like clean water, medicine and electricity, and just the rock bottom value of life here. Above all, soldiers must confront the fragility of their bodies or their friends', and the arbitrary brevity of human existence.

'It hit me that you can be talking to someone one moment and they can be gone the next day. It was the first time I realised that life is too short, you should really live it, say what you think,' Rob Soto, an 18-year-old US soldier in Kunar, concluded about losing two members of his company on one mission.

At the same time, many soldiers are curious to know their limits and push themselves to the edge, like a submarine captain taking a new vessel to the threshold of endurance, diving so deeply that the bulkheads groan under the pressure. How else do you find out what you are made of, some say? More than most things, coming under close fire for the first time tells you a lot about yourself.

'It depends what sort of man you were raised to be, on your mental strength and your dedication to the mission whether you'll fight or sit there and cry,' said Sgt. Gary Fordyce of the 1-4th Infantry in Zabul. And what comes after deployment is only expected to be lighter and brighter by comparison.

'I figured if I came here and had a tough experience I'd go home and even if the rest of my life is crazy it wouldn't be as hard as Afghanistan,' said Master Cpl. Flett with the engraved bullet. 'Every time a soldier goes to a war-torn country I'm sure they say the same thing, that these people have nothing and how can we worry about the stupid stuff back home? I was already grateful for the things I had before, but this has reinforced that.'

Recognition of the trivia of life is a recurrent theme.

'It has changed me, I don't worry about small stuff now,' Canadian Military Police

Corporal Elton Adams said in the summer of 2008. 'My wife called me the other day all distraught, she'd bumped the new car on the kerb and dented it. A year ago I might have been a bit upset, but now, what's a couple of hundred dollars? I will be happy if I go home with all my fingers, arms and legs.'

As is the theme of staying intact.

'Call me a pussy but I want to get out in one piece, go home to my wife in the same condition I came here in,' adds US Infantry Sgt. Farrel in Kunar. 'We're serving a purpose, doing a good job and it's exciting, but I could do without getting shot at, fuck that shit, I like musicals and dancing.'

Whatever the hopes and intentions, the experience of being at war will for many remain a hard one to quantify and manage after they go home. The short and long-term effects of post-traumatic stress disorder (PTSD), informally known as 'shell shock' in the world wars (in official WWI parlance as NYDN: Not Yet Diagnosed – Nervous), are still being observed and debated in countries that have sent units on successive postings to Iraq, Afghanistan and other theatres.

To help counter the possible fallout, some contingents do a 'decompression' course over a few days on Mediterranean islands like Cyprus or Crete. Here the troops get a chance to talk with counsellors and chaplains, swim, tour the sites and down a load of cathartic beer. The idea is to break up the return journey and ease the transition, unlock some of the trouble areas so they don't take the whole package of emotions back home with them, still sealed and untouched.

'I would fight with my wife about little stuff, like when my daughter complained about her food I'd remember the orphanages in Bosnia,' said a Dutch Sergeant Major who served in the Balkans before his country introduced its decompression programme.

But each person also detoxes in their own way, like the Scottish Military Policeman who told me, 'My idea of decompression is to get drunk and have a fight.'

During and after deployment a serviceman or woman can suffer from a range of stress-related symptoms like hyperactivity, hyper-vigilance, disturbed sleep, changes to appetite and gastro-intestinal disturbances, all

likely pointers to PTSD and more subtle than the rule of thumb applied by a US Marine Captain to his men that 'You've got PTSD if you shoot dogs and cats.'

In Canada's armed forces, symptoms must be displayed steadily for four weeks before a diagnosis of Acute Stress Disorder is upgraded to PTSD. Contrary to the popular public perception of PTSD, among soldiers, the primary cause is not combat stress but rather the strain of readjustment to families and relationships, and stable working environments that can be an acute anti-climax after the intensity of deployment. All Canadian troops get a mandatory check-up within half a year of coming home.

'There is a honeymoon period and problems can surface months down the road when they feel their work isn't fulfilling,' said Dr Colonel Theresa Girvin, a psychologist serving with the Canadian contingent in Kandahar in 2008.

Generally, about 80 per cent of affected combat veterans will adjust after nearly universal periods of sleeplessness and anxiety, US studies show. But 20 per cent have continuing difficulties, with post-traumatic stress, depression and alienation.

Often the problems simmer as a body of resentment the individual cannot easily break down and compartmentalise: 'I've had soldiers complaining of feeling very angry, anger at the locals, their situation and also at going home,' added Girwin. For one troubled soldier, it took a return visit to Afghanistan to bring any balm.

'After serving there during the Soviet campaigns, the nightmares remained for years,' wrote a former Estonian contingent commander in Helmand who fought as a Soviet paratrooper in Kandahar in 1986–87, coming back with NATO two decades later. 'After being there again, things have kind of clicked into place in a good sense. Now, some dreams haunt, but in general, my soul is at peace.'

While understanding of combat stress and PTSD is growing, tolerance is diminishing for those who cite it as grounds for clemency during prosecution for subsequent criminal offences back home. An American Colonel wrote to *Stars and Stripes*: 'There has been an overemphasis on post-traumatic stress disorder and traumatic brain injury for Operation

Iraqi Freedom/Operation Enduring Freedom veterans, and this may derive from over-compensation for the lack of emphasis on these mental conditions from previous wars. Unfortunately, this overemphasis has been taken advantage of by some veterans who may use PTSD as a contributing factor for their criminal activity…Bottom line, honorable service and having PTSD gives no one the right to break the law.'

The Canadian Mental Health Team Leader in July 2008, Captain Bruce Cleveland, raised a problem I heard among many troops who had been in combat in Afghanistan: 'Soldiers are not sure who the enemy is, they are crossing open farmland, one moment there are farmers there, the next there is a weapon pointing at them – the farmer has dropped his tools and picked up a weapon. There are often no front lines that are easily defined, our soldiers have taken casualties and there is no one to react to.'

It's a cause of huge frustration, not know-ing who you are supposed to fight while being forced by the very nature of the international mission to remain open to the broader popula-tion, without the support of which the whole effort is doomed.

'In Kosovo we were only helping people, we were liberators. It's very different here, we are also the enemy,' a Dutch Corporal said. 'And it's a lot harder because we are fighting against an invisible enemy. When we go outside we have to be careful of IEDs and ambushes. In Yugoslavia there was an enemy in uniform, but here they just have a beard, all look the same, and you can't tell who is who.'

The constant dilemma about who is friend or foe has a steady wearing effect on the for-eign troops. It's not right but understandable that after someone tries to shoot a patrolling soldier in the back he begins to tar whole vil-lages or districts with the same brush.

'There's a big danger of becoming cynical,' said Christian, a Danish infantry Lieutenant. 'The first patrol in the Green Zone after a TIC is the hardest. It takes a lot to go up to the locals and shake their hand after they tried to kill you the day before.'

six

TROUBLE TOWN AND THE DANES

'If there's danger the tower guards will sound a football horn and you take cover,' says the Danish Sergeant Major, a giant man in shorts with a red face, long nose and grey moustache. 'There's a firing range inside the camp, the US blow up their powder and ammo there, so if you hear something, look at the guys who have been here longest, they are the ones with the brownest legs – if they don't react, don't worry. Sometimes the cooks set off the fire alarms when they fry the bacon in the morning. If people are not running around, stay in bed and think of your breakfast.'

It's late May 2008 at FOB Price in Gereshk in Helmand province. A few months ago the British, Danish and US troops stationed here were still getting contact with the Taliban inside this city of some 30–50,000 inhabitants – no one knows just how many live in the slums that grew in the twenty years since the Russians left. But for now Gereshk has settled into an uneasy calm that allows for some headway on infrastructure projects. The hope is that these will help cement support for the Afghan government in the long term, but in the meantime the locals just seem inclined to take what they can get while the going is good, regardless of ideology. An 11-man Danish CIMIC (Civilian and Military Cooperation) team manages most of the construction of wells, schools and roads, and to the disapproval of some political parties in Denmark, also implements mosque repairs.

'We restored a lot of mosques, the reason is that the Taliban say ISAF are Christians, infidels, who want to get rid of Islam,' says the team leader, Major Peter. (There have been incidents of Danish troops being identified and harassed back home so that contingent uses only first names). It's a fair consideration in view of the publication by a Danish newspaper in 2005 of the controversial Mohammed cartoons. This sparked violent protests by Muslims around the world, and subsequent international reprints of the cartoons drew a crowd to the gates of FOB Price, until the Gereshk Mayor Said Dur Ali Shah helped calm and disperse it peacefully.

'We say we don't want to get into this discussion and if they need assistance restoring mosques we'll help,' continues the Major. 'It's very hard to measure if it creates a good effect but we think it does. When we started they didn't like speaking to us. Now they appreciate ISAF but they still don't want to work for us.'

A case in point is the garbage disposal project that the Danes helped the municipal authorities set up, comprising 60 small dumping points around the city that are emptied by trucks. The clean-up was a hit with the local population and is a pet project of the mayor, but he still can't raise more than 11 workers of 30 needed in this city of high unemployment.

'They are still intimidated by the Taliban,' the Major says. 'The insurgents are going for soft targets, they come at night when families are gathered together and go into their compounds and say isn't it better to support the Taliban and the Islamic war?'

Like most foreigners here, the Danish officer had to take a cultural jolt before he could start trying to effect positive change in a place that often seems firmly rooted in a primitive otherworld.

'I remember thinking this is like Europe 200 years ago, but you can go into a compound where they have no running water and flooring and they still have cell phones. The only thing that will change that is time, we just have to make sure we don't lose them. We have all this money for development, but money without time is worthless.'

Just getting the message across to the locals is difficult enough before anything gets fixed or built: 'I feel like a company that has a really good product but no one knows I've got it.' So CIMIC works closely with the Danish Influence Operations (IO) team that sits behind the next door in the stone-brick headquarters of the Danish Task Force Helmand.

Their pokey, windowless room is fitted with an A/C unit with no housing that dribbles water into one of those spouted plastic pots that Afghans use to wash their backsides. A dozen more pots hang in a bunch on the wall ('gifts', I am told) beside a poster of Kylie Minogue that is fixed with four ISAF stickers. On the shelves there are stacks of psychological operations ('psyops') leaflets warning locals not to tamper with any ordnance they find. Another flyer shows the black, red and green Afghan tricolour and pictures of the ANA and proclaims in Pashtu and English that 'The Government of the Islamic Republic of Afghanistan is fighting to drive the enemies of the nation from Gereshk and surrounding areas forever.'

The room also houses broadcasting equipment for Radio Gereshk 100FM, another means of local outreach. CIMIC helped the IO team to set up a ten-digit emergency number for the city that is manned by Afghan Police officers. It's taking a while for the idea to catch on though. The first caller wanted to complain that his house had no electricity and the second requested a song on the radio.

The next day the Major will conduct a visit to three of the city's 11 schools to introduce the new Afghan Civil Order Police (ANCOP) commander to the children, part of a bid to establish the local security forces as entities to be trusted rather than feared.

Peter is understandably nervous at the prospect of the mission. It's his first foray into town since a smiling suicide bomber walked into the middle of one of his CIMIC teams

in the bazaar on March 17 and detonated an explosive vest packed with ball bearings. Two Danish soldiers died instantly, as well as their Afghan interpreter and the commander of the detachment of Czech soldiers guarding them. Since then the Czechs have been confined to base by their Defence Ministry and do little but eat, work out and sit in a capacious plastic paddling pool sporting large Abba hairdos.

The outreach mission is an obvious target for any of the three suicide bombers currently believed to be on the loose in the city. The CIMIC team members are to be escorted by a few Danish infantrymen, a squad of British territorial SAS troops, and Afghan security forces. That evening at the HQ they hold the joint daily Danish, British and US briefing on upcoming business and notable incidents during the day in Helmand and Afghanistan as a whole.

The Taliban have been shooting at helicopters with small arms and RPGs at FOB Inkerman near Sangin (named 'Incoming' by the British because of the volume of fire it takes) and a few IEDs were discovered, including two mines suspended from trees to kill soldiers moving on foot.

A warning is issued to keep an eye on ANA soldiers after a pistol was taken from a Danish jeep in the night and another vanished from the quarters of a British soldier at one of the small outlying bases. That one was found during a search of the ANA barracks.

Meanwhile, the FOB Price notice board puts the next day's temperature at 40 degrees Celsius and recommends a fluid intake of 9.5 litres for those doing 'light office work', 12 litres for medium march and 14.5 litres for heavy march.

The CIMIC team assembles by its lightly armoured Mercedes jeeps at 0615 for the ride into town. I go in one vehicle with two guys from the IO team and Pia, a pretty blonde artillery Private with cropped hair from Jutland, whose inclusion along with another female soldier is aimed at creating a 'softer approach' during such missions, she says.

'When you go around in camps the ANA stare a lot. I don't think the locals notice we're women when we have our body armour and helmet on, but when they hear my voice is higher they pay attention,' says the 24-year-old, who has started to regularly help CIMIC to get in touch with women and girls in Gereshk.

The two Danish vehicles drive into the city with five British jeeps and Vector vans with the SAS and make a stop at the Joint District Control Centre (JDCC), a Russian-built fortified compound that is manned by seven British troops and more than 100 ANA and ANP. The March 17 bombing occurred less than 100 metres from here and a week ago they found a large arms cache round the corner. 'So anything can happen,' one of the Danes warns.

We are joined by seven Ranger pick-ups of the local security forces, one of which has been through 'Pimp My Ride' Afghan style and is decked out with a furry dashboard festooned with bright plastic flowers and Afghan pop music cassette boxes. The 14-vehicle column then snakes out of the JDCC compound and winds slowly through the bazaar to the first school.

Here we are to get a short speech of self-introduction by Sher Mohammed, the new chief of the ANCOP, a stocky man of about 40 with a livid five-inch scar that runs across his right cheek and under his ear. He will then hand out gifts from the trailer hooked behind my jeep. No toilet pots this time, but 60 small bags of flour, 60 of beans, 60 of rice and also 200 schoolbags and 20 footballs for the three schools.

The Danes emphasise that this isn't a humanitarian aid drop but a 'symbolic gesture of friendship'. I sense this approach with the limited gifts will backfire but say nothing; it's not my place to interfere. But I've been to a couple of HA drops before and they can get riotous, even when there's enough for everyone.

'Make sure you give the school kits to the children and not the teachers because they'll just store it and sell it,' a British officer advises before we leave.

We drive through the school gate and the Afghan and ISAF vehicles fan out across a grassy football field. A couple of ANCOP officers stand on the wall with Kalashnikov rifles and the SAS detachment set up a 7.62mm machine-gun on the roof.

This is where things start to go wrong.

Seeing the excited throng of hundreds of kids and youths crowded behind the barred windows, Sher Mohammed now refuses to hand out the items.

'He said it's not enough and threw it back at us, this isn't good,' Major Peter glumly tells the rest of the group after the interpreter finds out what's wrong. Someone manages to persuade the Afghan officer to go through with the presentation and the soldiers pile up 45 bags of flour, 13 footballs and half a dozen bottles of palm oil for distribution to the best and also the poorest students. In addition to the younger kids, the school has 300 youths aged 17 to 20 whose education was interrupted in the past and whose attendance of classes helps to exclude them from Taliban recruitment drives. The chief is unhappy at being co-opted in a handout that won't benefit the vast majority of the pupils, but he gives a short speech to the chosen recipients lined up before the piles.

'This is a gift for you today, it isn't much but we must accept it,' he tells them. 'Two things are important in this world, one is education, and the other is discipline. Discipline we can get from the family, but you must appreciate the teachers because they give you education, and you must try to be clever students.'

After the goods are given out, the school director Abdullah ticks off the Major for not bringing enough for everybody. The Dane apologizes to him as our group walks to the neighbouring compound, thinking it's school number two when it's actually the junior section of this one, with a total of 2,400 boys who study to age 16 and then go to the high school. The ANA chief addresses one class: 'We are proud of you young guys because it's a dangerous province, the situation isn't good but you still go to school. There has been fighting here for 30 years and our boys and girls are uneducated. My commander told me recently to find five soldiers for promotion who had been educated, and I couldn't find any.

'Education and praying are equally important. The Prophet tells us that if we are educated we can recognize Allah and know who we are. The ANA and ANP are trying to provide security in schools because you guys are the future of Afghanistan. If you get educated you can become a minister or a president.'

Danish CIMIC team distributes and demonstrates wind-up radios in Helmand province.

Danish troops descend from FOB Armadillo into the Green Zone in the Gereshk River Valley, Helmand province.

Danish light reconnaissance unit Saxo prepares to go 'night fishing' in Gereshk, Helmand province, June 2008.

The Danish Major steps up and clears his throat.

'Hello, my name is Peter, I'm an ISAF soldier, and I come from Denmark. My government and soldiers have been asked by the government of Afghanistan to come and provide security and help build up Afghanistan. I think it's a good cause so I left my family to come and help the ANA and ANP to build Afghanistan.

'We will help the ANA to provide security so you can get educated…Please don't go near the convoys, we are afraid you will get hit. Soon hopefully you won't need us and you can be yourselves again.'

Most of the boys are in exams but a couple of hundred crowd round as the trailer is uncovered and more stuff is handed out while the ANCOP keep the kids back with a mixture of jest and aggression. One officer chases them with booted kicks, another jumps forward and whacks the bolder kids round the head with an empty water bottle, or throws stones at them. They are scared individually but crow as a group, testing how far they can come forward without getting separated from the pack and hurt. This is how Afghans play.

The batch of gifts comes to an end and the Danes cover up the remainder, which should go to the next school. The kids see there's more but realising they aren't going to get any of it surge forward and start pulling at the tarpaulin. The cops start beating and kicking them in earnest but it's clear they will swarm the trailer at any moment. The Danish driver leaps in the Mercedes, guns the engine and lurches away with a mob chasing him, circling the school building at high speed.

The Major stands there aghast. 'This is a CIMIC nightmare – they're like wild animals,' he stammers, resembling the figure in Edvard Munch's painting 'The Scream'.

The jeep and trailer speed out from behind the school and pull up at the gate where the Afghan cops push forward and lash out in unison, holding back the mob long enough for the driver to exit the compound. Danish restraint prevents him from taking the direct, diagonal route across the football field to the main school gate, so he drives along the edge of the pitch and turns 90 degrees at the far corner, heading for the main exit.

The Afghan cop in the back of the nearest Ranger laughs with this buddy at the unexpected entertainment, cocks his rifle and points it at the children, who set off in a baying pack across the diagonal and head off the vehicle with the booty. With the way blocked, the yelling Danes and British try to shield the trailer while Gereshk's new Civil Order Police throw stones at the kids. Another officer points his rifle and chases them, striding along in the firing position. Hearts and Minds.

'I told you yesterday this would happen,' the Major is told by the Afghan NDS security agency guy who accompanies the mission. Eventually the plundering assault fizzles out and we can move again, a ring of soldiers escorting the trailer out of the school.

'You need a security perimeter to actually do any good, it's sometimes very frustrating,' one of the Danes reflects. 'They are opportunists; they grow up like that to survive. You know they are cooperating because it's viable, but if something better comes along they can just switch.'

We mount up and turn right into the bazaar's melee of stalls selling naan, fruit and carpets and a bustle of men and a few women in white, green and blue burqas. 'This is not a nice place,' someone says and I realise we are passing the spot where the CIMIC team got bombed three months earlier.

The next school has less than 100 male students who learn up to 16 subjects ranging from mathematics and English to car mechanics and electrics. There's no real prospect of a mob scene here but since most of the classes are sitting exams, the goods are left with the teachers. One of the older boys is taking pictures of the soldiers on his cell phone and sending texts, I'm later told he's thought to be an informant. Another kid asks one of the female soldiers what her family name is and gives her a piece of paper to write it on. It is also a concern – there have been cases in the small Scandinavian populations where families of serving military personnel have been harassed back home.

The third school is for boys and girls. It's recess when we enter the yard and the kids are milling around. The Danish public affairs officer says to a female British soldier who remains in full equipment, or 'battle rattle', 'Are you going to take your helmet off?'

'We're in Afghanistan. I don't like taking it off.'

'We take them off.'

'But my safety comes first.'

She does remove it though and goes with Pia and the other Danish woman to talk to some girls and their teachers while we go to the boys' side. The director tells us what we hear everywhere, that the staff are very poor, have low salaries and are not paid on time. The teacher of computing and geology comes up to us and tells us in very precise English that his wage is 2,500 afghanis (50 dollars) per month.

'I have to pay for the house and family. That's not enough even for one person. The Education Ministry has promised to build a house for every teacher but there are no houses and rent can be 3,000 to 4,000 afghanis a month. But I am proud to teach even without a salary.'

He then tells us about another suicide bombing on the street by the school while he was holding a class.

'There was an explosion outside, parts of the suicide attacker were all over the ground in here, his bones, brains, and all the children were crying. Two of them were hysterical so I pulled out my wallet and gave them my last money to calm them down, five afghanis each. We took them all back into the class and carried on. We have to work in these conditions.'

Back at FOB Price there is some new discussion of security. An interpreter was warned by a local contractor that he should not stand close to the CIMIC team, which suggests that a targeted attack can be expected. There is even talk of giving these 11 Danes British uniforms to help hide them among the overall body of foreign forces but they are not keen on the idea. A few days later a CIMIC jeep is hit by an IED in town and a member of the team is injured.

Night Patrol

Gereshk has suffered a rash of robberies at night so the Danish light reconnaissance unit Saxo goes out 'fishing', using themselves as bait.

'Two jeeps will have lights on, two won't, let's see if anyone bites,' says Rasmus, a young ginger-haired Sergeant who runs the scouting missions.

Four open-backed Mercedes mounted with machine-guns leave Price and motor down the highway into town. There are very few lights and most of the illumination comes from the half moon in a star-heavy sky.

The first stop is to pick up a Kalashnikov from a local man they found with the weapon the day before but who could produce no papers for it. The vehicles have to turn off the main road and crawl through a maze of dark alleys between compound walls, heaps of rotting refuse and stinking drainage runnels to reach his home.

They take the confiscated AK from its sullen owner and then push north to the outskirts and set up 200 metres from a gas station that was robbed a couple of times. Snipers cover the site while two vehicles move in and nose around. The only sign of life is the barking of dogs in the warm, gritty headwind so the patrol heads back into town to fish some more there.

As the Danes crawl through the deserted bazaar, dust devils dance around the deserted stalls and snagged scraps of cloth and plastic bags flap in the shadows. Everyone is jumpy enough without the violent electrical flashes that start when a power line is torn down by the rising wind. Suddenly the troops spot a man standing by a wall with a rifle and he's a moment from being taken down when they identify him as an Afghan policeman. The patrol drives back to base.

'It's an OK town but a few assholes spoil it,' says Rasmus. 'There are some suicide bombers who want to get ISAF so you have to stay sharp. But most people just want to live peacefully and send their children to school.'

The next evening Saxo goes out again and turns off the road into one of the quarters where sympathy for the Taliban is stronger. As dusk falls, the jeeps groan down a narrow rutted track by a canal, their side panels scraping against the steps of the mud compounds as they slip through. For 20 minutes the vehicles lurch through dim, tight alleyways where the local kids usually pelt them with stones. Today the urchins only run up with open hands to shout 'kalam kalam', pen pen. The Danes are extra vigilant because they have been warned

Danish patrol urges locals to report
Taliban movements and IEDS, Gereshk
River Valley, Helmand province.

of some vehicle-borne IEDs and an unmarked
white Toyota in particular, although this intel
tip doesn't help much.

'Have you noticed how many unmarked
white Toyotas there are in Gereshk?' one of the
soldiers points out.

It's already dark when two shots ring out
and the patrol stops. In front of them sits a
minibus with a flat tire and an injured driver
who had driven down the alley with no headlights towards the lead jeep. He failed to stop
as they flashed their barrel laser sights so force
was escalated.

'Warning shots were fired at the right-hand
side but unfortunately it was a right-hand
drive,' says a young soldier called Ziggi (his dad
is a big Bowie fan).

Of the two rounds aimed at the engine
block, one took out the tyre while the other
fragmented through the radiator and into the
driver's ankle, luckily missing the bone.

'I thought it was children playing,' the
20-year-old man groans, lying on the ground
with his foot in a pool of blood as the medic
gives him a shot of morphine and bandages
the wound. They call off the patrol and take
him to Price where the Danish medical team
led by Dr Nina patches him up in their tent.

Dr Nina

I met Nina at a gathering with a few bottles of
non-alcoholic 'near-beer' around a new picnic

bench the carpenters built for the HQ. An improvised signpost in the little yard indicates that Copenhagen is 4,769km to the west and the British town of Templecombe 3,682 miles.

Part Dane, part native American, the doctor was a reservist in the Danish armed forces for many years and volunteered for active service after returning from the US to start a new life. She had formerly specialised in emergency medicine in Rochester, New York, where treating gunshot victims of gang clashes was good preparation for her first tour in the Iraqi city of Basra. There her team got rocketed daily for months and felt like sitting ducks, she says.

Afghan officials in Gereshk were uncomfortable at having to interact with a female doctor until she treated the six-year-old son of a local administrator and was then cordially invited to the next joint meeting. It was the same in Iraq until she treated the Governor of Basra, after which he started to show up regularly to the meetings with the Danes.

'Being a woman works in different ways. I think it does create a lot of goodwill – women look at you, on the one hand they are thinking how can she not be like us, and on the other hand they see that you can be treated differently as a woman.'

But her gender is less of an obstacle than the overall attitude and practices of the Afghan doctors.

'The problem is that they think attending to basic hygiene is beneath them, so they'll throw away an organ in the garbage and it will stay there for days or weeks.'

I went to see Nina at the medical tent, which is fitted with an artificial response unit that monitors patients' vital signs and can give resuscitation shocks. But the tent can only take two patients with severe trauma at a time.

'Sometimes we have to line them up on the floor,' she says.

The facility is staffed by two doctors, two nurses and half a dozen military paramedics that the regular staff bring in to learn on the job. One of the biggest problems is the outbreaks of diarrhoea and vomiting caused by poor hygiene.

'If one soldier has it the whole tent will get it and it can actually close a camp if you're not on it immediately.'

And the dust. 'You can never clear it up totally, we try to clean at least once a day and at the end we ask ourselves if we even cleaned at all.'

The following month, Nina's team and the US military doctors at Price will pool resources in a new medical centre housed in metal containers with a large treatment room. But for now the casualties ebb and flow at the Danish tent.

In the late afternoon of May 28, an injured policeman showed up at Price with a flesh wound to his left shoulder, simple enough to patch up were it not for the added factor of rampant drug-use among the Afghan security forces.

'The only problem we had was that he was a heroin addict and we couldn't find veins so we had to give him medication intravenously into his feet,' Nina said.

Usually the doctors can spot the junkies from their failure to respond to morphine. 'When you give them the first shot you can easily tell they use something. They usually fess up when they start feeling the pain.'

But it was the circumstances of the injury that puzzled the Danes most. The evening briefing centres on tangled events that day at a Police checkpoint on the eastern edge of town. First two guys on a motorbike and carrying an RPG launcher were reportedly able to ride clean through before the cops could react. Then at least one ANP died and two were injured in a shooting incident, while another ran off from the same post with a PKM machine-gun. The casualties bore grenade shrapnel and gunshot wounds but the only explanation the ANP chief gives ISAF is that 'a gas cylinder blew up while the detachment was making tea'.

'You'll never get to the bottom of it, it's all about reading between the lines,' says a weary British liaison officer who has been grappling with the serial lies and evasion for several months.

The other injured policeman made his way to Gereshk city hospital where they sewed up his wound without realising that the bullet was still inside him, having passed through him from left to right and finally lodging behind his right clavicle, partly collapsing the lung. The Danes put in a drain and saved his life.

Dusty Dane. After journey across
the desert from Gereshk to FOB
Armadillo, Helmand province.

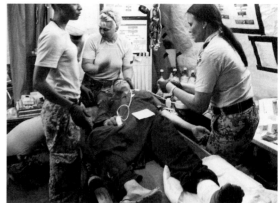

Dr Nina and team work on
wounded Afghan civilian,
Gereshk, Helmand, June 2008.

Before I leave FOB Price Nina gets another casualty, a member of the local militia that acts as a supplementary security force around the base. In another largely unexplained incident, a bullet went in one side of the man's head, through his jaw, opened an artery and exited from the other side of his head. The medical team was thrilled he was going to survive after they treated him. Then, against regulations, the Afghan militia commander passed him off as an injured Police officer, thereby securing his evacuation to the advanced medical facility at Camp Bastion for follow-up treatment. Now out of immediate danger, the casualty wasted no time in filing a complaint accusing the Danes of 'stealing his wristwatch and artificial leg'.

The evening before I leave Gereshk and move up the valley to a small Danish patrol base I sit with Nina outside the camp shop drinking fresh orange juice, a heavenly taste in these surrounds. The conversation turns to the dead rather than the living, something that is never far from your mind but which somehow gets blurred with its frequency.

'You see so many ramp ceremonies that you forget there's a person inside the box and that they're gone,' she says, referring to the formal loading of flag-draped coffins on transport planes for the journey home.

'It's hardening and it shouldn't be that way. When we treat Danish soldiers who ran over an IED and haven't been badly injured, it hits them hard psychologically, overnight they

realise that they're mortal. It's sad that they have that veil drawn away so suddenly.'

I didn't see the doctor again but got an e-mail from her three weeks later.

June 21, 2008
These past 24 hours have probably been some of the saddest of my life. It started out like any other day but proved to be very different.

At 0830 the phone at the infirmary rings with a heads-up that there was an explosion in town and that we might get some casualties. We had gotten a similar report the morning before and nothing happened. But as always when a report of that kind comes in we start preparing.

Then we were called again and told that we most likely would not get any as most were going to the little hospital in town. Fine we thought. Then the guard tower reports that they are seeing a convoy approaching very fast and in that moment we all knew that casualties were underway.

They come rushing in and when we get ready to unload the vehicle we realised that it was the US Marines from our camp who had taken a hit. We brought them inside and started to treat them. While treating them we got two more civilians, a child and a grown-up guy.

We got the Americans outside and waited for their helicopter pick-up, and then we proceeded to treat the child and the adult. The little six-year-old boy had sustained multiple injuries including an open skull fracture, severe traumas to almost all parts of the body and he died shortly after. A life that had barely begun. I focussed on the civilian to get him to the chopper. Then we washed the little boy and tried to make him look the best given the circumstances.

Then we had another American with a blunt trauma to his right abdomen. The fragment had actually gone through casings of ammunition and stopped in the fragmentation vest. He never realised that he had been hit. We send him with the chopper too as he could have internal bleedings that we couldn't see.

Then came the moment that I shall never forget as long as I live. Another Humvee stopped at our infirmary. On a stretcher in the back were a US soldier and one of the interpreters, both covered with a tarpaulin. We had to make sure that they were actually dead so we brought them into the infirmary.

We took the tarp off and I will never forget what I saw. The interpreter on top with a leg and arm blown off and with other injuries not compatible with life. We put him in the body bag, having to figure out what part belonged to which body. The second one had the stomach blown apart with its contents spilling out. We put him in the other bag. We made our isolation tent the mortuary.

One of their friends was sitting in a corner in the room and the sorrow in his face was heartbreaking. I must admit I cried whether I wanted to or not. The tears just flowed. They were my son's age and they should really have had their life ahead of them.

We had another American civilian who had been close to the blast and we sent him to the field hospital. All the injured Americans are doing fine and are out of danger. The rest of the day I spent talking to the Marines. They were all in shock and walked around like zombies. I can't help think that they had grown up today. The innocence evaporated as they all had to face their own mortality.

I think the lesson learned from today (if there is one to learn) is to live every day as if it is our last, as we never know what tomorrow brings.

June 22
I am slowly recovering from the ordeal but I think the picture of the two men has sort of burned into the retina and I wonder if that smell of burned flesh will ever leave my nostrils.

June 23
Things seem to have calmed down a little bit, at least for now. The only blast yesterday was a local rivalry; someone tried to kill one of the local mullahs but failed miserably.

Well, as you know, the Americans were hit and now even more so. The battalion commander, some Lieutenant Colonel or Colonel, went in a car with three others to attend a memorial service up here but the car got blown up near Kandahar and they all perished. Needless to say, it was an enormous blow to all the Marines here in camp.

I talked to one of the young servicemen yesterday and he had been in Iraq last year. Twelve out of the 22 in his platoon had died. He told us that he was going home in November, 'that is, if I make it that far'. This young person has had to face so much destruction in his young life, the innocence and youth has vanished. My heart was bleeding for him.

They came to the infirmary to ask if there was any way that I could get hold of a chaplain and luckily I could. Thomas arrived yesterday. I had never met him before but everyone worships him and I am starting to understand why. He has a very gentle way about him and he seems to really have a special rapport with the soldiers. I am so happy that he is able to help the Marines. He will also hold a debriefing for us today and I think that will be really good. We have had one, but I think he might be able to help us all deal a little better with the horrific experience that we have had to endure.

Having dealt with life and death makes you appreciate every day in a different way. A day that has gone by well can never come back bad. I think you learn to live in the moment and appreciate the little things that most people take for granted.

I think one of the hardest things of coming back is the fact that my boys don't want me to talk about what I have experienced. I know they are very scared for me when I am gone, and I think it confronts their fear when I talk about it. So in general I don't mention it unless I see some of the people that I was deployed with.

I am really excited about going back to my regular job in Denmark, and I know that my employers luckily feel the same way. It is really hard to tell what kind of impact that my experiences have had on me. I know I have changed but I think what I have cherished the most is the humor and the laughs. Without them I think it would be really hard but even in difficult moments, friendship and jokes are the best medicine. And that comes from a doctor!

Thomas, Ernie and the Green Zone

On June 3 two Afghan workers with a crane 'open the gate' at the back of Price to let in the armoured vehicles of the Fenris mechanized infantry company (motto: *Oderint Dum Metuant*: 'May they hate, as long as they fear.')

The Afghans hook chains onto the top of one of the Connex containers that currently makes up the back wall during enlargement work on the Hescos and they lift it out of the line. The first of the Danish Piranha armoured personnel carriers rolls through the gap in a cloud of dust. My ride to FOB Armadillo is here. After a 40-minute drive across the desert the Piranhas rumble into the little base where the crews shake off layers of dust and use compressed air guns to blast down the clogged weapons and equipment inside the vehicles.

Armadillo is perched on the edge of the desert above the Green Zone. This strip of arable land runs more than 400 kilometres, almost the entire length of the Helmand River, snaking down from the dam at Kajaki, through Gereshk and the provincial capital Lashkar Gah to the southern town of Garmsir,

and west through the desert through Nimruz province that borders on Iran and Pakistan. The Green Zone measures from one to ten kilometres in width, and as well as being the bread basket of the province it is its poppy-growing nucleus.

Helmand produces two-thirds of Afghanistan's poppy, and the country at this time produced 93 per cent of the heroin worldwide. So the value of this land's illegal agriculture is huge, amounting to hundreds of millions of dollars a year. Where possible the Taliban keep a hold over activities in the zone, which shelters, feeds and funds them, and provides concealed transit routes.

'It's their line of communication,' says the Danish commander at Armadillo, Major Morten Moeller. 'They can't use the desert because we'll see them; in the Green Zone they can put down their weapons and blend in with the locals. The locals live down there, so out in the desert the Taliban have no influence over them. It's also their way of financing their operations; they tax opium, take one kilogram of every five produced, and one in ten for wheat.'

The Danes mount one or two patrols a day into the fields below, which depending on the season can be ploughed and dry, or a riot of red and white poppy flowers, or covered in towering green corn plants that create a jungle effect. Before the afternoon patrol goes out I am billeted in a tiny windowless room in a tumbledown mud-brick house that is used by both the Danes and a small detachment of British troops. My cot stands between piles of rubble beneath a high vaulted brick ceiling with a single bulb dangling from the ceiling. A sparrows' nest is daubed around the cord and the birds flit in and out of the building through the holes and wonky doorframes and take turns to crap on my bed.

Through the wall I can hear the British signallers next door watching porn on a laptop, interspersed with snippets of Danish conversations that come through another hole in the wall to the kitchen area. Here there is a deep freezer which the soldiers fill with soda and water, a stove and a small bread-baking machine, piles of Norwegian and British ration packs and bookshelves stacked with dusty paperbacks and magazines.

Outside the house a tracked armoured carrier with Homer Simpson's face painted on the back is manned by a few soldiers of a Lithuanian fire support team who pick at a battered guitar between duties. Another 100 metres further on a British and Australian 105mm gun battery sits at the edge of the FOB by the mortar pits. All the barrels point towards the Green Zone and river.

I get a quick tour from the deputy commander of Armadillo, Captain Morten Haubro, who wears just shorts and boots and holds a leash with the camp dog, a skinny, mild-mannered mongrel called Fenris that chases cats for sport between long naps in the shade. On the way round I am introduced to a few characters like Henrik of the Mobile Electronic Warfare Team (MEWT – unofficial motto: 'In God we trust, the rest we monitor'), whose own lack of shirt in the 45-degree heat reveals a chest full of tattooed heroes from Danish mythology.

The troops live in dark mud-brick rooms and quarters built from Hescos, and the showers are a plastic curtain, chair and a hook for the ten-litre rubber water bags that warm in the sun and drain over you as you sit and soap. There are toilet cabins where you do your business in a plastic bag and throw it in a bin for burning, and parked near the medical post are three German-built Leopard L2A5 tanks, complete with improvised scrim-covered parasols over the turret hatches.

Some of the soldiers keep makeshift terrariums where they put lizards, camel spiders, bugs and other creatures they find on the base, which comes alive at night with creepy-crawlies. 'We had a few guys find scorpions in their boots in the morning so we always shake them out before putting them on,' one soldier tells me. Everything from the straggly non-regulation facial hair to uniforms bleaching on drying lines says this is the end of the line, far from the reprimands of zealous staff officers.

'We sort of make our own rules at the FOBs,' says a Dane with blonde hair and a full red beard.

At 1700 I go on patrol with a platoon of the First Brigade of the Danish Infantry. It's my first sight of the chaplain Thomas, a dark-haired, bearded volunteer from a Lutheran parish on a small island who blesses every mission that leaves the base. He then gives each soldier a good luck jab on the fist as they file out of the gate, through banks of concertina wire and onto the track that runs along the edge of the high ground.

The engineers go ahead and search the path for IEDs and we trudge through a 20-centimetre layer of moon dust toward a Leopard parked a kilometre along the hill. The tank sits menacingly on the crest, cloaked in armour and pointing its 120mm cannon over the Green Zone, but even these steel beasts cannot operate here with impunity. On July 25 one of the L2A5s based at Armadillo will run over an IED further up the Gereshk Valley, killing the driver.

A couple of armoured cars throw up choking clouds as they grind past and also take up a covering position on the cliff edge overlooking the fields. The platoon then moves down the steep paths into the Green Zone. It's only a 30-metre drop but it's like stepping from one dimension into another. Behind us lie thousands of square kilometres of desert and in front a lush and seemingly inviting garden of plenty. Even at 1745 a muggy 40-degree heat clutches at the fields but as the platoon fans out and pushes forward my nostrils twitch pleasurably at the heady scent of grass and hedgerows.

The troops had no contact here with the enemy for a month now since a new FOB called Attal ('hero' in Dari) was opened ten kilometres upstream. It quickly received a baptismal spate of attacks and ambushes as the Taliban shifted their focus from Armadillo. But there's no doubt the insurgents are still moving men, money and weapons through this neighbourhood and will reinitiate the fight when they are ready.

'The main threat is IEDs, they usually place them in canalization drains and tracks which is why we move as we do, through the fields and ditches,' a Sergeant tells me as we walk. It's two months since the last casualties were taken in this area, with one soldier killed and two injured in an IED blast.

The patrol works its way five kilometres through the fields where the farmers are gathering the last of the wheat harvest. The poppy was cut in the late spring and the dry stalks are piled everywhere, ready for use as firewood for baking bread once the bulbs have been split

Danish troops after patrol in the Green Zone, Gereshk River Valley, Helmand. In June 2010 the Danes were still there as partners of the 3/215 Brigade Advisory Group, but it was the Afghan National Police and the 3rd and 6th Kandaks of the ANA who were calling the security shots in Gereshk city.

open and the seeds extracted and stockpiled for the next drug crop.

But a strange economic tilt has confused the farmers about what to plant next: overproduction this year caused a glut in poppy with a resultant slump in the price, while a shortage of wheat in Afghanistan has pushed the price for that crop right up.

'Last year the price of wheat was very low, we couldn't make enough money, but next year a lot of people will grow wheat,' says Nasullah, a farmer we talk to through the platoon's Afghan interpreter. He has 6,000 square metres of land given to poppy growth which he says this year yielded enough raw opium to earn him 100,000 afghanis ($2,000). As elsewhere in Afghanistan, poppy cultivation here poses a huge problem for the authorities. Wholesale destruction of the crops will only turn the aggrieved farmers to the insurgents,

yet drug exports to Western markets pay for much of the insurgency and so perpetuate the war.

'If we don't get rid of the poppy there will always be something the Taliban can get financing from,' Lt. Col. Peter Boysen, deputy commander of the Danish contingent, told me a couple of days earlier. 'But if we just take the bread and butter from ordinary farmers their families are going to be hungry and we are never going to win.'

Meanwhile, Afghan President Hamid Karzai had to eat humble pie before western leaders after they rejected his requests for additional wheat donations.

'If we did not cultivate poppy in Helmand, Kandahar and Badakhshan and other places where there is cultivation, the president and cabinet would not have wasted three months begging foreigners,' Karzai said on

Afghanistan's Tolo TV that May. 'We begged for three months, dear brothers, your president sits and begs and tells them, "For God's sake give us a little wheat because we have no other option." The leader of one country told me "Brother, you should not cultivate opium. Work hard, and do not ask me for wheat."'

So now wheat is the fashionable crop in the Green Zone by Armadillo, even though debris of a bumper poppy harvest is evident all around.

After three and a half hours the patrol is instructed to withdraw across the fields. Before crossing the open ground we gather in the willows along a stream, where after the desert and baked mud villages I'm mesmerised by the smell of foliage, bird noises and croaking of frogs in the damp ditch below me. We are bathed in sweat and hungry when we get back. In the block where I live the platoon's cook has thrown together another of his all-in-one meals, frankfurter and mustard stew with rice. He's unimpressed by the mission to Afghanistan and doesn't mince his words. 'One day they will pull out the Danish forces and we will have achieved nothing.'

It's still dark the following morning as Lieutenant Martin Sorensen, the commander of Third Platoon, gives the next patrol briefing in the base's makeshift gymnasium. The soldiers sit around on weight benches as he explains the route in Danish punctuated by English words like 'high ground' and 'pressure plate'.

Am I nervous, yes, scared, no. I've been through places where there were huge fights days before but I have never been shot at. And as odd as it sounds, it still seems unbelievable that people have to dodge bullets, just as you can't appreciate the reality of a car crash until it happens to you, even though you've seen plenty of accident scenes.

Two British 105mm gun crews are setting up on the skyline in the first watery rays of light as we climb into the APCs, and at 0500 we set off along the cliff track, driving a few kilometres to extend the patrol range. We dismount and descend into the zone where it's a deliciously cool 20 degrees and dew glistens on the grass as the sun rises to the screech of cockerels. After 20 minutes we stop to talk to a farmer who at this early hour sits drinking tea with his young son beside piles of freshly cut wheat. He turns out to be a bit of a joker, asking me through the interpreter, 'Can you give me a print of the picture?' and when I say probably not, 'Well how about you just give me your camera then?'

'Not today I'm afraid.'

'Can't give me prints or camera, what good are you then?' he says with a twinkle in his eye before the Lieutenant cuts to the chase and asks him about insurgents. The farmer claims he hasn't seen any in weeks, when in fact they have been taking position in the neighbouring compounds since the previous evening. The aim of the patrol is to mask the extraction of two Danish snipers who have been staking out the farmland from a disused shepherd's hut on the cliff, waiting to pick off anyone they see planting devices.

'We found more IEDs in this area since February than were found in the rest of RC-South,' Sorensen says. 'The Taliban send out diggers on motorbikes circling the patrols to try to place IEDs to catch us on the way back. They place them on the high ground too in order to deny us access. Four days ago we caught two guys on a motorbike with an initiator and radio receiver. Normally they don't place them so that locals will hit them, they also know it's about Hearts and Minds.'

The soldier in front of me labours under a 25-kilo electronic countermeasures set that whirrs in his backpack. It will hopefully interfere with any radio-controlled attempt to detonate bombs planted on our route but it also hampers the patrol's radio communications.

'OK guys, we're going to wait 20 minutes, check atmospherics, watch for local nationals leaving the area, see if we can pick up any i-com chatter,' the Lieutenant says at 0600 as the patrol takes cover in a tree line between the fields.

Beside him sits the FOO (field ordering officer who directs auxiliary fire), a burly, affable guy called Christian who has his blood group tattooed prominently on his left upper arm. 'Hopefully that's not the one that gets blown off,' he tells me with a grin.

A few minutes later a local man approaches us carrying a whimpering two-year-old boy with a badly scalded foot which is now infected and weeping pus. Both are scared but for different reasons.

'I chatted to ISAF soldiers once before and didn't realise the Taliban were watching,' the man tells the Danes. 'Later they came to me and said it was my last warning and that next time they will hang me.'

The platoon medic does what he can for the boy using his first aid kit and we move on, encountering a couple more people on the way. An old man claims he and some others found three guys with motorbikes planting a device on a small bridge near here, but they packed it up and drove off when he said it would cause trouble for the villagers if troops got hurt.

'I think he was telling the truth but they are only telling us a fraction of what they know,' says Zabi the interpreter, moments before Sorensen gets word from the MEWT team above us about increasing enemy i-com chatter.

'The Taliban have had eyes on us for 40 minutes, twice they said they were in position to open fire on the patrol, so we are going to be cautious on the way out,' he tells me.

The likelihood of an imminent attack causes the hairs to rise on my neck and my mouth is uncomfortably dry as we pause at the next tree line. It's no longer an idyllic rural calm that hangs over the fields, but a razor-edged silence waiting to be ruptured by violence.

When the platoon moves again at 0725 an explosion rips through the air and we all throw ourselves into the nearest ditch, where I land in mounds of wet human shit. The Danes immediately open up in all directions with a deafening volley of suppressing small arms fire, and when it falls quiet again a minute later someone up the line shouts 'suicide bomber!'

I'm lying a couple of yards down the ditch from Christian who is calmly munching on a pepperami. 'Is this your first time in the Green Zone? Welcome!' he says, offering me a bite.

'No thanks, I kind of lost my appetite,' I say, motioning at the crap smeared down my legs.

'The Taliban are creepy, they shit all over the place,' says the Lieutenant, who then allows me to make my way along the ditch closer to the blast site.

I find a few more soldiers including the Danish casualty, a big, blond, bearded guy nicknamed Ernie who was standing about three metres from the blast source but amazingly suffered only a deep scrape to his cheek.

He had just stopped a local man on a motorbike, which prompted the initial report of a suicide attack. The soldiers shout at the Afghan to stay where he is and he stands awkwardly in the open.

'This is the second time this happened to me,' mutters Ernie, prodding the bloody patch beneath his right eye and protective glasses. He has only just returned to Armadillo and active service after his injury in the IED blast on March 31, when one soldier died and he had a metal shard go through his back. They later drained a half-litre of blood from his chest and evacuated him home for treatment.

'I got back to Denmark with a partly collapsed right lung – I wasn't worth much then,' he says as we crouch in the ditch, wondering what will happen now.

A few minutes later a cacophony of shooting erupts across the farmland but because the platoon is spread out over 100 metres it's hard to tell who is firing and from where. Only later do I find out that we were taking fire from three separate compounds, but I heard enough combat stories to know that the snapping noises overhead are bullets passing very close. Suddenly lying in excrement doesn't seem so bad.

The Danish APCs on the hill open up with their 40mm cannons and the barrage grows as the artillery guns and mortars at Armadillo join in, pounding the area around us. In the next few minutes a total of 75 high explosive and 65 smoke rounds crash down on the houses with enemy firing points and set light to piles of wheat, sending a pall of smoke drifting through the trees around us. A jet fighter screams overhead but instead of making a drop for the Danes it flies on and dumps its bombs by FOB Attal, where a British and Afghan patrol is being simultaneously ambushed. Third Platoon starts to pull out, moving a kilometre along the ditches toward the edge of the Green Zone and the inviting shelter of the high ground.

'Did you shit yourself?' asks a grinning lad called Tim who has a tattoo of Jimmy Hendrix on his upper arm.

'No, but I'm covered in someone else's,' I reply as we pant along the ditches. The patrol reaches the rock face and dashes up the steep trail to the top. Before climbing into the APC

I look back and see the fields beneath us enveloped in smoke and flames. So much for the garden of plenty.

Ernie is the one casualty and fortunately only had some dirt driven into his cheek. He's a very lucky young man – the IED was dug in too deeply and the force of the blast was channelled straight up rather than outwards.

Later at the debriefing the Danes are in high spirits after the engagement. Sorensen reports that four insurgents were killed by the barrage from the base and APCs, while two more were shot by soldiers on the ground. There were perhaps a dozen attackers, so some got away, possibly with a mortar tube that appears to have been used against the Danes. A dud round was found smoking in a ditch as the patrol withdrew and it was not of NATO origin.

In front of me sits Ivana, the Polish-born gunner of one of the APCs. Like others in the platoon she wears a T-shirt commemorating the last Danish casualty, Lance Corporal Christian Raaschou. The frontside of the garment bears the words PORK-EATING, WHISKY-DRINKING, PORN-LOVING INFIDEL CRUSADER, and on the back, 'In Memory of Rocco, 6.10.83-3.31.08'.

Hampered by the current water shortage I try to scrape the filth from my clothes and boots, gagging as I work. Once the worst is off, I change and stop by at the platoon's quarters where they are watching *Monty Python and the Holy Grail* on their dust-covered TV. We get to the scene where the knights are being bombarded with animal carcasses catapulted from the French castle and they flee, shouting 'Run away, run away!' I only just stop myself from blurting out 'Oh, like Third Platoon'. In fairness I should note that injury to one of the soldiers made the TIC an automatic withdrawal situation instead of them staying and counter-attacking. But Captain Haubro is still puzzled by the way the fight played out.

'It was unusual because they normally attack us from curved positions around the IED to engage the troops from 180 degrees. Also, there was no immediate shooting after the explosion, which might mean they were inexperienced or foreigners,' he says, speculating that this may have been an independent group of Islamic fighters operating separately from the Taliban.

The next day, June 5, I sit with Thomas the chaplain outside his quarters. Facing us stands the base 'church', a three-metre tower-like structure made of Hesco wire and holding a metal bell and next to it a large wooden cross that he made himself and painted with engine oil. A mechanic finished the cross with a metal plaque that says 'Put your faith in God and keep your powder dry.'

Aged 37 and attached to the military under an eight-month contract, Thomas comes from a parish on a small island with 4,000 inhabitants. A staunch monarchist and admirer of George W. Bush, he has an incredible grasp of English and speaks in a compelling, almost hypnotic manner.

I volunteered on December 12, 2001. I knew then there was a new world order rising from this episode [of the 9/11 attacks] and I thought Danish troops would be involved through NATO. I have no adventure in my blood, I don't need to run away from anything, I have a beautiful wife and three lovely kids, a wonderful parish, an island with beaches and big oak trees. I know it sounds old-fashioned but I wanted to do something for my country. I really believe each new generation are dwarfs but the reason we can see so far is because we stand on the shoulders of giants. If we want to be a people we have to walk the walk and not just talk the talk.

I think these guys here are being tested. Some of them fight because they believe in the fight, some of them fight to be able to say that they were here and fought, to some it's just a job. At some psychological level it's going to change them that they've been killing. But let's not make them victims, that's one thing I can't stand every time I hear that someone's father demanded this from his son or that George Bush wanted him there. These reasons are all there but it's shallow, we should just make them proud that they put on their boots and went.

You cannot walk down the street without being changed, every time you take a step you change, but these steps in the Green Zone are really tough. Of course we wouldn't be innocent if we stayed at home, you don't only get rough and raw by being here. But you don't necessarily degenerate being in a war. Maybe you become more firm in some aspects of life, maybe you don't smile as easily as you did at home, you've changed but not necessarily for the worse, maybe you got closer to the heart of the matter, I hope so.

I believe in being here and sharing life with them on a day-to-day basis, and showing them that you don't need to be the opposite of a soldier to be a Christian, that Christianity is like a roof with two pillars at each end, on the one side a Crusader with a bloodstained shield and on the other a fragile woman holding a lily. They don't need to change themselves to believe in the Lord, that's one of the most common prejudices. I would like them to think that if Thomas can be a priest with the amount of swearing, poker playing and gun-toting he does, then there's room for them too. It's not an act, that's who I am. And I don't care where the soldiers go, I'm not a Crusader, for me the important thing is the fact that when the boys go to war they need a priest.

In this theatre there is actually less death than back home but it's more violent. It's not so much death that is my task but giving them courage to live in spite of death. It's very vivid, there's a lot of angst to keep us sharp, and on patrol our guys are walking with their guns pointing down, waiting for the sting of death.

As a Danish soldier you don't die because you hate your enemy, you fight not because you hate but because you love your homeland and family. These boys are not raving maniacs, they are freedom fighters. They die because they love life, that's the paradox. A lot of these mujahedin die because they love death, they are looking for a front and they glorify death, they are a pack of renegades in a death cult.

At this moment Ernie passes with a large sticking plaster across his cheek. I ask him how he is.

'Physically I'm OK…I called my parents. They weren't thrilled.' He pauses, caught in conflicting emotions the day after his near miss.

It's twice it happened to me and I have to think about my family. I don't want them to get a call saying I'm dead. It's not worth fighting for. I think I'm getting closer to the IEDs all the time. I consider myself extremely lucky, I'm very glad to be alive. One of the great fears we have down there is that we will die very slowly in agony, or we lose a limb. Death is preferable to other things. Sure you can live without a leg or arm, but that's usually how we feel. When I walk out through the gate I'm scared, then training takes over and it's just work. When I came down here again after the first injury people called me crazy – I had to fight to come back to Afghanistan. But I cannot justify being here any more. I don't believe I'm having the impact on the place I was hoping to have and it's not OK any more. We should stick to one strategy, do something and keep on doing it, not keep changing.

We are not achieving what we are here to achieve. There are more IEDs on the high ground and in the Green Zone and the locals don't trust us, so we are losing ground. It was so much easier when it was a normal war down here, I wish I was on the last tour, they saw regular contact.

We destroyed a compound yesterday, shot at the locals, but what did we achieve? Every time we destroy a compound we destroy a home. We destroy it because the enemy are there. Of course there will be compensation but it takes time. But we don't have control down there, while they have freedom of movement, look at all the IEDs. If we had a good relationship with the local population they would tell us about the IEDs, we've got telephone numbers they can call. We should patrol more and concentrate on CIMIC efforts. I can kill as many people as I like but if I can't convince the local population that I am here for them and to support us, none of it matters.

I find out later from Ernie's commanding officer that this is in fact his third close IED encounter, having had one device burn out beside him during a tour in Iraq. He is formally entitled to request a transfer home, and the last I heard before leaving Armadillo was that he had done so. Few people could blame him, although there is clearly concern about how I would interpret this. Later that day Lieutenant Sorensen comes up to me and says he heard about the earlier conversation.

'I hope you realise that that's just his take on the mission, not ours. He uses a lack of faith in the mission to justify going home instead of saying that he's too fucking afraid to go down there.'

I will go out again the next day and am suitably apprehensive about the mission now that the insurgents have made their presence known again. That evening I ask the commander of Second Platoon, a young Lieutenant called Christian, how he prepares himself mentally for patrols in the Green Zone, especially after an attack.

'Denial…No, I'm just joking. I go out and do my job. The boys take comfort in the fact that they have no choice, if they didn't go out it would be deserting their mates, you do it for them. I never believed the stories of guys throwing themselves onto grenades to save their mates. But I believe it now, these guys would do it – it's amazing what they do for each other. I also learned to believe in God here because you are forced to face the reality of life and death.'

The next evening at 1730 I go on my third and last patrol with the Danes to an area a couple of kilometres up from the site of the previous day's TIC. The Green Zone is only a kilometre wide here and the river is just visible through the trees and grass. The farmers are all out gathering the last wheat and some complain to us of damage caused to their crops by stray flares or smoke rounds from the fight. One of the Sergeants takes photos of the blackened remnants of one old man's wheat which will be used to calculate a compensation payment.

The patrol lasts two and a half hours and we pull out as it starts to get dark. We suddenly have to change our route after MEWT pick up an enemy i-com message saying, 'Did you dig it into the track?' followed by 'Yes'. As the call to prayers drifts across the fading fields we can hear a lot of jubilation from the surrounding houses. The interpreter says they are celebrating the last day of the wheat harvest. As darkness falls the patrol regroups at the foot of the cliff under the gaze of a few curious farmers. Light from a sliver of moon picks out the antenna of the APCs which stand on the clifftop covering us, their motors running quietly as they scan the area. Back at base the platoon does me the honour of holding the debriefing entirely in English.

'The people I talked to said there are no Taliban in this area,' one of the squad leaders reports, and everybody laughs.

seven

COFFINS

I am booked on the 'Stampede 15' flight on a C-130 Hercules to KAF. Eighty minutes before the scheduled departure at 2000 a Mercedes jeep pulls up at the Camp Viking flagpole in a cloud of dust and a Danish soldier called Jeppe greets me. He drives out to the fringes of Bastion where there is only a runway, a couple of towers, a hangar with some fire engines and two large tents. We approach a British flight line officer standing by some pallets and ask if we should stack my gear already.

'We're going to be very busy, first we've got nine coffins to load on that one so you might have to wait,' he says, motioning to another C-130 that has just landed and is disgorging soldiers from its tail before heading north to Kabul.

I go and sit in the empty passenger handling tent, which has a television, a fridge full of water, a tea urn and three dozen chairs. Emerging from the Danish embed and finding myself in circulation with a shipment of bodies, I get an uneasy, spooked feeling that is compounded by the still surroundings. For the first time since starting this trip I find myself pondering the inherent risks and the random nature of the consequences.

It's a welcome distraction when 30 British soldiers noisily stream in, dump their kit and mill around, drink water and tea and watch the rugby. Fifteen minutes later they are led to a bus and driven away and I'm alone again. I step outside and watch a distant cart tow a UAV drone onto the runway and drive off again.

A Chinook sits in the distance with its rotors spinning for take-off and an RAF fire truck passes towards its hangar. A warm breeze tugs at the orange wind sock in the soft evening sunlight and the stones and dust exude a gritty smell as they also recover from the day's roasting. There is still no sign of the coffins, which

I'm told contain bodies of ANA soldiers. I jot this in my notebook and then ask myself if my anticipation of their arrival isn't a tad 'ghoulish'? It's rhetorical though; my heightened interest stems more from healthy introspection than reporting habits: because it could easily be my remains being moved in an ISAF plane now or on any other day while I'm in-theatre. The IED could have blown up directly under me or any of the Danes two days earlier instead of being dug in too deeply to cause more than a graze. Just being here is a roll of the dice, and while you can take certain precautions you also need a good portion of luck. The sixth vehicle in a convoy can run over the buried mine or an incoming rocket might against the odds kill a kitchen porter on base. And while being a civilian may help in some situations, as a journalist you pretty much run the same risks when out with the troops, as Nick Meo presciently observed six months before he got blown up.

A US press officer also reminded me of this the previous year: 'I know that in your role as media bullets flying is good for business but unfortunately that role does not offer a special force field to keep you any safer than the rest of us.'

Everyone I meet here has their own philosophy about the dangers, sometimes bound to their religion but more often just centred on simple fatalism. Sherry, the Canadian stewardess on the chartered plane that services Kamp Holland in Uruzgan, is aware that her aircraft is potentially vulnerable to attack as it lands and takes off at the base in Tarin Kowt, but says she doesn't let it bother her too much.

'I went to Vancouver to do some training, while I was there a helicopter fell out of the sky and landed on a guy. He had an iPod on and didn't hear anything. When it's your time, it's your time.'

Or your philosophy may rest more on simple suppression of worry: 'You try to put it out of your mind, because if it's in the front of your thoughts you'll never go forward,' a British soldier said.

I was personally more susceptible to the jitters when outside Afghanistan, before going on a trip or just after finishing one, with room to think about things that were coming up or happened a few days earlier. While embedded it was generally fine as long as I kept busy and didn't dwell too much on the frequent casualties in areas I was working in. And however wrong it is, people get used to it, blasé even. That said, a batch of nine dead soldiers of whatever nationality is a pretty good reminder of one's mortality.

I am finally called to board the RAF Hercules and find I am the only passenger, it's that kind of day. I can't help thinking it would be a fine twist if they now decided to route the ANA dead through KAF instead, just me and nine fatalities in the hold. But there's no sign of any coffin-shaped cargo and the British crewmen invite me to ride in the vacant third seat in the cockpit. We take off in the dusk, wheel east towards Kandahar and climb to 6,000 metres for the 35-minute journey. I sit behind the pilots trying to make sense of the mass of dials, switches and screens facing me. The only thing I understand is the altitude and that the operable weight of the aircraft is 41.212 tonnes, its fuel 6.859 and payload 3.225.

It's good to be moving again.

eight

BUNA ZIUA ZABUL

I realised the Romanians were special in June 2007 when I passed through FOB Lagman, the base their contingent shares with the Americans in Qalat, the capital of Zabul province. One of their soldiers was sitting by a small fire in the sunshine, carefully ripping pages out of a thick manual and dropping them into an ammo tin beside him. Every couple of minutes he'd get up and empty the tin onto the fire before he sat down and continued removing the pages. I presumed it was some kind of classified document he had been instructed to destroy. The two other soldiers who now joined him would surely just take the book from his hands and toss it into the flames and he'd smack his forehead and laugh at himself.

They also, however, seemed to relish the tearing process, first as spectators and then helping to burn the pages. I discreetly took 20 photos of the operation and when I flick through them in succession they make a jerky little movie of soldiers protecting state secrets with immense devotion.

At the time the Romanians had a few hundred soldiers in Afghanistan and were doing two important but often under-appreciated jobs: manning the perimeter towers around Kandahar Airfield and patrolling Zabul's 150-kilometre stretch of Highway 1, Afghanistan's ring road that connects the country's main cities. Many of KAF's occupants seemed unaware of the east European contingent's contribution and were bluntly dismissive.

'Other than go to the gym and eat I don't know what they do – I've never even seen them go outside the wire,' a US paratrooper said. But a Canadian officer I spoke to said the Romanians earned their keep a couple of months earlier when they spotted three Taliban who had obtained US uniforms and were trying to scale the fence.

'Those guys don't mess around, they shot their cocks off with Dragunovs,' he said, referring to the Russian-made sniper rifles the Romanians (ad the Taliban) use. I never managed to confirm either the attempt to infiltrate in disguise or the claimed emasculation.

It was not widely known but Bucharest's contingent was one of only eight of the 41 foreign armies represented then in Afghanistan that had accepted a combat role without caveats imposed on their use by their governments. The rest, including key troop contributors like Germany, Spain, Turkey, France and Italy, could not be deployed in a full fighting capacity like forces of the United States, Britain, Canada, Holland, Estonia, Denmark, Poland and Romania. On Friday June 13, 2008, the Romanians lost their seventh soldier in Afghanistan.

A year after my first visit to Zabul I had come back to Lagman to revisit FOB Baylough up in the mountains. It's a frustrating time, days waiting for helicopters that never fly and lots of kicking around. But the lack of transport means I get to see some more of Highway 1 and a glimpse into the Romanians' main job.

On June 11, I get attached to a convoy of four US Humvees that will drive up to Zabul with 14 American soldiers, including two I know from last year. We leave 1415 on what should be a 90-minute journey, although sometimes the convoys get attacked on the road, usually at night. They put me in the rear right passenger seat where I am squashed between a box of hand grenades and stacked tins of .50-calibre ammo for the Browning top gun.

'If we get in trouble we'll be messing with you a lot because we'll have to get all that ammunition up there,' the Lieutenant warns me. He tells all four gunners to switch weapons and grab their rifles when we reach Qalat to avoid 'collateral damage', i.e. harming civilians with the heavy weapons if we get attacked.

We roll out of KAF and follow the perimeter fence past a giant scrap yard with rusting remains of Soviet aircraft and vehicles, where a six-wheeled BTR armoured personnel carrier juts vertically out of the top of the pile like a toy. Gunners of a parked British column give us the thumbs up as we motor by them and through the ANA checkpoint, pass the MiG fighter that stands on a pedestal at KAF's main gate, swing onto the Spin Boldak road and head to the junction with Highway 1, or Ring Road South as it is known here. The first time I saw the country's main artery was from a small Huey helicopter a year earlier as we flew over a massive traffic jam caused by dozens of camels ambling across the two lanes.

Mine is the lead vehicle as we turn onto it, forcing Mercedes, Volvo and Kamaz trucks and cars to pull over and wait as we pass. Measuring 2,200 kilometres upon scheduled completion by 2010, the road links Kabul with Kandahar to the south, Herat in the west and Mazar-e-Sharif in the north. Our stretch is flanked by strips of farmland, weed-strewn desert and hills, mud houses and flocks of sheep and camels that gather at trickles of water in near-dry river beds. There are clusters of skin-covered dome tents of the Cuchi nomads, while occasional filling stations have 1970s petrol pumps that would fetch a tidy sum at collectors' fairs in the West. Straight and smooth, it's a pretty good drive, well maintained to prevent the insurgents from digging IEDs into broken patches, although they still blow up culverts, drainage ditches and bridges.

Since the Taliban were driven from power by US-led forces in 2001, safety and maintenance of the highway has served as one barometer of efforts to reconstruct the war-shattered country. Every day, a steady flow of trucks, coaches and cars passes through flash points in the fight between the militants and the Afghan government and foreign forces. As well as inviting harassment by common bandits and corrupt police, drivers are vulnerable to roadside bombs and ambushes. So it's a dilemma for the Taliban: they must hit their enemy but not alienate the local population by killing large numbers of civilians, or shutting down this commercial lifeline altogether.

'Of course we don't want to close the road to the locals, they are our own people. Our problem is with the Americans and NATO forces and in second place with the Kabul administration,' Taliban spokesman Qari Mohammed Yousuf Ahmadi replied when contacted in an e-mail. 'We are stationed in several places on the road and ambush and attack them – that's why it takes enemy vehicles ten hours to reach their destination when in the past they could do it in five hours.'

Today the sky is an overcast grey haze. I've become so used to the sun that I can't work out what it is until it starts spitting with rain. Just the smell of the damp and dust together is vaguely refreshing. Fifty kilometres up the highway from Kandahar we pass under an arch bearing the greeting in English 'Welcome to Zabul'.

Measuring 17,343 square kilometres, or half the size of Holland, Zabul has a 64-kilometre border with Pakistan. It has a population of 300,000 people in 20 Pashtun tribes that are split between the government and the Taliban in their allegiance. This was where the ousted Taliban established their first major re-infiltration route from Pakistan after 2001, and today it is a key transit and rest area for the insurgents as they move fighters and weapons west to Uruzgan, Kandahar and Helmand. Locked within chains of mountains, this is one of Afghanistan's highest provinces geographically and lowest in terms of development. It is bisected by the highway, which brings some trade, but is otherwise desperately poor.

Afghanistan has the third highest illiteracy rate in the world and Zabul leads in illiteracy nationally, while also having the country's second highest infant mortality rate. The province lives from animal husbandry and agriculture, growing fruit, almonds and wheat but not so much poppy, which does not like the terrain and climate. And that's Zabul in an (almond) nutshell.

Our convoy cruises into Qalat, 120 kilometres northeast of Kandahar, which apart from a mass of roadside stalls has a good number of buildings under construction and reflects some growth. Like a candle on a cake, the Roshan mobile phone network's tower stands on top of an old mud hill fort. And the modern fort that is FOB Lagman stands on a slight hill to

Transylvanian Orthodox church
built by Romanian troops at
Kandahar Airfield.

the edge of town, comprising the usual snaking lines of Hescos and concertina wire, and is filled with metal containers, wooden shacks, generator units, trailers and vehicle parks.

I go to report at the Tactical Operations Centre, or TOC, where the corridor walls are covered with newspaper cuttings about Romanian operations, with photos of troops of the 300th Infantry Battalion from Galati patrolling and mixing with the locals; but one article shows photos of soldiers carrying a casket and a young man's portrait. Another has a line of sobbing women in headscarves, ashen-faced husbands standing beside them. All I know in Romanian is *bună ziua* (hello) but a scan through the article isolates the key words: 'Humvee … dispositiv explosive improvizat'. An IED strike.

I am introduced to the Romanian commander, Lt. Col. Adrian Soci, a portly, moustachioed infantryman. Sitting at the bench outside the TOC he smokes and I make notes on a pleasant evening twelve weeks after Lt. Ionut Cosmin Sandu's vehicle was blown up on patrol on March 20.

'We had three IED hits in March and since January we found almost 50 IEDs in Zabul, mostly pressure plates,' Soci says. 'All this knowledge comes to you when you are on the highway and you expect to hit an IED at any moment. The Taliban want Highway 1 under their control, we want it under ours, so we are fighting. Especially during winter and spring they target convoys with supplies of food and water, it doesn't matter if they are military or civilian, they want the stuff for survival.'

The last serious ambush of a Coalition Forces convoy was three months earlier, while the last against the ANP was just two weeks ago, he tells me.

'Zabul province is a big challenge for everyone,' says the Colonel, who takes little comfort in the current lull in his sector. 'We know that after a quiet period a storm is coming.'

Some military officials are cagey when implicating foreign actors in the Afghan conflict, but not Soci. Since his AO borders on Pakistan and is one of the main in routes for fighters to the southern sector, he's more familiar than most people with the insurgent traffic.

'The Taliban spend the winter time in Pakistan. Foreign insurgents, Chechens,

Uzbeks, and Pakistanis also spend winter there and in spring they come here. Starting in March we saw a big increase in insurgent activity in Zabul.'

Like all commanders in Afghanistan, Soci would like more soldiers but that luxury was to fall instead to his successor that August, when in line with a Romanian pledge at the Bucharest NATO Afghanistan summit held in April 2008, the contingent grew in size from 480 to 630 troops.

'Romania is small, not as big and powerful as other countries in Europe, but we are here nonetheless. We just want to be equals,' the Colonel adds.

President Karzai made Highway 1 a priority in 2008 and asked the Afghan government forces and ISAF to step up efforts to secure the flow of traffic. But ask any Afghan truck driver and he'll tell you how fraught it remains, with frequent hijackings, robberies and executions. The Colonel insists the road is getting safer in his sector at least. A lot of work has been done to clean up the local Police force, which as in other places would often prey on civilian drivers for money, and he says his men patrol daily in armoured vehicles and rarely encounter trouble.

'There are some perfect spots for ambushes but most of the highway is on open ground where it's hard to set them up,' says Soci, inviting me to see for myself and join him the next day on a visit to a Romanian base located 70 kilometres up the road.

I leave at 1035 in a Humvee with three Romanians, one manning a 7.62mm machine-gun in the turret. We ride in convoy with some armoured cars to FOB Varner, which I'm amused to hear was unofficially renamed FOB Dracula by the last Romanian contingent.

Again, the highway seems almost civilized in places, with smooth asphalt, markings and road signs and little built-up areas with rows of stalls selling household goods, engine oil, firewood and bottles of garishly coloured soda. But then we see the burned-out wreckage of a minibus and some unmarked roadside graves made of rocks, and broken sections of the road that are prime spots for IEDs. In one place we detour around a bridge that was blown up a few weeks earlier. The Romanians later found the remains of the man who set the charge and must have accidentally blown himself up in the process. Documents in his pocket identified him as a Pakistani.

There are no surprises on the road today and 90 minutes later we pull into Varner, which is manned by two platoons of Romanian troops and 15 US trainers who work with the local ANA, plus a few interpreters. The blue, yellow and red Romanian tricolour flies over a small compound with some brick and plaster buildings with corrugated metal roofs, a few containers, armoured cars and jeeps and a couple of guard towers.

The garrison covers a 50-kilometre stretch of highway but it's generally pretty quiet, says Dedu Norocel, a 28-year-old Lieutenant who shows me round. There was some recent concern that the Taliban were planning to hit the FOB but there hasn't been any attack on the road in his sector for many weeks. This constitutes a challenge in itself, as far as the troops' vigilance is concerned.

'Routine is the biggest problem; we've been doing this since January 10. After six months of the same thing the most dangerous part is routine,' says the officer, a courteous, solid man with a neck thicker than his head. 'The soldiers know every inch of Highway 1 but I always tell them that they should ignore the fact they have been here 100 times before and imagine that it's the first time.'

The main concern today is the breakdown of the generator. Not only does it mean they lose communications but the fridges also go off *and they have no TV.* It's a critical matter now as the Romanian national football team is due to play Italy in the quarter finals of the European Championship the next day, Friday 13. It's unthinkable that they won't be able to watch the game and electricians are working feverishly to get the power back on.

He shows me the thick-walled officers' room, relatively cool by day but stuffy at night, except in winter. Varner is 1,800 metres above sea level and during that winter, the coldest in Afghanistan in decades, the temperature dropped below minus 30°C. There is a conditioning unit on the wall but it hasn't worked for two years, and the kitchen facilities are no better. Mostly they eat American MRE ration packs and cereals and fruit brought from Qalat. It's a very basic lifestyle, far removed from the comforts of KAF or even Lagman, which has a good kitchen, internet and a coffee shop. But the men don't complain too much, Norocel says.

'They are just frustrated that we don't have the gear the Americans have, their night vision is better than ours. They are like kids, they see the US equipment and ask how can these kids have this toy and we don't?'

He leads me out to the foot of one of the watchtowers.

'After routine the most dangerous thing is the kids, they throw stones at us or fire them at the towers from catapults,' the Lieutenant says, leading me up to the tower using a crude ladder made of planks. 'The locals say it's the children of the traders who come into the village to work at the bazaar. My biggest concern is that one day it might not be a rock but a grenade in that catapult.'

The view from the tower is very...Afghan. Mountains in the distance, desert, mud walls and mud houses, dusty tracks and a pack of grubby kids gathered beyond the perimeter, yelling up at us for food.

'We don't give them cookies and cakes because within 40 minutes we'll have the entire village at the gate,' says Norocel, adding that a similar principle applies out on the road, even if it's tempting to toss a few treats to the kids. 'Our rule is don't throw toys and candies from the APCs because then the children will crowd round them and someone may be killed.'

When they do foot patrols through villages further away from the base it's the opposite problem: 'We try to give them blankets, food and toys but they don't want to take them in case the Taliban come and beat or kill them for accepting anything from us.'

Varner doesn't get indirect mortar or rocket fire like other FOBs in Zabul, mainly because there is a hospital and school right over the wall.

'They don't have a mortar scope like we do, they fire it by instinct, so if they miss one and drop it on the hospital there will be a problem.'

The Lieutenant also heard that the Taliban are wary of messing with the 14.5mm cannon on the Soviet-model APCs used by the Romanians.

'They know it from the war with the Russians and they get frightened of it. But we get a lot of i-com chatter and always have a lot of people watching us,' he says, pointing to some nomad tents pitched 200 metres away.

'We tried to learn the name of the mountains here but they are too fancy. All we know is that Pakistan is 100 kilometres southeast beyond those hills, Kabul is 300 to the northeast, Arghandab is that way and Camp Lagman that way. And that's all we care about.'

It's a bleak view to behold for weeks on end, making even a trip to Lagman the equivalent of visiting the bright lights. After we climb down from the tower I tell him that in view of the base's nickname I'm sorry not to see even one picture of Count Dracula. The Lieutenant takes me into the main hallway and stops at a blank wall and looks puzzled: 'There used to be a painting of Dracula's castle there, it's gone,' he says. But in the yard, one armoured car has a bat sprayed on its turret. And back at KAF the Romanians built a Transylvanian church, a small wooden structure with a carpeted, icon-clad, A/C-cooled interior that seems a world removed from the wailing mosques of Afghanistan.

The troops unloaded the trailer of water that our vehicles brought and the column leaves at 1300, passing a 50-metre tall dust devil that spins by the side of the highway. Just outside Qalat we stop at a new ANP post that was completed four months earlier, a large square walled compound with towers set back from the road.

Deputy Police commander Sergeant Rozi Mohammed has been here four months and says he's got only 25 of 35 men that should be in his garrison. His officers are from Zabul, Kabul, Bamyan and Ghazni and speak a mix of Farsi, Dari and Pashtu. He says they most need night vision equipment, the same wish I hear from Police and Army units across the country. But ISAF is reluctant to provide this kit because of the inevitable transfer of units to the insurgents by treacherous or just financially desperate personnel.

In 2007 there were three dozen tiny Police checkpoints along the highway in Zabul, all manned by ill-equipped, erratically paid and demoralised officers who the Sergeant says were ranged against a mix of local Taliban and foreign fighters.

The small posts were dismantled and six large walled Police compounds created to cover the same area with a complement of up to 60 officers. Most of them underwent western-run training courses in Kandahar and were then reassigned. Wage arrears were gradually being made up but salaries were still as low as 5,000 afghanis (100 US dollars) a month, lag behind Army wages by a few vital dollars for family budgets, and are often delayed.

The Sergeant says he's now ten men short because officers often leave for the private sector once they have acquired their new skills, since security firms offer up to three times the Police wage: 'Much money is spent on a policeman in training, he then comes here, sees the deal and goes somewhere else where they pay more.'

The number of Police casualties speaks for the dangers of the job. The ANP bear the brunt of militant attacks as they are perceived as softer targets than Army units. Over the course of 2008 a total of 860 policemen were reported killed on duty.

An air of poverty hangs over these guys and it's hardly surprising that they might be tempted to shake down drivers for money.

'Our salary will just stretch to an 80-kilo sack of flour but we still have rent to pay for our families,' says another officer from Ghazni. He's been a policeman for nine months but says the money won't support him, his wife and four kids.

'I love my job and don't want to quit but that depends on my family's situation.'

The negative vibe seems to bother Colonel Soci, who now leans forward into the conversation and says through the interpreter: 'The government of Afghanistan is looking to improve salaries as the economic situation improves. He should stay in his job and do his best.'

Lieutenant Norocel had no way of knowing how grimly prophetic was his warning against complacency.

Eighteen hours later, in the early morning of Friday June 13, two dozen Taliban armed with AKs and RPGs launched a double-sided ambush against his patrol of four armoured vehicles on the highway near Varner. One soldier was killed and three were wounded. That morning, before I got word of the attack, I went to look for the Romanian priest in the small chapel at Lagman but heard he had gone to KAF. Later I realise he has gone to arrange the ramp ceremony for 29-year-old Private First Class Claudiu Marius Covrig. As I walk back I see Soci frowning by the TOC and when I nod to him in greeting he looks right through me. Later I see him smoking outside the library and he tells me what happened.

'They returned fire and called in close air support but the Taliban ran away,' he says with a heavy sigh. 'It's bad for morale but this is war. It's a risk we have to accept, we have no choice, we have to face the Taliban and beat them.'

Covrig had served for two years in the French Foreign Legion before joining his country's military in 2003. Married with a pregnant wife, he was on his first foreign tour. He was posthumously promoted to 2nd Lieutenant and awarded the Romania Star National Order as Knight in recognition of his devotion to duty. Romanian President

Traian Băsescu also decorated the three troops injured in the incident, which sparked a new and heated debate about the participation of the country's troops in missions overseas. Two opposition parties, the Greater Romania Party and the Conservative Party, promptly demanded the immediate withdrawal of its forces from both Afghanistan and Iraq.

I return unexpectedly that evening to KAF where on June 16 I go to the passenger terminal to catch a plane to Uruzgan to join the Dutch. After a British Military Policeman inspects my baggage I wander into the back yard by the runway and stop. On the tarmac before me hundreds of Romanian, US, Canadian and British soldiers are lined up behind the open tailgate of a C-130 as a casket draped with the yellow, blue and red flag is carried into the hold. Covrig is going home to Galati.

Private Claudiu Marius Covrig returns to Romania. *(Courtesy of Romanian Defence Ministry)*

nine

BAYLOUGH AND THE BOX

In June 2007 I promised the head teacher of the tent school at Baylough in Zabul province that if I ever came back I'd bring something useful for the kids. Beautiful it may be, but this area is as remote, backward, tormented and dangerous as it gets and if you are going to give southern Afghanistan an enema, this is where you'll put the pipe in. Most of the 800 children who attend the school in turns from across the district will never leave except to make occasional domestic supply runs or hospital visits to Qalat or Kandahar, or maybe visit Pakistan if they join the insurgency.

In Islamabad I had wanted to pack a globe so they could at least see there is a world beyond the provincial capital Qalat, but it was hardly a practical addition to my kit. After my request to visit Zabul was approved I went to the store at KAF and bought 3,600 sheets of paper, 360 pens, 240 pencils and some glue and scissors and taped it all together in a 10-kilo package. The ISAF press officer said it was good that I bought plain ballpoint pens without many parts: 'We give them things and they are used against us, components from wind-up radios and springs from biros are used in IEDs.'

Friday 13, 2008

A few hours after Covrig died. After six days of uncertainty and waiting I am slated to fly to Baylough tonight for two weeks. It is one year since I visited, the FOB has been attacked several days in a row and it promises to be quite a trip. I check in with the TOC at lunchtime and hear that my Chinook flight is still on.

Still I fight off a deep suspicion that something will happen to screw things up. My anxiety has nothing to do with the unlucky date or the Romanian casualties, rather my schedule is tight and I can't afford to lose any more time if I'm still to make the Dutch embed straight after this.

But the Americans assure me it's all looking good so I accept my apparent good luck. At 1730 I don my body armour, haul my two backpacks to my shoulders and hoist the box of stationery to my chest, grit my teeth and start the 100-metre walk to the PAX terminal, muscles screaming. Those kids had better study their asses off. A US soldier takes a look at the teetering pile of baggage on legs and takes the box for me.

The terminal is a wooden hut with benches, TV, a large Stars and Stripes on the wall and a counter with clipboards with manifests for today's flights to FOBs Baylough, Mizan and Lane, and also to KAF, leaving in that order. I add my details for Baylough and settle down with a copy of *The Bavarian News*, a paper for the US forces based in southern Germany, including the 1-4th Infantry that I'm attached to here.

On the front page there is a photo of a little girl with a hair bun pecking a man in a black helmet. 'Dressed as Princess Leia, Leighann Truesdale, 3, daughter of 1st Sgt Charles and Sgt 1st Class Christine Truesdale JMTC, gives Darth Vader a kiss May 4th at the Grafenwoehr Post Exchange. Members of the 501st German Garrison-Bavaria Area Star Wars Organization in full iconic costumes visited several locations on post.'

Two US soldiers and a young Afghan interpreter enter the hut.

'You heard about Baylough, it's pretty hot there, every night,' one soldier tells the other. 'That mortar Sergeant kept asking me what it's like, so I told him, "You're gonna fight".'

I gather from their conversation that they are working as embedded trainers with the ANA and have been trying to join their assigned unit for days. The beating of rotor blades grows louder and two Chinooks of the Royal Australian Air Force land, escorted by an Apache gunship, creating a dust storm on the LZ. The pilots promptly change the flight order, Mizan goes to the top, Baylough is pushed down to third place, and that sinking feeling begins.

'Don't blame me,' a Romanian transport officer says to no one in particular as he rubs out the FOB names on the board and switches them round. Show time for Baylough slips to 2030.

'They don't want to go, they've heard what's happening out there,' says the American soldier, who introduces himself as Jim. 'I've seen pilots come in and say they've got a malfunction, go to the dining hall, use the phones. They'll get back later and scratch the flight, say it's too late.'

He tells me that the last two flights to Baylough were cancelled and that nothing went out to the FOB since May. I ask if he thinks they'll really go today.

'I need to go there and I want to say yes, but I can see them weaseling out of it. The big bases, they fly there often, but the little bases, they're so isolated. Those guys are the ones in the fight and they get crapped on. And the guys who fight on the little FOBs get paid the same as US personnel in Kuwait. I guess that's the nature of the beast.'

The Perspex window of the terminal pumps in its frame to the throb of the Chinook's rotors as what should be our ride leaves instead for Mizan. There are 18 people waiting to go to Baylough, including nine Afghan contractors with sledge hammers and other tools. They watch American football on the TV as the three wall clocks show 3p.m. ZULU (GMT), 11a.m. Eastern USA, and 7.30p.m. local. It's getting dark, our bags are loaded onto the pallet and the Romanian officer says the flight will still go ahead. The soldiers discuss Bagram and its comparative luxuries with a civilian from KBR, the commercial firm contracted by ISAF to provide a variety of services.

'I went there and *wow*, they've got trees, roads and shops and while we're getting shot at they've got the nerve to complain to us,' one says before they trade tales of stupid deaths: a guy hit by a rocket while he was on an exercise machine; one killed in training by a fragment of mortar shell because he didn't have his armour on.

'I understand why we have to have it, but all this kit weighing 150 pounds [68 kilos] isn't conducive to agility, I don't care who you are, you're not going to run fast wearing all that,' says Jim, looking down at his pouches stuffed with M4 rifle magazines, grenades, compass, torch and other gear.

The next topic is how European troops are snapping up the dollar-priced goods at the American PX at KAF because of the strength of the euro. The other soldier tells how he saw one buy a brand new PSP game console and then mail it straight back home at the post office.

'I wrote to my Congressman about it, because I don't remember seeing it written anywhere in the government pledge to US soldiers that they have to provide cheap goods to the Romanian Army.'

The KBR contractor says there's now talk in the US Congress of taxing the earnings of the civilian workers like him, who are on $19 an hour. They can make good money working the shifts they do, 12 hours a day, 7 days a week for months on end, but he says lots of people will quit if they lose their tax breaks.

A 19-year-old Afghan policeman is also waiting to fly. He's from Ghazni province and based at Baylough and says he remembers me from last year when I visited their observation post at dusk as insurgents were gathering in the orchards to attack. They are still owed several months of pay by the provincial authorities and I assure him that if I meet the Zabul Governor I will ask him about the arrears.

At this exact moment there is a commotion as a group of American and Afghan soldiers and a US State Department official come in from the LZ escorting a man in a turban and wearing a suit jacket over his *payran tumban*. Zabul Governor Delbar Jan Arman, no less. I follow him outside and he agrees to see me in Qalat when I get back from Baylough. But since he has to wait for his car to arrive we sit down in the terminal for a mini-interview, the State Department guy hovering anxiously behind us as we talk.

The Governor and I speak in English which might account for the vague answers, although it's more likely just politician's evasiveness. I ask about Baylough's missing ANP salaries and he says there was a backlog due to 'problems

US CH-47 Chinook flies over eastern Afghanstan.

in communications between the provincial and central government' but these are now resolved and arrears will soon be paid. I ask about infiltrations of insurgents from Pakistan and this sets him on the usual diatribe.

'Pakistan should stop this but Pakistan is playing a two-sided game. Pakistan is the problem, the border is the problem. The Pakistanis are a double player, it's the Punjabi policy to defeat Afghanistan, they don't want a strong government here, and if our economy grows it will negatively affect Pakistan's.'

'And al-Qaeda?'

'They are all terrorists, whether al-Qaeda, Chechens, Uzbeks or Punjabis. How are they coming from these other countries? There is some source of support here, especially in Pakistan, every Afghan knows this. Our neighbours are not honest, especially Pakistan.'

Arman is whisked off to his car. The waiting US soldiers say they heard the Governor is here to discuss the disappearance of a large amount of money intended for ANP wages

and death benefits. I find out later that someone ran off with the entire payroll.

Two Australian Chinooks are to fly to Baylough, one with passengers and one with cargo. It's dark now as we stand in line behind our aircraft, its roaring turbines blasting us with scalding air. We are seated and our bags are secured down the centre of the cabin together with the Afghan workers' tools while an Australian military cameraman films us strapping in. After the anxiety of waiting we take off – after six days of nailbiting I am finally going to Baylough and I have to suppress a whoop.

The Chinook rises and hovers for a few minutes, lands again and the crew fiddle with something on the starboard side. 'Don't you dare scratch this flight,' I mutter to myself. The engines are left running so it looks like we are still in business. After a few minutes the crew get back in, open the floor hatch and attach the cable for some cargo we will carry beneath us. We take off again, hover at 20 metres for five minutes and land. They grab tools from a locker and go outside and we wait 10 minutes to the howl of the rotors. Then the pitch starts to decrease as the engines are switched off. Game over. With much shaking of heads and cussing we grab our stuff and disembark. The other Chinook leaves for Baylough.

I take my two backpacks and the now hated box of school supplies which I put down on the tail gate before I step down. The shift in equilibrium is disastrous and I somersault out the back and land heavily on my side, raking my left hip on the gravel and wrenching my spine. The side pouch on my small rucksack empties its contents in the dark for extra annoyance as I scrabble around collecting it all. Charity be damned. In considerable pain I hobble back into the terminal where we are told the next flight to Baylough won't be for about six days.

'I told you how it would go, step for step,' Jim says. 'The irony is that we're trying to get to the fight, not away from it.' He strikes me as an even-tempered sort but after two weeks of waiting his frustration erupts.

'All these caveats and stuff, if we don't get operational and effective we're not going to win this. There are too many chains of command, NATO, the UN, it's all a ball of bullshit. They kept the Marines at KAF for a month and a half, waiting at the gate because of bureaucracy. ISAF...We should keep the US, Canadians, Australians and the British, and all the rest can fuck off!'

What happens now is a fateful flip of the coin. The KAF flight is about to go and there is a space for me. I can count my losses and comfortably make the start of the Dutch embed, which if I read correctly between the lines, will involve a major operation. Or I can stay here and hope something comes up but probably have to wait for several more days and still have no guarantee of getting to Baylough, and miss the Dutch op.

I squeeze onto the helicopter which is packed to the gills with passengers and cargo. We fly for 40 minutes between the crags and over the desert. I am jerked from my thoughts by an intense whirring noise and it takes a couple of seconds before I realise the twin mini-guns are firing. The 7.62mm tail gun joins in what is likely a test fire. Then one of the mini-guns fires again a few minutes later, spewing out a stream of glowing tracer rounds that spark off the rocks below. The noise of the engines drowns out any talk but at that moment every passenger is wondering whether this is for real, that we are taking ground fire and should expect bullets to rip through the side panels and floor.

After we land I heave my gear off the Chinook and to the side of the runway. I don't want to drag the ISAF media Captain out of bed at 1 a.m. so I have to get to the transit tent and doss down there for the night. It's a kilometre away and I am still hurting badly from my fall. I ask two black American soldiers sitting in a little John Deere Gator all-terrain vehicle how I get off the flight line. They ask if I'm on my own and tell me to throw my stuff in the back and drive me all the way.

I don't know it at the time but Baylough has now gone for me. The US Major at Qalat is furious I jumped ship like this so the door to Zabul slams shut and I am blacklisted in his AO. The box of supplies remains jammed under the desk of a Canadian reporter at KAF for another 12 months before it finally goes with me to its destination.

ten

KAMP HOLLAND

Six young Dutch soldiers, four men and two women, and their Afghan interpreter stand spot-lit on the stage in white underwear and Army boots discussing their upcoming deployment to Uruzgan.

FLIPPER   We know what it takes
MARIEKE   To perform under pressure
KHADIJA   Discipline. Tough conditions
SIKKO   No acting, no bullshit
FOK   Real life experience
MARIEKE   And adventure of course
FOK   See something of the world
FLIPPER   Who else gets to experience
            such things?
MARIEKE   An unforgettable experience
ADRI   Exotic cultures
SIKKO   Always wanted to travel
FOK   It's almost like a holiday

SERGEANT DIRK (also in underwear)
            Quiet!

KHADIJA   Afghanistan
MARIEKE   And you are doing something
            for your fellow man
KHADIJA   Makes you feel good
MARIEKE   Helping people
KHADIJA   Poor people
SIKKO   We are so rich
FLIPPER   And when you come home
            you have a story to tell
FOK   If you come home
ELLIE   I just want to go somewhere
FLIPPER   I want to experience something
SIKKO   I can't wait
ADRI   Bring it on
FOK   I haven't a clue what, though
ELLIE   As long as something happens
FOK   We've got a real experience ahead!

SERGEANT DIRK   Quiet I said!

Six months earlier

The morning patrol in the Green Zone north of Kamp Holland in Tarin Kowt gets back to the harbour of vehicles at 1000. The Dutch soldiers have just shed their sweat-soaked body armour and sat down in the shade of the vehicles when there is a whizzing noise and a distant bang.

A 107mm rocket was fired at them from a nearby village but flew past wide and blew up harmlessly in the *dasht* desert between their hill and the town. Two Apaches gunships that arrive and circle spot a red pickup truck speeding away. An Australian unit intercepts the vehicle but has to release the passengers, four fighting-age males, as there is no evidence of their involvement. The soldiers stand down when they get reports over the radio that there is again a normal pattern of life in the fields, the best indicator that no Taliban are moving up to attack.

'Finally something happened,' one of the young infantrymen says.

The south-central Afghan province of Uruzgan has quietened down significantly since the current rotation of troops started their four-month tour in March, 2008.

There were some incidents that had a big impact. On April 18, a day after General Peter van Uhm took up the post of Dutch Defence Chief, his 23-year-old son Dennis died with another soldier when their jeep ran over a pressure-plate IED in the desert. Two more Dutch were seriously injured. The Australians at Kamp Holland also lost their fourth man KIA in April (17 by August 2010). But for the most part, those soldiers wishing for some action have been disappointed. Mindful that the enemy can punish complacency in the worst manner, the commander of Task Force Uruzgan, Colonel Richard van Harskamp, urges the soldiers not to let down their guard.

'Recently Uruzgan has characterized itself due to the noticeable peace and quiet. This is the result of weeks of hard work,' he writes in the Task Force newsletter. 'Many of you are at or past the halfway mark of your mission. The enemy will be here till the end of time and is not bothered by rotations. The results we achieve today are no guarantee for tomorrow. Therefore we must stay sharp till the end. To help you remember this I would like to end with a quotation from a randomly chosen counter-insurgency manual.

> Somewhere a True Believer is training to kill you. He is training with minimum food and water in austere conditions, day and night. The only thing clean on him is his weapon. He doesn't worry about what work-out to do, his rucksack weighs what it weighs, and he runs until the enemy stops chasing him. The True Believer doesn't care 'how hard it is,' he knows he either wins or he dies. He doesn't go home at 1700, he is home. He knows only the Cause.

There are plenty of 'True Believers' in Uruzgan, which, although overshadowed in news reports by neighbouring Kandahar and Helmand, is still extremely volatile. Since deploying here in mid-2006, the 1,600-strong Dutch contingent lost 16 soldiers killed up to my arrival in July 2008 (24 by July 2010).

The makings of trouble are present here at several levels. This Pashtun-dominated province of 350,000 people is home to various sub-units of the fiercely rival Durrani and Ghilzai tribes. Its six districts include Deh Rawood where Taliban leader Mullah Omar was raised, and it is surrounded by areas of high insurgent activity like the Deh Chopan district of Zabul province, the Ghorak district of Kandahar province and the Kajaki and Baghran districts of Helmand.

Uruzgan used to be the fruit basket of Afghanistan but war damage in the past 30 years and two recent heavy droughts more than halved the 1.6 million hectares of working agricultural land. Amid extreme poverty much of this was turned over to poppy, and the province is also a key transit route for opium shipments heading north from Helmand to Central Asia and Russia.

These days the insurgents tend to avoid direct large-scale attacks in Uruzgan after they failed to capture the remote US Firebase Anaconda in four successive attacks in August 2007, and a 500-man insurgent force was repelled by Dutch artillery and air strikes in the Chora Valley that October. Fighters increasingly roam in small groups, planting IEDs and executing hit-and-run attacks and melting away in the villages or mountains. Some pockets of entrenched resistance remain, like the Mirabad region to the east of Tarin Kowt, where in early June 2008 in the aftermath of a huge jailbreak by Taliban prisoners in Kandahar, 100 fighters attacked a patrol of Afghan and Coalition Forces.

A few days later, a major Dutch operation to flush out Mirabad gets cancelled because Chinook helicopters that were booked for it are needed instead for operations against prison escapees in Kandahar's Arghandab region. This deepened the sense of anti-climax among many of the soldiers on this tour after several months of intense training.

Uruzgan jumped back into the international headlines in February 2009 when a suicide bomber in police uniform walked into a Police training centre in Tarin Kowt and blew himself up, killing 21 officers and wounding at least 20. Nevertheless in the summer of 2008, IEDs were the main threat for that rotation of troops. EOD teams neutralized at least two dozen devices in the ten weeks before I visited, while others exploded with devastating effect.

'The soldiers' first mission was to recover a vehicle that was hit by an IED and torn apart,' said Gerwin, a Lieutenant of the 45th Battalion, Orange Gelderland Infantry Regiment.

> The injured had been recovered but they had to clean up blood, puke and wreckage. It really confronted them with the reality. One of our guys had to pick up some body armour that was draining blood. He said afterwards it that made a big impression on him, just the idea of holding the body armour of a guy whose legs had to be cut off him to free him from the vehicle. The same evening there was another IED blast with three injured, and their next mission was to recover that vehicle too.

Dutch infantry Sergeant
Dennis, Uruzgan province.

Dutch patrol, Uruzgan
province, June 2008.

From the very start we tell them this is not a safe place. Sometimes it's a bit surreal, you walk in the Green Zone, the sun is shining, the children are playing, the birds are chirping, but the guys have to be on the alert and look after themselves and the guys around them. Something can happen here in the click of your fingers. We didn't expect any kind of threat but a day ago a 107mm rocket flew over us. That was also a reminder for them that they must be sharp from beginning to end.

But the Dutch manner of doing business in Uruzgan, often maligned by ISAF partners and US forces in particular, is to concentrate on reconstruction and development and not invite trouble on missions outside the wire.

'We usually work in groups of 50 to 60 so that if the Taliban see us they think 'not today',' adds Dennis, a Sergeant from the same battalion. 'We're here to work safe, we are not here to get them all the time but to work with the people. But if they want to shoot, let them.'

On my first mission out of base I stand in the hatch at the back of an APC chatting through the intercom to Dennis, who I have not seen in person yet. He is a reporter's ideal interviewee, joking freely while also serious and opinionated, and I learn much later that the producers of the play *Kamp Holland* used him as the model for Sergeant Dirk.

'I think the public back home understand that we do some PRT work but especially last year they knew we do a lot of fighting as well. I don't think they understand us as soldiers, most of them think what the fuck are we doing here, young guys are dying.

'Maybe if we stay for the next 50 years we can do great things, us Dutchies can do something here in a couple of years but not much. The Afghans are a thousand years behind us, sometimes I think I'm walking in the Bible era, so this takes more than a couple of years to change.'

All the time he is scouting the road ahead for signs of an ambush – many of the prison escapees from Kandahar reportedly headed north towards Uruzgan and may have been re-armed and thrown back into the fray. While the Dutch may not go looking for a fight, they seem happy to get stuck in if it comes to it.

'It'll be like a scene from Braveheart, if 1,000 of them come at us in a line we'll show them our asses,' the Sergeant laughs.

After the patrol I sit in the Windmill Cafe in Kamp Holland. It is essentially a large air-conditioned metal hut with no windows, but to compensate for the close confines they have created an intimately lit and rather ambient interior with a strong Dutch flavour.

Above the door stands a metre-high model of a windmill, complete with sails that spin in the gusts that drive 30-metre tall dust devils through the base. Inside, the walls are hung with pictures of cows grazing on polders, fields ablaze with tulips, barges on canals and the narrow houses of old Amsterdam.

There is also table football, pool and poker tables, wicker chairs and a small altar with a large wooden cross. The Windmill offers free tea and coffee all day and has a bar that sells snacks and soft drinks. Soldiers eat fast food while watching *Hamburger Hill* and *Jarhead* on a large flat screen TV, and this month everything is decked out with orange balloons and Dutch flags because of the European championship underway back home. Matches are shown each night on a huge screen outside the cafe, where hundreds of soldiers gather to support the Dutch team, dressed in orange and waving orange flags. One guy even wears an orange burqa purchased at the camp bazaar, although he says fans at home are banned from wearing the head-to-toe veils because it is seen as provocative towards the Netherlands' Muslim community.

The Dutch troops live in 'chalets', roofed-in rows of steel containers with heavy doors, purpose-built with up to four berths in each. Surrounded and covered by Hescos, the chalets hold 24 containers in two rows and are the safest sleeping quarters I've seen in Afghanistan.

'Since we got the containers one year ago not a single rocket was fired at the base,' the Dutch public affairs officer tells me. That changed in April 2009 when a shower of rockets killed one soldier and injured four as they waited in line outside the dining facility.

This DFAC serves a general selection of European food but there are always individual packets of Edam (the Aussies jokingly refer to the Dutch as 'Cheeseboys'). I have seen notices at DFACs across the country about what attire must be worn at meals but this is the first time I saw a sign reminding civilians 'no dresses, no thongs'.

It was to this Dutch home-from-home that Geert Lageveen and Leopold Witte, producers with the Amsterdam-based Orkater theatre company, arrived on April 29, 2008. For two weeks they lived with the soldiers, gathering material for a production they hoped would wake the public to the realities of this deployment.

'We are not for or against the mission, we just register how things are being done,' they told the domestic media, stating their goal as breaking the 'Kamp Holland fatigue' that had appeared in the Netherlands two years after these NATO forces deployed in southern Afghanistan.

At Kamp Holland they found a duality of existence that was no less significant than that of being in the Netherlands and being in Afghanistan. The state of being inside or outside the camp, among things Dutch within its walls or things Afghan beyond them, was essential to telling the story, even if they hadn't planned on joining the patrols.

'Prior to our trip we promised ourselves and our wives not to go outside the gate,' Geert Lageveen wrote to me in 2009 after the play had completed its 60-show tour. 'That was in the Netherlands. After not even a day in the camp we changed our minds and we did want to go outside. Why? Out of a combination of a foolish thirst for adventure and an unbridled curiosity. Besides that, in the camp, the separation between Inside and Outside the gate was applied very strictly, so we felt the need to go 'Outside' ourselves in order to be able to write about it. That separation almost determined the actual shape of the play.'

Leopold Witte also noted the phrase 'On the desire to live something you don't want to experience', which became the play's subtitle: 'That sentence came to our minds after we'd been walking around camp for a couple of days. Strangely enough that concerns us too. Maybe that's why we went out of the gate…'

So the thespians donned body armour and helmets and went on patrol with the troops by day and spent their evenings chatting to the soldiers and gathering ideas about what really mattered here. Contingent commander van Harskamp told me that most people were actually enthusiastic about having the actors there because 'like every soldier they want to tell their story.'

Meanwhile, the Dutch had been taking a lot of stick from their ISAF partners for their softly-softly approach in Uruzgan, the battle of Chora notwithstanding.

'The Dutch are rebuilding the house while it's still on fire,' one American soldier complained to me in 2008. It wasn't an uncommon view to hear at the time, although interestingly the Dutch approach was singled out for praise in the US Department of Defense's January 2009 report to Congress, which stated:

> In areas such as RC-South, where resources are not sufficiently concentrated, security cannot be established or maintained. In such areas the full military, governance, and economic spectrum of the COIN (counterinsurgency) strategy cannot be implemented and the insurgents retain their hold on the local Afghan population. An exception in RC-South is Uruzgan Province, where Dutch forces have had significant success in implementing the COIN strategy.[11]

An ISAF survey among inhabitants of Uruzgan, however, published by Dutch media in July 2008, ran counter to the hopes the approach was working. ISAF was negatively viewed by 58 per cent of respondents, while 60 per cent said the security situation was bad compared with 40 per cent who said that in Helmand. And 60 per cent said the insurgents had more influence than ISAF or the Afghan government.[12] At the time the Dutch Command were unrepentant about their methods.

'We build where we can and fight where we have to,' Col. van Harskamp said. 'I do not buy into the statement that we're only here to be Mr Do-Good. My guys treat people with respect but if they are required they will fight as fiercely as the US troops. It is showing the guts to take a little more risk by not kicking the door down and knocking and asking to come in. The long-term effect is that you can come back.'

I went on to ask the Colonel if the Dutch approach was in any way influenced by the events in Srebrenica in July 1995, when Serbian troops massacred 8,000 Bosnian men and boys inside a 'UN-protected safe area' manned by Dutch troops.

'What Dutch society learned from Srebrenica is that the military was way too lightly armed. It's something that has become ingrained in us that we will never let that happen again,' he says, telling me of the enormous firepower at the disposal of his contingent, including Apache attack helicopters and 155mm Panzer Howitzers that are 'like an entire battery of artillery'. Though further down the ranks, the contingent's development-heavy platform was a cause of frustration for some soldiers.

'Look at how the British and US do things, we need to push harder, hunt the insurgents down,' a disillusioned infantry Sergeant tells me one evening outside the cafe. 'But instead we do PRT patrols and build wells and water pumps and then we're gone in four months.

'We have lots of rules, when to shoot, when not to shoot, and we have to make reports about everything. I'm not saying you have to bomb and storm everything but if you are going to do something, then do it,' he adds, blaming the politicians back home for tying the troops' hands. Then again, a couple of months earlier I got into conversation with a Dutch Marine at KAF who leaned entirely the other way.

'Every day here is a day too long, this is not my war. We came here to build the place up with schools, clinics, now all we are doing is fighting, in the Dutch sector at least. This is not for the people, it's about money, securing oil and gas routes.'

With this divergence of opinion in the forces, let alone the general public, a play about the mission had plenty to say, particularly as the Netherlands' four-year commitment as lead nation in Uruzgan was due to end by December 2010.

Two politicians enter a room in The Hague.

P1   So what do we call it without saying 'war'?

P2   How do you like this? 'Undertaking acts of violence against clustered enemy elements. Acts that, usually, are also encountered during a war'.

P1 You're saying it again! And I also hear 'enemy', too. We have no enemy. Let's use 'OMF', just like the Army Command: Opposing Military Forces.

P2 What was wrong with the word 'reconstruction mission'? It sounded great. Retro, very Fifties.

P1 Reconstruction doesn't sell anymore.

P2 Because of Srebrenica?

P1 Let's not use that word either. One more fiasco like that and we can forget about our place in NATO.

P2 If things don't work out in Afghanistan, NATO can forget about itself.

P1 Crisis Control Mission.

P2 Go on.

P1 We call it a crisis control mission bound by strict rules of engagement.

P1 Sounds a little feeble.

P2 Firm rules of engagement.

P1 Slightly more assertive.

P2 Robust rules of engagement?

P1 Until we think of something better. Were you in the Army yourself?

P2 No. I was truly glad; I have a hard time with authority.

[The current Minister of Defence, Eimert van Middelkoop, actually made a statement using similar words in an earlier interview, causing an uproar in the military and media.]

P1 Last item: casualties.

P2 Dead?

P1 Again, not a good choice of word.

P2 The Army uses KIA.

P1 Isn't that a make of car?

P2 Killed In Action.

P1 English is such a wonderful language.

P2 And WIA. Wounded In Action.

P1 But they don't count. OK, from now on we'll say it's a crisis control mission bound by robust rules of engagement, where actions initiated by the OMF may generate an unlimited amount of WIA and a limited amount of KIA.

P2 That's good. Nice and clear.

P1 How many KIA though?

P2 The Army Command is expecting 40.

P1 For the entire mission?

P2 Yes. That is also the tipping point for public opinion.

P1 How many are we on now?

P2 Seventeen. So we still have some way to go.

The politicians speak from a raised platform, presumably to symbolise their distance from the soldiers. I also hazarded a guess at the time that the decision to have the cast perform entirely in underwear was to show how war strips a person down to his or her essence.

'We did not want any realism on the stage,' Lageveen explained later. 'When you start with a uniform – even if it is a fantasy camouflage print – then you need weapons too, and so on. Apart from that, we felt we had to compete with the many TV images about the mission that are broadcast. Instead, the audience was supposed to imagine the uniforms, the desert, the armoured cars. We wanted to put their imagination to work. Besides, underwear made the military somewhat uniform and at the same time very personal, because one would recognize the physiognomy of each character. And that added vulnerability.'

A recurring theme is the raw youth of the troops, prompting one theatre critic to write, 'The producers portray the ordinary soldier as a school-leaver whose brains have not yet developed enough to oversee the consequences of his choice of profession.'

It's probably true for most of them. Maria, a civilian who had worked at the Windmill for 16 months when I met her had coincided with the deaths of 14 of the 16 Dutch soldiers who were KIA. She knew most of them from working in the café.

'It changes the boys. When they first come here they are all, "let's go!" Then one dies. Some of them kill themselves when they go home. They are 20 or 21 years old, it's too much for them.'

I heard similar comments from the soldiers' leaders about the raw youth factor.

'I told our guys that if they came here aged 20 they would be five years older when they returned home,' Lt. Gerwin tells me. 'They were just children if you look at their photographs, now you can't recognize them from those photos.'

'We had a family day back in Holland before deployment,' continues Sgt. Dennis. 'The mothers asked us to watch over their sons. We said maybe he'll be a bit different when he comes home, he's not your little boy any more, he became a man and he's had an experience that most normal people don't have.'

Like the producers, I was struck by the pronounced, almost parental concern of these men for their young subordinates. Perhaps in line with the demands of the job, the Lieutenant was the more reserved of the pair, while the company Sergeant, a stocky man with a round face that as easily creases in a laugh or tightens in a scowl, would encourage and berate the men in highly vocal fashion, making him ideal material for the stage version of Sergeant Dirk.

'One third of Dirk is Dennis, one third of him we created, and one third was shaped by the actor Kees Boot,' said Lageveen. 'The fatherly way with which he approached his men alternately hard and soft inspired us. His care, his strange sort of humour. Some of his statements literally ended up in the play's text.'

For that painfully young rotation of Dutch troops I met, one of the first, greatest shocks and growing experiences they endured was the loss of Lieutenant van Uhm and Private Mark Schouwink in an IED strike near the town of Khorma, nine kilometres north of Tarin Kowt.

'When you have someone killed in action, it's something that fortunately you will never get used to,' Col. van Harskamp said. 'If it happens to be the son of the Defence Chief that doesn't make the burden any heavier because it's already as heavy as it can be. It does mean you have to ensure that the whole treatment remains as worthy as possible.

'The General came here two weeks later and during his trip had some private conversations with the platoon. It was hard for him, he wants to be here as a professional soldier but he remains a father. I know he wouldn't want to have over-attention at the cost of attention for other families because his son died.'

But however sensitively the incident was handled, this high profile pair of deaths had a pronounced effect in Holland and was reflected by various polls at the time. The Defence Ministry's own survey in April 2008 showed a slump in support for the mission from 37 per cent in March to 25 percent.[13]

In a separate internet survey conducted in April on the Dutch MSN website in which 11,000 people participated, more than 60 per cent thought Holland should withdraw from Afghanistan when the death toll reached 25. Van Uhm and Schouwink were the 15th and 16th fatal casualties. One of the soldiers described that day to me during my stay.

'It was 8a.m., I was at the cafe drinking coffee and saw the Major walking past with the adjutant. I saw his face and already knew something was wrong. He said Unit 24 drove over an IED, 2 KIA, including Lt. van Uhm and Private Schouwink. It's your worst nightmare, two people killed by an IED. We are not afraid of contact with the Taliban, we are afraid of IEDs, there's nothing you can do about them. Some of our guys were in disbelief at the news; some walked away, some laughed in shock. The platoon stayed out that night. They could hear the locals in Khorma shouting and cheering. One reaction was to turn all the cannons towards them and blow the fucking place up but they didn't. When they returned you didn't know what to say to them, people were crying, still in disbelief. We all paid our last respects in the evening.

'The bodies were OK, intact, they died of internal injuries. There was a path made of candles, four men stood with the bodies as a guard of honour. Then the men of Unit 24 came first, then the rest of Bravo Company, 150 guys. Someone sprayed Schouwink with his favourite aftershave. It was so real. The ramp ceremony was the next day, the first ramp ceremony of the tour. It took Unit 24 two weeks to regain normality. The main problem was getting the boys focussed, they were scared, didn't have a big mouth any more. Some wanted to avenge the deaths – they took two of our guys, we'll take 20 of theirs.'

Overall, the incident represented a sharp wake-up call for many of the soldiers.

'We were here a while and everything seemed safe, then out of the blue one of the platoons drove over an IED, two killed and two wounded,' recalled Sgt. Dennis. 'After the ramp ceremony everyone is down for a couple of days and then you pick up the pace and carry on. The show must go on, the assign-

Last night of Kamp Holland
play in Amsterdam,
January 2009

Windmill Café, Kamp
Holland, Tarin Kowt,
Uruzgan province.

ments kept coming and three days later we went on another mission.'

This inexorable flow of duties and life was perhaps inadvertently mirrored in the pace of the play as it leapt from one tragedy or absurdity to the next in quick succession. It charted the course of the fictitious squad through all the factors and scenarios the real soldiers must have suggested to the producers: the shooting of an unarmed civilian approaching on a motorbike, treatment of a child victim of a mine blast, the reassignment of an attractive female soldier because the guys are squabbling over her, and ultimately the fatal injury of one of the soldiers. At that moment the 'Secretary General' appears on stage, in apparent reference to the Dutch head of NATO then, Jaap de Hoop Scheffer, who presents the case for the Netherlands' Afghan involvement:

Of course my thoughts go out to the victims' family and colleagues. But we must ask ourselves: in what kind of world do we want to live? Do we let children be denied school? People tortured for listening to music? Do we let homosexuals be stoned? Do we want to live in a world where women are shot because they looked at another man in the street?

The world is a village. 'Over there' and 'here' don't exist anymore.

If we don't fight Islamic fundamentalism over there, it will infect our society here. The authors of the attacks in New York, London and Madrid were all trained in Afghanistan. For this reason the United States responded to their violence. If this evil is not nipped in the bud more casualties will occur over here. And let's suppose we had let the United States do the job alone and that we would have stayed on the sidelines with clean hands. Would we feel morally superior towards the Americans but secretly glad they did the dirty work?

Luckily we are a civilized people and we decided democratically to help Afghanistan. The Netherlands have dared to take on an arduous task in the reconstruction. We can be proud of that. Let us finish our job. We cannot run away because the events are against us for a while. We cannot let Afghanistan down right now.

Therefore I appeal to your moral sense. Support our boys and girls in Uruzgan. If only for the simple reason that we decided to go there.

As a counterpoint to that argument, a young woman, the 'Demographer', then comes onto the stage and addresses the audience.

Let's look at this war another way, not as a battle between cultures and religions. Not about oil or terrorism. The reality is much more primal and simple. In Afghanistan there is a huge surplus of boys between fifteen and eighteen, full of energy, plans and hormones but without a job, a woman or hope. Look at the stats: every year in Afghanistan 500,000 boys turn fifteen years old. Let's say 150,000 of them find a job, which leaves 350,000 boys. In the best case scenario, let's say 90 per cent of them stay out of trouble, 10 per cent still join the Taliban. It gives meaning to their life. So that produces 35,000 new recruits every year. That's why war with the Taliban is like fighting a natural disaster. Look at Gaza, Iraq, Somalia, and Kenya, where a surplus of boys causes only misery. But in Afghanistan the reservoir of young men is now drying up as the birth rate decreases. The Taliban will eventually have to give up for lack of personnel and that's what we have to wait for. It's better than sending your – often only – son to a senseless war.

According to the Defence Ministry polls, support for the mission reached its lowest point in March 2009 when only 21 per cent of people supported the mission against 35 who opposed it. But by August 2009 support was back up to a typical level of 37 per cent (compared to 32 against, and almost as many 'don't knows'). At the same time, a relatively high 47 per cent thought the mission would contribute to the reconstruction of Afghanistan. Interestingly, the assertion of the 'Secretary General' that the military involvement in Afghanistan made the streets of the Netherlands safer from terrorist attacks seldom rose above 10 per cent in the ministry poll.

Against this fluctuating background of public reaction, Orkater's production got mixed reviews. The newspaper *de Volkskrant* slammed it as 'noisy one-dimensional theatre in which a group of actors in white underwear (why?) runs around the stage screaming out loud with panic-stricken eyes. *Kamp Holland* 'mostly addresses blunt Sergeants, dumb soldiers, the mutual frustrations, boredom and the ride "outside the gate" into the perilous desert.'

Military officials who attended the play were more upbeat, in their public remarks at least. In an interview with the Dutch VPRO Radio 1 in December 2008, former Dutch Defence Chief Dick Berlijn said he didn't recognize its assumptions about how the Afghan mission was being sold politically, or how the establishment wrangled internally about whether this was a reconstruction mission or combat mission. But he lavishly praised its contribution to bridging gaps in the perception of 'there' and 'over here', especially in the return home of serving soldiers.

> What struck me is the excellent way they sketched the feelings the soldiers have when they are there. They struck the right note...I think many men and women [who were in Afghanistan] will recognize the situation and themselves. What matters for them is that 'we' in the Netherlands feel what it was like to be there, for them. And this is something I learned to understand over the years, when Dutch society sends you on a mission, and one comes back with the feeling that everybody thinks that the mission wasn't worth it, then this is terrible. Look at our Indonesia veterans who had the feeling – for years – that what had been done there was terrible and wrong. That is a hang-over that stays with you for years or for a lifetime. The opposite is true as well, that when you come back and you feel society understands what it was about and what the soldiers experienced it feels as a heavy burden is taken from one's shoulders.

'I see all the emotions I have seen in Afghanistan in this play, and so that's a good job done,' Col. van Harskamp said after seeing *Kamp Holland*. 'It's not the kind of play you want to show at schools but as far as I'm concerned we will show it in the barracks as preparation of a mission.'[14]

Some civilian viewers felt the play came over in places as a 'list' of issues served up one after the other at the expense of forming a shaped story and characters. Then again, the amount of ground it had to cover precluded this. By and large, the producers were happy with what they achieved, even if it didn't revolutionize or even just touch public opinion on a large scale.

'I'm not sure whether our performance carried much weight,' Lageveen said. 'We've played it about 60 times with an average of 300 viewers. So, a large part of the 18,000 viewers will have another view now. A much-heard remark was that by living through the performance they gained an unprecedented view on the experiences of the soldiers in Afghanistan. On top of that, they felt a shared responsibility for "our boys and girls" over there and they were sometimes ashamed about their indifference for that ... A lot of soldiers attended, and though the play takes a critical point of view at the mission, they were usually even more enthusiastic. They recognized everything, and thought that we really hit the atmosphere of the military life and the complexity of working in Uruzgan very well. They often brought their families with them. To show them what they find so hard to explain themselves.'

Sgt. Dennis had this to say in an e-mail I received after my trip to Amsterdam.

> Maybe it's good to know that everything that's in the play really happened. We didn't walk around in white underwear, as I recall, but the rest of it is true! Most Dutch people don't have a clue what's happening in Uruzgan while they fight at the dinner table about nothing somewhere in Holland.

'At Last Something Happened' – Scene Two

As for the lads' longing to see some action, the Sergeant recounted how many got what they wanted a few days before the end of the tour when a fuel convoy they were escorting to Tarin Kowt from Kandahar was heavily ambushed.

Dutch patrol and loaded Bedford
truck, Uruzgan province, June 2008.

That IED-vehicle we recovered was our first mission outside. It helped the boys focus and they saw that it's serious shit over there. They stayed focussed the whole tour, although nothing happened. They were just young guys searching for action. So IF something happens, they feel a bit of a rush. But, after that big fire fight along the route KAF-TK, they thought a bit differently about it. When there are no WIAs or KIAs after such an engagement, the rush stays, they feel invincible. The next day they realised it was because of a lot of luck that they all survived. Don't get me wrong, they did very well during the fight. But, in all honesty, if the Taliban paid more attention during their shooting practice we probably would have had WIAs or worse.

We received the whole package during that contact, mortars, RPGs, PKMs ... everything. It lasted five hours over a distance of 15km. Everything went pretty well, although one mortar shell hit 50 metres away from us. The biggest problem came when we were halfway through the ambush. An Afghan (civilian) truck driver was shot in the head and his truck was standing sideways blocking the road, so we had a split convoy. Lt. Gerwin was on the good side and I was on the bad one. The Taliban concentrated their fire at that truck

and our vehicles that were nearby. I sent in the Apaches which fired everything they had and went back to base empty. We had to bring up one of our own truck drivers (a technician without any patrol experience) under heavy fire to the truck. He drove it with pieces of skull on the steering wheel and parked it at the side of the road. After that we could pick up speed.

It was the experience I needed as a soldier. It helped me realise that all those years of training had paid off and that everyone in the Army is important: the comms specialist kept contact with the opsroom and called in the Apaches; the medic saved the life of that driver, and if we had not had that brave technician I would probably still be fighting in that valley. It's the most important lesson I learned during that mission.

In February 2010, after 21 Dutch soldiers had died in Afghanistan, the coalition government in the Netherlands collapsed over disagreements on whether or not to prolong the Afghan mission.

NATO had requested the Dutch deployment be extended beyond the planned withdrawal date in December. Instead, the failure of the country's ruling parties to support a longer involvement meant a Dutch withdrawal was expected to start from August 2010.

Eviction

It's July 2, 2008 and I am holed up in a little guest house in Kandahar City between embeds, having arrived back from the Dutch earlier than scheduled and gotten booted off KAF by ISAF.

I had hoped to knock around the base for a few days doing interviews and tagging along with anybody who fancied a bit of impromptu press coverage, but my early arrival throws the public affairs office into extraordinary chaos. My main contact there, a pleasant Dutchman called Roland, is on home leave and no one else knows me there.

Joe, the public affairs man I speak to on the phone, tells me to wait at the terminal, so I take a seat opposite the International Military Police station. There is a constant flow of people with huge packs, and by the IMP's door a group of Canadian soldiers stand and discuss camel spider versus scorpion fights: 'The first night the camel spider won, the second night it didn't stand a chance.' They just found another scorpion in the Canadian compound and want to paint numbers on their backs to help place bets during the fights. It's a common entertainment down here, where ring contenders are plentiful.

I doze in the sun and wake at 1330, sweating and dizzy. A Canadian I recognise from somewhere advises me to go get some water, so I drink my fill and sit back and wait. In civilian life waiting in air terminals offers some of the best anthropology. At Kandahar or Bagram airfields there may not be the range of human interaction you see at say Heathrow airport (no joyous reunions and kissing), but there is the fun of watching soldiers of different nationalities mixing together.

At a low level of distinction between armies, I noticed that their demeanour and even equipment can reflect stereotypical national characteristics. Take the uniforms: Australians stroll round in a vivacious yellow, brown and green 'jelly bean' pattern, while the flaming red-brown swirls of the Egyptian kit emanates Saharan heat and rugged intensity. Finnish uniform is gruffly understated but imbued with a leafy love of the forest, while the French evidently wish to imbue a breath of stylish military élan with tight, figure-hugging tunics and drainpipe trousers tucked into tall black boots and set off with a natty slouch hat.

Once on KAF I was ushered with other passengers onto a German Luftwaffe C-160 transport plane by a polite young crewman who in precise English informed us that we will fly one hour and ten minutes and wished us to 'Heff a good flight.' The interior was immaculate, everything was stacked and ordered, oxygen masks and first aid kits were strung exactly overhead and belts clipped shut and hung neatly from the top of each seat, causing the American soldier beside me to gasp 'It's like a new Mercedes!'

Shortly after I flew to Helmand on a cluttered, dusty British C-130 with a distinctly 'lived-in' feel and stink of grease about it.

'We apologize as it will get hot because the air conditioner is broken,' the loader announced cheerily. 'As it's Sunday, the inflight meal is roast beef and Yorkshire pudding, seasonal veg, roast potatoes and a couple of pints of Guinness. The movie is…*Flight of the Phoenix*.'

I call Joe again.

'I've been busy with you all morning, the Canadians don't know anything about you, can't get hold of the Estonians, nobody wants to take responsibility for you. We are already understaffed and nobody is happy with you,' he informs me curtly.

Without asking me about the reasonable option, my staying somewhere in the city until I'm due to come back to re-embed, I am deemed a 'security risk', forbidden to leave the passenger terminal and with no mention of me being fed at any stage am told I will be put on a flight to Kabul the next day. I'm basically being frogmarched off the premises. After six weeks of schlepping from Army to Army in southern Afghanistan I sit in bemusement. If this is the panic caused by a journalist arriving a few days ahead of schedule then God help the place if 1,000 Taliban appear on the horizon. Maybe it is all just 'a ball of bullshit' as Jim said.

I shake off my stupor, leave the terminal anyway and get hold of a friend in Kandahar who sends a car for me. I'd have done it hours earlier if people had thought to treat me other than a fifth columnist. I inform ISAF I wish to

Dutch infantry Lt. Gerwin
wonders at the marijuana plants
growing on a police station
doorstep, Uruzgan province.

go to town and am told I will not be readmit-ted to the airfield for a week.

I put my body armour and helmet into a sack and root out my *payran tumban* and Afghan hat, advisable wear outside since a white west-erner in jeans is immediately noticeable and ripe for snatching off the street. At 1800 I get a lift to the gate from a couple of ISAF public affairs staff who had been instructed to 'look out for an Englishman who works for a German paper dressed as an Afghan.'

My friend's driver is waiting for me in a grey Toyota Corolla and we set off toward Kandahar at 1820 as the evening sun drops towards the hilltops. For the first time in weeks I'm at ground level as opposed to riding in a high military vehicle and I tell the driver to hang back from the US Humvees in front of us. I don't want to get shot by ISAF now.

Some British troops in Vectors stop us near an ANP post as a column of Police jeeps speeds past in our direction. We are at front of the queue of civilian traffic and looking directly up the muzzle of a British machine-gunner who fires pink flares onto the camber to deter cars from creeping up the roadside.

'Oh just let us bloody pass,' I hiss after ten minutes, and this is just one time I had to wait, the locals get it many times a day. After 15 minutes we can proceed again, passing an odd mix of sights as we head into town; flocks of camels, mud houses and Cuchi tents set up behind Western-style businesses renting out JCBs and cranes, and a refrigeration depot 'Built by India'. There are roadside billboards for milk and telecoms networks while others warn of suicide bombers and appeal to the public to report anyone seen planting IEDs. Brightly painted trucks and rickshaws jostle on the road while Soviet military vehicle wrecks rust in the adjacent wadi, all washed together by the feeble light of the setting sun's pale disc.

As darkness swallows Kanadahar we pull up at the guest house gate where the guard sus-piciously hefts the sack with my body armour until I tell him it's a carpet and am allowed through. Once I'm booked in, exhaustion sweeps over me. I shower, change and go and eat lamb, rice and chick peas in the restaurant and write notes in front of a TV tuned into an Iranian channel showing a Buster Keaton silent movie.

My week is monotone, consisting of sleep, food and writing in my little room. After my Zabul ban and the cancellation of the Dutch operation, things deteriorate further with the cancellation by the Estonians of my visit to Now Zad. I'm thinking of returning to Pakistan when the Canadians unexpectedly agree to take me in.

CANADIANS

Private Colin Wilmot was the 87th fatality for Canada's 2,500-strong contingent in Afghanistan. The 24-year-old medic was on an early morning foot patrol in the Panjwaii district near Kandahar City on Sunday July 6, 2008, when he was mortally injured in an IED blast. The tally would rise to 150 by July 2010.

Canadian troops based at Camp Nathan Smith in Kandahar City have only been patrolling the streets and fields on their immediate doorstep since March. Before that the suicide-bombing threat level was considered too high around this fortified installation that houses the contingent's Provincial Reconstruction Team.

So the closest the locals would see the foreigners was when they rumbled past in their LAVs, the 17-ton, eight-wheeled light armoured vehicles that the Canadians drive. But in these four months the PRT started 20 projects in the area to win local support, building wells, sewerage systems, roads and culverts. And now they go out on patrol beyond their wall. Early on Monday July 7 a Lieutenant picks me up from the media tent and leaves me at the vehicle park with the Platoon Sergeant, who nods silently when I'm introduced.

'He looks overjoyed to have a journalist along,' I say to the officer, who replies, 'He's just had a rough couple of days.'

I am told to walk behind the two CIMIC guys attached to the patrolling infantry, Captain Tylere Couture, a newly arrived, enthusiastic young man with six months of self-taught Pashtu under his belt, and one Sergeant Dawson.

At 0700 a LAV guns its engine and drives up a ramp by the camp's four-metre-high brick wall, ready to provide covering fire with its 25mm cannon if the patrol gets in trouble. More vehicles stand by with the rest of the platoon as 11 soldiers and I prepare to head out the back exit on foot. The troops put on their helmets and check weapons and radios before

we walk towards the double steel gates at 0710. They are padlocked and no one has the key so the unit radios for someone to come and open up. A helmeted head pokes out over the sandbags in the tower and a female voice calls out: 'Who wants to go on patrol?'

'US! The guys who are fucking dressed up at the gate!' the irate Platoon Sergeant yells back. We wait. Ten minutes later a small soldier runs up with the key on a chock of wood, opens the gate and then the barrier on the outer perimeter of wire.

The patrol moves along a narrow road made of crushed river stones and earth that has just been laid by Abdul Qadar, the local construction manager who implements projects financed by the PRT. It's supposed to be a small showpiece to illustrate how the infrastructure is improving. But a couple of men tell the CIMIC soldiers that people are worried that heavy rainfall will still turn the road into a quagmire. The Canadians refer them and others we meet to Qadar as part of a drive to involve Afghan officials more and break the dependency on foreigners to do everything.

'There is a semi-functional municipality in Kandahar,' Captain Couture explains. 'We want to spread local government, give all the credit to them. If they need our help we'll do it behind the scenes.'

We move on with fields and distant hills on our left, walls and compounds to our right. Men crouch in the street and watch while kids start to cluster around us, only to get abruptly moved on by the infantry.

'It's about time the government did something for you isn't it?' Sgt. Dawson tells more people we meet, drawing a murmur of 'Whoah' (yes). 'This road is an example of the local government trying to help people out, now we need you people to talk to them. You guys should start going to Abdul Qadar and tell him what services you need, wells, sanitation. It's your government and they have to work for you, tell them if you need wells and ditches, roads fixed. Have a wonderful day and be safe.'

After half an hour of this the CIMIC soldiers sit and have tea at the roadside with a house owner and some members of his family. Couture manages some small talk with them in his struggling Pashtu and with the interpreter's help they share a bit of genuine conversation and good humour.

A few metres away the infantrymen have thrown up a cordon, frisking anyone who wants to pass down the track, including children. Dawson tells me that two months ago a 12-year-old suicide bomber attacked this unit in another part of the province, killing one Afghan soldier and injuring two Canadians.

'They do that and now we have to pat down all these kids if we want to let them through.'

The Captain is still chatting over his tea while the soldiers at the cordon are being taunted by a bunch of teenagers fronted by a seemingly mentally impaired youth.

'Some village lost its idiot and we found him. Get out of here or I'll kick you in the fucking ass!' one soldier finally shouts, chasing the kids away.

The cranky Sergeant has perked up a bit and tells me the length of their tours has been extended from six to eight and a half months, much like the US stop-gap system, which in order to sustain numbers of available troops added three more months to 12-month deployments.

The Sergeant blames the Americans for the extra time to serve: 'They picked the fight and we're paying the price, longer tours and more time away from our families,' he says, before moving on to the topic of Zhari (pronounced Zari), an extremely violent district west of the city that I will shortly visit with the Canadians.

'If there's a place you want to have good insurance it's there. We got in a few scraps there, it makes you feel like a soldier,' he says, looking pumped at the mere thought.

The patrol turns back and makes for the camp. On the last stretch of road a man seated in a car with a woman revs the vehicle loudly and tries to pull out amongst the soldiers from an alleyway. The Sergeant steps up sharply to the vehicle, draws his rifle into the firing position and points the muzzle directly at the driver's head.

Vehicle-borne suicide bombings are an ever-present danger in Kandahar and the man is a whisker away from getting a bullet in the face. He wisely takes his foot off the accelerator and scowls through the windscreen.

'You'll wait there all fucking day if I say!' the Sergeant bellows at him as the patrol passes.

We carry on the last 100 metres to the perimeter. Despite the disturbance the Captain is still mindful of community relations, ticks off the interpreter for tossing an empty water bottle and makes him pick it up. When we get back inside he reproaches the Sergeant for the display of aggression but the NCO is unrepentant.

'One minute they are smiling and talking to you and the next they come at you,' he counters. 'The guys say fuck and things to them because that's the way it is.'

'Well it shouldn't be that way. They're our neighbours but they may be setting up mortar base plates there, all you have to do is tell them to fuck off and that'll start them off.'

'Sir, I realise you speak the language and all that but these kids are 18 or 19 and have had friends die in their arms and they will talk to them like that. You haven't been shot at, these guys have.'

'You don't have to be a linguist to understand fuck off.'

'Well you should raise the matter.'

'I am raising the matter.'

I am then led away from the exchange, which grows steadily more heated behind me.

Colin Wilmot was with 1 Field Ambulance of 2nd Battalion, Princess Patricia's Canadian Light Infantry Battle Group, based in Edmonton. He had not been scheduled to join the current rotation in Afghanistan but he still demanded to be sent.

'Colin wanted it known that should a spot become available on the mission, he wanted in,' Brigadier General Denis Thompson, Canada's top soldier in Afghanistan, told national media after his death. 'He was selected to fill a vacancy soon after, because he was motivated, he was skilled, and because he was eager to make a difference in the lives of ordinary Afghans.'

On the Tuesday evening the camp holds a memorial service. About 250 soldiers parade around the flagpole as their commanding officer says a few words and one of Wilmot's fellow medics, Corporal Genevieve Dureau, reads the eulogy, her voice cracking.

'He was always there for you, no matter what, always helped you, no questions asked – even if it wasn't in his best interest. He'd walk around with this really goofy smile on his face all the time, I don't know why, he just did. He was always happy, no matter what the situation was. Colin, you were the nicest guy I've ever met and you will be greatly missed,' the young woman finishes, breaking down in tears.

The next morning she is part of another foot patrol that goes out again with Captain Couture, this time in the warren of alleys to the west of the camp.

'If anything happens I'm sure that the LAVs will punch out of the gate and be on your asses in a second with their guns blazing,' one of the NCOs says as he sees the patrol out of the gate.

The brook that flows into the city from the fields is full of sewage but the kids still swim in this vile waterway and women wash clothes there. All the houses have a waste trench running into the stream.

'I'm not sure if the houses draw their drinking water from it but you see the kids drinking it, I nearly gagged the first time I saw that,' Couture says.

It's basically a goodwill patrol, with the same CIMIC pair engaging the locals in more chats about what needs doing in this run-down neighbourhood, and drawing a lot more *whoahs* of approval.

'It's good you do these patrols in town,' a man of about 50 tells Sgt. Dawson, who promptly gives the stock answer intended to build confidence in the 'Afghan face' of operations: 'It's the ANA and ANP who provide the security here.'

'Security is generally good but we have trouble with thieves, we had a car and a motorbike stolen from my son,' says the man, who is then asked if he reported it to the Police.

'We saw these same guys standing in the road by an ANP checkpoint with pistols, so how can we report it to the Police?' he protests, adding that on another occasion they also tried to stop his son's car and shot at him when he didn't stop. 'We don't want these thugs in our town.'

Then a man in dark Army-style protective glasses rides towards us down the dusty alleyway on a bike and is forced to stop at rifle point, taken off the bike and searched. He forces a smile but is shaking with fear and explains that he didn't see the patrol because of his eyewear.

As we pass along the streets I see that people are intrigued by Dureau, who despite her helmet, dark glasses and equipment is still discernibly female, blonde and shapely. The men stand and stare while the children crowd round to say hello and shake her hand. If she is inclined to shut off from the locals after losing her friend two days earlier it either doesn't show or her own giving nature won't allow her to do it. Amid so much childish excitement she greets the kids and beams at them as they take turns to clasp her gloved fingers. As we move on I ask her how it is to go back out there after such an incident.

'You start to get bitter and wonder why we're here and if we're doing the right thing. But you have to stay positive and focussed or you will completely lose faith,' she replies.

Back at Nathan Smith I shelter from the roasting midday sun in the small garden by the flagpole. Near me a notice board leant against the baking wall posts 'Todd's quote of the day': 'Never take someone for granted, hold every person close to your heart because you might wake up one day and realise you lost a diamond while you were busy collecting stones.'

And Todd's weather forecast: 49°C in the shade, 58 in the sun.

Bodyguards

'Of all the years I've worked here these are the dumbest fucking people I trained,' Rick, the Royal Canadian Mounted Police constable, exclaims into the heat of the morning sky.

He periodically boils over at the failure of the ten ANP officers to grasp basics, cusses them and dishes out the occasional kick up the butt as an aid to learning. He has just four days to turn them into personal bodyguards for Haji Baran, the government-appointed leader of Kandahar's Panjwaii district.

Coming mainly from the north and east of the country, the ten were plucked from mundane duties in Panjwaii like manning checkpoints to be groomed in aspects of client protection, from speed evacuation to hand-to-hand combat to detecting car bombs. Five of the group previously spent ten weeks at Police school in Herat. Five say they've had no training whatsoever and were just issued uniforms and weapons and put straight on the job. Most have been in fire fights and can absorb elementary drills with lots of repetition. Others, like the distinctly unAfghan-looking guy the trainer has dubbed 'the Russian' for his fair looks, seem beyond learning anything; and the youngest, a 20-year-old Uzbek, speaks neither Dari nor Pashtu and must have the gist conveyed to him by another officer who speaks Farsi.

'Your function and mandate is to protect the client at all costs,' Rick tells them. 'The Taliban, the bad guys, will look to see how you hold your rifle. If your uniform is smart and your car is clean and if you guys look like a hard target they will attack a softer target.'

On the first morning we sit in a sweltering classroom at Camp Nathan Smith as the constable's assistant, Sergeant Major Colin Norris, takes them through a compressed IED recognition course, speaking through an interpreter nicknamed Mojo.

'Always keep safety in mind. If you see something attractive it's probably mined,' Norris says during the hi-speed tour of pressure plates, tripwire and command wire-operated IED variants.

'The first thing you do is confirm it's a mine. That doesn't mean you put your hands on it. The day before yesterday an Afghan policeman was chipping away at a mine with a knife. I know he was trying to help but under that mine there might be another one. If you remember anything from this morning, DO NOT CUT ANY WIRES!

'As close protection operatives you must be aware of suicide bombers. Government officials are high priority targets. Suicide bombers may act alone or in a group, and may be used in conjunction with another event. There are two types, person-borne and suicide-vehicle-borne IED. In the first case it's normally a guy with an explosive vest on. He gets his mission from a boss, generally he is not afraid to die, and he doesn't care about himself at all. Please understand that he is not crazy, he has been through indoctrination, that is his destiny, he will do anything he can to get to his target and fulfil his mission – don't think he's stupid because he's not. He's usually male, early 20s. He used to shave his beard off before attacking in order to be clean in the afterlife. They don't do this anymore because we recognize that and can pick them up. The lone male usually acts funny, he may be stoned on marijuana or he may be nervous, wide open eyes, perspiring, doesn't respond to your instructions, he will do anything he can to get to his target and complete the mission.'

The session ends three hours later and despite the volume of information, it may be one of the easier of the four days – Norris is a patient man and close to retirement so he is hardly inclined to yell or kick anyone up the butt. 'If they remember even 40 per cent it will save lives,' he says.

Over the next three days Rick has the group doing a little of everything, including emergency evacuation of a client from a vehicle, during which 'the Russian' goes into a blind panic when he can't open the door. It's the trainer's fifth batch of students under a three-year, 99-million-dollar Canadian government programme to boost the Police and Army. And the more he berates them and shoves them around, the more currency his praise acquires. He's tough, but also makes sure they are fed regularly, lets them pray as prescribed and tosses in a few jokes between the reprimands, and before long they simultaneously fear and adore him.

'I'm taking techniques from a wide variety of Special Forces and I'm teaching you to implement them in a war zone – you guys are learning a lot,' he says by way of encouragement to the men, who are probably just happy to be away from checkpoint duty.

'Everything Mr Rick taught us was hard but it's getting easier day by day,' says Abdul Haleem, a 22-year-old from the northern

Canadian Captain Tylere Couture
(right) chats to locals on CIMIC patrol
by PRT Camp Nathan Smith.

province of Samangan, who the instructor rates as the second-best student. 'Panjwaii is very dangerous, full of insurgents, we didn't know how to fight before.'

The star of the class, Sergeant Noor Ahmad from Kandahar, says it's all useful stuff but he and the others are highly conscious of the difference between them and the ANA, who have permanently embedded Canadian trainers and get almost full-time coaching.

'We can't do anything here without the Coalition Forces. But why do just the ANA get to stay with the Canadians? We Police are in the front line, the Taliban shoot at us every day, so why don't the Canadians work with us like they do with the Army?'

And like his colleagues I met in Zabul, he cannot contain his dismay at the wages.

'I am a policeman, I fight in the frontline for 5,000 afghanis a month and I have a family to feed and clothe – do you think it's enough?' Ahmad asks me.

The instructors drive the men through drills with live ammo on the range in the beating sun ('the more sweat you leak the less blood you'll leak'), and the course winds down with final exercises before the graduation ceremony, including 'physical toughening'.

Rick gets Mojo to punch him repeatedly in the stomach and exhales sharply each time as the strength of the blows steadily increases, causing the trainees' eyes to light up with admiration.

For the piece de resistance he gets the interpreter to pound him viciously all over his body. He doesn't flinch and tells the class that they must learn to react with aggression and not pain. Then he gets them to do it and they mill around smacking each other and laughing like kids.

Before their new boss arrives they rehearse the acceptance of the certificates. This confuses the trainees even more than the bodyguard drills as they try to remember which way to turn, which hand to take the paper in and where to stand afterwards.

Finally Haji Baran arrives, portly, bearded and gruff, with a thick white scar plunging down his brow from under his turban. A widely feared and respected mujahedin fighter from the jihad, he is taken aback by the man-handling he gets when Sgt. Noor roughly bundles him to safety in a demonstration drill. He looks annoyed but he is gracious enough in his speech.

'I'm very happy the Canadian Police trained my bodyguards against the enemies of the country. We've had 30 years of fighting, my guys are uneducated but I would send them to this training any time. And so that my men look the part, I would also like you to give us boots, belts and other uniform, I know you've got Connex containers full of this stuff.'

Before the official leaves with his new personal security detachment he thanks the Canadian trainers, telling them that these are his most trusted men.

'Including the jihad, I've been injured three times. There have been a lot of attacks on me, IEDs and things, some of my guys have been killed. I'm a very important target for the Taliban and I heard rumours in the bazaar that they are again planning to kill me. I trust my men but I am a Muslim and I trust God more, my life is in his hands.'

After the group is dismissed the Canadian Police officers call over 'the Russian' and gently inform him in front of the district leader that he has not passed the course.

'He's a good man but he needs more work. You train with him and let us know when you think he's ready and we'll have him back,' they tell Haji Baran, who nods gravely and replies, 'Don't worry, this guy is mentally ill anyway.'

Arghandab

The change from the dusty stone plain around Kandahar to the Arghandab valley, which lies on the other side of these hills, is extraordinary, as nothing can be more wretched than the one and nothing more charming than the other.

The whole valley is a series of fields of the most magnificent crops of wheat and barley, meadows full of clover, and orchards of every imaginable description of fruit, apricots, mulberries, plums, grapes, peaches, nectarines, figs, pears, apples, quinces and pomegranates.

Each field or orchard has a rapidly flowing stream of clear cool water running through it, which is the cause of the extreme luxuriance of everything, and very [gratifying] to us who have been so long in a very dry and thirsty land… The people we met, though not actually glad to see us, were not uncivil, and many of them offered us fruit as we rode along. No doubt our being well armed helped to make them civil.

Diary entry of May 6, 1880, by Brigadier General Henry Francis Brooke, commander of British forces defending Kandahar City during the siege by Ayub Khan. Brooke died in battle on August 16.

July 10, 2008

'We've got a job to do so we're going to treat you like a ghost,' the Canadian Master Corporal tells me before the mission to Arghandab, three weeks after hundreds of Taliban massed here following the Kandahar jailbreak. Seemingly poised to move on the city, the insurgents were successfully driven out by international and Afghan government forces. After the area changed hands twice in the space of a few days, the objective is to visit a village that was seized by the Taliban in order to reassert ISAF's presence. CIMIC personnel led by a Sergeant Major will also go to ask the locals what they need in the way of new facilities.

Arghandab has calmed down since the June clashes but intelligence reports say a group of several dozen militants is now moving in this prized region located 20 kilometres northwest of the city. The scene of heavy fighting between mujahedin and Soviet forces in the 1980s, this territory with its concealing plantations and orchards is now wanted by the Taliban as a staging point for sorties into Kandahar.

'So we've got 70 Taliban who want to have fun with us,' the Master Corporal tells the soldiers at a briefing. 'Keep your heads up, hands on your guns, look like a hard target and we'll scare these guys into thinking twice about messing with us.'

At 0620 two LAVs and an RG31 mine-resistant truck leave Camp Nathan Smith and rumble through the roads and alleyways in clouds of dust. We drive at 40 km/h, the LAV cannons and the truck's laser-controlled 7.62mm machine-gun swivelling constantly, tracking movement as we pass a park with ponds and pine trees, stalls loaded with melons, cucumbers and pistachio nuts, throngs of bicycles, motorbikes and yellow Toyota taxis.

The city gives way to fields, plains and hills until Arghandab and its abundance opens up before us. As we pass lush fruit orchards and the occasional marijuana crop I am already thinking of Brooke's description, which I found in a collection of his letters home a few months earlier in a London museum.

The vehicles skirt round a wrecked culvert, and on either side of the spot there are billboards with a picture of an explosion and a sobbing child to warn people of the IED danger. Then at 0725 we arrive in the village of Juando Adira. As planned, the troops dismount, fan out and take up defensive positions before the CIMIC team leader goes to talk to the locals.

A farmer in his fifties says the village has fallen into disarray because its leader died and the mix of the Alokozai and Popolzai tribes there made it hard for people to agree on a successor. And because they don't have a figurehead they are ignored regionally, he adds, claiming that aid food delivered to Arghandab in recent months never reached them. They didn't get much of anything since Karzai came to power, although he says the president is still popular as he hails from a nearby village.

'We elected him, he is from our area, he's the best man for the job,' the man tells us before the conversation turns to the recent fighting that began one morning after the villagers woke to find Taliban moving outside their houses.

'There were lots of them with RPGs and machine-guns. They were hitting us and demanding food but I don't have even enough flour for my family. We asked them to leave and we sent our women away from the village, only the men stayed to protect the compounds. The Taliban also smashed my little portable radio that I used to listen to the Voice of America, BBC and Afghan Freedom channels.

'Then there were foreign soldiers in the desert, helicopters landed there and jets fired into our gardens. The Taliban came out and there was fighting and damage to our fields. Twenty of them were killed in an air strike,' the farmer recounts as a large black ant crawls across his *rakhchina* hat and onto the side of his shaven head.

'After the Taliban ran away we removed the bodies from the fields. They were chopped to pieces, beyond recognition, so we gathered them up and the ANA took them away in Rangers.'

The man can't say for sure how many people live here. Twenty years ago there were about 1,000 families in the area and he thinks there are probably more now. The locals have garden plots rather than fields, growing a little wheat, corn, pomegranates, grapes and tomatoes and even exporting some of the produce to India and Pakistan. Like most villages I visit in the country, water is the main problem. The two hand pumps are broken and people are forced to draw water from the filthy stream that meanders between the mud houses.

They have a tiny clinic but no doctor for women, and while the boys' school works, the building for girls stands derelict. The man says a contractor was paid to fix it up so it could be re-opened but he then scooted off with the money and hasn't been seen since. He points to a little girl of about four playing in a group of kids. 'I would send my daughter to school if there are no Taliban here, but if they come I'll keep her home.'

The CIMIC Sergeant Major asks him if there have been any construction projects in the area.

'A long time ago soldiers came in sandy coloured trucks like you, also asked us about our problems and made notes and left and nothing happened after that, so why are you asking me this?'

We mount up and leave, drive 20 minutes across the *dasht* (desert) bouncing violently over drainage ditches and past scattered nomad tents to a remote ANP post. Fourteen policemen sit sunning themselves in the courtyard of the mud compound while more keep watch from the roof. The Police Chief, Sergeant Ajmir, says they heard that 30 Taliban are on the way to destroy their vehicles.

'We can hold them off long enough until the ANA or ISAF Quick Reaction Force can get here,' he says, not visibly concerned at the prospect of getting attacked.

'Are your men happy here?' the Canadian commander asks through Mohammed the interpreter.

'Happy, not happy, it's our country so it's immaterial whether we're happy,' comes the stoic reply, coupled with a request for fuel and phone cards.

The Police all have cell phones so the Canadian leaves his number so they can ring in an emergency. The three vehicles move on again and the gunners are extra vigilant when passing shepherds with flocks.

'The Taliban are using an old mujahedin trick of tying IEDs to goats, they're getting desperate,' says the soldier manning the RG31 truck's machine-gun.

At 0945 we hit the main road from Kandahar to the Arghandab district centre and drive up to the district leader's compound, which is located near the restaurant and large blue-domed shrine built by the former Kandahar Governor Sherzai. We are late for the meeting and the district leader has already left, as have half of the 17 village chiefs who had gathered.

The official's desk is adorned with a framed plaque with the Canadian and Afghan flags, a small globe and an Afghan tricolour on a stick. A vase of plastic roses and orchids complements a garish portrait of Hamid Karzai set

against a purple sky, yellow sun and with the inscription 'National Hero of Afghanistan'.

The interpreter takes off his body armour and helmet but keeps his face wrapped in a scarf and his shades and baseball cap on in case he is recognized. While the Afghans are barefoot, having left their sandals and shoes by the door, we sit in boots and body armour, the PRT members wearing holstered pistols and radio headsets.

In such conditions it is hard to believe there can be a real connection between the sides. More likely the deference of some of these people here today is closer to the civility observed by Brooke in 1880, stemming more from the Canadians' well-armed presence in Arghandab. That and the wells and roads they can offer the communities, which means a tidy sum of commission for the contractors and village leaders. Without the district leader's participation the reduced meeting is a nonstarter. Before we leave, one of the Afghans makes an urgent request that the Canadians

Canadian Sgt. Maj. Bill Murphy inspects IED crater on Highway 1 in Zhari, Kandahar province.

fix the culverts and crossings where the LAVs drive on patrols.

'You are always welcome in the area, always have been, always will be. But you broke our bridge and you must fix it,' he tells the soldiers.

The town and road cling to the green waters of the Arghandab River, which in places is 20 metres wide. Kids swim in it, women wash clothes in it and drains empty there, but its murky flow still exudes a sense of life. With its shrine, restaurant and a few paved sidewalks, Arghandab feels relatively civilized – there are even small signs bolted on lamp posts (although it's unlikely they are working ones) advertising 'Internet on your mobile' with Afghan Wireless.

Mohammed seems happy to be leaving and keeps the scarf on his face until we are in the truck again and pass the town limits. But he says he'll be uncovered when he returns in a few days with his family for the weekly picnic, along with many other families from Kandahar that come to refresh themselves in this green and sometimes pleasant region.

'The women come to picnic on Wednesdays and the men come to play cards and relax by the river on Thursdays,' he says.

Never scar-off with the mujahedin

Haji Baran arrives again at FOB Wilson for a meeting with local Police and Army leaders, the Canadian Command and government officials from Ottawa. I only recognize the Uzbek boy in his security detail and we say hello. But knowing the way things can work here, 'the Russian' is probably driving Haji Baran's car. Before the proceedings get going I take the chance to ask the district leader if he knew Mullah Omar. He personally knows a lot of the local insurgents he is fighting, including the fugitive Taliban leader, who he says was born in the Uruzgan village of Terai and moved to Sangasar in Kandahar to fight the Soviets.

'I knew Mullah Omar for two or three years, he was a young fighter in the war, a third level commander at the time,' he says through a translator.

I ask him about his scar on his forehead and learn that it was from a rocket blast, one of the wounds he received in his many battles during the jihad. In turn I display a 30-stitch wound from 2006 that runs up my right palm and forearm and explain, 'I got this opening my kitchen window in Moscow while spring cleaning.'

Haji Baran nods appreciatively, stoops and pulls up his left trouser leg to reveal two bullet entry and exit points the size of pound coins. He evidently feels he must clinch our impromptu scar-off and despite the milling guests around us suddenly makes to raise his shirt but then stops himself.

I already know he's got a mortar blast injury up there. Its production would up the ante dramatically, forcing me to drop my pants and display my old chap with its lateral scar sustained in a rugby match around the same time as his Soviet rocket wound. My Royal Flush to his four of a kind, leaving Haji Baran to gasp *whoah* and deferentially bow out.

But it's not that sort of day or audience; we are here to consider prisoner detainment procedures after all.

Zhari

My 0700 wake-up call at FOB Wilson on July 16, 2008, is a series of explosions as five fuel tankers are destroyed in an insurgent ambush on Ring Road South.

The tankers were travelling from Kandahar to Helmand Province where ISAF forces have only enough fuel reserves to maintain full operations for a few more days. A total of 150,000 litres of fuel blow as the storage compartments are ruptured by RPGs fired at close range.

At 0900 I am writing an e-mail on one of the Canadian base's computers when another, louder explosion makes the window pane in front of me rattle in its frame. I go outside and see a doctor smoking glumly near the medical tent, no doubt wondering if he will now receive more casualties from the second attack on the highway that day.

A young woman has just died of injuries sustained during the tanker ambush and her mother crouches outside the tent, wrapped in a shawl and looking ashen and dazed.

'So-called collateral damage, she just had the misfortune to be there,' the doctor says.

I grab my gear and ride with the Quick Reaction Force a kilometre along the two-lane highway to the site of the blast, which was a remote-controlled detonation of homemade explosives stuffed into a wide drainage culvert running under the road.

The crater is long and deep enough to drop a bus into and chunks of tarmac and concrete slabbing are strewn over a 100-metre radius.

'Highway 1 is destroyed,' Captain Simon Cox reports on his radio and then tells me: 'They can do it wherever they want, all it is a couple of guys on motorcycles and they just throw it in.'

He stops to yell at an Afghan policeman who is reeling in the cable used by the trigger-man to detonate the IED, thus tampering with evidence that Canadian specialists will want to examine.

'It happens a lot, no matter how often we tell them the Police are always picking up the wire, they just don't get it.'

An ANP Ranger has been hurled off the road by the explosion, its doors blown open and the rear end caved in, having been clipped by the blast wave as it rode over the spot.

Sergeant Major Bill Murphy goes up to three survivors who are standing in shock by the crumpled truck, one with an injured arm. The body of a fourth man has been removed after his neck was broken against the roof of the cavorting vehicle. The flow of traffic has already resumed but is diverted along a parallel dust track so repair crews can get to work. It will take a day to get the hole filled and the highway reopened, so the Canadians put on a show of force, bringing in three Leopard tanks from the neighbouring base at Masum Ghar.

'I hate to say it but it's the norm, there have been four or five of these in the past few weeks,' Murphy says. 'This is the insurgents' way of saying we're still around, they are afraid to fight us one-on-one any more so they do shit like this instead.'

FOB Wilson is located in Zhari district, one of 17 that make up Kandahar province. Home to some 70,000 people, Zhari flanks Highway 1 and sits on the doorstep of Kandahar City, the centre of Taliban power until the movement was toppled in 2001.

A lesser-known landmark is the village of Sangasar, located 25 kilometres west of the city and four kilometres southwest of the spot where the tankers were hit. After the jihad ended, Sangasar was where Mullah Omar lived and preached at a local mosque before he roused followers against brutal local warlords in 1994. Sweeping up thousands more devotees in his wake, the one-eyed mullah led the Taliban to seize Kabul two years later.

He may not be here now – the insurgent leader is widely thought to reside in Quetta in Pakistan – but his loyalists fight on with great effect in this nest of resistance covering some 80 square kilometres.

'It's the centre of the Taliban and the people who support Mullah Omar and others like him who rose to power, it's culturally important to them, and that tends to be the rallying call that's used, something people fight for,' says Captain Darren Hart, acting operations officer for Canada's Task Force Zhari. 'I don't see them giving it up and abandoning it. Tactically, if you control Kandahar City you control southern Afghanistan, and if you control the population around KC you can potentially take control of the city.'

'This area was important in the Taliban era because many of their leadership came from here,' Haji Baran told me earlier. 'When the fighting started here two years ago the Taliban wanted to try to use it to gain control of the city. Then they took lots of casualties and now strive to maintain a mobile symbolic presence here, moving from village to village.'

Beyond its symbolic and tactical value, Zhari is simply superb terrain for guerrilla warfare. Walls, ditches and lush foliage offer the insurgents ample cover right up to the highway while the many grape-drying barns are distinctly fortress-like. Their baked mud and straw walls are so thick that only an air bomb or tank shell will pierce them, and they are full of narrow air vents that serve as firing slits. The grape fields themselves are grids of deep irrigation trenches that form ideal defensive positions and can often only be breached by tanks that crash through and 'unzip' them for infantry following behind. And if the insurgents don't want to fight they stash their weapons and blend into the local population.

'They wash the powder stains off their hands and act like farmers,' says Hart.

A 2000lb bomb
hits a Taliban
position by FOB
Wilson, Zhari, July
16, 2008.

Since 2006, Zhari was periodically flushed out by Canadian and Afghan forces in fiercely fought operations. But because there are insufficient troops available for a permanent and broad presence, the enemy quickly reinfiltrates the area, smuggling arms and ammunition in the trunks of cars and hidden under goods and firewood on trucks.

'It's like sticking your finger in a glass of water, as soon as you pull your finger out the water goes back to where it was before,' Hart continues. 'You can't declare an area cleared until the insurgents aren't having an effect on it any more. And if they can put out night letters and intimidate people then they are still having an effect.'

The backbone of the resistance could likely be broken by ploughing more troops into the district and keeping them there. But at this time the Canadians have only 2,500 personnel for the whole province and are thinly stretched. The Canadian Parliament only extended the Afghanistan mandate to 2011 after receiving a guarantee that an extra 1,000 NATO troops would be deployed here. With alliance members reluctant to commit more forces, it fell to the US to fill the gap in 2009.

At this troubled juncture of 2008 the 'who's winning' debate was as much a battle of perception and words as a hot fight, even within the ranks of the military.

'The trouble is we've lost the initiative and they've taken it, from high up the chain of command someone has said that's OK as long as we hold the Ring Road,' one Canadian soldier complained. But his CO at Wilson, Major Robert Ritchie, saw it differently.

'To say we've lost the initiative in Zhari is inappropriate. When the insurgents get in conventional combat with the Coalition Forces they are defeated handily. So they are working on the grates and culverts and striking where they are having the greatest degree of perceived success,' said Ritchie, who's 40-man Operational Mentor and Liaison Team (OMLT) is training the 3rd Kandak (Battalion), 1st Brigade, 205th Corps of the ANA.

Complicating matters, this was the first district in the south where Afghan government forces were officially put in the lead role, even though much of their manpower was woefully undertrained. And from what I saw, lack of available manpower had forced the Canadians onto the defensive in Zhari in mid-2008, pushing them right back to the road instead of holding a necessary buffer zone between this vital route and the enemy.

A small Canadian outpost at Sangasar was closed down in May because supply missions there by road usually came under heavy fire, sometimes lasting hours as vehicles ran the gauntlet. And despite a chain of fortified Police posts guarding the highway, the militants regularly encroached on the traffic, destroying vehicles with IEDs and laying waste to convoys carrying supplies for the military.

'The repeated pokes into the underbelly are like the 1,000 cuts that kill you,' Captain Hart observed.

The morning after the tanker ambush and IED, the Captain asks me if I want to go nine kilometres west to the Spin Pir Police substation that helps to secure the highway and is constantly harassed by the enemy.

He leaves me with Captain Chris Carthew of the 2nd Battalion of the Princess Patricia's Canadian Light Infantry which will send a platoon for three days to relieve the regular defenders of the post. Before we mount up in their four parked LAVs, the soldiers huddle together and one says a group prayer that 'we may perform our duties without any flaws and slaughter the enemy'.

'These guys are pretty religious, they say a prayer every time we go out and we've never been touched. I haven't had to open my med bag once, so…' Kelly the medic tells me.

I am jammed in the back of the first vehicle with seven soldiers, assorted weapons, stores and cases of food and soda before we leave on the 15-minute ride. I try not to think about the road we are travelling and the numerous culverts we must pass on our way through what the troops call Ambush Alley.

The substation is located less than a kilometre past the blackened wrecks of the five tankers that were destroyed the previous day and have now been bulldozed to the roadside. It is 150 metres square, with an outer wall of Hescos and towers that are still being built and an inner compound like a castle keep, with two fortified towers, one on the highway side that is manned by ANP and one facing the fields manned by Canadians.

Canadian Captain Chris
Carthew shaving at Spin Pir
police substation in Zhari,
Kandahar province.

There are concrete blast walls, a 60mm mortar in a sandbagged pit, a barbecue made from half an oil drum and a LAV with a boxing punch bag dangling from the back hatch. Along the Canadian side there are three tents, one for the interpreters, another with a shower and toilet and the largest one with shelves of tinned food, television, DVD player, fridge and a big dining table made from beams and planks.

'Welcome to Spin Pir,' someone tells the arriving infantry and is promptly asked if they had much trouble.

'No, just as long as there are no more mortars.'

Somewhere in front of us there is a hidden Taliban 82mm mortar position that is operated by a competent crew. In the past week they have been gradually zeroing in on Spin Pir, bracketing it by first dropping shells to the north, then to the south, then a couple of rounds that landed just outside the perimeter. They remove the mortar tube after each time they fire but have evidently left the base plate in place and covered so they can keep returning and ranging on the post.

'Tonight we expect them to get one inside,' says one of the relief group, a Corporal called Rafael who it turns out is an Afghan Canadian, born to parents from the eastern Paktya province.

The Canadian tower is built on top of an ISO container and is packed with weapons, including two 7.62mm machine guns, M72 rockets, an AR10 sniper rifle, boxes of ammunition and various scopes and sights.

'This is the fucking Alamo, man,' says Rafael, tossing a C-13 grenade in his hand. 'They won't attack us because we are fighters and have LAVs but if we go that way we'll be ambushed,' he says, pointing into the fields and compounds below us.

The Warrant Officer of the outgoing group takes me onto a small viewing platform and motions toward a tree line where they are guaranteed trouble if they push out that far.

'It's the Wild East. If we go 300 metres we come under sporadic fire, any further it's heavy fire, and we're under surveillance 24/7. They'll hit us from a distance with heavy weapons, RPGs, mortars, heavy machine-guns, but they don't come close. But as soon as we leave camp they are on us. They have people in that tree line, they can be anywhere any time and we can't see them.'

About 150 metres to the east of the substation a track dubbed 'Taliban Road' cuts down through this no-man's land at a perpendicular from the highway. It hosts some local traffic – cars, pedestrians, shepherds with livestock – but the Canadians don't go down there because of IEDs and ambushes.

The locals here are afraid to talk to them and there is no way of telling who really lives here anyway: 'We know some of the people are Taliban but unless they have weapons what can you do?' the Warrant Officer says in a lament that is by now all too familiar.

Two months earlier the Canadians cut down all the trees over the 300 metres of ground to the first wadi to deny cover to the enemy. A second wadi is 500 metres away and venturing that far, they stress, invites a determined attack. While the conflict in Afghanistan is often characterized by the lack of discernible front lines, the sides are pretty well dug in here, and the Canadians are the more vulnerable in this spot.

'Keeping a foothold on this area is all we've been doing,' another Corporal says.

I see from the tower map that Sangasar is just three kilometres south of the post but few of the soldiers are aware of the significance of the village, or even know who Mullah Omar is.

'It doesn't matter much when they're shooting at you,' a Sergeant replies when I tell him whose backyard we are in.

At 1445 we receive a situation report over the radio about the anticipated ambush of an 18-vehicle ANP convoy driving from Maiwand district past us to Kandahar City. The attack is expected to happen by the gas station 800 metres further on, close to the tanker wrecks.

A few minutes later we see the headlights of the approaching vehicles and count 17 Ranger jeeps and an open-back jingle truck filled with Police who wave to us as they speed past. As if scripted, the convoy gets as far as the gas station when the first RPG blast thumps, followed by a swell of small arms fire. A pall of smoke rises above the location as the soldiers in the tower scan the flashpoint with scopes.

'I got him, I got that guy! He's firing at the ANP!' Private Glen Kirkland tells the Sergeant as he hunches over the telescopic sight of the AR10 rifle.

'At the ANP?'

'He's firing at the ANP.'

'OK, shoot him.'

'Take him down,' another soldier urges, 'Take him down!'

'SHUT UP!' Kirkland yells, regulating his breath before depressing the trigger. There is a crack as the 7.62mm round fires and, according to him, hits the man in the side.

'Get him?'

'Got him.'

Someone laughs.

'You just fucking dropped him Glen.'

Waves of crackling gunfire issue from the spot as the Police defend themselves and Captain Carthew tells the four LAV crews to mount up. Ten minutes later the armoured cars swing out onto the highway and set off for the gas station.

'Last year a buddy of mine lost 17 guys in his platoon to IEDs, dead and wounded,' someone says as our vehicle rumbles along to the sounds of shots and blasts outside.

I wonder if I'm safe in a LAV but yesterday's crater indicates that not even being in a tank would help. Still, it's a good vehicle to be in if you get into a conventional fire fight, as we seem about to. (The Canadian Department of National Defence says: 'Canada's LAV III is a state-of-the-art combat vehicle that really packs a punch! The purpose of this fighting machine is to transport infantry on the battlefield while providing defensive protection and offensive firepower. Is it up to this task? You bet! The LAV III is armed with a 25mm stabilized cannon and capable of speeds of up to 100 kilometres per hour. Our soldiers and allies love this Canadian-built piece of kit!')

Ten minutes later the tail gate is lowered and we see a Ranger burning fiercely on the road in front of us. A group of ANP approaches, dragging the body of a bearded man in pale blue *payran tumban* and chest pouches with AK magazines. He's been shot through the side, his pants have slipped down to his ankles and his genitals flop around as they pull him along by an unwound turban tied to the left ankle. The medic is about to dismount to examine him when Carthew calls 'He's dead'.

I initially think he's a cop because of the grave air about the ANP. But he's Taliban and their faces are in fact set in predatory satisfaction as they proudly lay the trophy at our feet, like a retriever with a pheasant.

By some miracle the Police are all unhurt and lost only one jeep to the enemy fire. It's not clear whether the fight is even over. When I get back in the vehicle the medic says they were observing four men with weapons pulling crates in the distance as if preparing to set up.

'We were tracking them with the gun all the way, if they'd tried something they'd have been fucked,' the medic assures me. I wonder why they didn't take them out immediately if they had weapons, but guess that since the fight was happening around houses the LAV cannon could cause civilian casualties.

Nothing more happens in the next ten minutes apart from ammunition cooking off in the burning Ranger so we return to Spin Pir. It may be a happy day for the post as far as the mystery mortar is concerned. While the vehicles were out they spotted plumes of smoke rising from the trees 500 metres south as rounds were launched at the road. So the Canadians plastered the spot with their own mortar and 155mm artillery rounds fired from Wilson. But I heard much later that the elusive mortar or at least its replacement was working overtime during a subsequent bid by the insurgents to storm Spin Pir.

'Normal pattern of life has returned to Ring Road South, no activity to be seen south of the road or in the wadi,' Carthew reports over the radio an hour after the ambush began.

The Sergeant says to Kirkland: 'Don't you just love it when I say 'Let him have it'?'

'Yeah, but not when I'm adjusting my breathing.'

'You're not a sniper, you don't have that luxury, just take the shot.'

I ask the soldier if he shot anyone before.

'I fired a lot of rounds at people but I don't know how many I hit. That was the first time I shot with that rifle, the rest of the time was with machine-guns. It was a lot different. My heart was going through my chest, but there's no emotion trying to take that shot, you try to concentrate on your breathing.'

'Tell him about the first person you shot,' Rafael interjects.

'Shut up, I didn't do that for my benefit, mention that again and I'll punch you in the fucking mouth,' Glen snaps, boiling over instantly.

The Captain comes into the tower and asks 'What's up?'

'Nothing sir,' he says and they fall silent. I never hear the end of that story, which Rafael discretely avoids when we are standing in the tower that evening.

He's 21 years old, green-eyed with even, well-defined features in an olive complexion. I imagine him without Canadian camouflage and with a beard and suddenly see the Afghan. He says the locals always stare at him in villages and try to draw him into conversation, some-times he plays dumb, sometimes he engages them in fluent Pashtu.

'I think people think it's odd that I'm here fighting, but my family has been here fighting around Kandahar for a long time so it seems kind of natural to me. That's the difference between the other guys and me, the Canadian view is that there has to be justification for killing. War is war to us, it's a way of life, there's always been fighting, there doesn't have to be love or hate, just respect for your opponent.

'Different people deal with things in differ-ent ways. Some get all emotional about it but I don't let it bother me, if some dude is shoot-ing at me I'll shoot him. You train to come over and kick ass. You've got to come home

alive, not just physically but mentally. If you come home a wreck emotionally you're just a burden to your family.

'The guys who fly the Predators don't seem to suffer. I've seen those things kill civilians before and no one seems to suffer about it. They go on about using excessive force but then they'll drop a 500lb bomb on one dude.'

In the late afternoon the soldiers cook burgers on the oil drum barbecue and then prepare for a possible engagement, anticipating that the enemy will test them to see how they react. From 1830 they stand-to, five men scan the fields and highway from the tower and five LAVs are parked at the outer wall, their can-nons trained over the Hescos and ready to fire.

'If they are going to attack they've got to do it in the next 30 minutes,' Captain Carthew tells me at 1910 as the sun starts to dip beyond the horizon.

'With practice they are getting better, the level of coordination, sophistication of ambushes,' he continues. 'It's hard for us to maintain influence here without a massive amount of troops. The grape fields make it very difficult and the people are very poor and susceptible to anyone who offers them a job. It's close to routes of influence from Pakistan – assuming it's Pakistan – and it's close to Kandahar City. This highway is a lifeline and the effort to safeguard it is very taxing. It's almost like a Roman system of forts, you have to have line of sight to control everything they protect. The best defence is attack. The secret is to go and disrupt the enemy so they can't mount these sorts of attacks but that depends on the amount of resources available.'

He then says something that I firmly believe to be true, and certainly everyone who laments the US decision to go into Iraq in 2003, leav-ing the work here half-finished.

'We missed an opportunity in the first six to twelve months [in Afghanistan in 2001/02] when there was so much hope, but the oppor-tunity was lost,' Carthew says. 'Now it's going to take 20 years of blood, sweat and tears to achieve that.'

I am reluctant to go to bed in the claus-trophobic ISO container where there are 12 bunks and a heavy fug of body odours so I hang out for a while in the kitchen tent read-ing the lads' mag *Maxim*. I duly learn that if I

Canadian mentor explains map reading to Afghan National Army officer in Zhari, Kandahar province.

Canadian troops on patrol in Kandahar City.

let a partner throw hoops over my manhood and 'belittle my package' it will show her that I'm comfortable with my sexuality. But does she win a goldfish?

I spend another couple of hours in the tower with the sentry who scours the fields with night vision sights and then turn in. Even with 10mm of steel armour the container is little more than a 12-berth coffin if it takes a direct hit. The corner right above my head has a large dent where it had been struck by an RPG that didn't explode. A year later in a Kabul bar I meet a Canadian cameraman called Al who also slept in the berth under the dent, and had identical thoughts to mine.

Before driving back to FOB Wilson the next morning I talk to Lt. Hussein, the 28-year-old commander of the ANP unit that mans the front tower and perimeter.

'This is the heart of the Taliban, villages here have links with the Taliban and shelter them – when we go there they lay anti-tank and anti-personnel mines so we don't try,' he says.

The enemy here are all local, he claims, but their leaders are Pakistani and take men by force to Pakistan for training to fight ISAF, one son from each home.

It turns out the Lieutenant was driving behind the Ranger that got blown up two days earlier and that the man who died was one of his friends. Later that same day his unit found some insurgents preparing an ambush two kilometres further on with a command wire operated IED dug into the roadside.

I catch a ride back to base with a couple of LAVs on a supply run. To our right we see artillery rounds tearing into the trees around the village of Pashmul as a patrol I am supposed to be on is ambushed in the infamous graveyard there.

My freelance photographer friend Louie Palu shot and filmed the fight, which lasted three hours as the Taliban brought in reinforcements on motorcycles, working their way so close that the Canadians had to use hand grenades to fend them off. At least 11 enemy fighters were believed killed in targeted barrages of more than 50 artillery rounds and half a dozen laser-guided bombs dropped by jets.

It seems suicidal for the insurgents to attack so close to the bases and Police posts, given the speed with which the artillery and the Quick Reaction Force can bear down on them. But the Canadian intelligence officer at Wilson says detonating IEDs so near and staging ambushes this audaciously is a deliberate part of the insurgent strategy, aimed at discrediting the Afghan government and its allies.

'If you blow up and kill somebody close to a government facility, people will ask didn't the Police see anything and who is responsible for training these Police? And they only have to get lucky once, we have to be lucky all the time – that's the beautiful thing about an insurgency.'

I ask how many insurgents he thinks they are up against.

'It's impossible to quantify, are we talking about $10 farmer-insurgents or hard-core fighters? A Tier-1 fighter is a top of the line hard-core fighter, there are not that many here, there doesn't need to be. Tier-1 are rare, they are like technicians who go around fixing people's photocopiers. Tier-2 are the devoted, permanent staff and Tier-3 are casual $10 fighters.

'We've heard about 120 insurgents in Zhari and we've heard about hundreds. There aren't many foreign fighters though, foreigners are not welcome and are earmarked by locals. And you don't see a lot of ability to 'cross-border shop' by the enemy here, you can't just jump in jeeps and drive to Arghandab. You've got to know the ground well; if you don't then we'll kill you.

'Do they have an unlimited supply of men? No, a very large supply, yes. Is the insurgency as big down here as we think it is, no. I doubt there are more than a couple of thousand altogether. I'd hate to think we are exaggerating. We're hearing upwards of 8,000. How many are there in Waziristan? And are they all coming over here, no. But an insurgency doesn't count on numbers; it counts on the support of the people. Until the people take their country back this is all about the grassroots. Whoever causes them the least grief will win.

'This is not our fight to win. It's their country, they'll make it how they want it. This insurgency will never stop until the people take ownership, it's like all insurgencies. I just can't believe they support the insurgents, they know who the Taliban are and they know what they will do to them.'

As far as Zhari is concerned, he's frustrated like many of the Canadians that they can lose the initiative because the fight here is so dependent on the less skilled Afghan forces they work with.

'The mentors come here and lay their lives on the line, everyone comes to Zhari ready to kill but these guys don't want to fight. They've got to step up.'

Brothers in arms

The next day there is a Canadian and ANA mission along the highway to the site of the tanker ambush to deter any attempt to attack 50 loaded World Food Programme trucks that will shortly drive through to Helmand. It has come down from the Canadian Command that President Karzai is so concerned about the situation on the road that guarding it now takes precedence over missions into the Taliban ground to the south.

I go with one of the Canadian mentors and a US Army Major from the Center for Army Lessons Learned, Fort Leavenworth, Kansas. Working as an advisor at the Afghan National Training Commission, he's visiting Zhari to observe the performance and training of the 600 ANA based in and around FOB Wilson.

The three of us sit in a ditch opposite two of the burned-out tankers while the Afghan soldiers are pushed out to the edges of the fields. The roadside is strewn with garbage, poppy stems and bulbs, and a few yards away the Canadian spots an indented trail in the earth where the line for a remote-controlled IED was once laid.

'Their section battle drills are absolutely deplorable,' says the Captain, fatigued by long months of trying to instil basic soldiering skills into the Afghan soldiers in combat conditions.

'I had to physically show them an extended line and arrowhead, they only know single file. The Sergeants don't have any idea about placement of heavy weapons, how to direct fire and how to win a fire fight, no concept at all. They should at least be aware that in contact you immediately return fire until you are directed. But when they get in contact they take cover and don't shoot back until they're told, that's happened in fire fights. Their NCOs don't

take an active role. They have platoon leaders but no concept of squad leaders.

'Their officer corps is a lot better than the NCOs, but they don't weed out the good ones from the ones who are deficient. Every Afghan we've met has trouble reading a map, that's an endemic problem, so that's one of the cornerstone skills we try and help them with. Some of the officers know map skills but don't use them. They struggle with the whole concept; their mortar platoon doesn't see the value of using maps and calling in fire. The common answer is "we don't need to call in fire because we've got you guys here".

'They'll train every second day but it'll be a couple of hours maximum, getting them to do more is like pulling teeth. I don't know if it's a get-out-of-work thing or they are too proud to accept help. A lot of them are completely uneducated.

'Usually we have a TIC three or four times a month. Some soldiers are really good at shooting but they are few and far between. When they're in a fire fight they'll shoot in the general direction which is OK in the beginning because you need the volume of fire. If it is close contact or accurate the firing dwindles because most of the soldiers are hiding and that's when you need the volume of fire.

'The only person who knows how to fire the PKM machine-gun is the PKM gunner, I've told the commander this and he just says "it's his weapon". I've had weeks of promises that they'll do PKM training and they don't do it. But they had their first lesson yesterday. I got it done by promising them that we'll let them use our range.'

The Major points out a man in *payran tumban* and turban who is approaching us from the field and the Captain orders an ANA soldier to search him. He waits for the guy to almost reach us before he stops him, a screaming error if the man is wired to blow himself up among the infidels.

'I'm not militarily trained but I know you don't let him come up to us,' I say.

'I've got to the point where I've given up trying to change that, even though I tell them that every time,' the Captain replies, and recalls his first patrol with this new batch of soldiers. 'We got sent to do a counter-ambush and there I am teaching them to do an extended line.'

Canadians remove a wrecked Afghan police jeep after an ambush in Zhari, Kandahar province.

Locals pass wrecked oil tankers on Highway 1 in Zhari, Kandahar province, July 2008.

'How did that make you feel?' the American Major asks.

'Pretty much like I feel every day here,' the Canadian laughs with the same weary air of foreign trainers of the ANA that I encounter across the country. One US mentor I met in Helmand seemed to be on course for a breakdown, so acute had his frustration become.

'They're stupid because they've had no education. Some of the guys from the mountains have never used a toilet before and just drop their pants where they are and go. If I could shoot one of them a week, just wing him with a pistol, then I'd be able to get the message across, because that's all they understand, force,' he said.

It's the same story with the ANP, only worse. 'They want to be good policemen but a lot of the time we're just teaching them to live, get up, wash, get dressed,' another Canadian mentor told me.

The Major calls over the interpreter and asks the ANA Lieutenant sitting near us what the training centre in Kandahar should do to improve his soldiers.

'They must mainly show them firing tactics and how to deal with an enemy ambush and to fight their way out,' answers Iambek Khan, a 40-year-old from the Panjshir province north of Kabul. 'They don't know how to use radios and clean their weapons properly and clear them when they are jammed. But my soldiers have experience in fighting and can aim well.'

Khan has been in the Army for almost four years and earns 13,000 afghanis (260 dollars) a month. He says he saw a lot of combat in Uruzgan and Zabul and is tired of fighting and would like to join his brother and farm the family's land in the north. The answer to Zhari's problems is more soldiers, he believes.

After an hour the 50 WFP trucks start to rumble through, guarded by three dozen jeeps with Police and privately contracted Afghan security guards. The escorts are mostly clustered at the ends of the two-kilometre procession, rendering the middle section highly vulnerable to attack.

'They have 30 SUVs full of guys, 15 at the front, 15 at the back and they wonder why they can't protect the convoy,' the Captain says, shaking his head.

As we drive back to Wilson the American Major is unimpressed with what he's seen in the past few days.

'On the scale of 1 to 4, these ANA are at 3.5, trip over their laces, drown when it rains. They seem to be on the "hey, who wants to work?" programme. One thing I see is soldiers who need more battle drills. The biggest single problem is the NCO corps. The NCOs do not lead at a team or squad level so if you have an inefficient platoon leader the platoon is doomed. The platoon leader is supposed to be thinking two moves ahead, while the NCO is fighting the fight right now.

'In the western culture it's our mindset that we want to do better, we want to win. The Afghan culture lacks that drive and therefore they have little initiative. It's all about the past history of this country; go back to Alexander the Great, strong leaders run the whole show, one commander and 50 followers. Then the Soviets came in and made it officer-centric.

'What slows it down is that the officers don't take what they read and teach it to their soldiers. I do know there's a big pride issue. I find ways to make them look good, tell them their General is coming to see them and will be really proud of them and then they really want that and they try. I occasionally bribe them with trinkets like military notebooks but that only goes so far.

'When I'm dealing with Generals they are like smart nine-year-olds, Majors are seven to eight-year-olds. They're smart enough to know what the right thing to do is and smart enough to know how to get out of it. They need people like me to stop giving them things; we have to get them to earn it. We've got to get them to stand on their own feet. The sad thing is that they are doing combat operations with people who should go back to basic training.'

Later I ask Major Ritchie, the commanding officer at FOB Wilson, if he thinks it is right to secure such a strategic area with soldiers from the lower end of the proficiency scale.

'The Afghan government forces are in such great demand that we can't afford to have them in a stable training ground indefinitely. Zhari offers a more realistic environment while training them,' he tells me, insisting that they are making 'massive strides.'

They just trip on their untied laces while striding, I think to myself.

A few days later I meet the Afghan General in command of the 205th Corps and ask the same question I asked Ritchie, which he evades entirely. The interpreter says the officer found the topic 'uncomfortable'.

Outside the entrance to the Canadian Command Post at Wilson stands a tiny hut built of Hesco caging. This is where the executive officer of the Afghan Kandak, Major Toreliy Sadiqi, sits between duties, listening to Taliban radio chatter and playing chess with his fellow officers. The hut frame is covered in *zos*, the prickly green bush the locals cut in the desert and use either as feed for their livestock or like Sadiqi, to cool their quarters using a technique I call Afghan A/C. An officer in the hut pours water from a jug down the zos-lined walls and cool air starts to gush inwards. It's a simple heat exchange principle, just as the soldiers put bottles of warm water into a wet sock to cool them, but the effect on a larger scale in the hut is truly wondrous.

The Major is slight of build and has neatly parted jet black hair, a lean triangular face, straight nose and protruding ears. He has been a soldier for 19 years and worked in the Defence Ministry in his home city of Kabul before he was posted to the south.

'Life is a book, we must study it,' he says in proficient, self-taught English. 'My country's people have problems; we can deal with them with good training, good fighting. I like to work with these guys, US, Canadian, Italian. At first the difference between us wasn't easy but my soldiers and NCOs now work with them like brothers. After one, two or three months the soldier gets a certificate, he goes and a new soldier comes. Seventy per cent of my soldiers are good at fighting, 30 per cent are not,' he declares, putting the losses among his men at four killed and three injured in the previous two months.

'My Army is very young, the Defence Ministry system is very young, we need vehicles, ammunition and weapons, body armour, helmets,' he says, adding that he's no fan of training his men in combat conditions.

'That's not good, first they should be trained, and then we can use them on missions. These soldiers had one month training before they came here, they should get three months. This place is very good for the enemy, it has a lot of gardens, grape fields, it's very important for the Ring Road, and they are fighting for that. I think the foreign troops should stay 20 years because the Taliban is a bad enemy and my Army can't do it alone. We don't have aircraft, artillery, good armaments. Every time defence ministry Generals come I make requests for vehicles and weapons. The soldiers still don't have A/C, fridges, tents, and the two showers are broken. Why do I sit in this small house? Because I don't have A/C either.'

Not everything is to be concentrated on guarding the highway it seems, despite Karzai's demands. A day later some of the Canadian mentors take a platoon of ANA two kilometres west along the highway from Wilson, turn into the fields and drive 600 metres south, pushing directly into enemy ground in an open invitation to fight.

We dismount from the vehicles which harbour up defensively, leave 10 ANA and Canadians there while the other 30 soldiers start moving down the track into the nearby village. As we walk there is a distant explosion and we find out later four ANP died in an IED blast on the road a few kilometres east.

Several fighting age males vanish from sight as we enter the village. Captain Cox tries to talk to a man on a bicycle who is sweating and agitated at our appearance and assures us through a forced smile that there are no Taliban or IEDs around here.

'That guy's fishy,' the Captain says when we move on, a Reaper drone scanning the ground ahead as the patrol follows a long track heading south. There are cornfields to the left, grapes to the right and a large marijuana plantation at the next corner. Around us the farmers and locals start disappearing from the fields and there are no sounds apart from the chugging of irrigation pumps.

'See how the pattern of life has changed, that's a bad sign,' Sergeant Paul Sprenger tells me.

At 0840 the troops get positive identification (PID) from the drone on three insurgents in a compound ahead of us, two with AKs and one with a PKM.

'They're gathering – it looks like they are moving into a flanking position,' Sprenger says as they receive report of more movement,

Canadian L2A5 Leopard tank, Kandahar.

so Cox radios for permission to engage with artillery and weapons on the Reaper.

Some top brass are visiting Wilson and the request clearly bothers someone there. The Captain has to report three times that they have positive identification of three armed insurgents and that there are no civilians in the area and so there is no risk of collateral damage.

'Grow some fucking nuts man,' someone mutters as the troops get increasingly aggravated by their Command's sluggish response.

The enemy are now popping up all around the patrol. More are spotted 400 metres ahead while another four men with weapons start moving down our right flank. Still no permission to engage.

'Shit, there are loads of guys,' Sprenger mutters, while the patrol picks up enemy radio chatter about setting up an ambush. According to the original plan the troops are supposed to push another 500 metres south, which would take them into the open ground and directly toward the main enemy position.

'I don't believe I'd cross that field for all the money in the world based on how your Command is doing,' the American Major says.

Just before 0900 one of our would-be ambushers gets impatient and looses off a couple of shots in our direction. The troops finally get authorization to call in fire in self-defence.

'All right, it's time to make some magic,' says Bucky the JTAC as he starts coordinating aviation and artillery. At the same time someone spots a glint in a tree across the field, more shots ring out and a few rounds zip past. The Canadians and Afghans engage the suspected sniper and chop up the tree foliage with small arms. Then 155mm rounds start howling in and plaster the location where several more armed men have been spotted, erupting with thunderous bursts and sending huge banks of smoke and dust swirling into the air.

'Fire was effective, no more enemy fire from that direction,' Cox reports at 0915.

'I just don't understand how he missed all of us,' the Major says about the sniper, who is likely armed with a Dragunov with telescopic sight. 'If they'd just waited until we'd crossed that field in our leisurely way they'd have had us in a good spot.'

There is a discussion whether to continue and while the open field the patrol has to cross is extremely uninviting now, no one wants to give the encounter to the Taliban.

'If we don't push up they'll reinforce and stay there and it'll be a victory for them,' Sprenger says. But Cox decides to withdraw and the troops move out under the cover of artillery smoke rounds that throw up a giant billowing white curtain behind us.

'We only had 40 guys and they had dug-in defences, so we were basically moving into their kill zone,' he says, adding that he also didn't have much confidence in the ANA holding formation while crossing the field. 'I also thought they could be moving up to the west to ambush us on the way out.'

Sure enough, as the patrol pulls back the Reaper spots more insurgents moving down its west flank with an 82mm recoilless rifle. Resembling a bazooka, the weapon is powerful enough to punch a hole through one of the Canadian vehicles so they request permission to engage again.

'We're just going to kill these guys and then we'll go home,' Bucky says before calling in another strike by a $75,000 Hellfire missile which explodes on target and pumps a black mushroom cloud into the air. The Reaper's camera relay shows that the two men carrying the 82mm were killed on the spot and two others ran off. Astoundingly, one of them went and fetched a PKM machine-gun and came racing after the Canadians and ANA as they mounted up and drove off.

'They wanted to keep us out of there and they did,' Sprenger says as we leave.

Back at Wilson they weigh the balance of the mission. About 20 insurgents were spotted manoeuvring on the patrol in small groups. Half a dozen are believed killed and others injured by the Hellfire, a GBU12 500-pound laser-guided bomb, 16 high explosive

artillery rounds and 8 smoke rounds, so more than $130,000 worth of munitions in total.

It's a pretty standard contact for Zhari, lots of noise and a few enemy fighters taken out. But what excites the Canadian Command is that after the patrol left, the drone spotted farmers pelting the Taliban with stones as they removed their dead and wounded. This suggests that the locals are tired and angry at the insurgents for fighting in their fields because that draws destruction of property. In the broader picture, the Canadians hope this could signal the gradual onset of the 'tipping point', where the Taliban will no longer be welcome here and therefore unable to operate as they are accustomed.

But for now it's business as usual for the insurgents. That night, acting on a tip-off to the ANP, a Canadian EOD team removes nine 20-litre canisters of homemade explosives from a culvert on Highway 1 and destroys them. The controlled explosion is five kilometres away but the ground at Wilson still shakes.

★ ★ ★

That August I came across a story in a newspaper in a Canadian pub in London headlined 'Canadian military claims victory in major Afghan offensive' and detailing a large-scale operation into the main insurgent grounds in Zhari.

Brig.-Gen. Thompson, who accompanied Canadian and ANA troops, said in an interview that the three-day offensive was not aimed at reclaiming Zhari but was intended to disrupt insurgent activity, neutralize their ability to mount further attacks, and to serve as a final show of force before the end of the fighting season in September.

'We're showing them we can go wherever we want, whenever we want,' Thompson said.

twelve

YOU CAN'T FORBID LOVE

'**D**id anyone tell you about the Swedes' gender policy?' the naked Finnish Captain says through the steam in the base sauna. 'They can't look at porn mags or dirty movies but they can have sex freely. We can look at porn but no sex. So they are the fuckers and we are the wankers.'

Just as alcohol policy varies between the ISAF members (it's allowed in Kabul, in some northern and western bases but not generally in the east and south of the country), intimate relations between military personnel are something of a moot point within ISAF. Each contingent sets its own regulations, ranging from formally sanctioned consenting intercourse to the prohibited but grudgingly acknowledged variety. And apparently in the Finns' case, chronic self-abuse (who did the survey?) while some of their Scandinavian neighbours let down their hair and trousers at will.

Whatever the ruling, it will happen. 'You can't forbid love,' said the Dutch public affairs officer at Kamp Holland in Uruzgan, where there are plenty of women but conjugal relations between troops are officially frowned upon. I later learned, however, that at one time the armoured car crews there were doing a tidy business leasing their spacious vehicles to couples for trysts.

Porn is everywhere of course, voluminously downloaded on laptops and iPods, but mostly also forbidden, despite the impossibility of enforcing that ban. This seamier side of soldiering life came to my notice at a small US base when I went to borrow some DVDs from three guys living in a small mud-walled room. I asked after one of them, another smirks and said 'He's busy', motioning at a bunk that was blanketed over and rocking to a gentle rhythm. I looked through their DVD stack and took *Pirates of the Carribean*, although what I later found in the box was definitely not Johnny Depp. I suppose it could have been Keira Knightly, I couldn't see her face.

As you could expect from a nation that goes into societal psychosis at the sight of Janet Jackson's unveiled, unremarkable breast, the ban on sex has been more zealously enforced in the US military. In December 2006 in Paktika I was driving to the front gate of the base in an ambulance with a nurse who saw a female soldier sweeping the memorial area with a broom. She stopped and wound down the window.

'Were you a naughty girl?' she asked, and the other complained that a male soldier ratted on her for having a fling. After we drove on, the nurse told me that if the offenders are married the penalties are harsher, including loss of pay or rank. But usually it's just chores.

In other mostly European contingents the issue of intimate relations is more relaxed. The Norwegians are told to be discrete, and the Swedes are likely told not to flaunt it in front of the Finns, who as an exclusively male contingent in 2009 could only dream of the opportunity anyway.

As for gay relations, there are certainly homosexuals in the military but they are for sure the discreet yet tough-skinned variety. Above all in the US forces the majority of humour is at the expense of gays, so prevalent that it reminds you of being back at school; laboured, clichéd, incessant. It's only the 'your Mom' jokes that break the monotony ('Leave my Mom out of this, and I'll leave *this* out of *your* Mom'). In May 2010 the US Congress voted in favour of repealing a 1993 'don't ask, don't tell' ban on gays and lesbians in the forces, which in effect meant you could enlist as a homosexual as long as you didn't advertise it. Despite opposition by Republican elements in the house, the move was also backed by the Senate Armed Forces Committee.

At Kamp Holland, the Dutch PRT included a lesbian whose orientation was something one Afghan interpreter couldn't get his head round. Male homosexuality, however, is a prominent feature of Afghanistan's highly repressed gender culture and is embraced by many in its security forces on what western troops call 'Manlove Thursday'.

Good-looking teenaged foreign boys can find themselves being followed by shy ANA or ANP admirers, while bolder ones will just suggest 'jiggy jig'. But because conventional dating opportunities with females are non-existent for most Afghan men, male sodomy seems to be more a case of 'something to do' rather than an indication of deeper preference. The presence of women in the western military bewilders most Afghan soldiers and policemen, but they generally relish the sight of fair women in trousers, unthinkable in their villages where the burqa is the rule.

The female presence also poses certain practical challenges in the foreign forces. In many armies the place of women in front-line units is still hotly debated. Some countries like the United States and Britain do not allow females to serve in the infantry, even though many still end up in combat situations as drivers, mechanics and medics. Change in this respect is slow and draws reservations from even open-minded officers.

'The fact is you're always going to get that boy-girl dynamic, someone likes someone, someone else gets jealous,' one British Major said. But since any such objections voiced publicly by the High Command would get minced in the equal opportunities grinder, resistance is generally couched in terms of most women being unable to meet the physical demands of the job.

There are also provisions in US regulations saying that in view of their additional sanitary requirements, women should not serve in places where there are no proper toilet facilities. It's viewed by some people as a means of allowing opponents of equal male–female deployments to keep women away from front-line outposts.

By contrast, a Danish woman can serve in a combat unit and the only dispensation is an extra minute to do the running test in full kit. Women I met in that contingent were pretty offhand about the more intimate gender

challenges, even though in the forward positions they lived in the same cramped accommodation as their male platoon buddies.

'The only way we have privacy is if we have a shower and draw the curtains. But I don't think about it, nor do the guys,' said the Danish armoured-car gunner Ivana when asked if being seen in shared digs in her underwear is a problem. 'I think the situation would be worse if there were more women here.'

The basic Norwegian approach is don't introduce regulations you can't put into practice or enforce. At the shared Norwegian/ Latvian/US base in Meymaneh in the northern Faryab province I noticed a couple of male and female soldiers cosying up in a quiet corner. And the sunbathing area on one roof had Norsemen in shorts lounging and smoking around a single curvacious, bronzed woman lying on a sunbed in a bikini, with no signs of any excesses or rioting. But having women around still makes waves, one officer told me: 'It's a big problem, someone falls in love, everyone is gossiping.'

A female member of an American EOD team said the implications of her gender in a predominantly male environment were contradictory but by no means unmanagable.

'I've been in the Army for five years and I've never deployed with another girl, I've always been with like 12 guys and maybe I had a sheet round my cot but that's all. They'll offer to escort me to the toilet for a bit of privacy in case anyone sneaks up on me, even though I say I can go on my own. They kind of expect you to look after yourself but at the same time there are a couple of luxuries.'

But I heard plenty of tales of clandestine encounters, including actual prostitution allegations made informally against nurses of one European contingent. And not forgetting the legendary comforter of US servicemen in Iraq and Afghanistan, an ample girl known to the ranks as 'Clearing Barrel', (the term refers specifically to an oil drum or other receptacle dug into the ground for clearing weapons when entering a base).

In spring 2008, even the US military seemed to be shifting towards some kind of formal recognition of the status quo, i.e. that sexual relations will occur wherever mixed crowds of humans are thrown together, and especially in tough conditions. The corresponding measure remained convoluted and vague in its definition and effect, and prompted *Stars and Stripes* to run a story in May headlined 'Ban on sex for soldiers in Afghanistan is lifted ... sort of':

JALALABAD, Afghanistan — Single soldiers and civilians working for the U.S. military in Afghanistan can now have sex legally. Sort of.

A new order signed by Maj. Gen. Jeffrey Schloesser, commander of Combined Joint Task Force-101, has lifted a ban on sexual relations between unmarried men and women in the combat zone.

... Previously, under the (General Order No. 1 for Afghanistan) regulation, sexual relations and 'intimate behavior' between men and women not married to each other were a strict no-no. The regulation also barred members of the opposite sex from going into each other's living quarters unless they were married to each other.

... The new regulation warns that sex in a combat zone 'can have an adverse impact on unit cohesion, morale, good order and discipline.' But sexual relations and physical intimacy between men and women not married to each other are no longer banned outright. They're only 'highly discouraged,' and that's as long as they're 'not otherwise prohibited' by the Uniform Code of Military Justice, according to the new order ... A cursory reading of the order would seem to suggest that unmarried men and women could have sex in their living quarters, as long as all other persons who live there agree, or if they left the door open, if they were otherwise alone. But that's not the case, said Lt. Col. Rumi Nielson-Green, a spokeswoman for Regional Command-East and Combined Joint Task Force-101.

'Sex in both scenarios would be a chargeable offense under the UCMJ,' Nielson-Green said, referring to the Uniform Code of Military Justice ... 'The expectation is that troops should behave professionally and responsibly at all times,' Nielson-Green said, adding that while the new regulation does not condone sex, it 'does recognize that such behaviors happen,

and if they result in any chargeable offenses, then appropriate actions will be pursued.'

... Said one soldier of the apparent change on policy: 'I think it's a bad idea,' said Pfc. Shane Inman, 30, of Fort Dodge, Iowa. 'I think there's going to be a lot more pregnancies going around. Not that there already isn't. But at least they won't get in trouble for it.'

The move seemed to throw observers into some confusion about its repercussions. One US Captain stationed in Baghdad wrote to the paper with a touch of sarcasm:

'This is a victory for unmarried soldiers. It's interesting to note that the roommate of the one engaging in sexual activity must have no objections. This is a success for voyeurs as well, or at least a passive endorsement of the ménage à trois.'

A further dynamic to sexual tension within the US military was added in spring of 2008 by model and Army spouse Alessandra Bosco, who was to release a lingerie calendar containing 12 photographs of her wearing a mixture of lingerie and military items.

Married to Sgt. 1st Class Edward McCoy of the Germany-based 12th Combat Aviation Brigade, the young Italian bikini model said she got the idea for the calendar from soldiers who e-mailed her after checking out her Web site, which features a gallery of sexy photographs.

'I received a lot of messages from military personnel who wanted to see me in their gear. I thought about it and after some time I decided it was a good idea to do a calendar using some items they use in their jobs,' she told the paper. 'If [the troops] have good taste, they will definitely enjoy the calendar,' she added, clarifying that the item was intended for 'the military public, mostly male soldiers, rather than families.'

The project unleashed a storm of objections, primarily from the wives of serving soldiers, much to the amusement of some of the intended recipients of the calendar.

'Me and my buddies had a good laugh when we read their letters, which seemed to ooze jealousy,' wrote a US soldier based in Qatar. 'They are complaining because a military spouse, who happens to be a model, made a calendar (at the request of deployed soldiers), for deployed soldiers. One states she is appalled that the paper "thinks this is something families of deployed soldiers would want to see". If I read the original article correctly, the model made the calendars for deployed soldiers, not their families…The goal is the morale of the troops, not fear of offending some bored housewives who have nothing better to do than write jealous letters.'

After a story about the calendar appeared in *Stars and Stripes* in 2007, Bosco said she found threats posted on her Web page and that she was awakened in the night by women banging on her front door (in Katterbach, Germany) and yelling abuse. Her husband's car, a distinctive blue Chevrolet that sports an Italian flag, was apparently vandalized several times with side mirrors snapped off, keys dragged across the doors and the windshield smashed, she said.

Her husband said 'I've never been in this situation but I've been told my career is on the line. I'm probably going to be relocated because my wife is a disruption to the community and it is affecting wives' morale and they can't have that in [the 12th CAB] rear detachment at this point.'

The irony of a bikini calendar generating so much controversy when thousands of adult magazines are sold by the Army and Air Force Exchange Service did not escape McCoy.

'There is hard-core pornography everywhere and nobody cares. Every soldier could back me up, but they don't want their wives to know that and the Army doesn't want the public to know that.'

The problem is that Bosco is living in the community, he said.

'One wife said: "If my husband is in love with Angelina Jolie I don't care, but if he is in love with Alessandra Bosco then I have a problem because she is in my community".'

★ ★ ★

One summer evening in Afghanistan there is a gathering on one of the smaller bases. Various US units are passing through at this time and before nightfall I chat to a 20-year-old soldier called Amy. She's both pretty and pretty upset after someone spread the rumour that she's been 'whoring around' and as

a result she's being sent back to one of the main hubs. Another malicious rumour is that she's been instructed to carry a glowing cyalume stick everywhere at night so they can keep tabs on her.

Amy is adamant she did nothing to draw such gossip and is so pissed off that she now feels like doing what she's been branded with anyway. I tell her it's not a good idea to substantiate the accusations. Then she discloses a longstanding crush on one of the soldiers, says they are both due to be on the main base at the same time, and that she can't contain herself much longer.

'I thought your idea was to indiscriminately do what was alleged, but if there's someone special, hell, go for it, just don't get caught,' I say, tired of being the voice of reason.

'I'm glad you agree with me finally,' she replies, and then wonders where on the main base might be suitable for a tryst after she returns there. She heard the phone cubicles have a lock on them. I remember those little booths, and picture the whole cabin shaking on its foundations while a dozen callers turn and stare. Not very practical. So I tell her that when she gets there she should at least rethink that bit.

For what she has in mind, Amy can get what's called 'non-judicial process', get busted in rank without there being much real proof against her. But she can still resist this outcome if she's prepared to stick to her guns and take the case to the brink of court martial. The next morning she comes up to me with a conspiratorial air.

'You know that thing we talked about? I just did it today. I was walking past his room with a bag of garbage and he asked me if I'd like to pop in for five minutes, so we snuk into the armourer's cubby hole.'

I joke that she should walk around all day with a sack of garbage as the secret signal for a reprise. She looks at her watch. 'I think I'm all right for today, although maybe later…'

Thirty minutes later I am crossing the base and see Amy moving around with a 'purposeful saunter'. We pass in silence, I grin and she looks sheepish as we both glimpse a whistling, bare-chested young man cleaning a machine-gun inside a doorway.

thirteen

RISKY BUSINESS

'There are animals in Afghanistan I don't understand,' says Staff Sergeant Joshua Wyly, peering into an empty water bottle at his catch, a five-centimetre bug that looks like a locust wearing a WWII Wehrmacht helmet.

It's August 3, 2008. In the preceding three months the United States' 24th Marine Expeditionary Unit (MEU) rolled through Garmsir in southern Helmand, smashing heavily entrenched Taliban forces that had resisted two years of British efforts to dislodge them. Pushing out of the British-run FOB Delhi on April 29, the Marines had 170 engagements with the enemy in the next month. More than 400 insurgents are estimated to have died in the onslaught with infantry, helicopter gunships, jets and artillery. Now opposing forces gather for a further clash of Titans in the Command Post (CP) tent of the Marine artillerymen living alongside the British garrison at Delhi.

'Try to take Ukraine now,' Wyly defies, placing a large, black, dead cockroach on the *Risk* game board set up between him, me, four more Sergeants and Lieutenant Bonecutter. Around us the tent comes alive with fauna and the players intermittently jump up from the table to chase camel spiders and other weird stuff that scuttles around the gravel at our feet.

The Americans have refined the rules with their own additions and play with the keen grasp of people who have not only studied military tactics but also played the game ad nauseam; all except my partner, a thick-set Sergeant called Reynolds who insists on launching lavish and futile thrusts into Siberia.

I'm groggy with tiredness after three days of broken sleep at Delhi, spending muggy, blustery nights under a giant netting canopy with 30 Marine gunners and then on a cot by the CP, lulled by tendrils of noxious smoke from the burns pit. But playing *Risk* is the most familiar thing I've done in weeks so I fight until late for world domination, in spite of Reynolds' inexplicable invasion of Yakutia.

It's already surreal enough to be skirmishing for *Risk* territories in Garmsir when a large Afro-American officer enters the tent and raises some perimeter security issues. A minute earlier the teams had buzzed with talk of reinforcing their borders, now the battalion landing team commander, Lieutenant Colonel Anthony Henderson, gives instructions to reinforce the side gate and tower with a .50-calibre machine-gun, SMAW-D rockets and Claymore anti-personnel mines.

The next day they will reopen the Civil and Military Operations Centre (CMOC), the facility that processes compensation claims of locals for damage caused to their houses, fields and crops in the fighting. The CMOC started work on June 23, less than a month after the last engagement with the enemy. By late July it had received over 1,200 visits and paid out some $520,000 to 400 families throughout the Garmsir area. The system could only infuriate the Taliban, who need a subdued population to operate in, not families who receive generous payouts from the Americans and visibly warm to them.

Because Garmsir and many surrounding villages were largely deserted for two years, the chief spoiler of relations between locals and foreign troops in Afghanistan – civilian casualties – was according to the MEU limited over the campaign to one man shot dead for failing to stop at a checkpoint. The Marine Command also went to great lengths to ensure the soldiers were well briefed in the dos and don'ts of interacting with Afghans.

'Everyone in Garmsir loves the Marines now, taking shoes off in the mosque, saying Salam to the elders, not looking at the women, not going into houses without permission,' an Afghan military interpreter tells me.

US Marines of Charlie Company, 24th MEU, return from patrol by Jugroom Fort, Garmsir, Helmand province, August 2008.

So it surprises no one to hear that the Taliban are reportedly planning a double suicide bombing with cars packed with explosives, first to decimate the queue of claimants waiting outside the gate and then to hit US troops as they help the casualties. The threat is so acute that they briefly consider leaving the CMOC closed for a few more days following its recent relocation from one side of the base to the other.

'I'm not so into the idea of giving money to locals that I want to risk the lives of Marines,' a Sergeant says after the Colonel leaves. I transfer my doomed armies to Reynolds and bid the players goodnight as they talk through preparations for mass casualties from a bombing.

The compensation process starts way out in the fields and villages of the Green Zone of farmland along the River Helmand. Anyone can make a claim by approaching a US checkpoint and getting the Afghan interpreter to write down the alleged damage on a piece of paper. The claimants then have to wait for a passing patrol and show them the site for visual confirmation, get their paper signed and take it to the CMOC. After a final round of questioning, a successful claim is valued and payment made with rubber-banded wads of crisp afghanis. After the expense of deploying almost 2,500 troops of the MEU, the money paid out barely dents the pocket of the US military. But by local standards the sums are considerable and help to breathe new life into the former ghost town.

After the Americans arrived, a few thousand people returned to their homes and from its abandoned state the bazaar in Garmsir grew to 60 working stalls by mid-July. The Marines were satisfied with their rapid purge of the area but knew the enemy could re-infiltrate and disrupt at any time, if not in head-on fights then using IEDs and suicide bombers.

'It could all go to hell tomorrow,' their public affairs officer told me before I flew from Kandahar Airfield to Helmand in late July.

Troops moving to Garmsir from the main British base at Camp Bastion travel south through the desert to FOB Dwyer, either by convoy or in one of the Marines' CH-46 Sea Knight helicopters. A smaller version of the CH-47, these 40-year-old helicopters feel like the inside of a garden shed. The door gunner even sits in a metal framed canvas chair with a big bucket under the .50-cal to catch the empty cases.

From Dwyer it's a 45-minute drive east in a 7-tonne Oshkosh truck through more desert, over the river to FOB Delhi and then the final leg into the Green Zone. I get dropped off at Jugroom Fort, a colonial-era British site that had been an iconic Taliban stronghold until it was seized by the Marines on May 30. Not much remains of the high-walled complex and watchtowers, having since been largely bulldozed by the Americans to prevent it from ever being resurrected by the insurgents.

The commander of Charlie Company, Captain John Moder, gives me a quick tour through the ruins where his three platoons sleep in the few remaining buildings or in one-man tents in shaded corners, and along the bank of a gurgling stream where I am given a cot under a low tree. Now I can at least sweat in the shade. Garmsir means 'too much heat' in Pashtu, and with the mercury hovering around 50 degrees everyone is lying low. There are a few mens sleeping farther down by the tail section of a Soviet air bomb, and 20

metres upstream I hear the clank and gush of the hand pump where Americans now wash instead of Taliban fighters.

Originally the Marines were supposed to spend no more than 10 days in Garmsir but because their presence was needed to keep it clear after the fighting they have been here for nearly 100 days. There has been no contact with the enemy for two months, Moder tells me, adding, 'I'm surprised they haven't dropped some mortar rounds.'

A couple of hours later I go on patrol with a platoon and Master Gunnery Sergeant John Garth, a stocky, moustachioed reservist artilleryman who has three combat tours under his belt and now helps run the compensation programme.

At 40 years old Garth is already such an uncompromisingly grumpy old man that I can't help liking him. Importantly, he has the kind of no-nonsense manner that ensures that most of the fraudsters get weeded out and genuine claimants receive their dues.

'About 60 per cent of claimants get something while 40 per cent show up because they think we are giving money away or they are trying to bullshit us,' says Garth, who in his distant civilian life works for a mobile phone provider.

'You get these guys all the time, they jump on the band wagon and make claims all over the place, but we are not going to create a welfare society here. It's a difficult process because there is a lot of damage that wasn't done by us. We want to help these people but some of the stuff that comes up is like from ten years ago, this place has been bombed for ever. And a lot of the time the house has been more weathered than destroyed by us.'

Bathed in sweat after a few minutes on the move, we cut across fields that are still covered in dry poppy stalks.

'We're going to get bombarded when we reach that compound,' Garth warns, and I tense up – isn't the shooting supposed to be over? He's talking about claimants though, and we don't even reach the buildings when men clutching scraps of paper converge on the patrol from different sides, reminding me of the *Jurassic Park* scene where the velociraptors attack.

They halt the first man at a distance and make him lift his shirt and sleeves to show he's not wired to explode. Abdul presents a claim for a house with six rooms, three of which are standing and three are wrecked. But the paper says the damage was done before the poppy harvest and before the MEU arrived, so it's clearly a matter for the British who must have caused the damage in an air or artillery strike months ago. The man is told through the Afghan interpreter to take his ID and property deed to the separate British CMOC in Garmsir. Dangling the carrot of a cash reward for information, Garth asks him and others whether they have found or know of any caches of Taliban weapons and munitions.

'Tell him I've got a lot of money, I'm trying to give it away but only to people who tell us where there are bombs,' says Garth, who has a pocket full of afghanis and can't understand why no one is talking. 'Everywhere I've been, every time I've offered money people come forward. You can't be here for two years as a Taliban strongpoint and not leave something behind. And we took them by surprise, it's not like they had time to move it all out with trucks. There's got to be something somewhere – we're probably walking on it,' he says as we cross another ploughed field.

A couple more men have their claims confirmed, and then a guy who already received 20,000 afghanis ($400) tries to get more for supposed losses to his livestock.

'We can't pay for everything, they are free now and they should be grateful for that,' Garth tells him and then relents when he hears that after two years living in Kabul the man just returned with no job and nine children to support (his offspring mill around us).

He gets a one-off 'humanitarian payment' of 60 bucks to fix the water pump in the compound and is offered the chance to do some paid maintenance work for the Marines.

Back at the checkpoint near Jugroom we are approached by a toothless old man dressed in a grimy *payran tumban*, black turban and plastic sandals.

'My house was here where you built these Hescos, this belongs to me,' he mumbles, motioning at a new fortification that will be manned by British soldiers. 'I know it's difficult for you to verify but I can prove it.'

'That's what the other guy said this morning,' Garth replies and tells him to come back the next day with a second man claiming to own the land the post was built on.

We return to the ruined fort along a track covered in deep moon dust and criss-crossed with snake trails, reminding me to check my bedding and boots before use for a roving krait or cobra. It's dark when I turn in and as I sit down on the cot my heart almost bursts when I glimpse a long slender silhouette draped over my sleeping bag. It's the drinking tube from my Camelbak. Around me the stream and undergrowth come alive with chirruping, rustling and splashing and bugs shower on my head and notebook as I scribble by torchlight.

Because of the savage mid-day heat the work starts early here. The next patrol goes out at 0600 and the first 'client' appears immediately, a slow, dopey young man with heavily bloodshot eyes.

'Man he's baked,' one of the Marines laughs.

The stoned guy leads us along a filthy ditch into a disused compound and tries to claim for a collapsed wall, arguing that although he left his house 22 months ago the damage is two months old. Shrapnel and bullets are lodged in the walls but the place is mainly intact and Garth is firm.

'Tell him sorry but we can't do that. None of the damage is preventing him and his family from moving in and living safely. All of his roofs, windows and doors are in good shape,' he says. Looking closer, he then tells the man that the rounded, weathered brick edges mean that the collapsed wall has been down for at least one rainy season so it can't have been wrecked by the Marines.

We nose around some abandoned compounds that are full of poppy farming detritus, dried plant stems, containers, tools. Someone finds a souvenir sickle and I pocket a little wooden-handled scraper they use to scoop up the opium sap from the cut bulbs. There is a small marijuana bush outside one room which inside is piled hip deep with weed the Taliban had no time to move. And to think what I would pay in my college days for a tiny bag...

We stop on our way back to Jugroom while Garth sits down with the two claimants for the land where the Hesco strongpoint stands. They wrangle over who owned what on the site, which according to the Afghans once held four mud houses and a couple of shops built

1 Northern Alliance soldiers take cover
behind a dead Taliban fighter in the
early years of the war.

2 Taliban prisoners of
war, early 2007.

3 Gurkha of 1RGR during mission to Taliban village of Tambil, Kandahar province, Operation Southern Scorpion.

4 Farmers passing Gurkha column, Kandahar province.

5 Royal Marines laying down fire courtesy of a 51mm mortar, 2007.

6 Royal Marines advance across a waterway in southern Helmand, 2007.

7 Polish troops distribute aid to villagers, Paktika province, December 25, 2007.

8 Khakrez shrine at dawn, Kandahar province, January 2008.

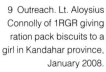

9 Outreach. Lt. Aloysius Connolly of 1RGR giving ration pack biscuits to a girl in Kandahar province, January 2008.

10 Girls pause in front of patrolling Danish infantryman, Gereshk River Valley, Helmand province, June 2008.

11 Danes on patrol in the Green Zone, Gereshk River Valley, Helmand province, June 2008. The patrol was ambushed shortly after

12 Danish patrol prepares
to leave FOB Armadillo,
Helmand, June 2008.

13 Dutch patrol,
Uruzgan province,
June 2008.

14 Canadian
artillery in action.

15 Canadian artilleryman,
FOB Wilson, Zhari, Kandahar
province, July 2008.

16 Canadian medic
Genevieve Dureau on
patrol in Kandahar City,
July 2008.

17 Canadian artilleryman pauses during heavy bombardment of Taliban fighters, FOB Wilson in Zhari, Kandahar province, July 2008.

18 Canadian police officer trains Afghan police in body guard drills, Kandahar City, July 2008.

19 Canadian patrol under sniper fire in Zhari, Kandahar province.

20 US Marine on patrol by Jugroom Fort,
Garmsir, Helmand province, August 2008.

21 Lieutenant Colonel (retired) Oliver North
travelling with his FOX TV crew in Garmsir,
Helmand province, August 2008.

22 Crashed US Marine Chinook CH-46, FOB Dwyer, Helmand province.

23 Taliban being detained by Afghan and US forces, Khost province.

24 M240 gunner
Brandon Jackson of US
2-506th Airborne Infantry
watches border with
Pakistan, Khost province,
September 2008.

25 US Army medic
Robert Kidwell attends to
wounded Afghan soldier
during Taliban attack on
OP5, Khost province,
October 2, 2008.

26 US Army medic Robert Kidwell waits by smoke signal during helicopter evacuation of wounded Afghan soldier during Taliban attack on OP5, Khost province.

27 UH-60 Black Hawk helicopter drops food and water in body bags for US and Afghan troops in Qalandar, Khost province, October 2008.

28 New Zealander standing near empty alcove of the Large Buddha, Bamyan.

29 Swedish soldiers distribute Nowroz
New Year congratulation cards to Afghan
villagers, Balkh province, March 2009.

30 Norwegian troops bogged down by
heavy rainfall, Faryab province, April 2009.

31 Afghan police officer, Maiwand, Kandahar province, February 2008.

32 Helmand heat. Estonian mortar crew training in the desert at Camp Bastion, May 2008.

33 An American Cougar MRAP (mine resistant ambush protected) truck undergoing proving trials in the US.

34 The aftermath of an IED blast.

35 US Special Forces dismount from an Army UH-60 Black Hawk while executing a pinnacle landing on a mountain peak in Zabul province, January 21, 2010. The Black Hawk crew was assigned to Company A, 2nd Battalion, 82nd Aviation Regiment, 82nd Combat Aviation Brigade. *US Army photo by Staff Sgt. Aubree Clute*

36 As seen through night vision, US Army soldiers review map data
while conducting an operation in the Panjwaii district, Kandahar
province, July 10, 2010. *US Army photo by Sgt. David Russell*

37 US paratroopers and Afghan forces patrol in the village of
Bakshikhala in Kherwar district in Logar province, April 12, 2010. The
mission was to provide medical care to village residents. *US Army
photo by Sgt. Russell Gilchrest*

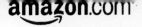

Your order of March 5, 2012 (Order ID 105-8283546-4089026)

Qty.	Item	Item Price	Total
1	**Embed: With the World's Armies in Afghanistan** Hardcover (** P-2-P80H368 **) B005HKV0UC	$11.98	$11.9

This shipment completes your order.

Have feedback on how we packaged your order? Tell us at
www.amazon.com/packaging.

Subtotal	$11.9
Shipping & Handling	$3.9
Order Total	$15.9
Paid via credit/debit	$15.9
Balance due	$0.0

161/DFPWlnlBN/-1 of 1-//1SS/std-n-us/8761426/0306-12:30/0305-22:32

V4

by the Russians when they ran a checkpoint here in the 1980s. The Sergeant's exasperation grows as they then speak of a third man who apparently also has some rights over the plot.

'No matter how many questions you ask, as soon as you think you're done they throw in one more monkey wrench,' Garth sighs, and tells them they all have to show up for another talk in a couple of days.

'When can all 3½ of you come?' he asks, raising the fingers of his right hand, the third digit of which was chopped in half by a vehicle hatch in Iraq. The joke sails over their heads into the blue Helmand sky.

The next day I drive to Garmsir with a platoon that pulls security while the British search the bazaar, acting on a tip-off that 'something you can strap on' is hidden there, suggesting suicide bomb vests. The market was sealed off the previous evening and now the British troops work their way along the ranks of shuttered stalls, cut the padlock off each one and send in a sniffer dog. The search takes the whole morning and nothing is found.

'I'm unhappy for the whole bazaar, it was wrong to close the market on a Friday, lots of people have lost food, meat, ice,' says Mohammed, one of a handful of traders who managed to slip in and open up shop. He sits with a couple of friends by a table loaded with rancid tomatoes, while the only other sign of life is a pair of camels lolloping down the main thoroughfare.

'We don't know who's better for the country but the Taliban certainly didn't give us anything,' says the vegetable seller, who moved back six weeks earlier from Lashkar Gah after a two-year absence. Those soldiers who know Garmsir describe the recent transformation as a wonder.

'This is the first time I've ever seen changes during a tour,' adds Sergeant Major Barry Lynn of the Scots Guards. 'You hear about Afghanistan and the casualties but what the British public doesn't hear about is this deserted market town and how the next day a couple of hundred people came back. They think we are just coming here to kill and get killed and don't see these people returning to the bazaar.'

In the past Garmsir was where the Taliban would send new recruits 100 kilometres up through the desert from Pakistan to be blooded before they went to fight around Sangin or Kajaki in northern Helmand. In April the insurgents were still attacking from fortified positions 800 metres away and would sneak in as close as 300 metres to fire at troops in the empty streets.

'You don't get many frontlines in the world today but there was one here, with bunkers and so on,' says Lieutenant Oliver Bevan, who is running the search operation.

Garmsir's Police Chief, Colonel Guli Khan, grew up here and took up his current job four months earlier. The town may have changed for the better in recent weeks but he's worried that the gains will be lost if they don't expand on the successes.

'If we move forward from here now the Taliban can't come back, if we don't they might,' he says, claiming that the foreign and Afghan government forces still only control 20 per cent of the Garmsir district. He is sure the Taliban have spies in the town and are just waiting for the opportunity to hit back. According to the chief there have been about 15 IED attacks and suicide bombings in the past four months and he expects more. Today he is writing numbers on the stall shutters so the owners can come and collect new replacement padlocks from the Police station. But he's not happy because he expects the traders will allege thefts of goods by his men during the search.

Most of the stalls sell a hotchpotch of domestic supplies, cooking oil, biscuits, washing powder, torches, nuts and bolts, shoes, baby bottles, flour, sugar, shampoo. But one has racks full of radios, cassette players and wiring circuits. The sniffer dog doesn't find anything incriminating here but the British take note of this abundance of components: 'This is an IED-maker's dream,' Bevan says.

Before we leave the bazaar, one of the search team tells me that many of the British troops based at Delhi think the Marines stole the show in Garmsir.

'The Americans came and took everything,' he says. 'The thought of doing a whole tour without firing a single shot is actually pretty depressing.'

The 24th MEU had been in-country six weeks before they reached the front, forced to wait at KAF while NATO debated how best to use them. Once dispatched to Helmand they drove hundreds of impatient soldiers from Dwyer to Delhi and pressed on immediately with Operation Azada Wosa ('Be Free').

The assault that began on April 29, 2008 was backed up by air and artillery power drawn mainly from the Marines' own resources, thereby making them dependent on no one. The 24th MEU was a self-contained, fast moving and highly aggressive force that just had to be set on task and left to do its job. And the Marine esprit de corps dictates that they don't stop until it is done.

Over the next weeks four companies pushed out from Garmsir to the east and then south through the 'Snake's Head', a tangle of small irrigation canals, destroying the enemy in their path and creating an extended front against hundreds of fighters based out of Jugroom Fort located a few kilometres to the west.

For a month the sides fought daily battles until the insurgent numbers were depleted enough to allow a direct assault on the fort, located ten kilometres southwest of Delhi. The first major success came on the opening day with the capture of the madrassa (Islamic religious school) four kilometres east of the town, a key element of the Taliban defences.

'It was a staging post manned by an estimated 30 men but they were coming in from the desert in vans, basically taxis bringing a steady flow of reinforcements,' said Moder, the Charlie Company commander.

One evening at Jugroom a young Marine Corporal called Steve from Texas asks, 'Do you want to hear about our first fight?' (I tried to get his surname from his Captain later, but he wouldn't give it.) This is his account of the taking of the madrassa on Tuesday April 29.

They drove us from Dwyer to Delhi; we got there at 11p.m. We didn't even go to sleep but moved out on foot to take the madrassa. We had way too much gear, I'm a SAW gunner and I had my 800 rounds of ammunition and 200 7.62mm rounds for the machine-gunners. By the time we got close to the objective we were nearly dead just from the walk from Delhi.

My platoon's mission was to take the madrassa but on the way our job was to form an echelon on the side of the road and search for landmines and IEDs. The satellite images they gave us were all wrong; they must have been from a long time ago. We were supposed to walk on flat fields but when we got there they didn't look like that at all, just thick grass. We decided to proceed to the madrassa on the road.

I'm the number four man in my squad. All of a sudden I heard a hiss right in front of my face; we looked at each other and then heard machine-gun fire. That was the most frightening time; we could see the bullets coming through the grass. I was crawling and looked up, the grass a foot above my head was being cut by bullets.

We were in our first fire fight and were stuck in the middle taking fire from both the Taliban and our guys. When the bullets stopped flying we could barely move, our packs were so heavy, but we still had to sprint to a compound to clear it. I remember we looked down and in the middle of the yard there was a 'pressure cooker', a gigantic homemade IED, all wired up. We were skirting round the outside walls and for a while we didn't even notice it. We said 'fuck this' and ran out of the compound.

The firing was subsiding and the squad leader told us to get in echelon, we told him that wasn't a good idea and in the end we just stayed where we were. Then we saw three guys running 900 metres away from us holding a little mortar tube and they started throwing rounds into it. We saw them loading the shells and then heard them whistling down and they started hitting all around us.

Our guys started firing mortars back at them, they were firing airbursts and those exploded right over us. The squad leader kept his head and told them to adjust fire and then they killed those Taliban. We stopped and smoked and then had to move again.

We were trying to get permission to drop our packs, the Lieutenant sent us to leave them in the Humvees so we had to run 1,000 metres all the way back down the track we'd just come up. We dropped them there and came back and at that point

Hesco fortification in Garmsir, Helmand province.

felt we were about to die from exhaustion, we couldn't even sweat as there was no more moisture left in us.

We cleared the compounds after blowing a guy out of a chimney with a rocket. Inside one of them there was something under the carpet and some wires under the floor mat. It was a Taliban landmine wired to a pressure plate about one foot from where one guy was standing, so we got out of there too.

By that time we had run out of water. We were just dying, sitting in the sun, boiling in our gear, we couldn't move. But we cleared the row of compounds, and then we spotted two Taliban, shot one and then the other as he was loading a mortar to fire at Third Platoon.

Later we had to supply the company with water; we had to run across a log over a stream as the Taliban were firing. We ran across with cases of water and started tossing them over the compound wall to the guys, bottle after bottle.

We could see the madrassa now, it was 800 metres away. There was a constant stream of vans bringing up their men. Then we got the order to fire, we unleashed hell on that place, using helicopters, artillery, mortars, but they just kept coming and coming. I opened fire and my belt of 100

rounds was gone in seconds, I just kept my finger on the trigger. After we lit up the whole area we went into a little house that we nicknamed Grandma's House because we finally felt safe in there.

At 3p.m. we got the call to move up to the madrassa. The helicopters were shooting at other targets to create a diversion for us so we got up there pretty much unnoticed. The only contact we had was some guy with an AK who popped up over a wall, we all opened up on him and he got blasted.

I remember we were excited to take the madrassa because it was supposed to be a big staging point. We were going to charge in victoriously but before we could the weapons company drove up in Humvees and busted through the gate, shot the place up and left. We were kind of pissed that they took our glory. Inside we found what looked like a little shop with food, soda and cigarettes. We could still hear firing but it was far away.

When the sun came up the Taliban were all running round like chickens with their heads cut off. We were in the middle of them, we didn't even take any fire, they seemed too confused to shoot. There was just a sniper in a tree who started to take shots so two .50-cals and three

SAWs opened up on that tree at once and blasted him.

Then we were told to clear a village one kilometre away and first search for IEDs, which was a slow process. All the village elders came out and told us the Taliban had run away. At first we got nervous about them being around us, then we gave cookies to the kids.

People were really happy to see us, the kids were playing with us, touching my tattoos – they'd never seen tattoos before – and older boys of about 16 were chatting to us. We went back to the madrassa and thought we'd be going back to KAF – it was only supposed to be a 7 to 10-day operation.

The company spent four weeks in this area before the order finally came to take Jugroom Fort. It was already a legendary site in Afghanistan, having long served as a redoubt for Taliban and al-Qaeda fighters moving men and weapons north from Baluchistan province in Pakistan and opium shipments in the opposite direction for export.

'Jugroom in the minds of our enemies and the minds of the locals was a citadel of Taliban military prowess,' said Lt. Col. Henderson. 'Psychologically, taking it from them was one of the most important symbols of the failure of the Taliban to be able to stand up to Coalition Forces and continue to dominate here.'

The last attempt to take the fort was in January 2007 when a 200-strong British force led by the Royal Marines tried to flush out the enemy from these heavily fortified positions. Even with the support of Apache gunships, B1 bombers and artillery, the ground assault was repulsed by withering defensive fire which killed one soldier and injured four more. The attack was called off but four British soldiers then performed an extraordinary feat, volunteering to be strapped with harnesses onto the outside of two Apaches and landing by the fort under fire to retrieve the Marine's body. Jugroom remained unconquered for another sixteen and a half months.

At 0500 on May 30, 2008, Charlie Company began the assault by driving straight down the road from Garmsir. Engineers moving with them removed 10 IEDs on the route, mainly pressure plates attached to mortar rounds, and the closer they got to the corner of the road that leads to the fort, the more enemy fighters appeared.

'There were Taliban coming out of the woodwork, crawling in the grass trying to sneak up and throw grenades,' recounted Moder. 'I got out of my truck and there was one on his hands and feet in the grass 25 yards in front of me. We shot him and then he blew himself up with a grenade.'

The company called in helicopters with mini-guns to sweep the defenders away from the road and then at 1100 Third Platoon made the final move on the fort in the blistering heat.

'Instead of attacking after the platoons had consolidated their positions I made the decision to rout them all in one day, continuing our momentum,' the Captain added.

To clear suspected IEDs on the final stretch of road to the fort, the Marines used two Mine Clearing Line Charges (MCLCs), 100-metre long lines containing 770 kilos of high explosives which are fired out to their full length and detonated to clear a path.

The 'shock and awe' effect of these huge blasts was compounded by a few dozen rounds of artillery fire, four large air bombs and strafing by helicopters and jets armed with machine-guns and rockets: 'We knocked the shit out of them, they'd hunkered down but there was still was an RPK in a bunker which the platoon destroyed with small arms and grenades.'

Jugroom was now not so heavily defended as before since many Taliban had been thrown into the fight against A and B companies to the east. A number are believed to have escaped during the storming of the fort, where the Marines later gathered ten dead insurgents in body bags and rolled up one in a carpet. No Marines were seriously hurt. This storming operation took 12 hours to complete, but Moder was modest about the achievements of the MEU, describing its success at breaking the stalemate in Garmsir as a 'manpower issue'.

'We had our own helicopters, jets and trucks while the British were just a rifle company with trucks. They were at the limit of what they could attack, seize and hold, then we came with 800 Marines and were able to push out.

'We were supposed to be here for up to ten days but if we'd left then there would have been a lot of progress that would have collapsed. We don't want to win and then turn a win into a loss by backing up and leaving.'

His boss, Lt. Col. Henderson, also downplayed any idea of British inability to do the job.

'We came in and did what we were asked. It would have been a lot harder if we hadn't had the resources of the British. They really understood the ground and helped us understand the situation,' he said while cleaning his pistol in the ruins of Jugroom.

There is also no disputing the fact that UK troops did play an important role pushing out from Delhi and holding a wider security perimeter around the town as the Marines stormed farther forward. But subsequent headlines like that of *The Independent* newspaper, 'British forces took Garmsir from the Taliban' were absurd. Regardless, the main thing was that the insurgents' grip on the area was decisively broken, something that both the British and the US wanted to consolidate by keeping it heavily manned during the stabilization period that followed.

'Our staying here longer was designed to build the confidence of people, and that confidence takes time and has to be based on deeds not words,' Henderson continued. 'We've been working to build a level of trust and support that eventually becomes intolerance of the Taliban presence. The group that will eventually eliminate the Taliban as a threat to Afghanistan will be the Afghan people – when they no longer tolerate the insurgents, then they will have true security. I'm pretty convinced that the Afghan people we encountered in the last couple of months don't want the Taliban back. I don't think from our Western perspective we can fully appreciate the psychological effect of taking this place,' he said, motioning at the ruins of the fort. 'I do know the floodgates really opened afterwards, with the locals returning from all directions within 48 hours.'

After many months spent in a state of siege, FOB Delhi suddenly had queues of Afghans at its gate waiting to make their compensation claims. The camp itself is a bombed out former US-built agricultural college which had changed hands several times and was once a Taliban madrassa. It made the world's news headlines in February when amid a news embargo agreed between the British military and the national media, an Australian women's magazine reported that Prince Harry was secretly serving there. His cover blown, the third in line to the British throne was promptly flown home after just 10 weeks in-theatre.

Situated on the east side of the River Helmand beside a long bridge, the base is made up of dilapidated brick buildings with sandbagged windows and dark A/C-cooled interiors where the British troops decorate their dens with pin-ups and the flags of St. George and St. Andrew.

Delhi is gravelled, has four corner towers and is surrounded by Hesco barriers, concertina wire and 100 metres of buffering dead ground up to the houses. As one testimony to the amount of fighting that took place there, all the seats inside the 'Hell Man's Kitchen' cookhouse are made from empty Javelin missile tubes, while 20 more of the weapons are stacked outside. It was during his two-month stay with the Gurkhas in this spartan, dangerous place that the 23-year-old British prince found his niche, stating to a reporter (after not having showered for four days), 'It's very nice to be sort of a normal person for once; I think it's about as normal as I'm going to get.' (The base would be transferred to the US Marines of Task Force Leatherneck in June 2009.)

After the search of the bazaar I get dropped off at the FOB where I decide to spend the weekend until the CMOC reopens for business. The head of the US compensation programme at Delhi, Lieutenant Healey, shows me the facility, which is just a few plastic chairs and a couple of tables set up in a Hesco-walled enclosure by the back gate. The roof is a large net that is propped up by a pole and collects sun-dazed dragonflies, praying mantis and giant grasshoppers. Tall and now super lean like most of the troops after these months in Helmand, the Lieutenant tells of some of the shenanigans observed in the compensation process in recent weeks.

There has been a steady flow of fraudulent claims and an increasing incidence of fake ID papers. The six-man team of Marines at the centre became adept at spotting forgeries with bogus photos, suspect printing and inconsistencies and slip-ups by those presenting the claim.

In one day they received six consecutive forms that were accompanied by apparently bona fide ID papers. Everything checked out and sizeable sums were almost released until someone noticed that the would-be criminal mastermind had added the exact same serial number and holder's signature to four of the claims.

Another claimant already received a one-third advance on a cash payment of 150,000 afghanis ($3,000), but when he arrived to claim the balance he inadvertently gave his real name instead of his fake identity.

The most far-fetched demand came from a man who overstated the size of his vineyard by thirty times and argued that because the grapes were special he should get 100,000 afghanis per damaged vine instead of the 1,000 usually paid. Another man sought 'ten hundred thousand dollars' for two square kilometres of wheat he said burned up at once.

'All we can do is kick them out, that's the frustrating thing,' Healey says in amused exasperation.

Since the start of business on June 23, the centre received about 50 claimants a day who were covered by Marine snipers as they approached, searched, fingerprinted and got a biometric cornea scan before they were allowed in.

'They don't really know what technology we have which helps us out,' the Lieutenant tells me, just as the troops' Afghan supplier brings in a wheelbarrow full of ice he drove here 60 kilometres from Lashkar Gah.

'I buy it for 600 afghanis a block and sell it for 700. Two days ago my whole load melted because they closed the road,' says the man, who is making a killing providing goods to the Marines and will be subject to one if the Taliban catch him.

'The guys used to order melons from him until they heard rumours or threats that the melons would be poisoned by the Taliban…I

Author with abandoned
Taliban crop of marijuana,
Garmsir, Helmand province,
August 2008.

hope he doesn't mind getting his head cut off when we leave, he could well do,' the Lieutenant says as we watch him trundle his empty barrow out of the FOB.

Just after 1700 thunder rumbles over Garmsir, the air gets rapidly warmer and a driving wind carries a billowing brown wall of dust towards us from the east, hundreds of metres tall and stretching a couple of kilometres. I film until the last moment from one of the towers as the *tufaan* roars in, wondering if we'll see bin Laden's contorted face in the swirls. Then nature's fury engulfs Delhi, hurling untethered items around for the next ten minutes and choking the occupants like every Army that passed this way over the centuries.

'Imagine the delights of an immense cloud of dust a mile square, or more, driven along by a red hot wind and forcing its way into every hole and corner,' Brigadier Henry Brooke wrote in May 1880. 'While it is passing it is quite dark, even in mid-day, and when it is gone everything one possesses, every table, chair and book, is covered in an inch of dust, and one's hair and beard turned into a whitey-brown colour and stiff with dirt.'

When we open our eyes again the tattered base is still cloaked in an orange haze until heavy black rain clouds burst and try to drown us with 20 minutes of torrential rain. Hysterical chaos ensues as the Marines run around hollering and dousing each other with water and handfuls of grit before they fetch a ball and start playing American football with some of the British. The players roll around in mud and clouds of moon dust that sliding tackles throw up from beneath a top layer of sludge. One nose is broken and a wedding ring is lost in the process but the soldiers are having a grand time. Meanwhile, the British Commanding Officer at Delhi, Major Neil Den-McKay, stands frowning in the main yard.

'This is exactly when we need to be on the line – this is when the fuckers will move,' the CO says before striding off to reinforce the perimeter guard.

On Monday August 4 the CMOC reopens for business. There are ten men waiting outside and at 0710 they admit the first claimant, a man with a limp and a stick who gets the 100,000 balance of a 200,000 afghani ($4,000) claim for the repair of four rooms, four doors,

six windows and a pump. The damage happened after two cars full of Taliban came and took over the house and then fled after the Americans bombed the building, killing two insurgents.

'Thank you so much for helping us, when the Taliban were here we had to feed them and couldn't leave our homes,' says the man, who has two wives, five sons and five daughters.

Echoing what the Americans hear from a few people, he says that the insurgents still come to his village because there is no US presence that far out: 'The Taliban patrol every day, there are a lot of Punjabis and they come five people in a taxi and two on a bike.'

The man has some trauma injuries on his body that he claims were the result of the explosion, and his legs shake so much he can barely hobble along with a stick. He says he already went to go to Karachi in Pakistan to get head surgery he says cost over $10,000 and still requires expensive treatment. But the compensation programme only covers property, not physical injury.

'I had to sell my tractor, car, and my 15-year-old daughter,' he tells me, crying in anguish or shame at the sale of his child to an unspecified buyer.

Another old man with a grin so wide that it threatens to force out his remaining few teeth today sports a shiny new watch acquired since he received the first 100,000 of a 250,000-afghani payout. He also thanks the Americans for driving out the Taliban.

'They took over our village, they used to beat us and we had to cook and feed them. There were many strangers, we couldn't understand their language.'

And so it goes on. Of the ten claimants seen in the morning, three are turned away either for ID irregularities or because they hadn't had the claim undersigned by a patrol. The number of fraudulent cases grows in the final days of work at the centre, which will close down in a week's time.

'You can tell we're getting toward the end because most of the legitimate cases have been in, now we're getting more fakes,' says Munro, a hulking, good-natured black Sergeant who disburses the money. The team seems to have fun doing the work, bantering with the locals, giving out extra gifts of calendars, pens and radios, and generally relishing no longer having to live out in the desert where they spent weeks crewing the guns.

'Being an artilleryman and having caused a lot of the damage down here it's just rewarding for us to help them rebuild their homes and lives and help them get back on track,' says Corporal Greg Allen from Wyoming.

The next morning the CMOC stays shut because of the heightened bombing threat. Intelligence reports indicate that a black Toyota Corolla will be blown up among the waiting claimants before more attackers wearing explosive vests run in as the Marines help the casualties.

'People are packing and leaving,' Munro tells me. 'Something's going to happen, that's the word. They know before we do. But we're ready for them.'

That afternoon a landowner who has already received 175,000 afghanis complains about the size of the payment.

'False claimants come and get money but people who lost property don't get full compensation,' he tells the soldiers, who are adamant that they've been more than fair with him.

As the man leaves he stops and turns and tells the soldiers: 'I know you have left your families to come here and help us and for this we thank you.'

There was a thoughtful air about many of the Marines as the deployment wound down, about the nature of the job they did and what the Afghans really expected from it all.

'They just want a piece of the pie, put on a new roof or glass in the windows, while we go and bitch about having a steak and a beer,' Garth says. 'Back home people don't just want a piece, they want the whole pie. I'm sick of people complaining they haven't got stuff. If they haven't got it they haven't worked for it. Here they work but still don't even have a crumb of the pie. The poorest people in America are way better off than these people.'

He's convinced that the Blitzkrieg approach of the Marines is the key to breaking the Taliban's grip on places like Garmsir.

'The Marine Corps hasn't been fully deployed in Afghanistan for two and a half years, they thought we were too aggressive, and then they called us in. Our guys met some resistance at Jugroom but not so much because the Taliban know how we fight, we go in with everything we've got and don't stop until it's done. We clear, hold and then hand over to someone. You're going to see us back again here soon,' he predicts, correctly. Within a year the Marine Corps was back in Helmand in much larger numbers.

'The Brits don't dismount enough, they go down the same roads and if they get hit by an IED they don't go down there. Our approach is that you should go down there the very next day and every day after that. If you get shot at while on patrol you should go back there, twice a day, regardless. Sure people are going to get killed and injured but they will anyway sooner or later if you don't do that.'

After operating in the Garmsir district for more than 130 days, the Marines returned responsibility for the area's security to the British Army at a ceremony on September 8, 2008.

'We are not going to solve all the problems with 2,500 Marines for seven or eight months,' said Colonel Peter Petronzio, the commanding officer of the 24th MEU. 'But what we can do is eat this elephant one bite at time, and we took a big bite and we did some great things in Garmsir, and for the people there it will be a lasting, lasting success.'

But no one knew for sure whether this success could really be conserved once the MEU left.

'When we go they'll take a swing at the British and let them know they're in town – they're not going to let them have an easy go of it,' Captain Moder predicted, while another Sergeant said, 'I hope the British can hold all of this, but I think we are instilling people with false hope.'

The following summer I met a British Army Lieutenant at KAF who had just been in Garmsir and asked him how far you could go before you run into the Taliban. He reckoned ten kilometres.

Al

I met Al in a guard tower during my stay at Delhi. Like many of the 24th MEU, he had done two tours in the Iraqi city of Ramadi

'Tufaan' dust storm sweeps into Garmsir, Helmand province.

from August 2005 to March 2006 and from August '06 to March '07.

'When I finish this it'll be 25 months in combat,' he calculates. 'This is by far the hardest deployment I've been on, Iraq is built up, living conditions are good. And this is much hotter than Ramadi because that's on the Euphrates.'

We chat and watch the dead ground and mud houses at this corner of the base. It's quiet but the suicide bomb threat is high. Al is quiet, controlled and pensive and, it turns out, a member of one of the four six-man teams of snipers that operated way out in enemy territory when the fighting was at its most intense. His profession fits him in as much as you don't imagine snipers to be extravert loudmouths – apart from anything else they are not especially liked among their own side even. Historically, theirs is viewed as a less than noble trade, the stab in the back from an invisible hand, so it's not something they tend to advertise.

'There are a number of things that get to you, it's a shitty job but somebody's got to do it,' the 25-year-old from North Virginia says.

His reflective air is due in part to things that had happened to his unit in Helmand, includ-ing the death of his best friend in an ambush. In addition to some terrifying encounters with the enemy they had to endure long days in the insanity-stoking 60-degree heat in the brushwood where they would lie motion-less for hours. Or they would hike with more than 70 kilos of equipment, including a rifle, pistol, body armour, chest rig and pouches with ammo, and the 'Ghillies', the camou-flage draping of Hessian scrim you see Tom Berenger wearing in the 'Sniper' movies. The daily ration issue was two MREs and six litres of water: 'That's not enough when you are carrying that load.'

At least the task was made simpler knowing that the civilian population had long since left the area and only the enemy remained: 'If you saw someone you knew it was "that guy".'

At night the sniper teams would probe the enemy positions, creeping forward across the farmland and scrub, not suspecting that ahead of them lay reinforced earth and log bunkers with firing slits that made the Taliban fighters practically invisible.

'We were right in their back yard and didn't know it. They had dogs chained to trees as an early warning system, or dogs in a hole, that

US Marines play American football
with British troops at FOB Delhi in
Garmsir, Helmand Province.

was really scary. As soon as the dogs started barking we got out of there.'

His team even lived in a chicken coop for a month.

'When you have chickens running over you, you know your life sucks,' he says, laughing as he remembers how a bird scampered right over the face of one of his buddies in the dark, scaring him half to death. Above all, Al's experience of Afghanistan is hallmarked by the ambush of May 19, when his unit walked into a screen of fire from concealed Taliban positions and 'All havoc broke loose, everybody was firing, it was like WWII.'

Corporal William Cooper, the second man in the advancing group, was hit at close range by Kalashnikov bullets and fell. Moving fifth, Al also 'flew back, punched in the chest' as his body armour absorbed the blow of a round. He jumped up and started pulling Cooper back with another man.

'I saw in his eyes he was unconscious, he'd gone into shock. The bullet had gone through his chest and hit every vital organ. We got him out of there but I knew him so well, I knew it by looking at him it was going to be…'

Al pauses and says nothing for a bit. He then leans out of the tower and shouts 'Hey! Stop!

No!' as some passing kids try to pull back the coils of concertina wire on the road to let a push bike through. They let go of the strands but the bike slips through anyway.

'He was a good guy. Another thing that got to me was building his memorial cross – that's something you don't expect to be doing for your best friend. It was a good cross. Things like that kind of make you want to go home.'

Al said a few words at the parting service for Cooper that was held at FOB Dwyer. Halfway through, one Marine who was generally the butt of the jokes fainted, fell over flat on his face and broke his nose.

'I'd just said Coop's whole name. That was his way of letting us know that he was still with us and that we were taking it all too seriously.'

At the service they placed his knife and dog tags with the cross, which Al says they will take back to their base at Camp Lejeune in North Carolina. There they would hold another service, send the cross off into the sea and torch it like the Vikings would do for their fallen comrades.

Same for the cross made for their Lieutenant, who in one of the most tragically random deaths among the Coalition Forces in Afghanistan that year was killed in his sleep by a collapsing roof at Dwyer when the troops were on their way to Delhi.

Al's family and girlfriend attended Cooper's funeral in the US and sent him photographs. 'I couldn't say goodbye properly, I wished I was there, but I was stuck here fighting the good fight,' says Al, who now wears a set of his buddy's dog tags with his own. 'I see that picture of him lying there over and over, get flashbacks.'

Another kid starts pulling at a fencing stake below us so Al reaches for the M240 machine gun on the ledge in front of us.

'I've got to scare him a bit,' he says, moving the weapon so the barrel jogs the scrim netting as if he's about to open fire. The boy isn't scared in the slightest and flashes a sly Afghan grin up at the tower before moving along with an 'I'll be back' air about him.

'He's the third kid who's tried to take that.' (The stake is stolen the next day, as is the metal spike strip that is now drawn across the road to puncture tyres of any vehicle that might be used to ram the compound.)

It's 1915 and dusk is falling, a tractor chugs in the nearby field and the call to prayer floats over Garmsir. I stare for a minute at the corner roofing post that has a crude skull carved into it and the scrawled inscription DEATH BE UPON YOU. Suddenly the tower radio hisses with a message that a Humvee has been blown up on patrol in the area.

'No one was killed but we just heard the weapons company ran over a landmine. Two guys got their legs mangled,' comes the clarification.

'That's the thing I hate about being here or Iraq, the IEDs, landmines, pressure plates, that's what everyone fears the most,' Al says before I feel compelled to put the inevitable question.

'I'm afraid I have to ask you this Al, did you notch up many kills?'

'I don't really like talking about that. I had a lot,' he replies. But he puts the overall tally of the sniper platoon as 83 confirmed kills and 17 possibles.

'I feel so bad, we did so much work here, gained so much ground. It's going to be hard to hold on to it. I pray for the Brits that they'll make it through. We have ten times as many forces as they'll have.'

Al's recollections of the tour have me so riveted that I'm scribbling in the dark and can't see that I'm writing on the same page twice. I will write to him when I get home but for now ask him how he sees his immediate future. He says something I have heard from other young men who have been in heavy combat.

'After being in the military I just want to have a common job when I get home, something like school teacher.'

The following April Al wrote to me:

I'm currently attending School in Northern Virginia where I grew up. I finally got the cross in January. It came over on a ship so by the time I got it I was already out of the Marines. All my friends had gone their separate ways. When we returned in October some of William's friends and I went to his parent's house and spent Thanksgiving with them. We all are heading back on Memorial Day in May; I'll bring the cross with me then and go from there. I plan to give part of the cross to his parents, and keep the rest in order to send it off to sea like I mentioned.

It's still very difficult for me to think about it. I had a friend ask me what I plan to do with my life now, and do I think about returning to the service. I told him that a part of me had died over there and it still feels like I belong over there until I feel it's time to come home. But another part of me wants to leave it behind, finish school, find a good job and raise a family. I'm not sure, but as time passes I know the pain I have will heal.

Oliver North

It's my last day in Jugroom Fort and I wait for a convoy to pick me up and take me to Dwyer. The trucks eventually pull in, it's another sweltering day in Garmsir and the other passengers have already climbed down and are standing in the shade by the time I haul my gear over. I meet two guys from Fox News and it turns out that one, Christopher Jackson, a 35-year-old cameraman from Toronto, was in the Humvee that hit a sizeable charge of homemade explosives on August 3 while I was talking to Al in the tower. One of the Marines in the front was badly injured and the top gunner was blown clean out of the hatch, but Jackson emerged unhurt.

'I'm lucky to be alive, I don't know why I am, it's just one of those things. I remember *boom*, there were flames and suddenly I found myself outside.'

All of the passengers escaped the flaming vehicle with the exception of Sgt. Courtney Rauch, who lost his lower leg in the blast and was knocked unconscious.

What Jackson omits to say is that it was he who dragged Rauch from the truck which then burned out, but his producer tips me off.

'It's what anyone would do, there were rounds cooking off in there,' the cameraman says with a shrug.

He instantly became a local hero among the Marines and for his actions he was later presented with the Distinguished Public Service Award, the second-highest award given to civilians by the Navy. But he's not too comfortable with being made into a poster boy.

We are told to mount up but they are still waiting for their presenter, a former Marine Colonel. Not being a Fox viewer it doesn't dawn on me until I'm sitting in the back and see an older man in Marine camouflage climbing up the ladder, and I get a flashback to a 1987 court scene centring on a handsome, square-jawed officer.

I quickly dredge up what I can remember about Oliver North and the Iran-Contra scandal involving the illegal sale of arms to Iran and diversion of the proceeds to rebels in Nicaragua, not a very pretty chapter in US political and military history, but I took to him immediately.

Now in his mid-60s, the retired Lieutenant-Colonel pokes fun at himself about his advancing age and lack of agility. He is extremely attentive and courteous to everyone he meets, regardless of their rank or position, and is just down to earth, despite his near superstar status in military circles.

'He washes our clothes sometimes, takes our socks and soaks them,' one of his team tells me. 'Despite all the shit that happened he's still a Marine.'

I don't remember exactly how many trips the Colonel said he made to Iraq and Afghanistan in the past few years as presenter of the channel's *War Stories with Oliver North* programme, around a couple of dozen. But he seems annoyed at himself that Jackson was in the truck that got blown up: 'I usually take the lead vehicle because I'm old and my kids are grown up,' he shouts to me over the groan of the Oshkosh engine as we drive.

Before we set off across the desert for Dwyer we stop briefly at Delhi. The first thing North does is get out his Leatherman knife and fix the broken water pump with a young Marine. The boys there are in awe of him and Master Gunnery Sergeant Garth also makes a beeline for the visitor for a chat. It's the happiest I saw him during those ten days.

We then leap and lurch along for 40 minutes in total dust madness that prompts us all to say what the hell and take photos of each other in the choking clouds, despite the inevitable clogging of our lens shutters. When we drive into the camp we pass the gutted wreck of a 1968 vintage CH-46 which, as a pilot later tells the Colonel, developed a problem with its compressor and crash-landed from 20 metres. Amazingly, the only serious injury among the full complement of people on board was a broken arm suffered by one of the pilots when the shattered rotor blade smashed the cockpit glass.

'You probably had your share of rough landings,' I shout to North.

'Shot down once, crashed twice,' he says, and with a laugh, 'If they weren't leaking they weren't flying.'

I tag along with the Fox team and for a couple of hours enjoy some red carpet treatment, or the closest Dwyer has to offer, as troops keep coming up to meet the Colonel and shake his hand.

'It's hard to do stuff on time because people always want to schmooze, but it's an important part of the job,' sighs one of his crew. 'On bases in Iraq we'd have queues of 50 soldiers waiting to have their photo taken beside him.'

Another Master Gunnery Sergeant comes up and tells us: 'I know you guys heard enough hero stories but this man here is the reason I joined the Marines.'

I'm pleased though when an officer comes up, greets the Colonel but then turns to Jackson and thanks him for pulling Rauch from the stricken truck. We then eat MREs together in the chow tent and enjoy some shade until the late afternoon when we are due to fly, they to Kandahar Airfield and I to Camp Bastion. As we walk to the flight line we pass three young British soldiers sitting by the path and North pauses and turns to them.

'Get home safely boys, thank you for your service to your country, I love you,' he says solemnly, shakes the hand of one and walks on with his now slightly stooping yet dignified stride.

I somehow doubt the Iran-Contra affair and the founder of the Freedom Alliance mean much to these lads and I chuckle at the thought of them staring behind this silver-haired guy in fatigues with FOX printed on his breast, and then a gruff Yorkshire voice saying: 'Oo the fook was that?'

We say our goodbyes and I jump on a Vietnam War-era CH-46, my fingers crossed that its compressor is in working order.

fourteen

NEGLIGENT DISCHARGE

February 2008, Maiwand District, Kandahar Province

A dawn raid on a village by the Gurkhas and ANA yields nothing except an ancient breech-loaded rifle that is found in a house. It's a cold morning and although the soldiers have searched his compound and disturbed his family, a local man invites us in to warm ourselves by his stove.

I am about to step into the room when three shots thunder right behind me. Thinking it's an ambush or an opportunist trying to bag a few infidels I jump through the doorway and then peek round the wall to see what's up.

Waheed the ANA Lieutenant accidentally loosed a burst into the ground two metres from my heels. In typical Afghan form he was swinging his cocked AK by his side with the safety off, finger on the trigger, and all it took was a slight pressure to fire the weapon as he walked. He gives me an 'oops' grin and that's that, just another negligent discharge. This I quickly learn is a speciality of the Afghans but is by no means exclusive to them.

Later that day I attend a meeting between the British Colonel and some elders. I notice that I am sitting with the muzzle of an Afghan soldier's rifle pointing at my crotch so I discreetly move out of harm's way. The weapon now points at a Canadian military historian travelling with us, but with so many firearms around, it's every man for himself when it comes to personal safety.

Two days later we move to the Maiwand district centre Hutal, where another bullet zings over our heads during a patrol through the fields, fired by a careless Police officer. The following afternoon I am talking to an Afghan truck driver who just delivered a load of water and concertina wire from Kandahar when there is an explosion across the road from our compound. We rush over to the build-ings occupied by the ANA to find the Afghan soldiers milling around and shouting. One has accidentally fired an RPG in a room full of his comrades and eight men are injured, several of them critically.

The Scottish doctor with the Gurkhas, Major Doug Reid, and two medics from the Canadian training team attached to the ANA set about helping the wounded who lie moaning or unconscious on stretchers. Because the round exploded off the room's concrete floor, most of the shrapnel injuries are to their legs and abdomen, and they will probably all be suffering from internal percussion effects. There are pools of blood and drenched field dressings all over the ground and in this chaos it strikes me how thin and puny the stricken soldiers look with their uniforms cut off them. The only heavily built man among them is their Colonel who stands to one side, grim-faced and shaking his head as the medics take turns blowing air through a tube into the lungs of the most badly hurt soldier. They hold his leg up to help stem the bleeding and a yellowy-white foot sticks out above the circle of bent backs. Despite their efforts he is clearly dying.

As the medics move between the stretchers a Canadian tells the Afghans to talk to their comrades to keep them conscious. Two don't get any pain killers – in the confusion one of the Afghan troops has stolen Reid's bag of controlled drugs, including his morphine. Another medic's first aid pack also vanished.

'This is a hell of an introduction to Afghanistan,' mutters one Canadian who has just arrived in theatre.

The blast occurred at 1220 and the medevac chopper arrives an hour and twenty minutes later. Reid has triaged the casualties to ensure those with a chance of survival are loaded and flown out first but the order is lost as the Afghans press forward and grab the stretchers.

Soviet tank wreck, Kunar
province.

The man on artificial respiration goes on before the others but is immediately called dead by the medic on board and has to be removed. The rest are taken to KAF for treatment, where I later heard from that three more died and a couple had limbs amputated.

Despite the best efforts of the foreign troops to organize the first aid and evacuation, the incident became widely known as an example of how things shouldn't happen from beginning to end. Amazingly, after such a harsh demonstration of the need for weapons safety, the ANA soldiers were found passing round a second RPG shell with a shard of shrapnel sticking out of it. British sappers made them place it on the ground, cleared the area and blew it up.

It still wasn't known how the first round detonated without the requisite few seconds of flight time to allow it to arm. Most likely the Afghans tampered with it to allow them to use it at short range.

'They are told not to do it but they put their rockets on instantaneous arming because they are nervous about the threat of attack,' Lt. Col. Bourne says in the aftermath.

But gun-toting is such a part of the male ritual in Afghanistan that it's hard to break the macho, sloppy habits of old.

'If we tell them to be careful with their weapons they just say they grew up with war and guns and know what they're doing,' complained a Gurkha Sergeant, while the Canadians could only wonder at the lack of basic drills among the troops they were supposed to knock into serviceable shape in a few weeks: 'I hate to quote the posters, but safety rules are written in blood,' one told me. 'Give these guys a little training, then maybe...'

Negligent discharges happen among the international troops too. I was told the fine for an ND among the Canadians was 1,500 dollars and about £350 ($450) for a Private in the UK forces.

A few months later I jump again when a shot cracks close by at the US Marine encampment at FOB Delhi in Garmsir, Helmand. Ironically, this ND is by a member of the sniper team, who in view of his profession you might think would never slip up like that.

'He knocked the safety-catch off as he unslung his rifle and had his finger on the trigger. Although he wasn't a shooter it makes the unit look bad,' his Corporal said. After several weeks of hard fighting and savage summer heat no charges are brought against the soldier, who works as a spotter. But for appearance's sake, he is made to dig an oil drum into the ground on a sweltering day and sandbag it as a clearing barrel.

While embedded with US forces in Kunar, I come across a 'Safetygram' pinned to the wall of the computer room which puts the NDs of the Afghans in perspective. The fact is that rounds will always be inadvertently fired wherever you have thousands of soldiers in a combat environment. But this is often due as much to screaming stupidity as careless handling of weapons, as the cited cases illustrate:

May 26, 2008 – A soldier was engaging in horseplay at an isolated FOB in Afghanistan. He pulled the trigger and discharged a round into his roommate's stomach. The injured soldier died of the gunshot.

July 1, 2008 – An Afghan Police officer approaches an RC-E medic stating that he had knee pain. The medic withdrew his pistol, jokingly pointed it at the officer's leg, pulled the trigger and the weapon discharged. The round passed through one leg and into the other. The unit reports the soldier had a history of drawing his weapon and pointing it. He had been corrected for such actions the day before the accident.

To 'hammer home the point', I saw this entry in another Safetygram:

While performing construction duties a US Service member was shot in the chest with a three-inch nail from a pneumatic nail gun. The Service member disconnected the gun from the pressure hose. The person assisting him picked it up and jokingly struck him in the chest. There was still pressure in the detached gun portion and a nail discharged into the Serviceman's chest, just missing his heart. He was flown to Germany for immediate attention and then to the US for further treatment.

fifteen

KHOST AND PAKISTAN

'To go to Khost two years ago used to mean death. Now I want it to be the model for all Afghan provinces.'

Afghan President Hamid Karzai, quoted in US Army newsletter in December 2007.

September 18, 2008

It takes four hours to fly from Islamabad to Kabul, take my body armour from storage and drive up the Shomali Valley to Bagram, where I am escorted to the Media Operations Centre (MOC) with CNN's Nic Robertson and his cameraman. I sit for the customary signing of rules of conduct and agreements to respect operational security, but this time there are *three* separate forms where I pledge that the US military will not be sued if I get killed or injured. They issue my new media badge and book me on the next day's Chinook flight to Camp Salerno in Khost province, which I last visited the previous December.

As usual I am billeted next to the MOC in the 'Hotel California', a hut with three little rooms with bunks for journalists in transit that has become a kind of home from home. Shortly before midnight I hear a repeated message over Bagram's public address system: 'There will be a fallen comrade ceremony, all available personnel are to report to Disney Drive. Taking of photos and PT kit is not authorised.'

Hundreds of mainly US and Polish troops are lined up on either side of this end of the road, the reflective sashes of the Americans gleaming in spotlights that cast a lattice of human shadows across the asphalt.

At 0020 they come to attention and salute as a Military Police car with flashing lights motors along slowly in front of six open-backed Humvees, each carrying eight US soldiers and a casket covered with the Stars and Stripes that will now be flown home for burial. These are the latest fatalities in Regional Command-East, four of whom died in an IED strike near FOB Wilderness in Paktya.

September 19

I spend the day waiting to travel, visit the PX, drink coffee and check my e-mail in the media centre where the US staff are trying to explain 'camel's toe' to the Afghan interpreter.

At 1730 I go to the Rotary Terminal where the helicopters fly from, dump my gear on a rack and take a seat with two dozen soldiers who are watching AFN television. In an ad highlighting the dangers of mental stress, the chairman of the US Joint Chiefs of Staff, Admiral Mike Mullen, insists that 'There's no shame in needing help, the shame is not asking for it.'

The Admiral has lately been busy in this part of the world. Two days earlier he was in Islamabad to discuss the fight against terrorism and to 'reiterate the US commitment to respect Pakistan's sovereignty', his embassy said.[15]

Tensions have steadily risen between the two allied governments because of repeated US drone strikes against Taliban and al-Qaeda targets inside Pakistan's tribal belt. The American military action, including the first known ground raid over the border which reportedly killed 20 people on September 3, stoked demands in Pakistan to abandon cooperation with Washington's war on terrorism. The drone attacks continued the day after Mullen's talks, prompting further protests.

Roll call for the Khost flight is at 1935 and 90 minutes later I take off in a CH-47 packed with personnel and cargo. We fly in darkness with a few tiny lights glimmering in the cockpit and a two-thirds moon that pours a watery orange glow over the hills as we chug eastward. Tired of blind flights, I scribble in my notebook WHERE ARE WE? and pass it to the door gunner who obligingly identifies each base we stop at: Phoenix, Shank, Gardez, Zormat, Sharana, Orgun-E and finally Salerno, where I'm billeted for the night in the empty media tent.

The next morning I get a briefing from a public affairs Major about the situation in the six eastern provinces covered by the US 101st Airborne Division's Task Force Currahee – Paktika, Paktya, Ghazni, Khost, Wardak and Logar. The US are the lead nation in the Area of Operations but are assisted by contingents from the Czech Republic, Turkey and Poland, some 5,500 foreign troops in total but still not enough by far to pacify this 67,000-square-kilometre expanse of mountains, valleys and plains.

'If we look at how vast this area is, we can't be everywhere,' the Major says, motioning to a large wall map of the provinces. Enemy forces are constantly on the move and although they cannot win head-on fights with ISAF, they are impossible to contain, let alone eradicate: 'You've got an ant trail and you throw a rock on it and they just go in different directions.'

The east has seen a 40 per cent rise in Taliban attacks in the previous four months compared to the preceding year. This has been partly attributed to cease-fires between the Pakistani Army and the militants, allowing the latter to send more forces this way.

Since I last visited Khost it also heated up in terms of 'kinetics', or fighting, mainly owing to the efforts of Jalaluddin Haqqani, who is regarded as the second-ranking insurgent leader after Mullah Omar. This prominent mujahedin warrior and former ally of the US against the Soviets served in the Taliban government and also led its armed forces when the US-led Operation Enduring Freedom began in October 2001.

US hopes to try to win him over again to head a splinter faction against the rest of the Taliban quickly evaporated that same month. During a trip to Pakistan, Haqqani told reporters: 'We will retreat to the mountains and begin a long guerrilla war to reclaim our pure land from infidels and free our country like we did against the Soviets…We are eagerly awaiting the American troops to land on our soil, where we will deal with them in our own way…The Americans are creatures of comfort. They will not be able to sustain the harsh conditions that await them.'[16]

So while a certain stability was attained in Khost in 2007 when Karzai spoke of it as a model, Haqqani and his allies stepped up efforts to split it away from the rest of the country in 2008. Operating from bases in the neighbouring Pakistani tribal area of North Waziristan, the Haqqani Network co-run with his son Sirajuddin hit the province intensively from May onwards.

Insurgent groups would cross the border using the old jihad transit routes known by the US military as 'rat lines'. Haqqani's men also established remote hill bases inside Khost that the US forces could only reach over vulnerable ground or through air assault missions.

Things were expected to hot up further in the overall south-eastern region in 2009 with the deployment of the 3rd Brigade of 10th Mountain Troops, bringing 3,500 more personnel to the AO. The plan envisaged that some of the extra muscle would be pushed out to new Combat Outposts (COPs), while other resources would be used to reinforce existing but lightly manned bases. According to the Major, the injection would ideally allow the reinforcement of vulnerable outposts to avoid a repeat of the incident at Wanat in Kunar province in July 2008, when 200 insurgents overran the outpost and killed nine US soldiers and injured 27.

Before I leave, the officer mentions that Narisah COP by Khost's southern border with Pakistan took 22 rockets that morning. I don't know at the time but Narisah is a good example of several problems rolled together – a remote COP under construction like Wanat, located on a major rat line over the border from insurgent bases, and far from any ground forces that could lend assistance. It's where I wind up for a week.

After the briefing I'm left in the hands of the 4-320th Field Artillery Regiment, 4th Brigade Combat Team, 101st Airborne Division ('Guns of Glory – Willing and Able'). They in turn hook me up with one of their infantry elements, Third Platoon, Delta Company, 2-506th Regiment, which is based at the Mandozai

An Afghan man rides through a dry river bed and meets a patrol led by US paratroopers of Company C, 1st Squadron, 91st Infantry Regiment, 173rd Airborne Brigade Combat Team and ANP near the village of Bakshikhala in Kherwar district, Logar province, April 12, 2010. *US Army photo by Sgt Russell Gilchrest*

district centre, located in farmland 40 minutes drive west of Salerno and Khost city.

I'm joining a unit with an illustrious history, the descendants of the famous 'Band of Brothers' that was led by Captain Dick Winters from the hell of the 1944 D-Day landings through the defence of Bastogne to the capture of the Eagle's Nest redoubt of Adolf Hitler in the Bavarian Alps in 1945.

Outside Battalion HQ I'm shown to one of four parked Humvees by Platoon Sergeant First Class Ryan Hendricks, a big burly son of Alabama who likes to throw apocalyptic one-liners into the mix, probably for the benefit of embedded reporters.

'One IED hit in the centre and you're all dead. But don't worry, we'll take care of you,' he tells me with a broad grin as I get in the back seat. Ours is the lead truck and tows a large, full fuel tank in a trailer, so if we do get blown up it will be spectacular.

In the front is Lieutenant Shane Oravsky, a slight, easy-going 25-year-old from New York state, who says the road is paved so there's no big IED threat apart from a couple of pits where they could be planted. But the drive through the city itself is dodgy at this time of day. I tell him that the previous December the main worry was kids throwing stones at the US trucks by the university.

'Things have changed a bit since then,' Oravsky replies.

We leave Salerno at 1700. The top gunner swivels the turret with a clatter of ratchet and bearings, his .50-cal trained on the tall grass and pines that surround the base and with an eye also on dozens of local workers streaming out of the gate and a few arriving for the night shift.

Memories are still fresh of the August 18 incident when multiple suicide bombers attacked Salerno in unison from different directions. Some were cut down before they could detonate their charges, one killed 10 civilians and wounded 13. ISAF later said seven insurgents were killed, three when they detonated suicide vests and four others by troops, while the Afghan Defence Ministry said 13 suicide bombers died.

The autumn sun is descending fast as we pass through the concrete blast walls and razor wire cordons on the perimeter. Hills rise in the distance behind flat expanses of ploughed land that are dotted with flocks of sheep, goats and mud compounds. While much lusher than the deserts of Helmand and Kandahar, the Khost Bowl is still recovering from scorching summer heat and the cornfields are struggling to push up the next crop.

More Afghan guards sit by a row of shops watching as we turn onto the main road where clamouring, gap-toothed kids give us the thumbs up. The civilian traffic obediently pulls over as the Humvees cruise along three kilometres of paved road into the provincial capital, passing mud-brick kilns with blackened chimneys and a big billboard with a picture of the provincial football team in yellow jerseys. As the working day comes to an end, local men sit hunched at the roadside and stare as we drive into Khost City. The stalls get denser and mingle with lines of metal containers, JCB excavator parks and wood depots that have vertical stacks of neatly graded boughs. Further into the city we pass messy quarters of mud-brick shops and houses and a few squat, plastered five-storey buildings protected by high walls and metal gates.

The convoy passes down the main two-lane carriageway with a central reservation of bare earth and eucalyptus trees. But I can't see the curious sight that caught my eye in December, a large swinging longboat fairground attraction that rocked frantically near the bazaar under the weight of dozens of Afghan men.

It's still busy at 1730 as we cruise through the 'Have a Safe Journey' gateway at the other side of town and past crowds of youths and men by the Al Nahyan University, built with money donated by the late president of the United Arab Emirates. The roadside stalls give way to car dealerships with yards full of Toyota saloons, jingle truck repair shops and some fortified Police checkpoints, before we are flanked only by fields and tiny villages.

The vanishing sun is now perched on a hilltop, creating an oddly charged and brooding twilight that I can't fathom. Fifteen minutes later the trucks pass a skinny dog with the usual beaten air of Afghan canines and weave into the Mandozai COP through the staggered Hescos that should slow suicide car bombers.

Located beside the offices of the district sub-Governor, Police, doctor and vet, the COP is a small walled compound with a one-storey central block labelled the 'Dawghouse'. There are two operations rooms, a kitchen and dining area and a couple of long side rooms and outhouses where the platoon sleeps. There's just enough room in the yard to park the Humvees and a five-ton truck, and altogether the COP measures about 40 metres

squared and is secured by rooftop sentries and video cameras.

Dusty brown patterned sofas and armchairs in the cramped dining area surround a television and beside them juts a Chinese-made 82mm recoilless rifle on a stand, a trophy from the platoon's August raid of an insurgent camp in the Qalandar district to the north. Their armourer, Specialist Merriman, is wiping down the weapon as I comment on its good condition.

'It's in good condition because they were using it to shoot at us.'

The other weapon they found on the operation, fully loaded and pointing toward the US helicopter landing zone, was a DShK, a Russian-made Degtyarov-Shpagin 12.7mm heavy machine-gun. This piece went back with the Afghan troops who accompanied them, but according to local information and judging from the ammunition recovered there are still two of these crew-served weapons up there, including a 14.5mm variant that the troops call the 'Super-DShK'. The thought of these visibly troubles members of the platoon because they can potentially bring down the Chinooks on the next air assault into Qalandar. The August raid also saw the capture of a handful of scared Pakistanis who were left behind at the camp while the main insurgent force went down to the plains for the attack on Salerno two days earlier.

I meet the company's outgoing commanding officer, Captain Nicholas Howard, a friendly, almost too confidently spoken young man who tells me I 'came at an interesting time'. I don't know if he means the next day's transfer of command ceremony, some upcoming operation or the general activation of the insurgents in the company's AO.

I still have no real idea of the dynamic of where I am but can tell that Qalandar is the main hornets' nest and source of trouble. Howard estimates there are a couple of hundred of Haqqani's men up in the mountains.

'We think they are partially funded by…' he begins, but leaves the sentence unfinished.

Over the next few weeks I hear numerous officers and soldiers claim that Pakistan's ISI intelligence service assists the insurgents based in the hills. It's the kind of assertion that sparks instant outrage in Pakistani political and military circles, with authorities in Islamabad vehemently denying any links with the Taliban and Haqqani.

But out here it seems to be taken as common knowledge that Pakistan is involved at some state or semi-state level, possibly through rogue elements in the ISI that used to work closely with the Taliban when the regime ruled Afghanistan. Pakistan was, after all, one of three countries to formally recognize the Taliban government before its demise in 2001, together with Saudi Arabia and the United Arab Emirates. The soldiers even refer to the Qalandar site as the 'ISI camp' and I'm told that documents were found that directly implicated the intelligence service. While browsing Haqqani in the internet, I find a reference to a demand supposedly made by the CIA in the summer that the ISI leadership explain apparent evidence of links with the militant group. I ask about this in Khost and hands wave in the direction of Qalandar: 'It all came from up there.' The next May, US Secretary for Defense Robert Gates directly linked Pakistani intelligence with the insurgents.

'They're maintaining contact with these groups, in my view, as a strategic hedge,' he told *60 Minutes*. They are not sure who's going to win in Afghanistan. They are not sure what's going to happen along that border area, so to a certain extent they play both sides.'[17]

Generally, Pakistan has an intangible, almost mythical quality for the US soldiers, who cannot set foot there unless it's in hot pursuit of a fleeing insurgent group, and then only for a few kilometres under an existing but little publicised agreement with Islamabad. A running joke they never tire of is likening Waziristan to a kind of Mordor-like entity, with three red suns and skies dotted with harnessed pterodactyls ridden by Pashtun tribesmen who spit death from DShKs mounted on the beasts' wings.

I want to have a chat with Howard before he leaves and I join him at dinner. Today the platoon's cook, Sgt. Jonathan Brodeur, has done steaks and people are cautiously trying a new addition to the condiments, a rack of absurdly hot sauces called 'Dave's Insanity Gourmet'. Last in ascending order of potency, the fifth bottle bears a black label that says

'Warning: use this product one drop at a time. Keep away from eyes, pets and children. Not for people with heart or respiratory problems.'

On a high about his move to a new command, Howard scoffs at the danger, puts three drops on one bite of steak and swallows it. Nothing happens for a few seconds and then he flushes fiery beetroot, chokes, jumps up and runs off and is not seen for the rest of the meal.

He later invites the soldiers to join him for farewell cigars and near-beer around a fire in the yard and a few of us sit puffing and watching the flames, the cigar and wood smoke mingling with a dusty tang that permeates everything. I now understand the weird murky sunset of earlier as Khost gets what I'm told is a typical summer storm, no rain but sheet and ball lightning flashing on the horizon and yielding later to a clear, star-laden sky.

'I can whine as much as I like about not having enough men but you just have to make do,' the Captain says. 'We're just about treading water and waiting for them to empty the pool,' he adds, meaning the authorities in Pakistan, where many insurgents come from, working out of remote training and logistics hubs in the tribal belt. This high level of insurgent activity was at least finally acknowledged in 2008 by the new leadership in Islamabad after years of contemptible denials by the government of ex-president Pervez Musharraf that there were any militant camps in Pakistan.

According to the platoon's intelligence officer, the insurgent bonus pay rate is 26 dollars per mission across the border. Even if nothing else deters this traffic, Howard wonders if the one-day Muslim burial rites complicate things, forcing the insurgents to rush their dead back to villages in Pakistan before sunset.

'Maybe they'll look at the 26 dollars and think twice about having their soul stranded in Afghanistan away from their tribal homeland,' he says.

Meanwhile, shocking news is coming in from Pakistan, for me at least. Earlier that day terrorists crashed a suicide truck bomb into the Marriott Hotel in Islamabad, killing 53 people, including the Czech Ambassador, two US Marines and a Danish intelligence officer. More than 250 were injured in the attack, which was thought to be retribution

Humvee of Delta Company, US 2-506th
Airborne Infantry drives through hostile village of
Shembowat, Khost province, September 2008.

by the Taliban for Pakistani military operations against its strongholds in the tribal belt.

On September 21 a helicopter brings Brigade Commander Col. John Johnson and Battalion Commander Lt. Col. David Ell for the change of command ceremony, which is also attended by the district's Afghan sub-Governor from next door. The soldiers carry the captured 82mm rifle outside and place it in front of the rostrum for added solemnity, and after a few speeches Howard passes the company's flag to the new commanding officer, Captain Ricardo Bravo.

Later it is decided to postpone the day's planned mission to pick up a low-level Taliban thug who was repeatedly detained in the past but always had to be turned loose for lack of evidence. He will get a visit the next morning instead.

That night there is a further incident at the border where Pakistani security forces and tribesmen reportedly shot at intruding US helicopter gunships, forcing them to turn back. Military spokesmen later denied the clash or any violation of Pakistani airspace by US aircraft.

Two days later a US drone crashes in South Waziristan, reportedly shot down by tribesmen and Pakistani troops. On September 25, NATO and the Pakistani military confirm that their forces exchanged fire on the Khost border by North Waziristan, so right in our area. Pakistan again alleges that its soldiers opened fire on helicopters that crossed the border while ISAF denies any violation of airspace.[18] This is the week when Secretary Gates tells members of the Senate Armed Services Committee in Washington that the United States faces committed enemies in the tribal areas of Pakistan and until those safe havens are removed, insecurity and violence will persist.

'If you asked me today, after the successes that we have had against al-Qaida in Iraq where the greatest threat to the homeland lies, I would tell you it is in western Pakistan,' he said.[19]

In turn, Pakistan's new president, Asif Ali Zardari declares, 'We cannot allow our territory and sovereignty to be violated by friends.'[20]

And all the while, things are hotting up in the 'model province' of Khost.

September 22

At 0600 the four trucks leave to drive a few kilometres north to pick up the Taliban suspect from his home, although people expect him to get tipped off in good time to disappear.

We roll out of Mandozai and together with two ANP Ranger pick-ups head across the plain in the early morning haze, passing some Cuchi nomad tents, herds of goats and a few camels. First the vehicles have to go through Shembowat, a hostile market town where insurgent activity is high and where they often plant IEDs to try and catch the US and ANP vehicles. Shembowat is a filthy sprawl of mud houses, stalls and rutted, unpaved streets where scores of young men stare and scowl as we crawl through, drivers and gunners scanning the road for signs of an ambush or IEDs.

Twenty minutes later the column pulls up in the hill-flanked wadi that runs north. With no homes around, the troops test fire their weapons, sending up a roaring barrage from two M240 machine-guns, the .50-cal and the Mark 19 automatic grenade launcher. The Afghan Police also open up with their AKs, and one officer fetches an RPG launcher and fires an armoured piercing round at the facing slope.

We mount up again and drive on for another half hour, passing logging trucks and tractors and a few houses and corn plots on the river banks. There is a slight trickle of water in places along the makeshift road, which winds through narrow choke points between steep inclines, perfect sites for an enemy attack from the high ground.

I can feel the tension growing now, this is also only a few kilometres short of Qalandar and the spot where the platoon was ambushed by an estimated 150-plus insurgents on July 20, when their executive officer Lt. Nick Dewhirst was killed by an RPG.

At 0720 the trucks park and the troops dismount and prepare to walk up the path to the suspect's house on the hill. Suddenly he appears, a medium-set young man with a styled head of dark, full hair worthy of a Vidal Sassoon model, who flashes us a welcoming smile and extends his hand to Lt. Oravsky. If he had been hoping to deflect the visitors with charm he is mistaken, and with escape now denied to him he trails morosely behind the Police and US troops as they climb up to his little stone house. At the top the ambiguous mood suddenly shifts to rage as the ANP start pummelling him with fists and boots.

A search of his shed has turned up two men from a neighbouring village who are chained together by the ankles. As they are released they tell the Afghan interpreter that the man abducted them nine days earlier and was demanding $15,000 ransom from their families. There is a lot of shouting and the accused is finally knocked to the ground by the Police. He is still yammering in protest and now starting to annoy one of the Americans who shushes him with the warning, 'Scumbag, I don't want to hear you talk!'

The man is taken into custody by a 26-year-old Police officer called Arafat, who has a strong, bulbous nose and neatly trimmed black beard. Smartly uniformed and wearing helmet and body armour, Arafat is a favourite among the US soldiers for his fearlessness in fire fights with the insurgents.

The new detainee and another young man, supposedly his driver, have their hands taped and are blindfolded and marched down the hill. He continues to bleat until Arafat hops onto one foot and deals him a kick to the head with the other, looks at me and says, 'No problem, Afghanistan good.' This time the man holds his tongue as the cops shove him and his accomplice into the back of one Ranger and help their victims into the other.

'We're doing good things today, we just saved their lives,' observes Dave McNeil, a tall, ginger-haired Staff Sergeant with a quick and tireless tongue and plenty of combat experience under his belt. The convoy sets off back down the wadi towards Shembowat. It's quite likely someone laid some IEDs for us in the last hour and the column stops at a suspect pile of rocks that could mark a plant. The Police dismount, spread out and advance on foot, scouring the river bed for wires and pressure plates while the trucks creep along behind. To our surprise we see that the two kidnap victims have been given rifles and are walking with the cops.

Back in Mandozai we prepare to drive that night 15 kilometres west to Dwawmanda, the Sabari District Centre where Fourth Platoon is stationed. Third will mind the DC for a few days while Fourth flies to the border and relieves a US detachment from Tani who have been holding the Narisah COP construction site.

Before we leave Mandozai they get yet another warning of an impending attack with a VBIED (vehicle-borne improvised explosive device), a massive car bomb the insurgents are supposed to be assembling for use against Dwawmanda. It's only the latest of many such tip-offs but they have to take it seriously.

'Let's hope we don't get blown up this week, that would be cool,' says Lt. Oravsky, who thinks that if the warning is accurate it will be the enemy's 'last hurrah' before winter. There are also reports of hundreds of gunmen moving up through Spera in the southwest. 'But they always exaggerate,' he adds.

Then again, there was the 100-man insurgent night raid on Spera in the summer when the District Centre was almost captured. A Predator drone circling overhead filmed the attackers storm one of the ANP observation posts and hack off the head of a captured officer. Then, inexplicably, they pulled out in a long neat line along the nearby wadi, presenting the arriving Apache gunships with a neat turkey shoot with their 30mm cannons. More than 70 dead militants were counted in the river bed the next day.

Night of Power

The soldiers watch an episode of *Dr Phil* in the dining area before mounting up and driving to Dwawmanda shortly after midnight. It's dark when we arrive at the austere 'home' of Fourth Platoon, a small, fortress-like compound perched on the edge of a ravine.

As the platoons bustle around in preparation for the changeover I stand in the hall and read the snake posters on the wall, surprised to see how many deadly nasties live in Khost: two species of cobra, kraits and Russell's vipers. Soldiers from this outpost tell me how during

recent building work in the COP an Oxus cobra reared up from inside a roll of roofing paper they had just carried into their compound, and had to be killed with a shovel. I am to go with Fourth Platoon to Narisah as Third will stay inside the Dwawmanda DC for the next four days and not do any patrols.

'You can choose between being killed by a car bomb or a rocket,' Lt. Oravsky offers, only half-joking. Neither option appeals but since I want to get up to the border I pick Narisah.

At 0300 I get in one of the trucks which drive down to secure the helicopter landing zone in the wide river bed beneath the compound. The night is clear with a half moon and the only signs of life are a few vehicle lights up on the new 100-million-dollar main road that passes through the DC, linking Khost with Gardez in Paktya province and then Kabul. It's called the K-G Pass and was the route that Haqqani's group successfully denied to the Soviets in the 1980s, effectively cutting off Khost from the rest of the country. Today he has the same goal, hence the high insurgent activity in these parts.

I wait in the wadi with my backpack among the shadowy figures of the soldiers until the Chinook lands, blasting up such a storm of grit that we are blinded and buffeted as our group of 18 grabs the gear and boards for the ten-minute flight south. Apart from me and the interpreter, there are 16 US soldiers, a tiny number to defend a strategic object against potential groups of 200 attackers, as happened at Wanat. It could be worse: with men on leave the platoon typically only has a dozen on any given patrol or flight.

Narisah COP is built in the form of a short fat arrow, an 80-metre-wide square of double-stacked Hesco walls with another broader triangular section up flush against one of its sides. We land inside the triangle at first light, leave our packs and quickly move out and round through the wire to occupy the square. Barely visible in the gloom, the departing US and Afghan troops run onto the Chinook and return to their base in Tani, and Fourth Platoon inherits its half-completed castle. They spent plenty of time here before but my first impression is of about as bleak a place as I've stayed in. The COP walls are finished but in places already lean at a wonky slant, with some Hescos holed and torn open by rocket bursts. There are no towers or gate yet, just a 15-metre wide gap in the wall that is blocked with concertina wire. Nor is there is any solid accommodation, just two large tents with cots set up beside a small concrete rocket shelter, a generator and piles of MREs and cases of water. Three MRAP trucks stand idly around the square.

As it gets light the platoon leader, Lieutenant Gabe Stultz, a humorous 'dip' tobacco-chewing 24-year-old from Pittsburgh, Pennsylvania, cusses the mess left by the departed occupants. Food remnants and MRE bags are strewn everywhere and the single portable toilet cabin is so smeared with excrement that he gets someone to dig a trench behind the fuel trailer until it can be cleaned up.

One of the Sergeants finds four grenades, a walkie-talkie, a SMAW-D rocket and a night vision sight dumped on top of the Hesco berms. No one has bothered to reinforce the corners of the square that the last detachment used as sentry points, and piles of empty sandbag sleeves lie around trodden into the dirt. The general impression is one of shitty hygiene and shittier soldiering, and the platoon does a lot of swearing as it clears up.

Stultz immediately pushes two of the guard positions out from the square to the corners of the longer adjoining triangle base. This now gives each of those sentries a clear field of view right down the COP, connecting from either side of the apex of the triangle. Neglecting this was a key error of the last group's security and did not go unnoticed by those watching us. By placing men only on the points of the square, the last commander created a huge blind spot around the sides of the triangle, one of which is near the entrance. The Lieutenant says our predecessors here were not infantrymen but rather a maintenance detachment that shared the tedious job of guarding the COP while it was being built.

'Their platoon leader told me he'd mastered infantry skills in the two weeks he'd been doing this,' he says, annoyed also by the request of the departing group to 'keep it clean' during our stay.

There isn't too much to see over the Hescos, just a plain to the north-east and a couple of kilometres of dead ground before the hills rise in the southeast toward the border with Pakistan, located six kilometres down the facing pass.

It looks quiet enough but this is the place that took 22 Chinese-made 107mm rockets on the day I arrived in Khost. A pile of jagged shrapnel and bent motors lying by one of the tents reminds that we are in someone's sights.

'Let's hope we get rocketed so you have something to write about,' Stultz says dryly, while a Sergeant adds, 'Let's pray we don't, that's some bad shit. If we do get rocketed, hide in the shelter or behind the Hescos, like they told us in Iraq, adopt the foetal position and wait for it to be over.'

The platoon spends half an hour gathering and burning the garbage and then I go with a couple of men who try to start one of the trucks. Neither has MRAP training and they just stare blankly at the space-age console and randomly poke at the controls in the hope of turning over the engine.

'Dude, you might as well put me in a helicopter, there are billions of buttons up here,' one calls to his buddy.

The soldiers are busy through the day and by nightfall the outpost has some semblance of military order. Even the toilet is serviceable, although faced with the flies and stench of the oil drum that catches the waste, I decide to stick to the spot behind the fuel trailer. Just before 0200 I'm dozing on my cot with my iPod on when there are some blasts and shots. I sit up to see the soldiers throwing on their kit and running to their positions.

'There's something going on,' is all I get from Stultz, whose cot is opposite mine.

I kit up and climb the ladder to the nearest corner post and sit beside Corporal Frank from Alaska who is manning the M240 machine-gun that points across the plain toward the border.

It's not clear what happened but there's no incoming fire and we wait in silence, staring into the darkness. The stars are out and a few house lights glimmer in the distance but the hills in front of us that denote Pakistan are a solid inky mass.

We hear that someone tried to sneak through the wire toward the gateway but was sent running by fire from a soldier manning the new post Stultz set up. Within a few minutes a couple of Apaches buzz past and scan the area, having been on patrol near the COP when the incident occurred. They circle for 20 minutes and leave, and when the Lieutenant gives the order to stand down at 0300 it's clear that the platoon has just been probed by the enemy.

Specialist Adam Schreib was on duty when he spotted four moving blobs through his night vision equipment. The images sharpened into four men with rifles who had crawled up and were pulling on the outer cordon of wire about 50 metres from the Hescos. In accordance with regulations on escalation of force, he shouted before opening fire.

'At first it seemed like dogs so I didn't do anything,' Schreib tells me later. 'Once they got closer to the wire, I thought that's not right, then I saw their heads and AKs so I started yelling, fired a couple of shots and then two .203 (under barrel grenade-launcher) rounds. They got up and ran like crazy.'

There's no mystery why they came directly toward the front gate – someone had worked out the blind spot under the security arrangements of the last detachment and intended to use it to get in.

'They could have taken out the corner guard and 30 more guys could have followed them in a heart beat,' Stultz reflects later. 'One man with an AK wouldn't even need to go into the tent; he could have just sprayed it from here and shot the guys while they were still lying in bed.'

The next day we learn that back at the Tani detachment's base someone even climbed most of the way up one of the watch towers that same night but was spotted and chased off by Afghan soldiers.

There is a disused school located about 200 metres directly in front of the gate which Stultz thinks the enemy are using as an observation post. It's also quite possible that while the four crawled up, a larger force was waiting behind the building ready to rush up in support if the first group made it to the gate. No one is surprised that the insurgents have such a close working knowledge of the area around the COP. During the day they can send unarmed people posing as shepherds and villagers along the track past the school, check out the route and generally spy on the

Americans. Again it's the old dilemma, if they don't have weapons, there's nothing much that can be done about them.

'The enemy have the luxury of being able to observe the pattern of life in the compound, see that we don't wear body armour when walking around inside, that the tower isn't manned until whatever time, where the toilet is and so on,' Stultz says.

The incident sharply focuses the need for attention before the next evening, which in this fasting week of Ramadan is known as Lailat al-Qadr, or the 'Night of Power'. In the Muslim faith, this is the anniversary of the night the first verses of the Koran were revealed to the Prophet Mohammed.

The defenders of Narisah COP are told by their superiors that the insurgents regard it as a good night to meet their maker, thereby demanding extra vigilance by the platoon. Just as Wanat was probed before the attack in July that inflicted mass US casualties, the move on the corner post could precede something much bigger on this special date. The next day I go out with Stulz and three other soldiers to inspect the school. They search the rooms and whip their rifles round in unison when an old man with a long white beard appears.

We gather he's the day watchman and call out the platoon's Afghan translator to talk to him. The man says he knows nothing about the previous night's events but that the night watchman might know something. The soldiers also tense up when a Toyota pulls up to the wire near the school and a man gets out and starts towards us. They make him lift his shirt to show he's not wired to blow up and let him approach.

He proves to be the contractor who is building the COP and asks if he can bring in a truck with his men and some guards and stay overnight. It's a timely offer and adds several more rifles to the overall defences before any Night of Power antics coming our way. The platoon already has Claymore mines set up at strategic positions around the COP walls, each of the devices ready to riddle attackers with 700 ball bearings propelled at supersonic speed by its 650-gram plastic explosive charge.

They dig in flares at an improvised HLZ inside the square for helicopters that may arrive to collect wounded, sandbag the firing positions on the Hescos for extra protection and zero in their weapons, firing at a board standing in the corner of the compound.

Stultz and Platoon Sergeant First Class Chandler discuss how to place the soldiers. Not including the few Afghans, their force of 16 men will barely stretch around the 300-metre perimeter.

'I don't want to concentrate too many of us in one place in case they get a lucky hit,' says the Sergeant, while the Lieutenant points out that 'If one man at the corner gets shot in the neck he's not going to be able to tell the others.'

The platoon is getting ready for a big attack and I wonder what I'll do if turbaned figures race in the gate with blazing weapons. Most likely get brutally murdered, since I don't reckon my chances of averting it by holding up my press card. Consciously preparing to break the reporter's obligation not to carry arms, I go to Stultz when he's alone and ask, 'If things get really bad can you make sure I get a weapon?'

'If things get really bad there will be weapons lying around,' he replies.

The interpreter, a good-natured lad of 20 the Americans call Prince has an AK that they gave him once he'd earned their trust. This is officially frowned upon and if interpreters are injured or killed while carrying weapons they don't get any insurance payouts. But some feel safer and carry them anyway – their chances are definitely not good if they get captured. Prince calls to the soldiers working up on the Hescos and asks for oil for his rifle, so they take a break from the work to tease him.

'Prince, if you kill any of my guys on the Night of Power so you can get to Heaven quicker, you ain't going to Heaven,' one of the Sergeants shouts down. 'I'm going to find a way to get you out of the country and then I'm going to torture you for the next 30 years, I'll take you to the edge of death and then get you better and start over again, you'll spend the next 30 years in agony.'

'First we'll strip you, cover you in honey and put you on an ants nest,' joins in another.

Prince just laughs, flashes a big white-toothed grin and calls them all mother fuckers. He learned fluent English over the border in Peshawar during the Taliban's rule and his American-Pakistani accented cursing amuses the men as they debate the fabled rewards of a warrior's death on this day.

'They are supposed to get 72 virgins times 72 so it's a good night for them to die,' ventures Chris Nelson, a chirpy Sergeant with a resemblance to actor Mark Wahlberg. He is adjusting the telescopic sight on his M14 rifle, not exactly a sniper's weapon but far more accurate than the M4s that most of the soldiers carry.

'There's no 72 virgins dude, you don't go to Heaven until Judgement Day,' Prince objects. 'Your soul just goes out of your body and goes wherever it goes.'

As I work on my laptop in one of the tents, Sgt. Bruce Hunter comes up and asks me, 'You ready for the Night of Power?'

Aged 27, he's a big beefy guy who I suspect has a serious temper when wound up, but fortunately we get on OK.

'You expecting trouble then?' I ask.

'They already probed us, just like they did at Wanat.'

Hunter says he was overrun at Najaf in Iraq and wounded twice. He walks a bit unevenly, the result of a ruptured eardrum from an RPG burst, which damaged his sense of equilibrium.

'I preferred it in Iraq although I lost a lot of friends there. It was an urban fight, more fast paced, more chances to kill the enemy – here they shoot at you from a ridge and you'll never catch up with them.'

On his right arm he has a tattoo of a rifle dug into the ground with a helmet over the stock, a pair of combat boots and dog tags hanging on a chain with the names of six of his Army buddies who died in combat since 2005. He says he has five more names to add below. Like many of the American soldiers he's frustrated by the Rules of Engagement (ROE) they must abide by: 'The amount of guys who got killed because they were afraid to shoot, I can count 20 in Iraq, and then some here.'

He seems quaintly set on convincing me he's nuts, or maybe he just is. Later when he passes on the way back from the toilet he points at the M4 slung over his shoulder and says, 'Isn't that a thing of beauty?'

What is clear is that the platoon is actually spoiling for a good fight to break the tedium of Narisah.

Soldier of Delta Company, US 2-506th Airborne Infantry watches Taliban infiltration route from Pakistan, Narisah COP, Khost province, September 2008. The Taliban probing attempt described came from the school building ahead of the position.

'I hope they try it,' Nelson says to me. 'We're close to the border so it's easy for them to bring up men and rockets. They've threatened to destroy this place many times but didn't do anything yet. You're here at the right time.'

Lt. Stultz tells me that his Command are looking into the previous night's incident to ensure it was handled correctly. He gets Platoon Sergeant Chandler to gather the men and read out the rules on the escalation of force. It can't be put in print for security reasons, although it's widely believed that the enemy know the ROE to the letter. Chandler reassures Schreib that he did everything just right.

'And whatever other regulations there are you always have the right to defend yourself,' he reminds them all.

I am frankly amazed that there can be such worry at recriminations after four men with rifles crawled up and tried to enter a base at night.

'ISAF ROE are choking us,' says Stultz, adding that his bosses would object to battle preparations like zeroing in weapons inside the perimeter, even though to do this outside now would be inviting trouble.

'There are steps of escalation and they don't appreciate that sometimes we need to jump right through them. I'm here to help win a war and get my men home alive, whatever it takes, and if people don't like that they can go and fuck themselves. Respectfully.'

I ask if he'd like their enemy to attack now.

'Hell yes, this is ideal, we're in static positions, not trying to take a shot while bouncing around in a truck, we know where the enemy's coming from, and we'd have to hold out for 20 minutes before the Apaches get here and start cleaning them up. I don't care if there are 200 of them, my guys have had their share of bad ambushes, they'll fight hard.'

It gets dark and we wait and wait and nothing happens. That's life at the front. Our four-day stay is extended to September 28 and for the next two nights the soldiers are on alert and must sleep in their boots.

On the Friday Staff Sergeant Eric McWilliams says they had reports of a couple of hundred insurgents with mortar tubes beyond the next village, and although it's most probably a false alarm he also brightens at the prospect of them moving on the COP.

'We've got machine-guns on the corners, if we cut down 40 or 50 of them that would dissuade the rest and they'd turn tail.'

Orders come down to double the guard. That evening I put on my body armour and Kevlar, climb up onto the Hescos and join Sergeants Nelson and Smith, who have a six-hour shift at the Mark 19 grenade launcher. The conversation jumps between Afghanistan and Iraq, pets, cars and women. I explain how you get your porn star name (name of first pet and mother's maiden name), and so that evening Hamish Batson, Dude Mueller and Buster Labart sit in the tower and talk for six hours.

'I've been shot at, IED'd , RPG'd, rocketed and suicide bombed,' Nelson says. 'I haven't been car bombed yet, I'm still waiting for that.' (It happened the following March, resulting in two KIA and another man seriously injured.)

I think Nelson's five IED strikes and survival is plenty enough until Smith counts his – ten in all and nary a scratch. He could be understood for being a bit rueful since the State of Texas would automatically pay for his son's education if he wins a Purple Heart medal for a combat injury. But no one in their right mind wishes for injury here.

Over the radio comes a report that a group of men is moving toward the COP from beyond the nearest village.

'Grow some balls…just one rocket even,' Nelson growls. 'We've had a thousand threat warnings, we get kitted up and nothing. I'd like one to be confirmed.'

September 27

The NCOs overturn the toilet cabin while one of the soldiers is inside. I come out of the tent to investigate the howls of laughter and see Specialist Burgess crawling out with his pants round his ankles. But thankfully for him the drum underneath isn't attached to the booth. The soldiers spend another day doing guard duty, eating, sleeping, playing cards and watching movies on their PSPs.

September 28

I pack early in readiness to leave, then our relief is pushed back another day. The mood isn't too good, we've been out here six days now and because Dwawmanda's shower unit broke over a week before they came to Narisah, some of the soldiers have forgotten what hot water is. We all stink.

It's not even the primitive conditions or the amount of time here that bothers them so much as the lack of available time this will leave before the start of the next scheduled operation. On October 1 both platoons are due to fly from Salerno right up to the border at Narisah on a three-day operation.

'We'll go back to Salerno and they'll send us up into the mountains without even having showers,' someone predicts.

By contrast, plenty of people are happy around us as today is the last day of the Muslim fasting month of Ramadan. At dusk dozens of fires appear on the hills to the west and north and singing and music can be heard along with the distant crackle of gunfire. We watch as streams of red tracer rounds fly across the sky in an impromptu display of fast-free joy.

'Waste that shit, it's less to shoot at us with,' says Stultz, who is standing near the gate watching for any signs of hostility in our direction. 'It's going away from us but if it comes this way we'll give them something to celebrate about,' he tells someone over the radio and then turns to me.

'If they want to attack tonight, bring it on, all they'll find behind these walls is a load of aggravated mother fuckers!'

September 29

We get up at 0515 and prepare to leave. The Chinook arrives three hours later, drops off the Tani crew once more and flies us out. Three hours after that the COP takes eight 107mm rockets, two of which land by the fuel trailer and obliterate my improvised bathroom.

A week later I run into two of the Tani guys on Salerno. They are not only convinced the enemy are watching the COP round the clock but that they also know exactly which platoon is manning the outpost, presumably because their spies monitor movement in and out of the platoon bases. The maintenance unit knows it is regarded as the weakest link by the insurgents. As they started to position their sentries after relieving Fourth Platoon they even heard the Taliban say over the radio, 'We'll never get a better chance than this.' But the ground attack didn't come.

Night of Powerlessness

September 30

Mandozai comes to life at 0430 as Third Platoon gets ready to leave for Salerno for the start of Operation Rat Trap, a helicopter drop at the border beyond Narisah COP to hamper enemy infiltration. The soldiers do the usual weapons drills on the trucks before setting out and get a pre-op briefing from Oravsky and Hendricks.

'This time around were going to Narisah COP, not to the COP itself but to the mountain where we got rocketed and mortared before, on the back side of that near the Pak border is where we're going,' the Platoon Sergeant says, digging at the earth with his knife to illustrate.

'Lately they've been rocketing and mortaring Narisah COP extensively, they just got hit with rockets yesterday and twice when we've been there and that one time when we got hit with 25 rounds. So they're trying to move in, they've probed the COP with a recon element. Now we're going to be at two OPs, we'll infil on one, stay for a couple of days, get picked up by the birds and go to the next. That's

going to be the real hairy one, we're going to be somewhere up by the Pakistani border and we could find ourselves in the shit on this one, unlike when we were in Spera and just ran into a few dudes. We're going to be near the border where the Taliban and their little al-Qaeda buddies come back and forth because they've got that rat line and all that AO to come and do what they've got to do, and they know they can get back into Pakistan real quick before we can bring the rain on them.

'We'll have 10 ANA with us this time, it's not a whole lot but hopefully we can get some more, we'll do what we've got to do, shoot up what we've got to shoot up if need be, and get back home.'

'We're a small element, if it comes to the point where we're outnumbered and out-gunned well find a spot, we'll Alamo up and fight to the last. No surrender, it's like I said before, you'll get your head lopped off with that dull butter knife, on video, so you might as well go down fighting.'

The troops start to mount up for the drive to Salerno where they will hook up with Fourth Platoon before the air assault starts the next morning.

'The Alamo didn't really work out for those guys, they got fucked – I think we should find another fortress comparison,' Staff Sgt. McNeil points out.

An hour later on the main base they empty the trucks, stow all the weapons and ammo and leave the vehicles parked up. The new Captain has upset a few people by ordering dry rehearsals of boarding and deplaning from the Chinook. They've done this many times before but he's concerned about keeping it smooth with 10 ANA soldiers in the mix with each platoon.

The US and Afghan soldiers meet and greet each other before moving to the flight line under the already beating sun and then run on and off a stationary Chinook several times before Captain Bravo is satisfied.

I'm racked with worry at this stage, not at the thought of the operation but because the air transport officer has vetoed taking me. The passenger limit has been reduced from 30 to 25 as the aircraft will fly above 3,000 metres altitude and the thin mountain air affects load-bearing capacity.

And this looks like a good one, not to be missed. The platoons will be dropped as close as 800 metres to the border, and although there are some Pakistani observation posts up there, no one informs them in case information is leaked to Haqqani's side.

The track record of the Pakistanis is heavily compromised by previous incidents of blind eyes being turned by some units and alleged active assistance to the insurgents by others. Consequently, there's a lot of speculation among the US soldiers as they get ready.

'I hope our allies don't kill us,' one says.

'They'd have to be pretty ballsy to shoot into Afghanistan.'

'Then again, if they're on target and kill us all, who's to know?'

'I don't think they killed any of us yet.'

'Their troops have shot at ours though.'

That afternoon Third Platoon does more training outside its temporary barracks on Salerno and the soldiers take turns to strip the weapons down and change barrels.

'This weapon is terror for the bad guys,' Hendricks says about the M240 machine-gun. 'If we are on the high ground and shooting down at them on the low ground then God help them. And they will concentrate their efforts on trying to find the gun.'

The Captain returns and gives me the thumbs up after pressing the issue of me flying. I'm cleared to go. My notes for the day say: 'I am paradoxically elated at being given the green light to be dropped into the middle of Taliban territory.'

October 1

There were a dozen people crammed into one tiny room so a few of us slept the night on cots outside, getting sucked anaemic by mosquitoes. We pull our boots on at 0500 and go to the flight line where the platoons do last preparations as the sun rises over rows of silent Apaches and Chinooks beside us.

The soldiers test the night observation devices (NODs) that attach to the front of their helmets, rearrange their packs and check the radios until they are told 'Get your gear on.'

The engines of our CH-47 start with a click and a whir and the rotors slowly turn, gathering speed until the noise drowns out all else.

Everything moves quickly now. At 0723 we take off and do a ten-minute run to Camp Clark near Mandozai to collect the ANA soldiers before climbing into the mountains.

The first chopper is carrying 15 US soldiers from Third Platoon, eight ANA, an ex-special forces guy called Mike who is there for intelligence gathering, a young Afghan interpreter they call Josh, and the reporter.

The two helicopters split up and at 0803 our rear wheels touch down on a grassy hilltop just long enough for us to race off the back ramp, fan out and take cover behind the rocks and bushes. There is no hail of AK and PKM fire, just silence among an endless span of mountains and valleys under the azure sky.

Two escort Apaches circle overhead as Bravo surveys the area and then gets the ANA to push up to another peak 250 metres away. Once the Afghans secure it the rest of the group follows, the US labouring under huge loads of equipment, weapons and ammo.

Twenty minutes later we reach the crest, which is dotted with stumps from the logging that goes on all over these mountains and a few stunted holly trees.

'It's pretty up here, if they just stopped fighting and put in a couple of ski lifts,' Private First Class Alex Maldonado says as he sweats up the slope with the SAW 5.56mm light machine-gun.

Aged 28, the San Diego native is a shade under two metres tall, balding with sideburns and big glasses. He's a gun enthusiast and seems to know the specifications and modification of every modern weapon there is, and happens to have just ordered new grips for his deactivated AK from a Russian friend of mine who deals in military surplus in London. He's also a big fan of Depeche Mode and his arms are covered in tattoos honouring these, my fellow Essex men.

The Chinook is long gone now but a pair of Apaches drones around for two hours after we land, scanning the area for trouble.

'I love air support, when I hear those blades it's a huge relief,' Maldonado says as the soldiers dig in at some of the tumbled-down rock fighting positions on the hill. These could have been built by the Taliban or remain from the days of the jihad, when mujahedin groups would pass through here from Pakistan to fight the Soviets. Narisah COP is five kilometres north-west from here.

'Where's Pakistan?' someone asks.

'The top of that hill,' says Sgt. John Yeager, pointing to a ridgeline one kilometre south. Along with Staff Sgt. McNeil, he is probably the most experienced member of the platoon, having served in Iraq and then in Afghanistan during 2005 when the Airborne fought heavily in Helmand, a year before the British established a permanent presence.

'Are you fucking kidding me? If they fire at us from Pakistan can we fire back?'

'Not really.'

'So we just have to take it?'

'Pretty much,' Yeager says with his customary half grin.

It's 1020 in the morning and already 34°C. The troops set up the Command Post and I go back along the ridge to collect my pack. As I pass a few of the ANA going the other way I catch a waft of marijuana, stop them and get the guy who's smoking to hold it up to me and sniff it again. Weed indeed. And these stoned dorks are covering our backs?

'What are you doing, this is an operation, look, "dushman" [enemy]!' I say forcefully, motioning in all directions.

'Sorry,' he says and walks off grinning like schoolboy that teacher collared puffing a Marlboro.

Imagining the scandal if Sgt. Hendricks learns they are smoking dope in the middle of bandit country I let it go, but ask Josh to tell them to cut it out. But it turns out the US soldiers are well aware of what's going on, it's usual for the ANA to smoke it, even when out on operations, and admonishments and complaints change nothing.

We get reports of a shoot-out between some insurgents and locals at a village a couple of kilometres away and two Apaches show up and circle for a while. But it's quiet where we are and we have a pretty mellow day.

We are sitting in the grass eating MREs when Mike the ex-SF guy asks me if I think if the war is religious. I tell him I think it is but maybe by default. I don't know any Taliban or other insurgents personally but my impression is that while there are certainly religious fanatics in the mix, many insurgent

commanders and mullahs will have their own agendas with the usual earthly motivating factors, lust for power, influence and money. But since preaching jihad to village boys is the easiest way to stir them up and recruit them in sufficient numbers, then maybe for them it becomes a de facto Holy War against 'foreign invaders', who are portrayed as trying to crush Islam.

We see four goat herders to the west on the opposite hill. 'If they're goat herders then where are their goats?' someone asks, while at the post on the east side of the hill we can hear the ANA's portable radio blaring a jangly Afghan pop tune.

One of the US goes to tell them to turn it off but the best he gets is a slight reduction in volume. I really hope we don't have to rely on these guys too much if there's a fight. Their Sergeant seems to be the only serious one among them and, as fate would have it, he is the only one to get hurt.

Later that afternoon Lt. Oravsky and a few US and ANA go on a short patrol down a draw in the hillside where they'd seen a guy wandering with his animals.

Anxious to avoid any repercussions later, the Captain rejects an idea to go up to the very borderline so we dip into the gully which is wooded and perilously steep, sending cascades of shale beneath us as we clamber down.

It soon becomes clear it's a big waste of energy and will be a grind on the way back up so we turn around, but the ANA Sergeant and four of his pot-head Privates have raced right down the hill and out of sight before Josh can call them back. Ten minutes later they reappear, chests heaving, and we press back up the hill before looping round as close to the border as we dare, passing maybe 300 metres short.

After dark the US set up Claymores, collapse the far post and draw in the security perimeter as tightly as possible in case anyone tries to sneak up on us.

I'm lucky not to have to get up every couple of hours to do sentry duty and at 1900 I burrow into my sleeping bag and borrowed waterproof bivvy sack and doze off to the sound of grating entrenching tools and the distant braying of donkeys. Others leave their sleeping bags open when they go on duty

US Army medic Robert Kidwell attends to
wounded Afghan soldier during Taliban
attack on OP5, Khost province.

and later find their bedding has been soaked
through with heavy dew that falls before dawn.

The soldiers had good air support today,
covered twice by Apaches for two hours, then
a Predator drone, then two F-15 fighter planes,
then more Apaches. Who's going to mess with
them with all that fire power up there?

September 2

The sleeping members of the platoon rise
around five and the soldiers pack their kit, dismantle the Claymores and kick down the rock
walls of the emplacements to deny them to the
enemy.

The soldiers head down the hill and reach
the HLZ at 0645, an hour before the Chinook
swoops in, preceded by Apaches which sweep
the area for enemy forces.

It's only a three-minute flight to what is
designated OP5, a hilltop over a small village

that isn't even marked on the map. In some
places there are areas with the printed legend
'border disputed'.

It's an awkward place to land, flanked by
some cottages and overlooked by a large slope
on the hill that denotes the frontier. Again, the
Chinook doesn't set down completely, just the
rear wheels touch the grass and the screaming aircraft sways as we jump off and spread
out. The crewmen shove off two large boxes
with water, American MREs and Halal boil
in the bag meals for the ANA, ten times more
supplies than were requested. The helicopter
flies off and everyone has to load as much into
their kit as they can before the rest is burnt
to prevent it from falling into enemy hands.
Captain Bravo relents slightly and decides to
leave the cases of water for the villagers, so
Josh calls in a man standing 100 metres away
watching us.

He tells the soldiers that the village is called Dwah Neshtarah and is in a perpetual state of conflict with their neighbours over the hill in Pakistan, who he says steal their livestock. Generally the border makes little difference to daily life here, since the inhabitants are all Pashtun and maps are of no consequence.

But something is going on around us. An elder tells several men who drift up close not to touch the water that is offered and they obey. Either they are scared the insurgents will punish them or they intend to hand the cases straight to them. Or they are insurgents.

The remaining contents of the boxes have to be incinerated with a thermite grenade so we all move away. Sgt. Hendricks strikes a dramatic pose and pulls the pin, tosses the grenade in the box, loses his balance and rolls down the slope like a drunken bear, sending a ripple of laughter through the platoon.

We set off round a 400-metre path through the village and to the foot of our hill. Once again it's heavy going up the slope and we only reach the top at 0900, soaked in sweat and sucking at our Camelbak tubes. The troops set up posts around the crest where there is a rock wall enclosure and what looks like a prepared firing position. We are under a kilometre from the borderline on the top of the next hill.

From here we can look down at the Pakistani OP on the facing slope, located a few hundred metres into Afghanistan under agreements between Kabul and Islamabad to help interdict passing insurgent groups. There is no sign of life at the post although they are certainly watching us through binoculars as well. No one expects any help from the Pakistanis if we get in trouble.

The sun is starting to really cook now and we are allowed to take off our body armour and helmets as we settle in. I leave my gear in a tiny ring of trees just behind the rock enclosure on the top of the hill where the Captain sets up the Command Post. Intel Mike is a few yards across from my spot.

There's nothing much planned for now and I'm tempted to take a nap in the shade when a guilt pang lifts me to my feet to do some work. I walk up to the Captain and his Fire Support Officer (FSO) and ask about the game plan.

Bravo says the whole area is criss-crossed with insurgent rat lines through the moun-

tains from their sanctuaries in Waziristan, hence the operation code name Rat Trap. The Lieutenant, whose task as FSO is to coordinate artillery and air support, pulls out a map and they show me where we are and infiltration routes that the insurgents are known to use.

Haqqani and his son are known to run a training camp a few kilometres over the border by the North Waziristan village of Mazdak so we are practically sitting on an ants' nest. But the Captain feels that with all of the auxiliary firepower at his disposal, his tiny group has the initiative even here.

'We will ideally spot a mule train with a couple of hundred insurgents moving in from Pakistan and destroy them as a lesson to others not to try,' he tells me. It all sounds very serious and rather improbable to me, since our arrival will have been widely reported already.

At 1415 we are still talking when we pause and cock our heads towards a bang that comes from the east. Everything seems to hang for a few seconds, then suddenly the air is saturated with the crackle of automatic weapons and the first RPGs slam into our hill.

I bound over to my little copse and dive onto the ground. It was the right call – the rock enclosure I would have sheltered in takes a hit a couple of minutes later. My heart is pounding insanely and I have to ride a surge of adrenalin that spins my head. As in the other TICs I'd been in, the surroundings leap in a moment from tranquility to boiling fury, and I have to rein in my racing mind and choose a course of action.

I struggle to get into my body armour while staying as low to the ground as possible, but because my spot is so close to the hillcrest it seems to be at the centre of the opening barrage of fire. Bullets hiss and whine past, cutting through the foliage around me. This is closer and more intense than anything I've experienced before or since and we are utterly on the receiving end, caught unawares, with many of the soldiers unkitted and weaponless and perhaps now leaderless – I have no idea if Captain Bravo is even alive. I writhe around in the dirt, trying to pull on the heavy Dutch vest without having my head burst by one of the rounds fizzing through the grass. Only when I finally fasten the plates do I take a proper look around.

Mike is crouching in the same tree line as me, and 10 metres down the hillside I see Sergeants Hendricks and Kile, Josh the interpreter and the FSO lying pressed to the ground. Only Kile has his weapon and body armour.

For now their spot is shielded from the brunt of the barrage, which is increasing steadily in intensity, coming from the hill where the Pakistani OP is and also from the village below. I crawl at high speed on my elbows and join the knot of soldiers. My camcorder is still in my hand but the bag with my stills camera gets left back at the crest.

Mike is hovering at the tree line behind the Command Post when an RPG explodes a few metres away. The shock wave sends him flailing down the slope but he's uninjured and clambers over to our prone line. My sense of time now evaporates as explosions boom all around the hill and the snap of the passing bullets is now directly overhead as our attackers work their way round to the rear.

Then I notice the ANA Sergeant crouching behind me with blood pouring down his leg after a round went through his kneecap. He looks at me with a half blank, half quizzical expression on his face but makes no sound, not even a groan. I don't think he could have had any morphine as the platoon medic, Robert 'Doc' Kidwell, was not yet with us on this side of the hill.

I later recall the words of a British Captain in Helmand who said of the ANA: 'Their resistance to pain is incredible. I've seen guys with a leg blown off or they've been shot to bits, and whereas a Western guy would be screaming his head off, they are at most whimpering, as if someone's nipped them.'

The Sergeant applies a field dressing to his wound and a couple of minutes later Doc appears and cuts off his trouser leg, applies a tourniquet and bandages it properly.

'Are they on the hill with us?' Hendricks shouts and we turn our heads in unison to look down the slope. At that moment there is a distant bang of an RPG being fired, followed by a whoosh and mighty blast a few metres behind us that causes the ground to shudder.

'Everyone OK?' Sergeant Kyle calls out as more rounds then ricochet off the stony ground around us.

The insurgents have now shifted the focus of the attack from the front of the hill and sent a flanking group through the village and round to our side. More bullets course up the slope and leaves and twigs begin to drop from the branches above us as we scan the ground below, still unable to make out any movement in the trees. So much for holding the high ground… Then something hums right over our heads, droning like an angry bee, its explosion down the slope absorbed into the general cacophony. Some of the soldiers later reckon there was an 82mm recoilless rifle at work as well as RPGs, AKs and PKM machine-guns.

But the platoon's own heavy firepower is mostly silent because the FSO is lying here clutching a hand grenade for dear life instead of getting on the radio and coordinating the big guns. I often replay this scene in my mind, sorry for him that he lost his composure but also angry that people could have died because he didn't do his job, myself included. He tries to shout a few instructions up the hill but the Americans still have no artillery and the only reason they get air support is because Fourth Platoon hear the shooting from their OP a few kilometres away and call it in.

Maybe it's easy for me to expect the Lieutenant to get up and run to the hillcrest in the middle of this maelstrom and join the Captain. Then again, that's exactly what the interpreter does, sprint to the CP and retrieve the Lieutenant's body armour, helmet and rifle but not his radio.

Josh makes it back OK and I also take my chances and dash for my camera bag. It's foolhardy but I know I have to keep myself busy and focussed rather than freezing up and waiting to get hit. As I do a running slide back into my spot by the others, Mike looks at me and says, 'You're either very brave or very stupid.'

This was probably the day I learned that fear is not the problem and can actually help to hone your reactions. The problem is not controlling your fear. But I still feel it, and wrest off the tendrils that try to grasp and incapacitate me, force myself to concentrate, do my job, stay in the moment, and just stay alive.

There are more scattered shots and a couple more RPG bursts but the attack now tails off as the estimated 40 to 50 insurgents disperse. It can have lasted only 25 minutes at most but it seems like an eternity before two US Kiowa helicopters swoop into view and search for the retreating insurgents. Some men are spotted but they are unarmed, and it's clear that while part of the attacking force pulled back into Pakistan, others dumped their weapons and hid in the village and outlying compounds.

Our little group on the west slope of the hill lost contact with about eight soldiers on the opposite side, including five who had been patrolling 50 metres down the east face when the attack began. Their exposure and the ferocious intensity of the firing over there would say that someone had to be hurt, but by some miracle the only serious casualty that day was the Afghan Sergeant.

Lt. Oravsky's small party took much of the opening barrage, having been badly caught out in the open.

'I was stuck down below with Sgt. Yeager, Maldonado, Fortiz and Tardif,' he recalled much later. 'We had no cover initially except for a lone skinny tree on the side of the mountain and the five of us were huddled behind that little thing. I'm sure that 80 per cent of our bodies were exposed, literally.

'I can't speak for everyone else but a PKM opened up on us and they hit *everywhere* around us but not actually us. We saw the insurgents as well. They were wearing black manjams and green chest rack systems, very generic. I remember being extremely mad that the rest of the guys weren't opening fire to take some of the pressure off of us five. Then the RPGs started hailing in within 10 metres of our position. I remember thinking 'I hate these fucking things' after my truck was hit with seven of them in the July ambush. I don't crumble mentally, but since Qalandar the outgoing sound of an RPG nearly makes me want to shit my pants. When the insurgents finally shifted fire up to your position we five were able to get behind a huge rock. The tree and the damned rock were the only cover on that barren side of the mountain…'

Brandon Jackson, the M240 gunner and at 19 years old the youngest member of the platoon, was told to hold his fire during the bombardment. He has only 700 rounds which would have been eaten up in a few seconds of rapid fire. As Hendricks said earlier, the enemy's priority would be to locate and

neutralise the gun, so he has to save his ammo for a determined attempt to overrun the hill.

But some of the soldiers there managed to hit back. Sgt. Dan Firkus shot one of a group of armed men coming up the slope from the village. He fired again as two others tried to drag the injured man, and they dropped him and ran off.

At 1511 Captain Bravo radios Battalion HQ with a situation report: 'A lot of RPG rounds pushed my guys off position so we're tightening security. We received small arms fire from the east and south, also at least 10 to 15 RPG rounds. The ANA is stable and we are preparing to medevac him.'

At 1525 a Black Hawk arrives for the casualty but since the helicopter can't land it hovers above us as they winch up the Sergeant on a stretcher.

'He'll walk again with some surgery and a cane,' Doc Kidwell predicts.

The two circling Kiowas then leave and the troops dig in for an anticipated follow-up attack.

'This was round one, they'll be back tonight if not sooner now those birds have gone,' Sgt. Hendricks says. 'I'm supposed to be going on leave – if I get killed now my wife and kids are going to be pissed off.'

I help Fortiz, the platoon's shortest soldier (small in stature, big in spirit, as I tell him), to hack out a shell scrape into the roots and earth and reinforce it with a few rocks. It's less than 30 centimetres deep but it's cover of sorts, and since I need cover as much as the next man I will dig what must be dug, alongside the Americans.

Meanwhile, recriminations are starting to surface, although no one mentions the fire support debacle in front of me, it seems that's too bad to touch.

'It all came from that training camp we've been telling people about. And the ANA said those villagers we gave the water to were supplying the attackers with weapons – all Hearts and Minds, eh?' Oravsky says.

'The Pak mil were 300 or 400 metres across the hill from them,' adds Doc. 'They were probably saying 'wow, look at the rockets'.'

A second imminent attack becomes likely as villagers are spotted leaving the houses below. It's usually a pretty reliable sign of trouble

Soldiers of US 2-506th Airborne Infantry drive to helicopters for start of Qalandar operation, Khost province, October 2008.

since the insurgents try not to harm the locals so as to retain their support, although this time they did not seem to have forewarned anyone.

'We just picked up on the radio that the Taliban are regrouping for a second attack,' Hendricks confirms at 1604, ten minutes before a whistle and explosion send me diving for cover.

'It's ours,' Fortiz says without flinching and continues to dig.

I don't see much of the Captain, who is up at the Command Post coordinating artillery ranging before contact resumes. Better late than never. The sun is already sinking at 1700 but the only sounds are mooing and barking in the valley, and the clang of Maldonado's entrenching tool in the trees just below me.

A contracted Mi-8 civil aviation helicopter flies in and drops supplies, including extra Claymores and trip flares, but not the .203 under barrel grenade ammunition that was requested, nor the requested RPG launcher with 10 rounds for the ANA, and definitely not the three additional loaded AK magazines for each Afghan soldier. But they all have enough Halal burgers to last them a week thanks to this morning's logistics screw-up.

'Anyone carrying a weapon and you have eyes on, you're clear to kill,' Lt. Oravsky tells his platoon.

At 1727 shots ring out from the east slope above the path from the village. Four men with rifles try to make their way up to where they earlier had to drop the injured man, and Josh can make out soft calls of 'Commander, where are you?'

Firkus gets a clear shot on one of the rescue party and drops his second man that day.

'That's two down, let's hope our luck holds out. It's going to be a long night,' Hendricks warns.

The dusk deepens and a few of us are sitting round the trench I helped dig and now occupy.

'War, Nick man, it fucking sucks,' the Platoon Sergeant says.

'Are you feeding me quotes Ryan? Just don't say it's hell…'

'War is hell Nick.'

The group laughs but it rings hollow as we all wonder to ourselves what the night will bring. Before it gets completely dark the soldiers untape their hand grenades ready to use

and switch on their NODs. The night vision capability gives them the edge if their enemy tries to scale the hill. But if 200 fighters come from Haqqani's camp with sacks full of magazines, ammo belts and RPGs to loose off at us from a distance, we are almost as exposed as earlier. And once resistance here has been sufficiently battered and depleted, they will come up for the remainder of the unit. And that will be that.

'How good do you think these guys are at night?' someone asks.

'I don't, there might be harassment fire though,' Maldonado answers.

By six it's pitch black and a few of the soldiers talk quietly around me.

'I feel like I'm in Bastogne,' someone says. 'I just want to go back to Salerno – I don't mean right now, but in the future, along with everybody else.'

'One thing is for sure,' Hendricks adds. 'In typical 101st style we are low on ammunition, surrounded and outnumbered.'

The troops get reports that Haqqani's men are setting up rockets over the border and we prepare to be pounded from afar. Not to be outdone, the US artillery at Camp Clark drops 20 rounds to deter any ground attack, battering some of the earlier firing positions on the facing slopes. The shellbursts erupt just a few hundred metres away but are oddly comforting, their splitting roar telling us that we have backup and the insurgents that they will be torn apart if they try to use the slopes again. And when a couple of hours later two F-15s race past low overhead in a show of force and drop some flares, we really feel better. But what will happen at dawn?

Then the landscape echoes to the crump of distant explosions and the Americans can only presume that someone is taking out rocket launching sites. Unawares to us, Hellfire missiles fired from a drone have destroyed a house where according to the Pakistani military at least half a dozen al-Qaeda fighters of Arab origin and several Taliban militants were among more than 20 people killed.

I think there were more types of air strikes that night but in view of the political sensitivity of US border incursions into Pakistan, no one would confirm that to me. But I did hear later that Pakistani military helicopters were buzzing along the frontier watching this situation unfold. Pakistani news reports citing 'sources close to the militants' also said US jets launched strikes in the area, killing 'women and a child'.

But for all we know right now, Haqqani's entire camp is mobilizing for an all-out attack at first light, in which case this position will surely be overrun and heads will literally roll.

My own fuzzy, exhausted head recalls the scene in the Mel Gibson movie 'We were Soldiers' when the North Vietnamese pour out of their underground bunkers and converge in a seething mass for a final assault on the Americans. There are hardly that many militants up here, but still. Then I recall Spike Milligan's observation that this kind of trench fighting is quite convenient as they just need to fill in the hole over you if you get killed.

Huddled inside my helmet and body armour I sleep fitfully in this shallow depression with its rich earthy smell, sometimes staring up at the night sky and picturing how small we are in this vast landscape. A couple of commercial airliners fly high above our hill, their passengers oblivious to what is happening below. I think I may have flown the same route while travelling from Islamabad to London and at some point that night I scribble in my notebook in the darkness: 'There are people up there drinking tea, watching movies and reading the papers.'

I wake for the last time that night at 0417 and the first glimmers appear over the horizon around five.

'I guess this is now Operation Getthefuckoutahere,' I say to Hendricks, who spent part of the night sat next to me in the hollow.

'This extraction has got me worried, it's got the makings of a disaster,' he replies. 'We're a small element deep inside bad guy country, Heaven knows how many dudes they've massed in the night.'

Captain Bravo requests permission to find another place for the Chinook to land so we are not presented on a platter for anyone positioned on the slopes where the initial bombardment came from. But his bosses don't go for it. We will have to come back down the hill and through the same village whose men drank their fill of the Americans' water

before attacking us, then take that long path to the HLZ and wait to be picked up. We will be bunched up, totally exposed on low ground with no cover, and if Haqqani's men work it out in time, we'll be taken apart.

At 0720 we start the descent, moving cautiously through thickets on the east slope and fifteen minutes later we take position on the edge of the village, which the ANA now search.

Some of the locals complain that the troops shot their mullah during the fight and that he bled out from a stomach wound. It's effectively an admission of their participation in the fight, and several young men sitting by a house stare hatefully at us as we trudge past.

'Eight people urged the CO to have the ANA search those houses before we went up,' someone says.

For all our tension, Dwah Neshtarah is the essence of tranquility, like nothing happened, its snooze lulled by the buzzing of insects and distant mooing, while two camels amble knock-kneed along the path above us.

We push out to the HLZ at 0817, but before we hear the chukka–chukka sound of our ride out we have to wait 30 minutes, anxiously scanning the hilltop until we can climb on. Huge relief shows on the faces of the men as the loaded Chinook finally alights and swings down the valley, over OP5 and back to Salerno.

Despite the din of the engines I try to do a filmed interview with Jackson, who is sat beside me with the M240 upended between his knees, unfired because the big assault didn't materialise.

'What do you think?' I shout.

'About what?'

'The operation.'

'The what?'

'The operation.'

'That?'

'Yes.'

'I'm just glad to get out alive,' he says with a big grin.

There's a lot of discussion of these events over the next couple of days and criticism is levelled at the new CO. The lack of immediate artillery response is one point. I learn that even with the FSO out of the equation, the Command Post managed to get a call to the artillery. But because the request did not

Lt. Shane Oravsky, Third
Platoon leader, Delta Company,
US 2-506th Airborne Infantry.

specify 'immediate suppression', which would have brought down clustered fire on the given coordinates, the distant gun teams assumed it was an 'adjust fire' mission. After dropping one round they stopped and waited for further instructions which didn't come.

'I've never been pinned down like that before,' one of the platoon members tells me. 'Usually within a couple of minutes of getting hit you'll hear artillery shells coming in, but not this time. That was the epitome of a clusterfuck mission, I'm sorry you had to see that. They used us as bait, that's all they ever do.

'The problem is the Command, we're attached to the artillery, they use us to draw the enemy out and they kill a bunch with artillery and it makes them look good.'

I learn a year later that my video film of that incident has since been used in officer training at Fort Benning as an example of what not to do when you are needed most.

Because the US military generally do not confirm details of cross-border strikes, the actual sequence of events that day and night stays under wraps.

Meanwhile, eager to exact a crushing victory from the encounter, the militants informed Pakistani media of the following, which appeared the next morning in Pakistan's leading English-language newspaper *The News International*.

Afghan Taliban led by prominent commander Sirajuddin Haqqani, alias Khaleefa, claimed that their fighters attacked US troops in Narayzai area of Tanaee district in Afghanistan's Khost province, killing five soldiers and injuring eight others. The Taliban claimed they also fired at two US helicopters that came to airlift the bodies and injured US soldiers.

Sources said the US jetfighters and gunship helicopters later started pounding suspected positions of the Taliban inside Afghanistan in which some of the bombs fell on two Pakistani border villages – Kharseen and Mazdak.

The residents said two men, two women and an equal number of children were injured in the attack. They were admitted to various hospitals in Miramshah. However, Maj-Gen Athar Abbas, Director General of (Pakistan's) ISPR, denied any bombing by the Nato forces on Pakistani tribal villages.

Abbas said the Nato-led International Security Assistance Force had informed Pakistan it would be conducting an operation across the border from North Waziristan, and there was no intrusion into Pakistani territory.

Concerning the drone attack, the same report added:

Official and tribal sources said a US spy plane, also known as a drone or Predator, fired two Hellfire missiles on Mohammad Khel village, about 20 kilometres west of Miramshah, the headquarters of the North Waziristan Agency, in which 15 people were killed and several others injured. There were reports that those killed in the missile attack included some Arabs, who were invited to a dinner by the pro-Taliban tribesmen in the village.

Qalandar

'George W. Bush eh? Eight years later we're still chasing terrorists. I believe God allows terrorists to run unchecked because we've allowed ourselves to go adrift.'

A few days after our return from Rat Trap I'm waiting for a ride out to Mandozai with Fourth Platoon. I end up talking with a Sergeant I haven't seen before who is leaning against one of the trucks.

He proves to be an earnestly reborn Christian and impresses upon me the message of Psalm 9:17 that 'The wicked shall be turned into hell and all the nations that forget God.'

The Sergeant wants to become a military padre's assistant and says that since deploying to Afghanistan he has come to develop a respect for the burqa culture: 'I'm not saying they are right about everything but I admire how devout they are, I only wish the Americans, British, Canadians and French could be so devout.'

But my thoughts are elsewhere. Before I left Salerno I reread a story I filed about Rat Trap and was alarmed to see that at the late hour of writing I had inadvertently written 'Captain Ricardo Bravado'. The flawed story already went out to clients of the dpa news wire and although I immediately got the editors to run a correction, the fateful typo starts popping up on websites around the world. This is hardly going to endear me to the CO on the eve of the next operation called Snake Bite, a six-day foray up to Qalandar and the same insurgent camps they turned over in August.

Between the operations I spent a few days on base and did a couple of trips with other units. I was billeted in a room with a civilian contractor and a US soldier, my bed separated from my neighbour by a wardrobe with the sound advice EMBRACE THE MADNESS written on the back in marker pen. One evening Salerno takes eight or nine 107mm rockets, the first bombardment in a couple of months which I sit out in a dark concrete shelter with a Military Policeman. No one is hurt.

Meanwhile, there is some damage control going on in the higher echelons of ISAF in Kabul. The top commander, General David McKiernan, holds a news conference to dispel any defeatist talk about the mission in Afghanistan.

In a previous interview with *The Times* the departing commander of British forces in Afghanistan, Brigadier Mark Carleton-Smith, said that in his opinion a military victory over the Taliban was 'neither feasible nor support-able' and that the aim should be to 'contain the insurgency to a level where it is not a strategic threat to the longevity of the elected Government.'

His bleak prognosis followed a leaked cable by François Fitou, the deputy French Ambassador in Kabul, claiming that Sir Sherard Cowper-Coles, the British Ambassador, had told him the strategy for Afghanistan was 'doomed to failure', the paper reported.[21]

In the cable, Mr Fitou told French President Nicolas Sarkozy that Sir Sherard believed 'the security situation is getting worse, so is corruption and the Government has lost all trust.' Sir Sherard had told him Britain had no alternative but to support the US, 'but we should tell them that we want to be part of a winning strategy, not a losing one. The American strategy is doomed to fail.'

The media had a field day and McKiernan promptly appeared before the Kabul press corps to declare, 'I absolutely reject that idea and I don't believe it,' while acknowledging some of the obstacles to ending the lingering insurgency.

'It is true that in many places in this country, we don't have an acceptable level of security. We don't have good governance, we don't have socio-economic progress, and we don't have schools being opened up. But we are not losing in Afghanistan,' the US General stressed.

After the bustling impersonality of Salerno it's good to get back to Mandozai and see some familiar faces. That evening I'm tucked up in my sleeping bag watching a movie on my laptop when the CO appears and thanks me for the story I wrote.

'Just one thing, my name isn't Bravado, it's Bravo and unusual enough as it is without any changes,' he adds. I offer my apologies and he seems satisfied.

'I was more worried what quotes you might have used, sometimes people say things in the heat of the moment and some journalists quote them.'

The Qalandar operation is scheduled for October 15. The two platoons leave skeleton crews at their COPs and move to Camp Clark from where they will fly up to the mountains.

We spend two days packed into bunks in little fuggy tents with all the weapons, and a dark and portentous air hangs over the whole affair.

Intelligence reports say there are 150 insurgents up there and that they have been tipped off that we are coming, possibly by spies among the ANP the US are supposed to take with them.

The two DShKs are still thought to be in place and likely trained on the HLZ the Chinooks used last time and will use again now. There is also concern that that the landing site will have been sown with IEDs to blow off a few legs as the soldiers leave the helicopters.

Third Platoon has extra cause to dislike the target area, which is where they suffered their six-kilometre ambush on July 20. According to the locals, the enemy knew the US troops were coming in their four trucks and spent a day and a half digging in on either side of the road and test firing their weapons.

That was when the platoon's Executive Officer, Lt. Dewhirst, was killed by an armour-piercing RPG that penetrated his vehicle. Matters were made worse by the lack of available firepower from the top gunners to hit back.

The .50-cal machine-gun malfunctioned and another gunner who was since reassigned to a non-combat job elsewhere pretended his M249 SAW light machine-gun jammed and cowered inside the vehicle. Specialist Ashby's M249 locked up so he had to fire from the hatch using the Kalashnikov of a wounded ANA, while Private Tardif got hit in the arm but kept shooting with his rifle.

After his .50-cal went down, Perez, one of the platoon's two Puerto Rican soldiers, took driver Maldonado's M249 and fired all 900 rounds. Perez was a blessed man that day. A couple of weeks earlier the mechanics at Salerno obligingly welded some armoured plates around his turret for extra protection. It probably saved his head from being ripped off – after the ambush they found an RPG burst at the back of the truck that sprayed shrapnel scars right up the new armour, just behind his skull.

October 15

We get up at 0450 and are told at breakfast that we have to wait for two hours because cloudy weather prevented the Chinooks from leaving Salerno. People have been having uneasy dreams about this operation – during the night

someone calls out in his sleep, 'Fortiz, there's four of them, take them out.'

At 0645 we are told to move and load the gear onto the five-ton truck and climb on to go to the HLZ. Just before 0800 we are told the operation is scratched, which puts a big grin on every face present, US and Afghan.

'Nick, we're going to live!' one soldier says with affected Hollywood intonation.

'Same time tomorrow everybody, nothing's changed,' Sgt. Hendricks calls.

We sleep, eat, read and chat in the tents, apparently still on standby in case the weather suddenly clears. At 1330 it's definitely off until the next morning but there's some doubt whether we'll get the helicopters then because several operations are underway in the AO.

I see one of the Battalion HQ officers I know from Salerno walking toward me and I raise my arms wordlessly in the air.

'You've been around the Army long enough, hurry up and wait,' is all he says.

October 16

I wake at 0600 and see everyone is still in bed so I guess it's all cancelled again. Perez confirms and then by the latrines I meet Fourth Platoon Sgt. Chandler who says there's no transport available for us until the twentieth. I run into Doc Kidwell and tell him the news.

'I'm not going to shed a tear about this, I had a bad feeling about this one,' he replies.

The grey clouds in the sky were not the only ones hanging over us these past few days, and the feeling of relief is universal.

'No one's upset at all. It was a half suicide mission anyway,' says another soldier in my tent. 'They had the largest number of guys up there; if they'd decided to fight we'd have been fucked.'

I meet Ignont, a hulking black southerner who it seems had a particularly rough time in Iraq on his last tour. He's of the same mind: 'It would have been a slaughterhouse. With them having the intelligence that we were coming they'd have shot us down on the HLZ.'

The previous morning I had heard him say 'I didn't sleep well, I was nervous.'

'But you aren't afraid of anything Ignont,' someone tells him.

'I had a bad feeling about this one and that usually means something,' he replies. He does seem to have rather vivid manifestations in his sleep. Two days earlier in Mandozai I found him chuckling in the washroom because he'd just had a 'dream about monkeys'.

The platoon returns to Mandozai where they are immediately put on 100 per cent security in full kit after news come in of a suicide bombing at the Terezai District Centre in the east of the province. An Afghan security guard and a policeman died.

In the evening Captain Bravo calls a platoon meeting but it is an internal matter so I stay away. I later learn that among other business, an instruction was relayed to the men from on high to no longer refer to 'the Taliban' when talking to media. From now on they must only say 'the enemy'. It's clearly a dilemma for the ISAF chiefs how to refer to what American troops informally call 'the bad guys'. In the past few years they have been called Anti-Coalition Militia (ACM) and then Opposing Military Forces (OMF) and Armed Opposition Groups (AOG), and at the time of writing they were the Anti-Afghanistan Forces (AAF).

After the meeting the men are kept in the dining area to watch a DVD that the Company's rather stiff First Sergeant Glen Coleman brought back from leave, a 90-minute documentary about the construction of the Pentagon Memorial in Washington.

Platoon Sgt. Hendricks calls me in too. Sure, it's an occasionally moving piece about creating a fitting tribute to the 184 people killed in the 9/11 attack on the building, and another small piece of the overall healing process in the country. But with no disrespect to the victims and their families, it was frankly an over-produced drag to watch – we are not required to automatically like every tribute story and film that is made.

I can see some of the soldiers fidgeting, most would probably not have voluntarily watched it to the end but because of the theme and the fact it was the First Sergeant's event, they have to sit tight and be attentive. But Coleman at least stays on message. When the lights come on he gives the platoon a talk on remaining upright, soldierly and true to the task. Coleman says every day he's in Afghanistan he thinks of the regiment's three KIA during the tour, 1st Lt. Nick Dewhirst, Staff Sergeant Kevin Roberts and Sergeant Ryan Baumann.

'Whether we agree with these wars in Iraq and Afghanistan it doesn't matter, we're soldiers. The thing you can do as American soldiers is give your all every day,' he impresses upon them.

On October 19 we drive back to Camp Clark for another go at Operation Snake Bite. In the evening I sit down with Lt. Oravsky and the two Platoon Sergeants in the dining hall.

'We might get our asses handed to us,' one of them says with that joking tone soldiers have when broaching bad topics. 'People take these guys for granted, that they're no good with their weapons and so on but they just have to get lucky. We had an ANA guy and we put a water bottle on the hood of a truck at 100 metres and he hit it first shot. They must have guys like that too – and that was just a water bottle.'

Back in the tent there is some leg-pulling about the SMAW-D rocket Sgt. Hendricks has strapped onto his backpack. He is prone to sudden eruptions of anger over little things but he takes the ribbing with a big grin.

'If there's a bunker and I take it out with this you're gonna say 'that's one bad-assed dude'.'

Reveille is at 0450, everyone gets ready in silence, has breakfast and loads the gear on the truck before twenty of us clamber onto the vehicle and drive to the HLZ two hours later. The atmosphere is tense and there is still talk about the heavy weapons that can be waiting for us when we land.

'It doesn't really matter whether you get hit by a DshK or a Super-DshK, 12.7 or 14.5 mm, the result is the same,' someone points out.

I'm slated to fly on the fifth Chinook run with Lt. Oravsky, Sgt. Hendricks, McNeil, Yeager, Maldonado, MacLachlan, Fortiz, Villalobos, Jackson and a guy from the Paladin task force that does site exploitation, picking up physical evidence for analysis.

'All right bitches, mount up,' Yeager barks and we grab our packs and run onto the waiting helicopter. We fly less than ten minutes, land at 0842 on a large flat table among the hilltops that overlooks the track where the ambush occurred three months earlier.

The US and Afghan troops secure the site for the next Chinook that is carrying some specialists and five Afghan Police officers. One of these starts messing around with his mobile phone after he gets off but Captain Bravo makes him put it away. Distrust runs deeply as far as the ANP are concerned.

Two Apaches circle around the valley and the HLZ is obscured by dust after the last Chinook leaves. The hill where the insurgent camp is located is visible one kilometre to the southwest.

Fourth Platoon and their Afghan units have been dropped further up the valley so it's just Third Platoon, a few intel guys and 40 ANA and ANP who move out from this table at 0900.

We stop at a shepherd's hut that they know as the 'Flea Shack' after the platoon all got infested while sleeping there after their vehicles were disabled in the July ambush. Half an hour later the Apaches go off station and the silence is broken only by the sound of two logging trucks groaning up the track below us.

The artillery at Camp Clark drops a dozen shells around the objective hill to range the guns, and we set off down the slope to the infamous ambush track before we can start climbing up toward the insurgent camps.

We pass a couple of little closed stores, one of which is run by a guy once identified by his long, flowing hair who is known to sell tents and other supplies to the Taliban, or rather 'Anti-Afghanistan Forces' camped in the hills. When they raided the place in August the shopkeeper was surprised to see them after the July ambush and had the gall to ask 'Are you still alive?' The ANP promptly cut off his hair as a lesson in manners.

We clamber and sweat for an hour through pine trees to the target area where I go with first section under Sergeants McNeil and Firkus up to the far OP, a rocky nipple out on the fringes about 100 metres from the ANP and 200 metres from the main group.

We start to dig in but it's impossibly slow going in this rocky terrain.

'You know what the worst bit is?,' says McNeil, his entrenching tool bouncing off packed layers of shale that make up the hilltop. 'Expecting to get shot in the back while digging in.'

I help Brandon Jackson and Specialist Scott MacLachlan to dig another position a few yards away to cover the other slope. Once again, I am a non-combatant but I'm also a beneficiary of any cover that's created so it's fair enough that I hack at the shale too.

Over three hand-blistering hours the five of us manage to excavate two depressions that measure 1.5 metres square and maybe 20 centimetres deep, heaped around the edges with earth and rock fragments. The half dozen ANA with us work half-heartedly on their own position just beyond McNeil and Firkus.

At 1700 it starts to thunder, spots of rain fall, then two-centimetre hailstones beat down so hard I grab for my helmet. Our foxhole has a poncho strung over the top that affords some shelter but the two Sergeants lie in their ponchos, being pelted by hailstones the size of eyeballs and laughing like maniacs. We all get extremely wet and cold and it seems to us that any smart Taliban fighter will be holed up in a cave somewhere.

'That's the advantage of being an insurgent, you can choose when you want to fight,' McNeil says. 'If it's bad weather you don't have to, and most of the time they don't.'

As it grows dark and colder there is a general abandonment of camouflage and concealment procedures and groups of US and Afghan troops on the surrounding hilltops light fires.

Our ANA tear down whole trees and soon we are huddled around a roaring fire. We are a perfect target for anyone who does manage to sneak up but sentries scour the area with night vision equipment, allowing the rest of us to just about dry out before we take another whipping of hail.

That night Mac, Jackson and I cram into our soggy pit and rest uncomfortably until 0200 when I groan 'fuck this', climb out, stretch out and go to sleep on the open ground until dawn.

The next day I come down from the OP and join the main group just as a Uh-60 Black Hawk flies through and drops supplies in a body bag. The crew tosses the bag out at 30 metres, it bounces off a tree and splits open and most of the water bottles burst when they hit the ground. It's a total waste of a flight and they have to repeat the run later in the day, this time dropping the body bag from ten metres instead, preserving the contents.

Captain Bravo takes a patrol to the main insurgent camp. After a 30-minute hike up and

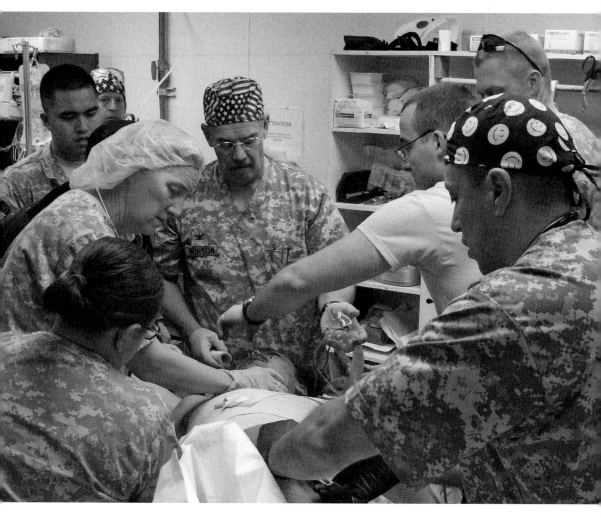

US military doctors treat Afghan wounded
in suicide bombing of Dwawmanda COP,
Khost province, November 20, 2008.

down the wooded slopes we reach the spot, encountering nobody on the way.

During the August raid they not only captured a few fighters but found rows of tents with equipment that they burned. But this time the occupants had several days' warning to vacate. The US already heard through intelligence channels that the last of the enemy fighters left the previous day. Now all that remains of the camp are some lean-to shelters made of tree boughs, a clearing with a large, neat semi-circular seat carved out of a bank of earth, a couple of fireplaces and a lot of garbage that the site exploitation guys fish through for evidence and tell-tale items.

I build my own mental picture of the insurgents from the scraps we find: despite their sweet tooth (candy and biscuit wrappers) they try to stay healthy (vitamin boxes) but are nonetheless…depressed? Among the piles are empty packets of Modrin tablets, 'For relief of depression, anxiety, tension.'

Carved into the fork of a tree are the Pashtu symbols for *Allah u Akbar*, God is Great. Sgt. Yeager gets out his knife and carves on the other stem of the fork 'John was here'. On the opposite tree Lt. Oravsky goes one better, carving his name and Afghan cell phone number, perhaps in case any of these glum fellows on Modrin needs to talk to someone who cares.

In another camp round the hillside they find a syringe with needle which according to the Paladin guy is either for medicine or bomb making: 'Sometimes they inject things into the explosives to make the blast bigger. If this is a suicide bomber camp it could be that.'

Or they could just be using heroin, which is in plentiful supply in this country.

We squelch back into our own camp a couple of hours later amid more thunder and heavy rainfall. After nightfall we receive the improbable warning that 300 insurgents are moving down from the north so everybody has to kit up and take position.

Then we see flashlights in the wadi and hear trucks moving in the dark. It could just be loggers but there are also get reports of 30 men moving this way from the next village. Some of the soldiers are tense, others are just annoyed at the fuss.

'It's always '300 Taliban' wherever I go,' the Paladin guy grumbles, while the ANA get unusually agitated and extinguish their fires. The consternation lasts for a couple of hours and then I give up and turn in for the night. But first I warn Fortiz and Villalobos that if it kicks off I'll be jumping in their hole, and I squeeze in for a 'test cower' before disappearing into my sleeping bag.

During the night there are some distant explosions and we hear the next day that the US bombed an ANA post by mistake, killing at least eight Afghan soldiers.

'They're really livid, they want American blood now apparently,' someone says.

'I'm not surprised, imagine if the ANA killed eight of our guys,' another adds.

We dry out by morning fires and leave the hilltop at 0700, sweat our way back down the hill and up to the HLZ where we are picked up two hours later and flown to Clark. The last

I see of that camp before I end my embed is a Chinook hovering in the blue sky against the haze of Qalandar's mountains, a 155mm field gun strung under its belly.

Back at Salerno we hear that the handful of ANP who came with us on the operation overturned their truck on their way back to Khost, killing two Police officers. They are blaming this on the Americans for having dragged them up to Qalandar.

* * *

Dwawmanda was finally bombed on November 20, 2008. A truck full of explosives rammed the gates of the COP and blew up, destroying most of the installation. Only a handful of US troops were present at the time, while the rest of Fourth Platoon was out on an operation. Two soldiers received minor wounds but at least four Afghan nationals were killed.

Mandozai's turn came on December 28 when an explosive-laden SUV drove to the checkpoint by the COP and blew up outside the sub-Governor's compound. The blast coincided with the exit of pupils from a nearby school on the last day of term. Fourteen children died, as well as an Afghan security guard and another Afghan adult; 58 people were wounded. The Taliban claimed responsibility for both blasts.

On Christmas Eve a member of First Platoon based in Margah, Paktika, was killed by a rocket. And in March 2009, a couple of weeks before the 2-506th shipped out, I received an e-mail from Lt. Stultz saying, 'I just lost two more soldiers to a suicide VBIED that hit the lead truck of my convoy. A third is at Walter Reed Hospital fairly beat up. We were so close to making it home.'

sixteen

BUDDHA BING

'**I**'m not too amazed by them, they're pretty much just holes,' the young New Zealander at the wheel of the armoured Toyota truck grunts as we pull up by the empty alcove of the large Buddha.

It's his first close look at the ancient site, even though the sandstone cliff face in Bamyan is less than two kilometres from the tiny NZ camp called Kiwi Base and is clearly visible. Most of the 130 NZ troops stationed here with the Provincial Reconstruction Team won't get a chance to visit during their six-month tour, unless like today they are chosen to scout the area ahead of the arrival of a VIP.

In one of the most heinous acts of vandalism in modern history, the Taliban deemed the Buddhist relics 'idolatrous' and dynamited and shelled the two giant figures in 2001 until there was nothing left.

But while only bare niches remain, it speaks of an enduring legacy that they are still referred to as 'the Buddhas' and draw a steady trickle of Afghan and foreign visitors, including former First Lady Laura Bush in 2008.

To say the place is magical or wondrous is an exaggeration. If anything, it's a rather pathetic spectacle to see the people of Bamyan hope on the absent statues to keep them on the tourist trail and bring in some extra cash. But as international forces fight the Taliban insurgency just an hour's drive from here, Bamyan is a curious oasis of relative calm that attracts any official who can wangle a business trip this way.

'Everybody loves to come here because it's a different atmosphere,' says Major Hamish Gibbons, the operations officer at Kiwi Base who meets me after my 50-minute flight from Bagram on a tiny STOL passenger-cargo plane.

The absence of broad hostilities stems from Bamyan's almost exclusive population by Hazaras, an ethnicity which according to some theories is descended from the conquering Mongol hordes.

As well as being physically distinctive from the Pashtuns, who form the bulk of the insurgent ranks, the Hazaras are Shiite rather than Sunni Muslim. And their brutal persecution by the Taliban during the militia's rule of Afghanistan from 1996-2001 means that today they guard their territory with ruthless efficiency.

'We're lucky that the Hazara people are even more anti-Taliban than we are – our main force protection is the Hazaras,' Gibbons says.

It's not all roses though. The Kiwis may be the only troops in the eastern command sector who patrol in baseball caps rather than helmets, but at least three IEDs exploded here in 2008, one of which lightly injured a New Zealander. Suspicion falls mainly on criminal gangs but the Taliban put in the occasional appearance. In 2007, two 107mm rockets fired from the hills above the alcoves whizzed over the base, serving as a reminder that they are still out there.

'Bamyan is still the most stable and secure province in Afghanistan but it would be naïve of us to assume we weren't being watched,' says PRT commander Colonel Richard Hall.

The province is also the place where a New Zealander first won a Victoria Cross, the highest military award for valour. In 2004 Lance Corporal Bill Apiata of the Special Air Service carried a gravely wounded comrade to safety while under fire from an attacking group of 20 enemy fighters. But generally the soldiers say that the public back home is rather removed from this far-off mission by members of the country's 4,500 regular military personnel. 'A lot of people don't know where Afghanistan is, and some might even be surprised to hear we have an army,' Gibbons says, apparently only half joking.

With so much combat occurring elsewhere in Afghanistan, there is some regret among the Kiwis that they don't get to engage the insurgents like other armies do.

'We haven't done any major fighting since Vietnam, people would just like to know that we can still do it,' says Corporal Shane Hutson of the 1st Battalion, Royal New Zealand Infantry Regiment.

Others are more vociferous.

'This is a bullshit mission,' a Sergeant tells me. 'The reason we are here in Bamyan is because [then Prime Minister] Helen Clark looked at Afghanistan and saw that it is the safest province.'

According to the Sergeant, there was once some discussion about sending 160 NZ troops to Kandahar to crew a unit of LAV armoured cars provided by the Canadians and to assist that overstretched contingent. But the idea got no further and in 2008 the Kiwis' job mainly revolves around providing security and planning assistance for the construction of schools, clinics, roads, wells and floodwalls. Plus the occasional mission nannying VIPs around the sites.

'The only time we get to see them this close is if we are escorting people,' Lt. Phil Bayly says as we drive past the empty alcoves and then go 12 kilometres out of town to view some hill ruins before a top ISAF official arrives the next day. I am later told I can't accompany him on his tour 'because he wants to relax', but in the end bad weather at Bagram scraps his trip.

The patrol dismounts and half a dozen of us, including the PRT's padre who is making his first trip out of the base, climb 25 minutes up steep paths to some red stone ruins thought to date back 1,000 years. At the highest point we find an old Soviet firing position which still holds the rusting chassis of a ZPU anti-aircraft gun. On the wall inside the derelict hut beneath someone has recently scratched in Cyrillic letters *russkie vernulis* (the Russians have returned).

On the road to town the patrol stops in a ragged little village to hand over boxes of school supplies and a few footballs. The soldiers spread out and pull security but my attention is caught by the behaviour of the padre, whose eyes dart about while his hand remains poised on the grip of a 9mm pistol holstered on his chest beside a sheathed bayonet. I wonder if he's just nervous on his first trip out or getting carried away with the Rambo thing.

He shrugs off my question whether his aggressive stance doesn't send the wrong signal at a humanitarian event in a low-risk area. Then one of the soldiers comments on his belt pouch with loaded magazines for a Steyr rifle that he doesn't even carry.

'If anything happens I can pick up one of your rifles,' the padre replies. But at least he lets go of the pistol grip long enough to present the footballs to the school teacher.

Dusty tracks take us back to town through thirsty orchards, mud villages and timeless Silk Road scenes of turbaned men driving donkeys piled with brushwood. No one is afraid of the patrols and the Kiwis continually exchange waves with farmers and kids dressed in sparkly, brightly coloured shawls and shirts.

We pass a wrecked T-62 tank, one of many knocked-out Soviet vehicles that litter the area from the days of the jihad. In the centre of Bamyan town there is a field where the rusting hulks of several tanks and armoured vehicles have been dumped.

They are essentially junk, but it occurs to me that the local administration would probably be mistaken to remove them as they clean up the town for tourists. They may want to accentuate the province's more distant, non-military past, but the wrecks are sadly as much part of its history as the statues that towered here through the ages.

'A shrine and shopping centre for 20 centuries,' reads a 1933 article in *National Geographic* magazine titled 'Afghanistan Makes Haste Slowly'. 'The Great Buddha at Bamyan, northwest of Kabul, is a colossal monolith higher than Niagara Falls and was a Central Asian rendezvous for pilgrims and tradesmen in the first century. Now motor cars are frequently parked around the bazaar at the feet of the towering statue.'[22]

In reality the figures were built in the fifth and sixth century, but the point is they have been the area's defining landmark and focus over the ages.

The main bodies of the two Buddhas, standing 53 and 38 metres in height, were hewn directly into the sandstone cliffs and details were modelled in mud mixed with straw and

Humvee of New Zealand PRT, Bamyan, against a backdrop of the Hindu Kush mountains.

coated with stucco. This coating, practically all of which was worn away long ago, was painted to enhance the expressions of the faces, hands and folds of the robes; the larger one was painted red and the smaller one in several colours. The faces were thought to have been made of great wooden masks or casts.

Local man Basir was 15 years old when the statues were destroyed over several days by the Taliban, according to some accounts helped by Chechen militants with demolition expertise.

'It was horrible, they forced all the residents to move from the villages because they were placing high explosives,' he said. 'It took them five days to organize all the bombs and finally they blew it. They used tanks and put explosives inside the statues, there were many explosions, everything was shaking. They were destroying Afghanistan's heritage. And they would have killed us if they knew we were watching.'

There was an international outcry at the destruction after the failure of diplomatic efforts to avert it. But local reaction was muted in the face of continuing persecution of the Hazaras by their Pashtun Taliban rulers.

'When the Taliban destroyed the Buddhas the people themselves were under attack, so preserving themselves was more important,' said Foladi Amir, Bamyan's Ecotourism Programme Manager.

In 2008, many locals were offended to see billboards go up around town showing a jolly turbaned Pashtun man urging them to register for the 2009 presidential election: 'Your participation in the elections is your share in the reconstruction,' the man proclaims in Dari and Pashtu, while motioning to a ballot box.

The driver I hire, Javed, is unimpressed by this campaign sent down from the corridors of Kabul.

'If the Pashtuns did something good for the country it would be OK but they just cause trouble, make explosions and kidnappings. So why are their fucking pictures everywhere?' he exclaims as we drive.

With natural resources limited to some minor coal and iron ore deposits, the development of tourism and roads is the priority for Bamyan Governor Habiba Sarabi, the country's only female Governor. Even in its Buddha-less state after 2001 the province still had some tourist base to work with before the security situation in the country worsened, receiving some 3,000 foreign visitors and 30,000 Afghan visitors in 2005.

Most of the foreigners were already working in-country rather than arriving from abroad, and would travel to Bamyan by air as well as drive the rough and increasingly dangerous route 240 kilometres south-west from Kabul.

To boost recovery, a major asphalt road is expected to be built by 2012, while a small international airport is to replace the town's landing strip. And Bamyan aimed in 2009 to become Afghanistan's first declared mine-free province.

Interest in this part of the country was expected to grow with the planned restoration and display of a 19-metre 'Sleeping Buddha' discovered in 2008 near the main alcoves. Unearthed by French and Afghan archaeologists, the find reinforced hopes of locating a horizontal effigy measure some 350 metres in length that was documented by Chinese monks in the eighth century.

Meanwhile, there were proposals to use some of the dynamited rubble remains to recreate the two large Buddhas. Alternatively, Japanese artist Hiro Yamagata negotiated with the Afghan government to project a series of giant Buddha images on the cliff with multicoloured, solar and wind-powered lasers in a weekly show.

It's arguably a better idea than trying to physically reconstruct the figures but this installation would present an enticing and obvious target for the Taliban. The laser project was already pushed back once five years to 2012 by the artist, who claims it will 'revive the great creative spirit of mankind which produced the Great Buddha of Bamyan centuries ago'.

The rapid escalation of the Afghanistan conflict probably means it will never happen. But Yamagata's website seems to indicate he would use the whole cliff as his canvas, creating images of Buddhas that didn't previously exist, and producing a somewhat self-promoting, even 'artistically idolatrous' display that perhaps has no place here.

The 'then and now' duality that characterizes Bamyan took another turn in spring 2008 when the New Zealanders had to sandbag and destroy a Pakistani-made 85mm rocket found buried in the ground about 60 metres from the small alcove, having deemed it too unstable to move. The provincial culture department subsequently accused the EOD team of causing damage to the historic site, although the controlled explosion left a crater the size of a small puddle and was judged by UNESCO as having caused no harm. Most likely, someone opportunely figured on squeezing more money out of the Kiwis as the contingent kindly rendered their town a little safer. (In July 2010 the Kiwis were still there – but in that month they declined to send 50 more troops to Uruzgan province, where casualties were being suffered, to strengthen Australian forces there as requested by former Australian PM Kevin Rudd. Were the Kiwis having second thoughts, was this another crack in the ISAF wall?)

With its calm-within-the-storm atmosphere, ancient sites and 21st-century armaments, Soviet tank wrecks and mobile phone towers, Bamyan represents a curious intersection of cultures and civilizations, and continues to throw up the oddest common denominators with the outside world.

As I walked up the path to the scaffolded alcove of the small Buddha, a party of Hazara students visiting from the neighbouring Dai Kundi province emerged from the cliff and walked toward me. As they passed, their grinning teacher stopped and took my hand and exclaimed 'Hello, Mr Bean!'

seventeen

WAR STORY CENTRAL

The four American soldiers are chatting in the stationary Humvee to 'Sweet Home Alabama' when 7.62mm bullets start smacking into the hood and turret at short intervals. One finally hits driver Alex Goduti's windshield panel dead centre with a splat, a few inches in front of his nose. The reinforced glass withstands the impact but the next round or two will shatter it so he slams the vehicle in reverse and sends it lurching back up the narrow track for protection from the shooter.

'I'm so lucky,' the 20-year-old from Maine repeats as he stares at the cobweb of cracks on the pane. I keep my camera rolling from the back seat, wondering at the speedy materialization of my story on the first mission out of the KOP.

Our hasty withdrawal is quickly reversed – a few minutes later we have to go forward again and round an exposed bend to find a spot wide enough to turn the truck without rolling down the hillside.

'Paradise City' by Guns and Roses comes on and the soldiers are laughing as Goduti per-forms a hasty 10-point manoeuvre over the precipice. Then a US 120-mm mortar shell slams into the slope just below us, spewing up flame and smoke from the pines.

'Please keep the rounds away from the road,' the Lieutenant requests politely over the radio.

Korengal Valley in Kunar province became known to me through stories by Elizabeth Rubin in the *New York Times* magazine and from pieces by *Perfect Storm* author Sebastian Junger in *Vanity Fair*.

Both were hard-hitting, gritty accounts of a daily fight-within-a-fight between US infantry and an array of enemies in picture-book surrounds, so I resolved to make my way there in 2008 and do a story on the media's mesmerised interest in 'Death Valley', as the soldiers call it.

With so much quintessential War on Terror on tap in Korengal, the US public affairs office at Bagram is inundated with applications for visits here. That year about half of all requests to embed in eastern Afghanistan specified the valley, although only a few bidders made it because the military can't overwhelm the single company of troops with a mob of reporters, photographers and TV crews.

'The Korengal Valley became a media magnet when word got out that journalists who went there were virtually guaranteed to experience combat,' Junger wrote in an e-mail to me. 'For a while, almost one-fifth of the combat in the entire country was occurring in the Korengal.'

I was offered a 10-day embed in Kunar with the Provincial Reconstruction Team with no mention of the valley, but once there I still hoped to wangle my way up to the famous KOP, the Korengal Outpost.

The place was characterized in my mind by an image from Junger's story of how troops originally built it under fire, heaving rocks over their heads into the Hesco cages until they had some basic cover. The site evolved into a reinforced hill base with mortar pits and a dusty helipad but is still so exposed to enemy fire that the soldiers are rarely completely safe – one man was killed by a bullet as he lay sleeping in bed. From the establishment of the permanent US presence in the valley in 2006 to May 2009, 40 US soldiers died in this beau-tiful, lethal backwater.

When I entered the Media Operations Centre at Bagram in late October I met Getty Images photographer John Moore who had left Korengal that morning on a helicopter and made it all the way back to BAF. Just a few hours before he was at the KOP shooting a shura between the US and local elders. The event ended when the base mortars opened up on insurgents attacking further down the valley, sending the guests dashing home in a startled flurry of henna-dyed beards.

It's more laborious getting out there. To reach Kunar you have to fly east from Bagram to Jalalabad Airfield and then north to Asadabad, the provincial capital. And to get to Korengal you have to go to FOB Blessing and then hop over the hills in a helicopter to the KOP or to Firebase Vegas on the opposite side of the valley.

I land in Jalalabad in the middle of the night after a 30-minute flight on a C-130 transport plane. With a large dining facility, gymnasium, stores and bazaar, FOB Fenty is like many other bases, but its runway is so close to the accommodation that the transit tent all but billows to the roar of aircraft.

On October 31 the DFAC is decked out with pumpkin bunting and witch and ghost streamers. The new Halloween movie is playing on a big screen and I wonder if I'm the only one who finds it unappetizing to eat as Jason holds a victim's head in a bath full of water, filmed from under the surface as blood gushes from his gurgling mouth.

I watch him expire over the back of a soldier whose T-shirt shows a Humvee and top gunner and reads, 'Life is like a box of ammunition, it's so good you just never want it to end.'

This is the Area of Operations (AO) of Task Force Duke, 3rd Brigade Combat Team, 1st Infantry Division. I get my obligatory media briefing on the four eastern provinces of 'N2KL' – Nuristan, Nangahar, Kunar and Lagman – from the Major in charge of public affairs, who seems to have a patchy grasp of the region and only a finger-hold on events over the border in Pakistan, despite their close bearing on the situation here.

But it's kind of useful to learn that there are 30 military bases and outposts in the AO and that Nuristan has only 15 kilometres of paved road, and I jot down a couple of platitudes she offers about counterinsurgency: 'That's what COIN is all about, people, relationship-building, how we can help you to help yourself.'

I stop outside the public affairs office the next day and chat to one of the staff who is sat by a video camera on a tripod trying to attract soldiers to record upbeat greetings for the folks back home.

Accustomed to the insistent procession of journalists heading to Korengal, he even thinks this makes the conflict worse.

'If reporters stopped going there it would probably go away. The insurgents know they get on TV and that they'll get bang for their buck.'

I fly to Asadabad on November 2 in a Chinook escorted by two Apaches, touching down half an hour later in Camp Wright, named after Sgt. Jeremy Wright, who was killed here by an IED on January 3, 2005.

The FOB is ringed by steep hills and has a couple of artillery guns pointed over the summits and two Soviet-made Afghan National Army T-62 tanks parked up for additional firepower if needed.

I'm left in the briefing room by Lt. Loren Crowe who comes back ten minutes later with the US commander in Kunar, Lt. Col. Brett Jenkinson, a tall, balding man with a slightly eccentric demeanour and a tendency to roll his face to accentuate points, often with a kooky grin. For someone charged with such a tough area he's pretty laid back, but the mere mention of Korengal draws a heavy sigh.

'We've been fighting there for years and brute force and ignorance don't work,' he says, and shows interest in my idea of a story on how the media cover the conflict in the valley. The public affairs Major in Jalalabad is now far away, this is Jenkinson's turf and if he wants me to go there I will, and vice versa.

Kunar province is in a state of busy logistic activity in November 2008 as the US troops prepare for winter, stock up their forward positions and help to organize the Afghan government forces.

After a summer of heavy fighting, many enemy have been drawn over the border to the Bajaur Agency where the Pakistani military under US pressure is waging a campaign against the Taliban as well as al-Qaeda elements said to operate across this area. Kunar and Nuristan are often mentioned in connection with the possible whereabouts of Osama

Author's first trip out of the Korengal Outpost, Korengal Valley, Kunar province, November 8, 2008.

Specialist Alex Goduti of US 1-26th Infantry examines bullet damage to his truck, Korengal Valley, Kunar province.

TIE-DOWN

B 36

bin Laden, after a video released in September 2003 shows the fugitive and his deputy, Ayman al-Zawahiri, climbing mountainsides with pines and dark rocks characteristic of these provinces. Then again, it has also been suggested that if bin Laden is still alive he may be hiding in Afghanistan's north-eastern Badakhshan province, Pakistan's northern areas or its Kurram Agency, Kashmir and so on.

Pakistani military action in Bajaur has created a breathing space for ISAF to resupply and reinforce on the Afghan side of the border, and over the past month additional ANA units boosted the Police presence in district centres during voter registration for the 2009 presidential election. Meanwhile, the remaining insurgents have been planting IEDs to try and hit the registration teams and disrupt the process.

The intensity of the fight in Kunar is evident even in the calmer spells. On the morning I arrive in Asadabad I go with Lt. Crowe's platoon north up the main road to FOB Monti, located close to the border.

'Holy shit there's a lot of birds over our heads, I mean Apaches, 1-2-3-4-5, and two Black Hawks,' the top gunner shouts. He ducks down through the hatch and asks me, 'Have you been in a TIC before?'

'Not in a convoy. Is that likely?'

They laugh without elaborating and the gunner tells me that as the only person in the back I will have to feed him boxes of ammo for the M240 if we get attacked.

The six vehicles stop in the Chagal District Centre at midday and the US register a 60mm mortar against likely Taliban firing points following a big attack from the surrounding hills in September. Beside the DC main compound stands one rusting Soviet T-62 tank wreck and in the middle of the next field sits the stripped hulk of a T-34 WWII Russian battle tank.

Our column continues up the main road to Monti but all my notes say about the ride is, 'I never saw a top gunner swivel so much.'

The next day the platoon drives to the Dangam District Centre which is located seven kilometres from the border and is only reached by leaving the paved highway and driving an hour down a narrow track. It's a lousy route by any standards, with dips and hairpin bends that strain the 160-horsepower

engines of the Humvees, and there is a high chance of running over one of the IEDs that appear at night.

Most of the 40-strong insurgent group that operates in the immediate area are thought to be fighting in Bajaur now, but locals still found four roadside bombs on this track in the past six weeks. A few days earlier three members of a Taliban IED cell blew themselves to pieces while planting a device. All that remained were mangled torsos that the ANP buried at the spot and which were later dug up and recovered by men from one of the more unruly villages in the area.

The District Centre still bears the scars of heavy attacks in August, including the 27 successive rockets that blew holes in the school roof and the wall above the window of the Police Chief's room.

The chief has about 60 men to hold the ground and a good armoury of weapons, from Russian-made PKM machine-guns to a ZPU-1 14.5mm anti-aircraft gun that stays trained on the hill crests by Pakistan. Crowe has also acquired a truckload of Hescos to make defensive walls around the official buildings.

'We'll make this place into a castle, the strongest DC on the border,' he tells the Police Chief. 'They're not going to fight in Bajaur forever, that's why we need to get those Hescos filled and defences strengthened before they come back.'

By contrast, the fight in the Korengal Valley located a few kilometres to the south-west seems to grind on independently of the ebb and flow of hostilities in greater Kunar.

Their ancestors having migrated here a century ago from Nuristan to the north, the estimated 6,000 Korengalis are a separate people with their own language and who are fiercely protective of their tiny swathe of land and way of life.

There is a hard core of local men who fight the Americans and ANA almost daily, their numbers never seeming to diminish despite the losses they take. As Junger writes, there are Pakistani cellphones painted on rocks in the valley as a means of recruiting volunteers, and Arabic graffiti urging local men to join the fight. The valley according to Jenkinson is also where various groups including foreign fighters come to 'get street cred', creating a cauldron of violence in this magnificent cedar-clad mountain panorama.

The ferocity of the conflict also echoes a tradition of entrenched resistance to outsiders in Kunar, which saw heavy fighting during the Soviet occupation in the 1980s. Some former mujahedin commanders came from the valley and the allegiances endure to this day among the local population.

Measuring ten by eight kilometres, the valley is located in the Manogai District, which has at times posted Afghanistan's highest numbers of 'significant acts', any form of contact with the enemy, including IEDs and indirect fire with mortars and rockets. It is also known for other records. At FOB Blessing, the 155mm guns of Charlie Battery, 3rd Battalion of the 321st Field Artillery, are trained towards Korengal. By late October, 2008, they had fired more than 5,900 shells since deploying to Afghanistan less than a year earlier, making them the busiest artillery unit in the US Army.

I fly to the valley twice, initially to the KOP with Lt. Col. Jenkinson to attend a shura meeting with two dozen village elders. The CO's party brings in Kunar Governor Sayed Wahidi and the Manogai sub-Governor in a further bid to win support for construction of a 43-kilometre road running through the valley and linking it to the main provincial highway.

Road crews already reached the mouth of the Korengal where they immediately came under fire and had to stop until enough willing labour can be recruited from inside the valley to push the project forward. No one expects to find a panacea to local troubles in the road but the bubble of armed resistance might be pricked with improved access to the outside world.

It could also aid the resumption of the Korengal's stalled logging industry, control of which was a core dispute between local factions. This first sparked the fighting here when a rival managed to turn the US forces against local landowner Haji Matin. After members of his family died in an air strike and others were arrested, Matin went into armed resistance and remains the key insurgent leader in the area.

But as importantly as anything else, the road project creates employment for young men who might otherwise pick up a rifle against the Americans.

'Most of the people in the province are fighting predominantly not for ideological reasons but for a job,' believes US Navy Commander Daniel Dwyer, who runs Kunar's PRT.

According to him, the average daily wage for insurgents here is five dollars, so the Americans are offering almost a buck more as an incentive to choose peaceful employment. But this isn't working either, so they call shura after shura to nudge local leaders to review their allegiances.

'It's a pity, money comes here and there's a chance for employment but people don't come forward,' Governor Wahidi tells the elders gathered in the dingy concrete 'shura shack' near the KOP mortar pit.

Appointed a year earlier, the official has a white trimmed beard, a wavy grey combover and small glasses, and combines an astute, scholarly air with light humour that seems to sit well with the Korengalis.

'Today I need 300 labourers but no one is coming forward – you must be very wealthy people indeed,' he says, stressing that the inhabitants of the valley stand to miss out entirely on 50 million dollars of US aid that is earmarked for development projects in Kunar.

'Today I flew here in a helicopter. It costs maybe 2,000 dollars for one flight, money that is better spent on building a school. It costs 100,000 afghanis for an artillery round, so this is wasted money. ISAF are a peacekeeping force, they are not here to fight. If you stop fighting this money will come here, so don't complain any more that there are no jobs and no money – it's up to you,' Wahidi tells the group.

There are a few more speeches, then a turbaned elder with a prolific white beard, beaky nose and his middle finger in a bandage rises to his feet.

'We have fruit on the tree but we can't eat it,' he says with near theatrical woe. 'We are very unhappy that construction of the road has stopped, we beg the fighters to put down their weapons but we are unable to force them.'

Reminiscent of the 'oh, the kids of today' lament of western parents, another insists that in Korengal, 'the young people don't listen

Troops of the US 1-26th Infantry direct 120mm mortar fire onto Taliban fighters, Korengal Valley, November 9, 2008.

to the elders, in the past we had a chance to impose decisions but not now.'

'We are helping as much as we can,' says a third man with a long red beard, glasses, grubby jacket and a stick. 'In the past the enemy had some bases, we could take the message to them, now they are scattered in different places and we don't know who to talk to or who their leader is. They are hiding in the mountains, they don't have representatives that we could approach, but if I can find them I will tell them.'

Since he became Governor, Wahidi has been up here four times to impart more or less the same message.

'If we don't have a continuous dialogue they will think we've forgotten about them,' he says before the meeting. 'The big hope is to bring

people closer to the government and start the actions planned for the valley, a community centre and roads.'

But these are people who are historically used to sitting on the fence and playing both sides for gain or simply for survival. The Americans have heard it all before and are sure that some guests at the shuras report straight back to the insurgents.

'It's the same old-same old,' Jenkinson says later. 'The United States will leave Afghanistan before that road goes through. We'll have to do a lot of killing first, it would be better to build a dam and fill the valley with water.

'We've lost six guys from the battalion already up there. And for what, how many more men do we have to lose? Nothing's working, we've tried fighting them into submission and talking them down from the mountains and giving them projects. Those people don't want progress or they'd fight for it.'

But later that month, after I left the valley, there came a vivid demonstration of why the locals are so afraid. The Taliban came to Loy Kalay, pulled the village elder who attended the KOP shura out of the mosque, accused him of working with the Americans and shot him. Then they beheaded his corpse in the centre of the village as a warning to others.

I return to the valley the next day on a supply flight from FOB Blessing and spend four days with Viper Company 1st Battalion, 26th Infantry Regiment at the KOP, which is still the oddest working environment I experienced in Afghanistan.

What strikes you is the compact nature of this struggle and how such a beautiful place can simultaneously twitter with birdsong and roar to exploding bombs and machine-gun fire; how kids in the villages walk to school while the sides shoot it out in the hills above them, and just how routine and almost ritualistic these engagements have become.

'You can get shot at every day, it might only be one guy with a rifle and five rounds, harassment fire, or sometimes it's ten guys with machine-guns and RPGs,' Executive Officer Lt. John Rodriguez tells me after I arrive the second time.

We are perched on a small roof at the top end of the KOP while Rodriguez stands with a radio and directs Chinooks bringing men and supplies here, to Outpost Restrepo located a kilometre higher up the ridge and to Firebase Vegas, which is just visible five kilometres across the valley. Vegas sits beneath plenty of high ground and as such takes the brunt of attacks on the bases themselves. In August, around 50 enemy fighters tried to storm it but were sharply repulsed.

'For the most part everyone would relish them trying to overrun one of our bases because if they attack with loads of guys it's easier for us to take them out,' Rodriguez says. 'If it's one guy and a rifle you can shoot mortars all day but where is he?'

The following morning at 0430 I go out in one of the Humvees with four soldiers from Viper Company's Second Platoon, including platoon leader Lt. Cliff Pederson.

'We are just providing cover, it should be boring, that's why we brought lots of music,' one of the soldiers says before we roll out to secure the extraction route for another US platoon and some ANA and their Marine trainers who will search one of the villages.

The Humvee groans along a narrow winding track over a steep drop, passing square little houses made of rocks and heaps of massive 70 centimetre square cedar wood blocks that have lain by the road since the paralysis of the lumber trade.

The iPod in the truck is playing 'Highway to Hell' by AC/DC when the other guy in the back says 'I have eyes on two PAX on 1705, 40 metres from the top, black manjams, no weapons.'

I don't know it yet but there are certain hills in the Korengal Valley that are out of bounds to the locals and where the troops can engage anyone spotted moving on them, even without positive identification (PID) that they are carrying weapons. Named after its metre elevation above sea level, Hill 1705 is one of these hills.

Instead of the usual wait for threat confirmation as happens in most other places in the country, the sighting almost immediately ignites a barrage of rifle, machine-gun and mortar fire, causing Korengal Valley to rumble and shake around us.

Some ANA soldiers run past the truck, shooting as they go, while someone out of sight is going crazy with a PKM, loosing off whole 100-round belts of ammo in one go. We halt by a disused saw mill on a bend in the track and wait for the dismounted US platoon to pull out past us.

The soldiers in the truck continue to chat when the first soldiers jog by and then take cover among the timber piles as insurgent fire pursues them. Right outside my window some guys let rip with M4 rifles and an M240 while we sit tight to more classic rock, and Goduti pronounces the fateful words: 'No truck of mine has even been shot.'

The Humvee's Mark 19 automatic grenade launcher has jammed and refuses to fire so the top gunner, 18-year-old Robert Soto from New York, ducks down inside the vehicle. Moments later rounds start thumping off the hood, turret and windshield and we have to get out of there fast before someone hits the damaged glass with something heavier.

After our laborious turnaround on the road, we start moving back to Dallas as 155mm rounds roar in from Blessing to hit Hill 1705 and other sources of insurgent fire. Several US soldiers emerge from cover and move with us, crouching between the truck and the rock face for protection, firing a few shots as they go. A Sergeant stares at me through the window and asks his buddy, 'Who's that? Oh it's a fucking reporter, I hope he's not filming, I've got my sleeves rolled up.'

It's one of those bizarre moments that will stay with me forever. Even in the middle of a fire fight they are worried about being shown in non-regulation dress. The top Command recently took punitive measures against units in RC-East where reporters photographed and filmed soldiers who were not wearing ballistic eyewear, had their sleeves rolled up or were generally unkempt.

'We had cases where injured guys got shaved by the doctors before they went into surgery in case some General came to see them and freaked out that they're unshaven,' one of the officers tells me.

The next spring, Specialist Zachary Boyd from Texas made the front pages of the world's newspapers in a photograph of him manning a position in Korengal during a surprise insurgent attack wearing a red T-shirt, pink 'I love NY' boxer shorts, flip-flops, helmet and body armour.

This surely earned him a severe reprimand by his Command, but Secretary for Defense Gates stepped in to say publicly that Boyd's job was safe. 'Any soldier who goes into battle against the Taliban in pink boxers and flip-flops has a special kind of courage,' he said.

On the drive back to base we stop in the village of Aliabad where the ANA and their Marine trainers are resting near the cemetery, which juts with its Kunar-typical headstones made of two-metre slivers of rock. A few months earlier, $10,000-worth of arms and ammunition were discovered in one of these graves.

The Marines pay little attention to the reporter as they gulp water from their Camelbaks and prepare for the enemy to resume the attack, requesting only that their

interpreter's face is not shown in any photos or film.

Second Platoon leader Lt. Pederson says the troops at Korengal have become used to camera-toting civilians who tag along on missions. If anything, the constant media procession is observed with detached amusement.

'It's almost become a rite of passage for journalists, so they can say 'I've been to the Korengal',' says the officer, whose company lost six men killed in action and 19 wounded from July to the onset of the calmer winter period in December.

But general indifference towards the journalists is tinged with caution that they can become a liability in an emergency. One prominent war correspondent got banned from the valley that year after panicking in a fire fight and running amok. The bottom line is that as a reporter you are as vulnerable to enemy fire as everyone else, and in Korengal it is usually upon you without warning.

'I was almost killed twice – both times when I least expected it,' Junger recalled of his own visits.

There are usually one or two TICs a day in the valley, shattering the calm with thunderous artillery, mortar and small arms fire, cannon bursts from Apache helicopters and the splitting roar of bombs dropped by NATO jets. And today is just another day of Viper Company's one-year tour, fairly unremarkable to the soldiers but an eye-opener to this newcomer.

Back at the KOP I am feeling a bit shaken after the lashing the truck took and flake out on my cot with my iPod for a couple of hours. I'm billeted in a wooden hut with two Army engineers who built it on the spot where the soldier was shot dead while sleeping in his tent. In the late afternoon the three of us hear small arms fire followed by outgoing mortars and we cautiously emerge to look across the valley.

The ANA are milling around near the towers at the lower end of the KOP where the camp's water truck has just been ambushed while collecting water from the river below. Twenty minutes later a pick-up speeds through the gate in a cloud of dust and brings the injured truck driver to the first aid point.

He's been shot through the arm and is moaning loudly, and once the doctor has patched him up he is flown in a medevac chopper to Asadabad. Two ANA soldiers are brought in later with shrapnel wounds from the same incident.

Another mission goes out that night and Second Platoon tramps down the hill in complete darkness, through an insurgent-friendly village, over the river and up another hill to provide overwatch when the ANA search a village at dawn.

I still wonder why they even took me along on this two-hour hike as there is no moon and I have no night vision equipment. All I can do is try to attune myself to the tiniest contrasts of light and shade between the depressions and rocks as I stumble along. It's a mystery how I don't break a leg as we cross a river and clamber up the steep slopes, but sixty minutes before first light the platoon and I make it up to the target peak without incident.

'Now we wait and see if they want to play or not, we'll know in the next hour or so,' Pederson tells me.

At 0630 half a dozen fighting age males leave houses in the nearest village and split up, some moving up the road to the next settlement while others go up the prohibited heights to retrieve their weapons from caches in the rocks. Twenty minutes later the Americans get word that the insurgents are trying to fix their positions and muster enough supplies for an engagement. Three men are sighted moving down the facing slopes and the Americans promptly plaster the location with mortar shells. There are reports of one injured man and then no further contact so the US and ANA units return to base.

In the mid-afternoon insurgents creep down the hillside opposite the KOP and rake the buildings with a PKM machine-gun. The base mortars immediately bring down a barrage of high explosive and phosphorous rounds and silence the weapon.

No one is injured on this side, although unbeknown to the engineers and I as we watch from round a corner, the incoming rounds are passing ten metres over our hut and impacting against the walls of the KOP's operations centre and Second Platoon's accommodation.

It's another characteristic of Korengal madness that you can be in a TIC and not even know it.

November 10: The Dallas Dash

Today is the official birthday of the United States Marine Corps. It's my last mission out of the KOP after two on the high ground as search parties went in, so I ask to join the team of Marine trainers and their ANA as they go into the village of Loy Kalay.

It's essentially a bait run, designed to flush out the enemy and draw them into an engagement with the US troops waiting above us so the Apaches, artillery and mortars can mop up a few before breakfast.

Our group should leave while it is still dark to maintain the element of surprise but the ANA are disorganized and late, and the four waiting Marines become infuriated as the first glimmers of daylight appear.

'Until they raise the standards of recruiting, this turmoil is going to go on for a long time,' one tells me forcefully and for the record. 'They are taking from the bottom of the pot, not even that but from the residue – these guys can't even get a job as farmers or shopkeepers.'

As we trudge along the track toward Aliabad I talk with Captain Clinton Cummings who commands the Marine Embedded Training Team. He tells me I am one of few journalists to go with the ETT and the ANA on a mission, usually stories focus of the infantry of Viper Company, although as he notes, 'The whole point of us being here is to get these guys to be able to do the job themselves.'

'There's a lot here that people don't know about and it's important that the story gets told,' Cummings continues. 'Although sometimes journalists ask you questions during fire fights when people have got other things to do.'

At 0530 it's already light as we reach the Vimoto Observation Post to pick up more ANA and another couple of trainers.

'So much for going in under cover of darkness, thanks guys,' someone mutters as we set off again along the track.

I fall in at the rear with Corporal Eric Russell, a twenty-year-old from Allendale, Michigan, who imparts the glad tidings that we will have to run between the trucks under fire on the way out.

Until now I hadn't put two and two together – my ride in the truck on the first day, the running infantry, the harassing fire. Like a python swallowing a brick, I digest the fact that I have signed up for the 'Dallas Dash', a 200-metre life or death sprint along the exposed hillside track to the Dallas OP.

The patrol moves down the hill into Loy Kalay just before 0600 and the ANA start searching a few suspect houses. Four men were spotted fleeing from the village as the troops approached, and they and others from the area will now be gathering their weapons for the looming shoot-out.

It kicks off at 0639 when the insurgents start firing at the infantry on the hill above us, filling the valley with the sounds of battle. The exchange lasts ten or fifteen minutes but for the next hour our group has to run and duck from house to house, manoeuvring into position until the order is given to withdraw.

The Americans learn that the enemy commander has instructed his men not to waste their ammunition on the troops on the high ground but to wait until we pull out on foot and concentrate their fire on us.

'Once they see us in the open they're going to start shooting,' Gunnery Sergeant Alexandro Magdaleno warns me as we wait behind a brick wall. Two Apaches buzz round overhead, rocketing and strafing the insurgent positions, but this won't deter them from trying to pick us off as we extract, he says.

It's nerve-wracking to stand around waiting to be a fairground duck while the shooters try for the cuddly toy. But the sun is shining and the Marines are in a boisterous sporting mood as they get ready for what has become a regular event.

'If you take it too seriously it sucks but if you have fun with it then it's more bearable,' Russell says, adding that the trainers try to beat their personal fastest time for the run.

'I don't mean to worry you but the last journalist who did the Dallas Dash with us got shot in the chest,' Magdaleno informs me as we prepare to go. But a few minutes later someone above gets impatient and opens fire on us while we are still crouching among the houses.

This draws a massive response from all positions of the US and ANA, including ours. The air above the village is thick with machine-gun and rifle fire and we start taking rounds

from the same saw mill we were parked beside during the TIC two days ago.

The ANA and Marines start unloading at the mill and Magdaleno fires a SMAW-D rocket which explodes on the slope a few metres short. I am crouching in a concrete passage by a house 20 metres away from him when the rocket launches but my right eardrum compresses into my skull with a stab of pain. Then as I grope in vain for my earplugs the left eardrum takes a battering from the machine-gun fire of the soldiers beside me, the long bursting reports amplified by the walls around us. (Weeks later my hearing was still impaired, as if my ear was stuffed with cotton wool, and grew worse after the next trip to Zabul. A hospital test in August 2009 confirmed a permanent 40-decibel reduction in my left ear.)

We get the order to move out in two groups and I move with the first, eager to get this over with. Half a dozen of us creep along with the last of the four trucks as they take up position at 60-metre intervals along the track to the Dallas OP.

'One-two-THREEE!' the burly Afghan Sergeant roars in English as he races off in the lead, and the rest of us follow one by one, pounding along the first stretch as fast as possible.

Despite roaring bursts from the truck-mounted .50-cal and M240s I can hear the snap-snap of incoming rounds somewhere close but focus on getting to cover as fast as possible without falling over. Pausing only briefly at each Humvee, I am one of the first to reach the shelter of the OP, my heart pounding even faster than my boots had. More men puff in behind me and the first group is home safe.

The soldiers then open up from behind the OP's Hesco wall at Hill 1705 but they are shooting blindly while the insurgents have a far more distinct target. The incoming fire intensifies as the second group starts along the road and at one point the rock face behind one of the trucks seems to explode with impacting rounds. But the gods smile on the runners and all the Afghan and US soldiers make it in OK, chests heaving, soaked in sweat and whooping with adrenalin-fused elation.

After a few minutes, jets swoop and drop 2,000lb bombs on the saw mill and one other target. The US forces try not to damage local

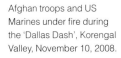

Afghan troops and US Marines under fire during the 'Dallas Dash', Korengal Valley, November 10, 2008.

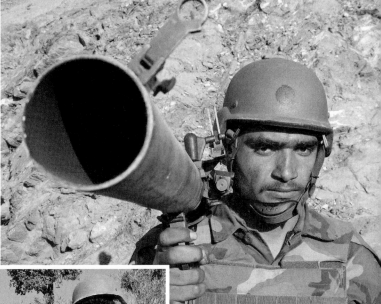

Afghan soldier with an 82mm recoilless rifle after the 'Dallas Dash'.

US Marine Gunnery Sergeant Alexandro Magdaleno with Afghan National Army trainees after the 'Dallas Dash'.

property but this disused facility has been used as an enemy firing point once too often and is now erased without ceremony. The trucks then pull out and we follow on foot, glancing back as the helicopters continue to strafe the smoke-shrouded hills with rockets and long burps of cannon fire.

It might be tit-for-tat or just opportunism, but that night RPGs are launched at the Dallas OP from somewhere in Aliabad. One American soldier suffers a shrapnel wound to the back of the head and is medevaced out.

★ ★ ★

'I think the people we are fighting are fighting for a lot of different reasons, a lot of foreigners, a guy trying to make a buck, anything to make a bit of extra money and if it's shooting at Americans it's OK,' says the commander of Viper Company, Captain Jimmy Howell, a calm, polite man of 29 who first came to Korengal three years earlier during initial probes into the valley.

'At any given time there are probably upward of 30 to 50 guys who live here who are ready to fight, the core group, plus a flavour of everything else like foreign fighters,' he tells me over a cup of coffee in the mess hut the evening after the dash. (Elsewhere I hear references to hundreds of insurgents based in the valley, but no one can say for sure.)

'Part of the reason they are fighting here so much in Korengal is to keep development out. I think the road will happen and that the only people who are against it are the Taliban, so they are throwing everything they've got at it. It'll take time.

'I think if we left they wouldn't move on, Korengal is in the middle of everything, they could launch a lot of attacks from here. The fight here keeps the heat off the Pech River Valley and Kunar River Valley, so it allows us to continue to develop the infrastructure and governance in more populated areas.

'There was a lot of fighting here before there was the amount of media coverage and I think that regardless, the Korengal is an easy place for them to fight and it is an area that they've been pretty successful at keeping progress, infrastructure and ties with the government at bay.

'But I also think that an enormous part of the enemy's strategy is to use the media to bolster their appeal and discredit the Afghan and US governments. The enemy wants media coverage of Afghanistan and the Korengal to remain negative, what they want is any report that shows the Afghan government or the US as incapable of securing the country.'

Amid discussions of how to present the Korengal in media reports, the common denominators are to be found in most accounts about the fight in the valley: natural beauty and bestial violence, suffering and sacrifice, hope and frustration, all punctuated with the stark snapshots of combat that this place serves up time and time again.

As photographer John Moore put it, 'In the Korengal, you photograph US troops doing what they were trained to do – fight, fight and then tomorrow, fight again. Every day their mettle is tested by the hostile local populace, the brutal mountain terrain and the Taliban, who seem quite unafraid.'

Perhaps another reason for the flow of journalists here is that even if the origins of the hostilities are complex, the story as it stands today lends itself to drama-laden simplicity as the sides slog it out blow for blow.

A lot of the soldiers feel that media accounts tend towards sensation and negativity and some wonder if journalists arrive with the story practically pre-written and just needing some gunplay to fill the gaps.

'They already just want to depict how bad it is,' one Private said. 'They focus on us killing their guys and our killed in action and wounded, rather than what we do for the people, giving them wheat and things.'

Adds Marine Captain Cummings: 'Sometimes it gives the impression that the whole of Afghanistan is falling apart, and that's definitely not true.'

Writer Junger agrees that the view of the Korengal can get skewed with potentially ruinous long-term effects.

'Reporters generally failed to acknowledge that there are vast swathes of the country that are relatively peaceful. But as the Generals say, perception is an important part of war,' he said. 'If the Taliban can pass themselves off as a tactically-skilled force that is steadily gaining power, support for the government among regular Afghans will begin to waver. Once that process starts, it will be very hard to reverse.'

There has been speculation that the Taliban might plough extra resources into the valley precisely because it receives so much media attention. But the movement plays down the issue and insist it does battle just as fiercely elsewhere.

'Maybe the reason you know or hear more about our fight in the Korengal is that journalists go there more,' Taliban spokesman Zabiullah Mujahed said by telephone from an undisclosed location, denying that the insurgent command has a special focus here. 'The fact is, we inflict casualties on the invaders every day in all corners of the country.'

'The high level of media coverage certainly does not discourage the enemy, and may encourage them to a degree,' Howell says. 'But I think the real reason they are fighting as hard as they are here is because a lot of their leadership have strong ties to this area and they have been able to really fight us to a stalemate. While we've made some progress, it is extremely minimal when put in the context of development in the rest of the country.'

For the soldiers, the basic result of all the dramatic, high-octane coverage is that they have to phone home and allay fears every time a new media story comes out.

While generally well received by the troops, a piece shown by the American television company NBC in October 2008 took some criticism for its handling of a friendly fire incident in which a US mortar shell hit a house, killing one American soldier and injuring six.

The immediate aftermath of the blast was not shown, but the pained cries of the survivors were aired.

'I don't think people back home needed to hear all of us scream right after we got hit, my mum didn't need to hear that, nor did the wives and kids of the people here,' said Specialist Thomas Richardson, 22.

'My inbox was full of mails from family and my wife was saying "you didn't tell me it was like that",' a Sergeant recalled after the piece was broadcast. But another soldier objected more to NBC's mention that some men at one of the more primitive Korengal outposts, Restrepo, wear flea collars on their belts to fight infestations.

The greatest concern, however, is that the notion of a full-on, 24/7 fight inflames the situation not just here but elsewhere in the province and also the country.

'It's a good story – but it's a story,' says Howell. 'We're not fighting for our lives every minute of the day. There is some intense fighting and hard times but I do think things are portrayed more dramatically than they actually are.

'I don't think the reporting on Korengal gives a fair representation of the progress in Afghanistan – you can't judge Afghanistan by Kunar province and you can't judge Kunar province by the Korengal. But it seems to be an Alamo for everybody; there have been a lot of reports from here.'

With no sign of a breakthrough in the Korengal stalemate for the following 18 months, reporters would continue to come seeking what they believed to be the essence of the war in Afghanistan, making it almost inevitable that a media worker would figure among the casualties before a victory, solution or withdrawal here was forthcoming. Then again, this would probably only enhance the valley's newsworthiness for editors sat in newsrooms far from the gunfire.

'I have found in the Korengal an area of spectacular, albeit deceptive beauty, where a seemingly tranquil paradise can turn into your worst nightmare in a heartbeat,' wrote combat photographer Keith Lepor, the person who in September 2008 took a 7.62mm round directly over his heart while doing the Dallas Dash.

His life was saved by the ceramic chest plate in his body armour and he keeps the metal bullet fragments that he retrieved from the vest as a reminder of the hazards of the job.

My advice to journalists regarding the Korengal is not to enter such an environment unless you are passionate for what you are doing and willing to pay the ultimate price. For me, capturing American troops on film and doing justice to the Marines and Army with whom I was embedded with was worth the risk. The world must know what American troops are doing to keep them safe against an enemy committed to the destruction of all

Insurgents on Hill 1705 receive
US mortar and helicopter
rocket fire, Korengal Valley.

that we in the West hold dear and further-more fight the enemy in Afghanistan and not on the streets of London, Paris, Berlin or New York.

A friend from *Time* magazine, Aryn Baker, describes in an e-mail her own Dallas Dash amid a fierce night time ambush in April 2009:

This is where you start thinking about the insanity of war. About the false sense of security that two metal plates and Kevlar webbing offer when they are presented in glossy catalogs. About how vulnerable flesh is to metal projectiles. It wasn't my life that flashed before my eyes, but all the descriptions of wounds I'd heard from the buddies of injured soldiers. Faces blown off, shattered shoulders and mangled limbs – all

the points exposed by the limits of Kevlar. What is more insane than running 200 meters through gunfire to reach safety? But we did. I felt like Bruce Willis in *Die Hard*, somehow dancing between the bullets that showered from below and behind. The Taliban can shoot, but they can't aim. We were lucky. All of us were.

Amid Korengal and Kunar's grinding fight, momentous happenings in the outside world seem far, far away. On November 4, the United States elected a Democrat as president to the dismay of many in the military who feared for the high level of funding they enjoyed under Bush and the Republicans. But this global event seemed to go over the heads of some soldiers, while others noted it and pushed it immediately to the back of their minds.

'At the end of the day, Barrack Obama's election doesn't change much out here,' infantryman Soto told me. 'We've already had people pass away and it makes it a whole different fight, not what the President wants or even the CO, you are doing it for those guys.'

The story I wrote about the valley was picked up by various media outlets. I came across it posted on one website with a reader's comment that is quite a masterpiece of brash presumption and judgment:

> I wish all these reporters that end up in bad places in the middle of Iraq and Afghanistan would all get killed. They put themselves in these situations and take up attention from soldiers who should be focusing on the mission at hand. They want to get out there to make a name for themselves at the expense of soldiers. I'm sure that every night they pray that tomorrow they will finally get that shot of an 18-year-old American boy in his final moments. Disgusting.

The next June I was walking up Disney Drive in Bagram when I saw the names Soto and Goduti on the back of the patrol caps in front of me. It could only be them on the way home after their tour but as I glimpsed Alex from the side I hesitated for a moment, seeing a much older guy, kind of worn and washed out, and definitely not the fresh-faced 20-year-old I met in November. They both seemed pretty happy, but from stories out of Korengal that I'd read since my visit I knew they had been caught up in bad things. We exchanged quick greetings and they ran for their bus. Perhaps soldiering is their vocation, but as I waved from the kerb I hoped they would never come back here again.

★ ★ ★

In April 2010, the US military pulled out of the Korengal Valley, saying the valley is too isolated and the American presence was even pushing the locals to side with the Taliban. The KOP and the firebases and outposts were dismantled and blown up.

eighteen

NORTHERN LIGHTS TO GHOWRMACH

I am riding my Honda 125 along the dual carriageway in Islamabad at 70 km/h when from behind the flowing vehicles a man wheels a motorcycle right across my path. I have time to think 'This is it' before I plough into his rear wheel, fly over the top of his bike and hit the road, my bike following a second or two later and landing on my legs. The cars behind swerve round us and a crowd quickly forms and pulls the gushing machine off me. I get to my feet in an eruption of pain from top to toe and, after establishing the guy's OK, slap him hard across the face. I then forgive him, clamber onto my bent but still functioning bike and ride home. I have an hour to pack my things before travelling to Peshawar by car for a Kabul flight the next morning to join the Finns. I should probably be dead. It's Friday 13 March. My new birthday.

There is a strong Scandinavian flavour about Camp Northern Lights by the northern city of Mazar-e-Sharif. The dining facility and 50-berth accommodation blocks are pre-fabricated but it is neat, durable work, fitted of course with IKEA furniture and exuding a freshly disinfected smell and sanitary exactitude that beggars belief after primitive conditions elsewhere. In the ablutions container by the transit tents, a notice in English on the wall gives these guidelines:

1   Make sure the toilet is clean after use, otherwise use the brush.

2   Pour some chlorine solution on a paper and wipe: the door handle; the door locker; the handle of the brush; the handle used for flushing the toilet; the toilet seat on both sides; the upper part of the toilet.

3   Wipe items but leave a thin film of chlorine remaining on the above mentioned surfaces. Are the cleaning conducted satisfactorily the next soldier will be pleased. All tissue may be flushed down the toilet and the litter removed. Please use the elbow when you open the door. Finally wash your hands before starting to work again.

In March 2009 this base on the edge of Mazar is home to 110 Finnish troops and around 400 Swedes. Both are non-NATO contingents that together with the Germans, the lead nation in Regional Command-North, are responsible for security in Balkh province where this historic city is located. The troops also patrol the outlying provinces of Jawzjan, Sar-e-Pul and Samangan, which together with five others form the more stable north of Afghanistan.

Military traffic bound for Northern Lights passes through the giant Camp Marmal, the headquarters of RC-North and Mazar's main ISAF base where in March 2009 the airfield is being enlarged to serve as an international airport.

In Marmal, the contrast with RC-East and RC-South is already tangible in the passenger terminal, which is brightly decorated with displays of Afghan art and the flags of other countries represented in the north, including Italy, Hungary, Latvia and the United States.

There are plenty of soldiers in transit but the atmosphere is not charged with the urgency and tension that pervades busy bases in the south and east. Nonetheless, the national flags here and across the northern camps fly today at half-mast in tribute to ISAF casualties in other sectors.

'Since we've been here the flags have probably only been fully up for three days in total,' says a Swedish soldier in his fourth month of deployment.

One immediately difference to more volatile parts of the country is the way the Finns and Swedes drive among the Afghan civilian traffic rather than forcing oncoming vehicles to pull over to the roadside like ISAF columns do elsewhere.

The psychological effect of this intrusive road policy on the population should not be underestimated. While necessarily aimed at reducing chances of vehicle-borne suicide bombings of military traffic, it places the whole environment on a war footing at all hours. It's unlikely the Balkh locals are constantly grateful they don't have to stop for the Finns and Swedes, but the absence of the practice certainly helps to consolidate a sense of normalcy and generally not aggravate people.

The Scandinavians often drive only in pairs of armoured Mercedes-Benz jeeps or Toyotas, which takes some getting used to after riding in convoys bristling with all manner of weapons. Nor do they wear helmets when on patrol, keeping them instead to hand inside the vehicle.

But the Finns who collect me still move fast and tight and the drivers are skilled at judging overtaking manoeuvres as pairs of vehicles so they don't get separated. Sure, it's generally quieter here, but they have had occasional attacks on them and they can't afford to get complacent.

'We have been quite lucky over the past year or two, there was shooting and IEDs and nothing happened, but we could easily have a couple more dead,' says the contingent's public affairs officer, Lt. Mikko. Petri Immonen was Finland's single fatal casualty to date, killed by an IED in Meymaneh in 2005.

Like most of the troops here, Mikko uses only his first name because among Finland's small population of 5.3 million it would not be hard to locate and harass people who served here. Like the Danes in Helmand, the Swedes and the Norwegians have the same policy after the family of a Norwegian pilot received threatening phone calls over his Afghan deployment.

It's a twenty-minute journey over potholed dusty tracks from Marmal to Northern Lights, passing sections of the nearly completed northern section of the Ring Road that runs west from Mazar to Meymaneh in Faryab province and then down to Herat.

After the eastern mountains and the deserts of Kandahar and Helmand, the area is soothingly green, with the toothy low belt of the Marmal mountains jutting in the background over a flat, fertile plain. But like everywhere else the villages are still mostly mud-built and ragtag, and dotted with occasional rusting Soviet wrecks. And still about 80 per cent of people are illiterate in Balkh.

At first I don't understand what the groups of kids running up to the road want as they hold their hands a foot apart in front of their faces, like excited anglers demonstrating imaginary carp. A driver tells me their prize is the footballs that ISAF units occasionally give out on patrols.

We pull into Northern Lights, where even the Hesco-built guard point at the entrance has Plexiglas windows and air conditioning. Inside the camp I meet a young Finn from the headquarters block who speeds around on crutches with his foot in plaster.

The last guy I asked about his crutches was an American who got shot through the leg in a firefight in Paktya. Sampo's cast is the result of a toe broken while playing volleyball. It really does feel like fresh pastures up here.

Since the Blue Mosque in Mazar-e-Sharif is a site of international religious importance, the contingents are preparing for one of the key events in the Islamic calendar, the Nowroz New Year celebrations on March 21. A few hundred thousand people may descend on the city, including many foreign dignitaries. This creates a major security headache but for the most part the ISAF troops will hang back from the proceedings.

'It's important that Afghan troops and Police do this by themselves,' says Finnish commander Lt. Col. Ahti Kurvinen, a sociable, tall, blonde 43-year-old from Helsinki. 'It's good preparation for the presidential elections, we see what these security forces can do on their own and we are ready to support.'

Kurvinen was deployed in Bosnia and Herzegovina in 2000 and has been in Afghanistan for less than one month of a six-month posting, plus an extra month assigned to cover the August polls. He is already busy

Finnish troops pause for lunch during patrol in Balkh province, March 2009.

preparing to receive another 100 Finnish troops to boost security during the elections, and outside his office construction crews are building the extra accommodation needed.

The Finnish contingent is comprised of 40 regular soldiers and 70 reservists. Other ISAF contingents envy the Finnish deal: The troops here get three blocks of two-week leave during their six-month tour, and a Private here will earn around 5,000 euros a month, which includes a per diem payment of 80 euros danger money.

But with the bulk of international resources concentrated elsewhere in Afghanistan, personnel are thinly stretched in the Finnish AO. A quarter of the Finnish contingent are involved in CIMIC work in the four provinces, reducing patrolling capacity yet further.

'Jawzjan alone is already bigger than Kosovo where there are 15,000 [foreign] troops today and which in its best days had more than 50,000 – and we have just 30,' the Colonel notes wistfully.

Fortunately, the demography of northern Afghanistan lends itself to marginalising the Taliban. The region is mainly populated by ethnic Uzbeks, Tajiks and Turkmen, although it has some scattered Pashtun districts and villages. While not all Pashtuns are Taliban, the vast majority of Taliban are Pashtuns, and these isolated settlements tend to overlap with both areas of ethnic tension and insurgent activity in RC-North.

ISAF are not the only ones activating efforts in the region – the incidence of attacks is nonetheless rising, regardless of the demographics.

'Even though it's safer than Helmand or Kandahar there are still insurgents who want to harm the local security forces,' says Kurvinen. 'If we compare what happened this year to the last, the number of incidents in January and February has doubled.'

Attacks on Police posts are not uncommon, the last occurring at an ANP checkpoint by the Pashtun village of Aqcha three weeks earlier. Then while I am at Northern Lights at least 10 policemen are killed at a checkpoint between Jawzjan and Faryab by insurgents wearing ANP uniforms.

But the Taliban are still not strong here. 'The biggest problem in the north is local power

brokers, criminals,' notes the Norwegian deputy commander of RC-North, Lt. Col. Stein Lauglo.

As in Bamyan, the much vaunted stability of the north works to its detriment when it comes to allocation of resources by the government and international donors. The lion's share of the money goes to the country's most turbulent provinces to help calm them with development and to buy the loyalty of Pashtun tribes. Yet to take the northern peace for granted carries a growing danger of backfiring.

From January 2002 to September 2008 Samangan province was by far the smallest recipient of USAID funds in the country, receiving just $13.1 million, calculated mainly on the unlikelihood that the province will flare in insurgent activity or revolt.

'And what do they get for being a peaceful province? Last year when it was the harshest winter in 30 years, Samangan was forgotten altogether from the list to receive food aid,' says the Finnish contingent's political advisor, Marco Pajunen. 'But there were reported starvation deaths in Samangan and then a drought that hit the province very harshly straight after the winter.'

At a meeting with President Bush in the United States in April 2008, Samangan Governor Enayatullah Enayat is said to have expressed his indignation over this neglect, asking whether he needed to actively stir up trouble in Samangan to ensure a decent level of assistance.

The north of Afghanistan has a violent history of being torn between a succession of warlords and other heavy-handed power brokers. The current Governor of Balkh, Mohammad Noor Atta, is a former mujahedin fighter and warlord whose tough-talking manner is backed up by implicit force. It's a combination that observers say works well here, since people feel more protected from their enemies by a man who can wield the stick, providing he doesn't oppress them.

'Where do people find security? In former traditionally powerful personalities who have money, power and also weapon power,' Pajunen elaborates. 'He's a warlord in the guise of a modern governor. He's popular, that's why he's a stabilizing influence, but there is an element of fear, that's the basis of his governance.'

Peeved too by the lack of resources given to his province, Atta delivered a scathing attack on Western management style during a ceremony in early 2009 marking the start of construction of a 30-million-euro runway for the international airport at Mazar-e-Sharif.

'Largeness cannot be expressed by words alone, words must be followed by deeds,' he said in the presence of German Defence Minister Dr Franz Josef Jung. 'The donor countries give money to Afghanistan but unfortunately the money is not spent on bare necessities but for splendid meetings, conferences and workshops and thus is of use to foreign specialists only. For the large wounds Afghanistan is suffering from, not the least ointment is left. Donors come and make promises, they prove their goodwill in expensive conferences presenting papers to show their activity, but this is only superficial and of no sustainable effect in the country, just words again.

'On the other hand, no funding is provided for regions where capabilities for reconstruction are available, where good governance rules and where there is no poppy cultivation, where security is ensured and effective management is provided. Assistance is reduced to absurdity and reconstruction degenerates into farce – complaining is of no use. Reconstruction teams in other provinces like Kunar, Parwan, Kandahar, Logar, Khost, Herat and Paktya have rendered greater deeds, for example construction of tens of kilometres of roads, building of schools and hospitals and other activity worth mentioning.

'To Balkh Province, however, such assistance is refused. It seems as if stopping drug cultivation, ensuring security, implementing good governance and showing positive attitude towards international forces is regarded as a mistake and is punished by not providing any assistance for reconstruction.'

The question here as in many parts of the country is how much more patience can the general population show amid a clear failure of the Afghan and international authorities to provide for them.

'If the slide continues people will look more to traditional powerbrokers,' warns the Finnish political advisor. 'I don't think we need more

soldiers, we need development, governance and capacity.'

Crucially, however, Mazar-e-Sharif and Balkh Province were due in 2010 to be the first region after Kabul to undergo what's called TSLR – Transfer of Lead Security Responsibility – and be passed entirely to Afghan control. (Kabul was transferred to the national security forces in 2007.)

Regional Command-North deputy commander Lauglo acknowledges that there has to be a change in how stability is rewarded region for region, even within the northern sector itself.

'We need to distribute the money in a more fair way. The problem will be if we put too much development in some areas, people in others will say 'OK, if we have narcotics and Taliban they will give us money, if we don't they won't'.'

As he tells me this I think how easy it is to cook up trouble when money is at stake. At one ISAF base in Helmand a local security firm lost the contract to guard the outer perimeter and approaches. Perhaps it was just coincidence, but the next day there was a rare rocket attack, neatly demonstrating the need for a wide security cordon. The contract was reinstated and there was no more trouble.

In the centre of Northern Lights stands the Suomi Talo, the Finnish House, a small one-storey building where the soldiers watch movies, use the internet, make salami sandwiches from the fridge and drink endless cups of rocket-fuel strength coffee.

'Finnish people drink the most coffee per capita in the world but we don't shake, as you can see from Formula 1 racing,' Kurvinen tells me proudly.

Like the Swedes in their adjacent bar with pool table, the Finns may drink a maximum of two alcoholic beers in the evening, helping themselves from the fridge and marking their consumption on a list taped by the door.

'It's easier to behave when you have limits,' says the Colonel. 'The Finnish nature is such that if we give more opportunity to drink it can affect operational capacity. So if someone opens a third can and even tastes it he will be sent home.'

Beside the Finnish House stands a rustic log cabin that houses the sauna, with another tiny

Swedish soldier on patrol,
Balkh province, March 2009.

wood-fuelled sauna like a Wendy house along-side it. In fact they have a total of five saunas, the two wooden ones and three in containers. Another log cabin variant is on order to cope with the additional 100 soldiers that are due to arrive for the elections.

I thought the Russians were crazy for their steam but the Finns are in a league of their own. Wherever the Army deploys the sauna is the first solid structure to be built, while the troops are still living in tents.

'The sauna is good for hygiene and it's also the Finnish way to relax after patrolling,' Kurvinen explains. 'Some contingents can't have a sauna because it's regarded as a luxury but for us it's like a shower, it's the very minimum.'

Over the course of six consecutive evening visits to the log cabin I learn how Finnish women gave birth in the sauna as late as the 1960s for the prevention of infection, how the sauna would be used as a death bed for the

elderly, and how the troops in the 1939-40 Winter War against the Soviet Union used to delouse themselves in the steam.

Like the sauna, the heroic resistance to Stalin's forces is still a binding part of the fabric of Finland's national identity. The two elements came together in the naming of the contingent's sauna in Kosovo after Simo Häyhä, the star Finnish sniper of the Winter War credited with over 500 confirmed kills.

Not being a NATO member, Finland is in Afghanistan out of solidarity with the gen-eral international effort, while at home the debate continues whether to join the military alliance or not. The prevalent opinion now, says Kurvinen, is that this step would merely bait the bear when relations these days with Moscow are pretty good.

The military's Afghan involvement also prompts occasional debates whether this is a peacekeeping mission or a counter-insurgency.

Dwarfed by the Hindu Kush mountains, Norwegian troops take position on the edge of Ghowrmach district, Faryab province, March 2009. Pot-shots are taken at them from the facing hills an hour later.

National authorities tend towards the former, partly because the usual western argument that fighting extremism here keeps it off the streets at home is hard to apply in Finland, especially given its tiny Muslim population. But regional variation of the situation around Afghanistan is largely lost on the Finnish public.

'Most people think of Afghanistan as a whole, they hear in the press of incidents that happened in Helmand and Kabul and don't see the difference between the north and the east and south,' says Pajunen, who can count the number of journalists who visited Balkh in his 18 months here on one hand.

'The Finnish press are only interested in Afghanistan if someone is killed, dies in a car accident, or goofs up in spectacular style, so people don't have an objective picture of what's happening here.'

Meanwhile, regardless of the international context, the core identity of the Finnish soldiers is very much that of the woodland fighter and defender of the past, rather than potential NATO forces. I ask the Colonel when Finland like other countries will switch from the heavier 7.62 mm calibre ammunition to the 5.56mm NATO standard.

'Never! In the forest the bigger the calibre, the more effective it is, because twigs and leaves deflect bullets off target,' he says without pausing.

Forest fighting tends to crop up a lot in conversation too. One evening broken-toe Sampo also sits me down to watch a classic Finnish war film about the resistance to the Soviet advance, which consists largely of the boys of one platoon creeping through the pines and dying one after the other in skirmishes with 'Ivan'.

'I was reading a book about the Green Berets and it said that after six weeks they can move in a forest with a compass. In Finland kids can do that in elementary school after two days,' says Christian, a Captain from the town of Turku who is sitting in the sauna on my first day at Northern Lights.

He commands one of several two-jeep mobile observation teams (MOTs) that the Finns send around their AO each day. I will join him next morning to drive up to the border with Uzbekistan, having already met most of his team this evening.

'Most of the MOT will come in here now so you'll see them all naked before we go out,' he informs me as we talk.

At this moment blaring rock music kicks in as this month's touring guest band starts its show, a Swedish outfit called the Night Wolves. The band is fronted by the former vocalist from the now defunct Rednex, who were known best for their 1994 hit 'Cotton Eye Joe'. The musicians all wear Army uniforms with insignia while playing, another example of the laid-back Swedish approach to soldiering that irritates some of the Finns.

'They regard it as part of their individual human rights to have long hair and beards. But once you give them that you can't take it back,' the Finnish officer says.

The Swedes can also sleep with each other, which contrasts sharply with Finnish military regulations and rubs it in that there are no women anyway in Helsinki's contingent at this time. But all of its soldiers are familiar with an issue of a gentleman's magazine that features one of the female Swedish soldiers at Northern Lights, a reservist who does glamour modelling.

My entire body hurts after the bike crash but it's my ribs that really torment me at every move, possibly cracked in the rough landing. So I just sit in the steam listening to a high-energy cover of AC/DC's 'Highway to Hell'. The last time I heard this song my truck was being shot up in Kunar.

I eventually dress and exit the sauna in time to see the Swedish commanding officer do a stage dive in a swirl of laser beams and be passed above a heaving crowd of happy soldiers.

The next morning at breakfast a Swedish Lieutenant called Martin is sitting opposite me. He also does road patrols like the Finnish MOT I will drive with today up to the Uzbek border.

'You always feel like you are going to a party overdressed, wearing your flak jacket and rifle while the kids are waving at you and giving you the thumbs up. But you have to always remind yourself that this is a dangerous country and stay on your toes because anything can happen.'

A testimony to this stands outside the hall by one of the paths, a memorial bell and the names of two Swedes, a Finn and a Briton who died in the north. Near it there is a little 'garden' of defused mines and rockets, mortar shells and grenades that were found in the area, like the TC6 anti-tank mine originally made in Italy but since copied by other nations and having a 6kg explosive weight. Or the Iranian-made YM-1 pressure operated pressure-operated anti-personnel mine, and the ubiquitous Chinese-made 107mm rocket with 1.26kg explosive weight. Outside the dining hall a pair of ballistic glasses hangs on the wall, badly pitted but not pierced by a demonstration shotgun blast at five metres, reminding the soldiers always to wear them outside the base.

I leave Northern Lights at 0738 with six Finnish soldiers riding in two armoured Mercedes jeeps. Iron Maiden's 'Aces High' thumps away in my vehicle, followed by 'Smoke on the Water' and 'Bad Moon Rising'. You can rely on the Finns to stand by the classics.

Christian's team usually covers between 500 to 1,000 kilometres of the AO each week. Today we travel 30 kilometres east on Highway 1, the same road I felt quaking to the explosion of giant IEDs in Zhari, and then 55 kilometres north on a smooth, straight road towards the border town of Hairatan.

The road is lined with pylons and the landscape on either side stretches out like tundra, a vast earthy plain with occasional smatterings of green. The soil is still laced with mines planted by the Russians in the 1980s to deter the mujahedin from ambushing convoys driving to and from Soviet Uzbekistan. The ambushes are still just about a thing of the past here but there are plenty of nefarious activities in the area.

'Don't ask the Border Police about the smuggling – the whole area lives off it, opium, arms, we don't touch it,' I am told before we arrive at the customs point at the River Amu Darya.

People in Hairatan are better dressed than most but are still visibly poor as they lead mangy camels through the dilapidated streets and bazaar. It's one of the country's few river ports so there is some infrastructure, dock facilities and buildings that are not made of mud, but the whole area is dominated by one structure, the giant grey-painted Friendship girder bridge. This is where Moscow's troops

in Afghanistan withdrew on February 15, 1989, after a nine-year war that claimed the lives of 15,000 Soviet soldiers and between one and two million Afghans.

The last soldier to cross was General Boris Gromov, commander of the 40th Army, who recalled the day in his 1994 book *Limited Contingent*.

Just after nine in the morning I called my adjutant and had him check me over in my uniform from all angles. He scrutinised me at length and then nodded, all good. The battalion was already waiting to roll out. The APCs stood in an even line and all the soldiers had to do now was jump on them. They informed me that we were ready to go, I glanced at my watch and gave the order, 'Start the engines!' The boys made a real effort, everyone moved off in unison, which rarely happens, and the whole column drove off past me. There were tears in many of their eyes, and not from the wind either.

I waited a while and at exactly 0945 the wheels of my carrier started to move along the last few hundred metres of Afghan soil before drawing up to the bridge. Some of our border guards were sitting in trenches on the slight bend there and as we passed I waved and shouted, 'Good luck, and remember there are no more of us left in Afghanistan!'

There was no one on the bridge itself, which was absolutely empty. But on the Soviet side in Termez a throng of people was waiting to meet us, including relatives of fallen soldiers and officers. Despite having received official notification of death and holding funerals for their loved ones, some still bore out hopes that they might now appear.

So that no one got hurt by accident I gave the order to drive as slowly as possible across the bridge. On the one hand I still remember today how the crowd met and congratulated us with hugs and kisses, and threw flowers before the tracks of the vehicles. But I also remember how not one single boss in Moscow had thought to organize an official reception for the 40th Army. This attempt to gloss over our

Friendship Bridge, crossed by General Gromov in February 1989 as the Soviets withdrew.

withdrawal from Afghanistan was just another example of the tactlessness of those sitting in the Kremlin. It seemed to me they wanted to casually heap all the mistakes of their predecessors and Gorbachev's cronies onto us, as if to say there's no need to greet those who survived Afghanistan because it's not the kind of war you want to remember anyway.[23]

Twenty years and one month later, Lt. Kadyr, the small, moustachioed head of the local Afghan Border Police's anti-smuggling unit, leads Christian and I round the bend where the Soviet guards once sat in their trenches, past a large portrait of Karzai and a sign in Russian saying 'Welcome to Afghanistan' and onto the bridge.

Like that morning in 1989, it is now completely empty ahead of us and I can almost hear the roar of Gromov's carriers as they make that final journey. There's not much traffic these days, says Kadyr, maybe 120 cars and trucks a day, mostly moving from Afghanistan into Uzbekistan loaded with lemons, raisins and other foodstuffs.

He assures me through an interpreter they have no attempts to smuggle here, and not wishing to rock the boat I leave the matter at that. Later I hear at the Finnish HQ that there has not been one single official confiscation of contraband at the bridge in two and a half years.

I ask the Lieutenant if he speaks Russian. His face cracks in a happy smile as he tells me of four years he spent as an Afghan Army cadet

Norwegian troops rest during mission in Faryab province, March 2009.

in Moscow, Vladimir and Sochi during the Soviet time.

'I would like to travel the world, go to Finland, but I'm stuck here,' he says sadly as we walk back to our vehicles. 'What is it that we have here in Afghanistan that everyone seems to want, and why does everything get destroyed all the time?'

I mumble something about his country being a crossroads between East and West, that things will steadily get better and he'll go to Finland some time.

Really perhaps I should tell him his people are fated to be pawns in dirty games and his country is a convenient battlefield, that he

won't ever go to Finland and will probably be stuck in shit for the rest of his days. Is that any truer than what I actually say?

★ ★ ★

I move to the Norwegians in Camp Marmal by Mazar and am left in a tent for a few days waiting for a flight to Meymaneh, where the largest element of their contingent of 600 soldiers is based.

Marmal is a huge base, occupied mainly by a couple of thousand German troops, but with a few hundred Norwegians, Latvians and Italians living in a smaller interior base called Nideros. March weather is fooling with Mazar, sending dust eddies across sunny parade squares one day and chill gusts the next, buffeting the portraits of the Norwegian King and Queen through the mess tent walls.

My accommodation is by a Latvian tent which has a few relics of the 1980s outside its door; a rusting Soviet heavy machine-gun on a tripod and a NURS rocket pod from a Hind helicopter that has a Soviet steel helmet with red star perched on its nose.

More tents are occupied by the Italian jet fighter crews and maintenance teams who I see more often in bathrobes and slippers than in uniform as they head to the showers in loud, gesticulating groups.

There is a tent bar called Little Norway that serves near-beer and has a pool table and table football. Meanwhile, the Germans up the road have 'Planet Mazar', a big open-plan brick sports bar complete with a large TV screen. At the 8p.m. start of alcohol sales the bar counter is already packed three deep with thirsty *Bundeswehrsoldaten* buying regular Weissbier and Pilsener for one euro a bottle.

Among the Germans' starling speckle camouflage you see the non-descript khaki digital pattern of the Croatians and the occasional green-patterned Italian, although the latter are technically not allowed to drink here. But as fighter pilot Gino tells me nonchalantly back at Nideros one night, 'Italians don't get drunk, we can have four or five beers and you wouldn't notice.' He says his contingent get on well with the Germans but not so much with the Norwegians, who they find 'a bit cold'.

The Italians are currently rotating back home, and one Latvian seems pleased to see the back of this batch: 'It's good the Italians are leaving, they take up lots of room and make a lot of noise, shower three times longer than anyone else and listen to music and sing in there.'

Across the German courtyard there is a bar restaurant called K2, which is more intimate with its subdued lighting, and the Oasis restaurant bar. Up the road there is the Beach Club, a tent structure with a lots of stand up tables and a gravel garden, about as tropical as Mazar can get. After the spartan conditions in the south and east Marmal is pretty relaxed, and is known for this among the Germans, who have

other large bases in the northern provinces of Kunduz and Badakhshan where Taliban activity is greater and things are more businesslike.

'A friend of mine came to visit here from Kunduz and said "Wow, it's like a holiday camp",' says Florian, a German Tornado pilot.

The Norwegian press officer tells me his contingent had to impose a strict ban on alcohol as 'Norwegians tend not to stop at just two beers'. With two spells of two-week leave during their six-month tour they only have to stay dry for six weeks at a time anyway.

'If you can't go six weeks without a drink you probably shouldn't be here anyway but in some institution,' he says.

But other national elements that visit Nideros can get carried away at the German bars, which are enticingly located five minutes up the road. One East European country's troops created a stir one night by getting plastered and then throwing up all over the Hesco walls around the tents.

How the Germans manage to keep their own troops in line is remarkable. With so many of them based here it is not possible to enforce the 'two cans rule' they are supposed to abide by, especially since they can buy cases of wine and beer in their camp shop. Their drinking habits came under uncomfortable scrutiny in 2008, when Germany's *Der Spiegel* magazine broke the story that the previous year's contingent of 3,600 soldiers had taken delivery of more than 1.06 million litres of beer and wine, and the current contingent was set to exceed this.

Matters were made worse by another report that 40 per cent of German soldiers were too overweight to meet physical requirements. The figures prompted Reinhold Robbe, Parliamentary Commissioner for the armed forces, to state: 'Plainly put, the soldiers are too fat, exercise too little and take little care of their diet.'[24]

Newspapers abroad like Britain's *Daily Telegraph* seized on the disclosures, running stories with headlines like 'German soldiers too fat to fight Taliban.'[25]

On March 22 I meet the Norwegian Defence Minister Anne-Grete Strøm-Erichsen in the Little Norway bar. She's just flown on a German helicopter to Ghowrmach, the main trouble spot in Faryab province where the Taliban made a comeback in recent years.

'We wanted to keep the insurgents in Ghowrmach and avoid letting them spread north into the rest of Faryab. Or we would have to wait for them to come and there would be shooting,' says the minister, a dainty, pleasant woman who agrees to be interviewed by me despite her evident fatigue. 'Hopefully with our presence we will let them know that we won't allow them to recruit more members among the locals, the young people.'

Measuring about 170 square kilometres, Ghowrmach is an artificial Pashtun concentration that resulted from the forced resettlement of unruly tribesmen from the south by Afghanistan's 'Iron Amir' Abdur Rahman in the late 19th century. Today these villages encroach on areas mainly populated by Uzbeks, creating considerable local tensions.

But as well as history, a mix of geography, recent politics and red tape helped create the current situation in Ghowrmach. Technically the district was always part of Badghis province, which is located southwest of Faryab and lies in the territory of ISAF's Regional Command-West. Since the Hindu Kush mountains cut off Ghowrmach from the rest of that sector it was seldom visited by troops based there. But since it was not part of RC-North there were too many administrative procedures for Norwegian troops in Faryab to simply pop in there as needed, which would have made most sense.

The result was the emergence of a small vacuum-like sanctuary for insurgent elements, a fact that only properly came to light in 2006 when emergency relief teams went into Ghowrmach to help during heavy flooding. By this time the Taliban had appointed a shadow Governor, Mullah Dastagir, who was killed in a US air strike in late 2008, plunging the nascent insurgent structure into disarray.

When ISAF mounted operations in the area the next January and February the resistance that remained scattered into the hills in panic. They could have been hunted down but the Norwegian approach was not to kill for the sake of it and thereby create blood feuds against NATO among families whose young men were just trying to earn a few bucks.

To control the rot, Ghowrmach was in 2009 incorporated into the rest of Faryab, and the stick and carrot of military force and

development was employed there. Norway spends $120 million per year on development in Afghanistan, 20 per cent of which goes straight to Faryab and Ghowrmach and the rest to the government in Kabul to disburse. (To the annoyance of Balkh Governor Atta, the Swedes send all of their aid money to Kabul). Concerning the money spent locally, it is known that villages that receive projects are forced to give the Taliban a 10 to 15 per cent cut of the funds, so Norwegian tax payers are in effect funding resistance against their own troops.

The additional economic attention to Ghowrmach draws resources away from other parts of Faryab and has upset communities that feel the Pashtuns are taking their piece of the pie.

'We need to distribute the money in a more fair way,' Strøm-Erichsen acknowledges. 'UNAMA [United Nations Assistance Mission to Afghanistan] has said it is important not to put too much money into Ghowrmach.'

Militarily, the Norwegians now send in heavily armed 'Task Units' every few days to push into the villages and make ISAF's presence felt. Compared to the east or south, the insurgency up here functions at a pretty low level, usually consisting of IEDs and drive-by shootings by men on motorcycles. And also kidnappings of Chinese and Koreans from road crews working on the section of the Ring Road that passes straight through the district.

The locals desperately want the link-up with the markets in Herat and Mazar and before his death began to complain bitterly to Dastagir, whose sub-commanders were behind most abductions. Eventually he had to instruct them to leave the road alone to avoid alienating the local population.

After a few days at Marmal I fly 35 minutes on a Focker 50 prop-plane to Meymaneh, a small PRT camp set inside stone walls and towers and manned by Norwegian and Latvian troops, with a small number of US specialists and liaison staff. It is located by the town of the same name in a fertile valley surrounded by long, grassy hills with triangular ends that undulate gently, like melting Toblerone bars. At this time of the year Faryab is covered in tiny white and mauve flowers which from the air give it a sugar-coated, fairy tale appearance,

Afghan elders shelter in the rain, awaiting examination by a Norwegian medical team, Faryab province.

Afghan troops train with a
recoilless rifle, Ghowrmach,
Faryab province, March 2009.

as if there should be canoes full of Oompa Loompas paddling down the landscape. But like many other places, there is a recent history of violence here too.

In 2005 during the international uproar about the Mohammed cartoons published in several western newspapers, the former site of the base in the town was attacked by a mob suspected to have been stirred up by local warlords with their own agendas. Norwegian and Finnish soldiers used tear gas and firearms on protesters, some of whom were said to have been firing with rifles at the soldiers from adjacent buildings. Three Afghans were killed and 22 were injured in the incident, which

was the first time foreign forces in Afghanistan had been mobbed at their base. From 2005 the Taliban also advertised a reward of six kilos of gold for anyone who killed a Norwegian soldier. So there is a lot of concern about insurgent activity in Ghowrmach, which is 'like water starting to drip down the hillside', I am told by the visiting Commander of the Norwegian National Joint Headquarters, Lt. Gen. Harald Sunde. (General Sunde became Norway's Chief of Defence in May 2009.)

Like the minister, he stresses, 'If we allow this to spread unopposed it could run into other dimensions. It's not an offensive or a huge (Taliban) operation, it's shuras, reconnaissance to see their freedom of movement and what they can do.

'None of them here are loyal, they are youngsters on motorcycles issued with AKs, they do harassment of checkpoints and the next day the same guys can walk round kicking stones in the bazaar. The enemy forces are still not connected to the east or south, but the locals are now being harassed, visited at night.

'The Afghans have their own strategy of survival and that's the strategy of alliances, "I am loyal to the one who can guarantee my tomorrow," they must be allied to the strongest, the crook or the Taliban who comes at night is the one you have to serve. That's why we must deal with this as soon as possible.'

It may not be Helmand, but the Task Unit I leave Meymaneh with on March 30 to go into Ghowrmach has still been attacked enough on missions this year to warrant extreme caution.

The unit is comprised of 14 vehicles and 70 soldiers of the Telemark Battalion, Norway's only fully professional battalion. For a while we follow the emerging Ring Road, passing Soviet wrecks and isolated encampments of excavating plant busy cutting the route through hills that are two-thirds grass covered and one-third bare earth, like balding heads.

The Task Unit's deputy commander, Captain Orjan, describes the administrative border with Ghowrmach as being 'like a magic line', the crossing of which usually initiates some Taliban response. The insurgents are accustomed to operating on their side of the line, which used to provide safety from ISAF forces that were not allowed to cross into RC-West. And for them to work any further out of the Pashtun belt also risks sparking retaliation from the outlying Uzbek settlements.

It's a mixed few days weather-wise, with some bright warm spells but mostly driving wind and steady rain that bogs down the Iveco off-roaders and Sisu APCs. The start of mosquito season is approaching so all the soldiers are taking daily doses of Doxylin, an antibiotic which, as well as averting malaria, also kills the Chlamydia bug. As a result, medical staff say the Norwegian troops are going home on leave feeling sexually invincible, with all the consequences that fallacy carries.

The objective of this latest mission to Ghowrmach is to try to push the Taliban's area of influence back from the Ring Road and make contact with the locals. No one knows how many insurgents operate here but it's thought to be no more than 200 spread between different villages and commanders. Unless these got coordinated, the expectation is to run into only 20 or 30 in any one place. But IEDs are the main threat, they tell me.

On April 1 the unit stops at a Pashtun village on the very edge of Ghowrmach, and the ANA and ANP riding with them set up a security cordon along the low hilltop that separates us from 'enemy territory'.

There's no love lost between the ANP and ANA here and there have been cases where one refused to help the other while under attack. But today with a bit of nudging from the Norwegians they seem to get along and after a bit of squabbling even manage to agree a few joint operational procedures.

The Norwegian doctor and his nurses perform a 'medcap' treatment of ten locals as a goodwill gesture. No women are allowed by the men folk to come for examination, and although a crowd of kids with various sores and scalp conditions stands round in the rain to watch, the ten put forward for treatment are all village elders.

As best as his equipment and experience will allow, the doctor diagnoses three cataracts, severe arthritis of the knee, dyspepsia, pneumonia, possible lung cancer or TB, two cases of intestinal worms, urinary tract infection, tinnitus, and two cases of prostatitis. At the end of the event someone brings in a five-month old baby girl with a probable viral infection or bacterial bronchitis. The pile of medications the soldiers brought diminishes rapidly and the doc seems happy enough with the balance.

'The good thing is we could do something for all of them, only one was a hopeless case,' he says later. But everyone is still dismayed that the old men hogged the available care.

'It's important for us to remember that 100 or 150 years ago Europe was just the same,' points out the commander of the Task Unit, Major Jan Helge Dale. 'In my own village 40 years ago there was a family where the old man would wash his youngest son first in the bath tub, then himself, then the horse's harness, then his wife.'

A Swedish CV 90 leaves its base on a long range patrol.

Quiet, bearded and partial to pensive pipe-smoking, Dale is super-methodical about how he operates. While he has 70 soldiers and a lot of firepower, it's hard to imagine him charging into anything and he is a good choice of officer to deal with the delicate local situation. There is an enemy here for sure, but a heavy hand will make matters far worse.

'I don't think the solution is to kill every insurgent,' he says, puffing clouds of tobacco smoke. 'The ones here are only hired to do harassment work; they are farmers in the day and fight at night. We need to take out the commanders and those hardcore fighters who fight because they really believe in the Taliban as a movement. Because for every farmer we kill, if we need to kill, there are left behind children, wives who will turn their backs on the government because they killed their relatives. The only solution is to give people work. We are winning lots of tactical battles but in

the long term we are losing support because people expect more than we just kick out the Taliban for a short time.'

It's still and soggy on the hills that evening as the Norwegians dig in, placing sentries and machine-guns on the high ground around their encampment. At 1930 shots are fired at us by four men who were initially spotted with rifles at 1,500 metres, then disappeared between the hills only to pop up at 900 metres and fire half a dozen AK rounds.

A .50-cal machine-gun hammers off a burst in return and a Norwegian sniper sets up to pick off the shooters as they pull back. But they timed it perfectly, it is now too dark and the sniper's optical scope too misted in the drizzle, which blots out everything beyond 600 metres.

The mission continues for two more days, moving right into Ghowrmach to the FOB, an old Soviet site that has been reinforced with Hescos into a 100-square-metre redoubt. Those few shots are the only real sign of enemy activity apart from a report that 16 construction workers were just kidnapped by an insurgent commander who lives 10 kilometres further west.

The rest of the mission is spent being wet and digging trucks out of the mud before it's finally called off because of the weather. The last unsubstantiated report of enemy movement comes while a few vehicles are camped up on a hill by a telecom tower as a morale booster to the ANP based up there.

The Norwegian Lieutenant comes up to me in the pouring rain and says: 'Fun fact – ANP intelligence says a group of 50 Taliban are heading towards us from the west.'

The troops man machine-guns around the perimeter and fire illumination shells all night although no one expects to get attacked in the downpour, which turns Ghowrmach into a giant quagmire. And the ANP are not exactly famed for their reliability here anyway.

'Three weeks ago we found Norwegian binoculars at the point used by an IED trigger man who forgot them,' says the Lieutenant. 'It was the same pair we gave to the ANP earlier. These are our allies but not all of them are loyal.'

As in Finland, there is some confusion in Norway about the nature of the Afghan involvement.

'I think most people think of it as a war since Norway is sending soldiers,' said Major Dale. 'I think some people at home think we are only giving humanitarian aid and others think we are doing only war fighting, they don't see the complex operation as the Norwegian media are not very good at giving the complete picture of what we are doing.'

Defence Minister Strøm-Erichsen noted that even though Norway's three-party coalition government evenly supports the mission, the country's pronounced home peace and stability amplifies every repercussion of the Afghan involvement.

'Even though we had a terrible time in WWII, we might too often take this home peace for granted. We lost two soldiers in Afghanistan, and both times the discussion starts from the beginning,' she said. (In 'bloody June' 2010 four Norwegian soldiers were killed by a single IED in Faryab, bringing the total to nine. At that time Norway had approximately 500 soldiers deployed in Afghanistan.)

'Sometimes I'm embarrassed by the community in Norway,' complained a medic with the Task Unit. 'We take a casualty, which isn't very often, and there's an uproar with people saying we should leave Afghanistan.'

The casualty figure would rise the next month after an IED blast west of Mazar killed two more soldiers. But for the most part the job in the assigned part of Afghanistan wasn't as bad as the soldiers and everyone else in Norway had been led to believe.

'The media made it sound worse than it is. When we first went into Ghowrmach here one newspaper wrote that there were 2,000 Taliban waiting for us here,' said Sgt. Bord, a 21-year-old from Lillehammer. 'And when something happens in Helmand, friends contact me and ask if it's dangerous.'

It seems most of the troops in the Scandinavian contingents have seen Ross Kemp's Helmand-based Afghanistan series, which while boldly portraying the fight down south give little indication of the variety of conditions across the country or the range of armies deployed here.

'I met some British people on holiday in the Canary Islands who didn't know that the UK wasn't the only Army fighting here,' one Norwegian said a little resentfully. But most soldiers just get on with their tour and count the days until they can go home.

'We joke that we'll come back here on vacation with our families in 30 years time,' another soldier says while on patrol in Ghowrmach. 'But it would be nice to see it happen, make all of this worthwhile.'

nineteen

AMONG THE AFGHANS

This land is Afghanistan, pride of every Afghan.
Land of peace, of the sword, its sons brave men all.
This is the country of every tribe, land of Baluch and Uzbeks,
Pashtuns and Hazaras, Turkmen and Tajiks,
Arabs and Gojars, Pamirian, Nooristanis,
Barahawi, and Qizilbash, the Aimaq and Pashaye too.
This land will shine for ever, like the sun in the blue sky,
In the chest of Asia, it will remain the heart for ever.
We will follow but one God,
Allah is great, we all say, Allah is great

National Anthem of Afghanistan

'The Afghan loves a gun and fondles flowers,' Maynard Owen Williams wrote in his 1933 article in *National Geographic* magazine titled 'Afghanistan Makes Haste Slowly'.

He can be cruel, yet will die to protect a guest. More manly than many Asiatics, he becomes almost effeminate when at the end of his long lean fingers there is not a knife but a fluttering square of bright silk. The Afghan boy, greeted at birth by a salvo of gunshots, is treated by his father with unusual tenderness.

Of all Asiatics we met, the Afghan seemed least concerned with copying others and most concerned with being himself ... He is so evidently more of a man and less of a barbarian than one expects that a liking for the Afghan was spontaneous ... How long it will be possible for a lone foreigner or a small party to cross Afghanistan from end to end in safety from everything but too much kindness I cannot say.

Even during WWII, the country enjoyed the relative peace and stability under King Zahir Shah that lasted 40 years before he was deposed by his cousin Mohammed Daoud Khan in 1973, before the final plunge into conflict with the Soviets in 1979. Their defeat gave way to the civil war of the early 1990s followed by the rule of the Taliban and now the snowballing insurgency that followed that regime's ouster.

In the 1933 piece, Williams describes Afghanistan as 'still divided against itself by snow-clad mountains and feudal customs under which tribal loyalty is more potent than patriotism.'

Today this still holds true in many places as the Afghan government under an elected president, ISAF and the international community pursue a giant nation-building project in a country that is still firmly rooted in its ancient past.

At one end of the spectrum, foreign leaders and Generals mix with erudite, well educated Afghan dignitaries in air-conditioned rooms in Kabul, Washington, Paris or Budapest. In provincial capitals across Afghanistan, military and state department officials make the best of constrained partnerships with warlords and mujahedin fighters who, now clad in sharp suits, serve as Governors and senior administrators. And then there are the foreign soldiers who patrol remote, dusty villages from another age, seemingly a million miles from anything more familiar than mobile phones and fake

Rolex watches that incongruously adorn the locals.

At this end of the scale the perception of the ordinary Afghan is seldom complimentary, and harsh generalizations are commonplace.

'They all have beards, they all lie and they all want something from you,' asserts a Dutch Sergeant in Uruzgan, while a Canadian infantry Corporal adds: 'They hold one hand out for things and stab you in the back with the other.'

They are typical comments, and for all their bluntness do reflect the very real and cynical survival instinct that has been bred into Afghan people over centuries of war and privation.

Yes, the ordinary Afghan will see what he can get from whichever foreign presence happens to be in his region at a given time. Because he is used to seeing armies come and go, possibly leaving whole villages marked for brutal retribution by old masters of the area. That is a chief problem facing foreign troops today, convincing people that they will not leave tomorrow or in a year, and that they can win.

'The local people will go for the strongest side, it's quite medieval,' a British infantry Lieutenant said. 'If we give more of a show of force the local people will turn away from the Taliban. Then the more you make them realise that you're human and you're here to stay, the more they start to warm up.'

Local leaders will often hedge their bets and work both sides to their advantage if they can, or think nothing of switching allegiances if this is expedient. Mostly it's just business, but there are other reasons.

'An enemy tribe is usually one that has been slighted by the government, but personal enmity goes a long way to explain why an entire tribe can switch sides,' said Michael, a Danish intelligence officer who specialises in tribal issues and took an intensive Pashtu language course in the United States before deploying to Afghanistan.

'We don't see that half fight with us and the other against us, it's usually 80 to 90 per cent, usually because of personal gain by the chieftain. People very rarely change sides as individuals; usually the entire group follows the chieftain.'

Since the Taliban were driven from power, learning what makes the tribes tick has been a major challenge for the United States and other armies in ISAF. It's no easy task, given that there are about 60 main tribes and 400 sub-tribes mainly in the Pashtun tribal areas in the East and South that may support ISAF, fight it bitterly, or sit on the fence. And all the while shifting alliances and fighting among themselves.

After much trial and error, the ISAF focus began to shift and be refined towards a better understanding of these nuts and bolts. In February 2008, General David Petraeus, then Commander of US Central Command, said that 'a nuanced appreciation of local situations' was essential to understanding 'the tribal structures, the powerbrokers, the good guys and the bad guys, local cultures and history'.[26]

Now the Pentagon is looking for a healthy dividend from deploying 'Human Terrain Teams' (HTTs), groups that study the tribal dynamics of a region and are comprised of contracted civilian anthropologists, political and social scientists, ethnic Afghan cultural advisers and regular Army officers.

In late 2008 there were 20 HTTs operating in Iraq but only six in Afghanistan, where in places there is no information about the local tribes and sub-tribes and the fractures within them, a shortfall that had to be redressed.

'The only way we can do this is by going out and talking to people, asking what are their grievances and the root causes of conflicts,' said the then leader of the HTT in Khost, Major Alex Wells. One challenge has been overcoming reservations about the human terrain concept among old-school soldiers: 'Even some of the hard-line infantry are now understanding that it's not just a matter of kill kill kill,' Wells said.

Translated into actions, this means for example that units are able to use HTT knowledge to quickly tap the real powerbrokers as they push into guarded and often fearful rural communities.

This up-close-and-personal approach carries risks apart from IEDs and ambushes. In November 2008, while on patrol in an Afghan village in Kandahar province, HTT social scientist Paula Loyd was doused with a flammable liquid by a man with whom she had been discussing fuel prices, and set on fire. She suffered second- and third-degree burns over

Girls in Helmand,
June 2008.

Gurkha 'influence officer'
Lt. Robert Grant gives
out biscuits to children
near Khakrez, Kandahar
province.

Children blowing bubbles,
Maywand, Kandahar
province, February 2008.

60 per cent of her body and died of her injuries in hospital two months later.

It is this exposure and vulnerability that creates the main dilemma for the foreign forces as a whole: how to protect themselves but not become too distanced from the people they must build relations with.

'To protect the lives of people we wrap them in a 20-tonne armoured vehicle, it'll protect you from a blast but it prevents you from talking directly to people,' said Captain Darren Hart, the acting operations officer for Canada's Task Force Zhari in summer 2008. 'And with the helmet, flak jacket, ballistic eyewear, mouthpiece and wire running to our ear, the kit makes us look like starship troopers, worlds apart from the people we are talking to. How do you be intimate enough without being too intimate?'

This is not new. The late former Soviet soldier and journalist Artem Borovik wrote in his 1990 book *The Hidden War*: 'If you want to learn about a strange country, say experienced travellers, disappear into it. But in Afghanistan we couldn't even manage to do that. During the nine years of war we were constantly separated from the country by eight centimetres of bullet-proof glass through which we stared in fear from inside our armoured carriers.'[27]

Today each foreign contingent has its own methods of narrowing the gap. The Czechs were distinctive by the unkempt, bushy beards most of them grew during their deployment.

'I allow the soldiers to wear beards to be close to the traditions of the local people,' said Lt. Col. Pavel Lipka, the contingent commander in late 2008. 'We always say we are not bringing our culture and traditions to Afghanistan but are trying to follow theirs.'

It's all well and good, but one of the keys is still dialogue. The amount of foreign soldiers who speak more than a few words of Pashtu or Dari is negligible, so working and social contacts with the locals are often hampered by bad translations. Conversely, interaction is greatly enhanced by an interpreter who strikes the right chord in conversation. Language, tone and atmospherics are crucial to a mission, and can result in success or dismal failure, depending on how the message is imparted to the Afghans or their responses relayed back to the soldiers.

'Often the interpreter will tell us what they think we want to hear,' said Michael the Danish intel officer, whose Pashtu was good enough to vet the quality of translations. 'One interpreter said the village elder was telling us "could Coalition Forces please not walk through the fields", when his exact words were "we don't want these infidel dogs polluting our crops". Our guys didn't know how upset he was and stood there smiling at him.'

Some say the golden rule is to keep the message short and sweet so that it will not get warped in translation and will stick more easily in the minds of local people.

'We are ISAF; we are here to help the local population. If you can help us throw the Taliban out we can help get you schools and doctors. We know the old ANP were corrupt, that's why they were changed,' British Gurkha Lieutenant Emil Simpson told successive groups of villagers in Maiwand district in February 2008 during a patrol to inform them that the district's rotten Police force had been completely replaced.

'All we can do is give them a simple message. I find in Afghanistan it's best to have one message and repeat it like a stuck record, at least you get it across,' he said. 'The media are fixated on fighting, but it is patrols like this that are going to get the locals on our side and win this war.'

At the same time, the international forces face increasing animosity from the general population over house searches, detentions, disruptions to trade, tolerance of government corruption, failure to fulfil promises made by previous troop rotations, and most of all, civilian casualties.

As the fighting intensifies, so does the number of innocent people killed. For example, the United Nations recorded 2,118 civilian deaths in 2008, an increase of 595 over the previous year. In the first six months of 2009 there were 1,013, expected to rise dramatically during the summer months.[28] 59 per cent of these were attributed to insurgent action, predominantly to IEDs which killed at least 400 innocent Afghans.

Air strikes continue to be the main cause of the deaths inflicted by Coalition Forces. The worst single incident of this nature was the May 2009 bombing in the western Farah province that resulted in up to 86 civilian deaths, according to the Pentagon, while President Karzai said the number was 130.

Far removed from the reality of waging the fight and in a typical outburst against the Americans calculated to boost his ragged public standing, the Afghan leader demanded an end to all air strikes after Farah. This was rejected outright by both ISAF Command and soldiers on the ground.

'They say we can't use air strikes, how about you fight your own war you clowns, we're over here fighting Taliban?' one US soldier said in an incensed discussion with his buddies.

Tragic incidents undermine the already weakened public faith in the Kabul government and international forces. After the Farah strike, which brought hundreds of protesters onto the capital's streets, US National Security Adviser James L. Jones told media in a classic sound bite that 'in one mishap you can create thousands more terrorists than you had before the mishap.'[29]

In February 2010, 33 civilians were killed in Uruzgan province by an air strike on a convoy of vehicles, leading then ISAF Commander General Stanley McChrystal to publicly apologise to President Karzai for the carnage and order an investigation. In May the blame was officially laid at the feet of Predator drone operators for their 'inaccurate and unprofessional' reporting.

Back in December 2008, previous ISAF commander David McKiernan issued a directive stressing that 'Commanders must focus upon the principles which attach to every use of force – be that self-defence or offensive fires. Good tactical judgment, necessity, and proportionality are to drive every action and engagement, minimizing civilian casualties is of paramount importance. Do not hesitate to pursue the enemy, but stay true to the values of integrity and respect for human life. Living these values distinguishes us from our enemies.'[30]

Successive commanders have tried to reduce numbers of civilian casualties in 'mishaps' by urging troops to avoid fights in villages and towns. But the sheer amount of ordnance tumbling from the skies and spitting from artillery pieces will keep producing these tragedies and turning people against the foreign forces.

This erosion has been accelerated by high-profile cases where ground troops killed civilians through unwarranted and indiscriminate use of force. On March 4, 2007, a unit of US Marines was travelling through a village near Jalalabad when one of their vehicles struck an IED. According to military investigators, troops responded by opening fire on several vehicles, killing at least 10 innocent people and wounding 33, among them children and elderly. Other accounts put the number of dead at 19. Drawing outraged condemnation from Karzai, the incident prompted thousands of people to take to the streets in protest.

Claims that the soldiers took small arms fire and saw armed men after the blast were officially dismissed, and compensation of $2,000 was paid by the US government to the families of each person killed. US Army spokesman in Afghanistan, Colonel John Nicholson, publicly apologised, saying 'I stand before you today, deeply, deeply ashamed and terribly sorry that Americans have killed and wounded innocent Afghans'.[31]

The unit in question was withdrawn from the country in an effort to both contain the backlash and also a culture of retaliation as emerged in Iraq, where as one soldier put it, a frequent response to IED attacks was to 'pop the nearest farmer'.

A more sinister incident took place in Paktika that August when Polish troops opened fire from a mortar and heavy machine-gun on the village of Nangarkhel, killing six civilians and wounding three during a wedding celebration. The unprovoked attack occurred a day after Poland took its first KIA in Afghanistan, and a few hours after an IED crippled a Polish vehicle near the village. There were subsequent allegations of a pre-planned vengeance attack by the Poles, possibly with US connivance, and claims that one Polish unit refused the task before another stepped in.

The trial of seven Polish soldiers began in Warsaw in February 2009, when prosecutors argued that there were no grounds for the bombardment of the village. Six of the defendants faced life imprisonment if convicted. At the time of writing, the trial continues. A story by award-winning Polish journalist Paweł Smoleński that was picked up by some of the media also said that then Defence Minister

Polish troops maintaining an Israeli-made Orbiter mini-UAV (unmanned aerial vehicle), FOB Sharana, Paktika province, December 2007.

Aleksander Szczyglo publicly stated the troops were fending off a Taliban attack, although this was duly ruled out. Smoleński further quoted an unnamed US Major as saying 'The Poles are performing excellently in Afghanistan and that is what should be the front-page news, not any Nangarkhel – something unfortunate but not of great significance.'[32] The Commander of Polish forces in Paktika province in late 2007, Lt. Col. Piotr Zieja, insisted the matter was concluded with no lingering ill-will.

'For local people the most important thing is compensation. They got $2,500, plus some sheep and flour in accordance with Pashtunwali [Pashtun tribal code of conduct]. The people were neutral toward the Coalition before and still are,' he insisted.

US forces based with the Poles at FOB Sharana in Paktika told me the same: 'Initially there were some problems when the incident occurred but restitution has been made and all parties have moved on,' a Major said with evident distaste for my question about how deeply this incident had scarred relations.

Observing tribal compensation codes might appear to settle matters, but such incidents only negate genuine and prolonged efforts by foreign contingents to build lasting ties, including by the Poles, who at the time had 1,600 soldiers in Afghanistan (rising to 2,500 by July 2010). But distinctions between the foreign contingents are largely lost on local people, and in rural communities in particular, where the collective consciousness may even be reluctant to separate ISAF and the Soviets.

During the Christmas Day patrol I did with the Poles in Paktika in 2007, the unit made a humanitarian drop of coats and blankets in a remote village that rarely saw outsiders. Some unidentified soldiers stopped and distributed wind-up radios here six months earlier, but the village elder of about 70 years old didn't know who these soldiers were now when I asked.

'Maybe Italian, or US...British? Ah, Poland, I heard about that country on the radio,' he replied. Then he added, 'The women and children are afraid of all foreign troops. When the Russians were here they would come to the village, kill people and take things.'

A priority of the international effort is to prevent the Taliban from stirring up a broader jihad-type movement, which could unite large parts of the population against the foreign forces, as happened with the Soviets. The same principle applied earlier, as shown by the following analysis of the jihad phenomenon found in British Army Field Notes written after the Second Afghan War (1878–1880):

The extent to which the Afghan tribes may combine will depend upon a) The degree of popularity of the war b) Whether a jihad has been systematically preached. In the case of a jihad, tribal feuds and jealousies are forgotten or buried, and the tribes combine against the common foe of Islam. All the tribes in Afghanistan, with the exception of those which are Shiah would probably join in a holy war.

As it stands now, most Afghans are still just tired of fighting and tribal feuds; divisions still heavily outweigh the prospects of a full-blown jihad, even in the Pashtun lands. Many communities remain split along tribal lines and locked in longstanding and often basic internal disputes that create a complex three-way interaction with ISAF.

'It's everywhere here, usually to do with water, one tribe uses the water and blocks it off to another,' said Nico, a Dutch Military Policeman working on the CIMIC programme in Uruzgan. Troops there even had locals take a rifle and shoot at them from beside a neighbour's compound in the hope of getting ISAF to arrest or even bomb him. This pervasive enmity within communities is echoed in British Brigadier General Henry Brooke's 1880 description of rural settlements.

Opposite from top

Helmand farmer studies a flyer urging locals to inform troops of any unexploded ordnance, June 2008.

Camels at Masum Ghar, Kandahar province.

An Afghan village is a collection of mud huts with flat roofs, and so arranged, and the huts joined together with high walls, as to form a kind of fort, as in this country every man's hand is against his neighbours, and everyone goes armed and prepared for treachery, and violence. The people are a distinctly warlike race, and fight bitterly among themselves.

With the foreign contingents being widely regarded as dispensing machines, local rivalries also escalate over who gets what. Giving one village a well and hoping this will serve as an example to others in the area that 'ink spot development' will in time reach them seldom works.

'You have villages with two tribes and if you give something to one of them the other thinks why not give it to us and will start threatening and fighting,' said the Norwegian contingent's Major Dale.

Even when such hostilities are absent, many communities lack the basic will to effect collective improvement. Perhaps it's born of seeing any construction of worth get destroyed over the years and wealth being taken away. Or maybe the notion of showing any initiative beyond farming crops and repairing the house was just never encouraged.

It baffles foreign troops to see small villages smothered with garbage and human excrement, suggesting that the residents have no stake in the immediate surroundings outside their walled homes. One Romanian officer in Zabul concluded that most rural Afghan men 'stand around in their villages and stare at the sun and do nothing'.

However, those who can read and write and live in or move to the larger towns and cities are anything but slow and unmotivated. For example, most interpreters hired by ISAF learned English at private courses in Kabul in a year and are impressively sharp-witted. The contrast with unschooled farmers is huge, and amply demonstrates that education is not just about learning a subject but also honing a person's overall ability to compare and categorize, evaluate and deduct.

Meanwhile, cunning comes naturally in areas where there is only the hard school of life for most inhabitants. In Paktya, one

Afghan soldier detains
suspected Taliban fighter, Zhari,
Kandahar province, July 2008.

American unit was admirably duped by a village elder who briefly cleared his house of his possessions and successfully passed it off as a mosque during a PRT visit. The building was duly fitted out with a US mosque kit, so got carpeted and had solar lighting installed, plus prayer mats and a loudspeaker system.

The lack of any activity other than farming in many areas does mean plenty of cheap labour for ISAF-sponsored construction projects. And the effect of these in a community goes beyond the mere creation of a new building or stretch of road.

'If you keep people in the area in work then they won't try to steal from you or blow you up, and it gives them a sense of pride,' said Joe Faustein, a member of the US Civilian Army Corps Engineers who was supervising construction of the Sabari district centre in Khost in 2007. But nor is it just a matter of going into a village and doling out contracts. Depending on the region and level of Taliban activity, just accepting a job from ISAF often carries a great risk.

'There can be Taliban retribution if they accept help from ISAF, quick impact projects are quite dangerous in that respect,' said 1RGR's Paul Pitchfork. 'We're in danger of trying to do good for good's sake and ending up doing harm.'

Adds a Canadian Corporal working with local contractors in Kandahar: 'The Taliban attack the road crews, they know when it's payday so if they find a guy with a roll of banknotes they'll beat him up or maybe kill him.'

A century ago, the implicit threat of punishment of errant partners was a cornerstone of the British strategy in Afghanistan, as evidenced by those same field notes:

Afghans are treacherous and generally inclined towards double dealing. Firmness, combined with bold and vigorous action, is the proper and only safe attitude for Europeans to adopt when dealing with them…In no circumstances should terms be made with Afghans, unless the observance by them of such terms can be enforced … The Afghans thoroughly appreciate and respect the disposition which can and does punish, and then makes friends and lets bygones be bygones.

Values espoused by the international community today obviously prohibit use of coercive force in building a humane, functioning Afghan state. The best definition of a winning formula I heard was from a Canadian soldier who simply advised: 'Give people something they don't want to lose.' Which comes back the basic truth that you have to provide jobs, roads, clinics and schools to prick the bubble of the insurgency. There are no shortcuts. Some who have served in Afghanistan think the cultural divide is so great that it's a lost cause, whichever path you take.

'We are ignorant if we think we're going to change anything, they are so steeped in their ways and tradition that it'll take a lifetime to do,' a British soldier in Helmand said. But others cite examples where the sides found common ground, if only for a moment, in the most unlikely circumstances.

'We were doing a house search in a hostile village that had 'Welcome Taliban' written on the walls,' recalled Lt. Stultz of the US 2-506th Airborne Infantry. 'There was a big panic as a cobra looped through the eves of a house. All the animosity was suddenly gone as we threw rocks at it together and for five minutes we, the villagers and the ANP were one big happy family.'

twenty

SPRINGTIME FOR OMAR

May, 2009

'**S**mile and wave boys, smile and wave,' Lt. Col. Robert Campbell, commander of US ground forces in Paktya province, tells his men as we drive through villages and crowds of sullen staring locals on his first road tour of his new AO.

Paktya is a tough one to manage, 5,500 square kilometres of mountains, plains and woodland that has a 38-kilometre border with Pakistan and is on the 'Zadran arc' named after Haqqani's tribe, which is causing considerable trouble to the Khost-Gardez Pass road project. Insurgent activity is currently rekindling here as it is throughout RC-East after the winter lull. Campbell's Alaska-based unit, the US 1-40th Cavalry, has recently taken over the AO and his personal detachment of trucks makes a three-day journey from Gardez to FOB Herrera in the north of the province, where I am to be dropped off.

'You came at a good time, we'll put you in a truck, we'll probably get blown up,' Campbell tells me cheerily as we wait at Salerno in Khost for a Black Hawk that will drop us at his headquarters in Gardez.

Khost is also feeling the effects of the Taliban's spring awakening. On May 12, a couple of hours before I land at the base, there is a coordinated attack by multiple suicide bombers against municipal buildings in the city, resulting in eight insurgents killed, six dead local nationals and 18 wounded locals and Afghan soldiers. At 0700 the next morning the base itself shakes to an explosion as a car-borne suicide bomber kills seven local workers queuing at the front gate.

Gardez is quiet by comparison when we arrive. The next morning I go with Campbell on a walkabout in the bazaar where he strides around chatting to shopkeepers and being mobbed by kids as he hands out sweets and pens. I am uncomfortable about walking around like this; a bomber just has to be on the ball to take out a top US commander and me with him. But I am assured by one of the soldiers that the town is 'secure'.

The Colonel also stops at the Governor's compound and talks to the ANP at the gate, urging them to keep vigilant at all times. It's good advice – on July 21 multiple suicide bombers, some dressed in burqas, attack this site and other government buildings in secure Gardez, killing five Afghan guards.

The Colonel's road trip starts at 0815 on May 16. I am in the second of four MRAPs, tall, heavily armoured trucks with V-shaped hulls to deflect the upward blast of IEDs, windows fitted with steel grills against RPGs and seats suspended on taut ropes to reduce percussion effects of explosions on passengers. Opposite me sits Jan, an Afghan from Paktika who has worked as an ISAF interpreter for seven years, been in a few dozen fire fights and survived an IED blast that killed three US Special Forces. Hands held out palms up before him, he recites a quick prayer from the Koran, sees me looking, smiles, points upwards and makes the sign of the cross. Above us top gunner Mike Notrica cocks the Mark-19 grenade launcher and we set off.

It takes us a day to drive 60 kilometres up the province, stopping off at district centres for meetings with sub-Governors and Police Chiefs as we go. All the way there are reminders of the spring awakening, stories of prowling insurgents and IEDs, while reports of attacks across the province are relayed to Campbell over the radio by his headquarters. As I listen through my own pair of headphones, snippets of information like 'FOB Wilderness, 35 enemy using AKs and RPGs in 10 fighting positions' jar against the seemingly tranquil, panoramic views we drive through.

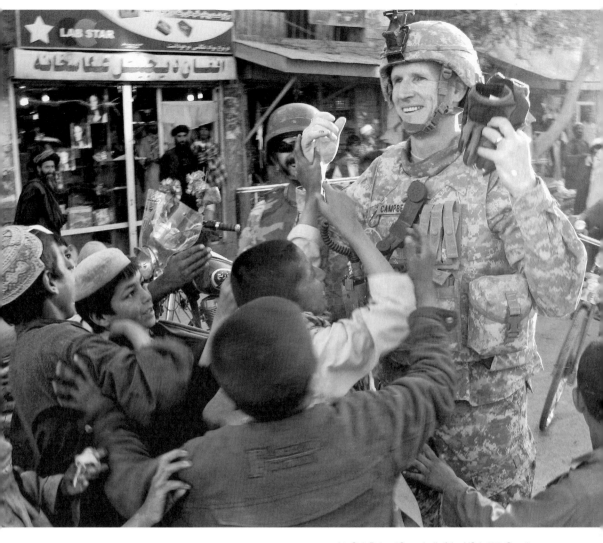

Lt. Col. Robert Campbell of the US 1-40th Cavalry
being mobbed by children while giving out pens
in Gardez, Paktya province, May 2009.

'It's a good job no one's shooting at me now because I couldn't shoot back, I feel so peaceful, the river, the mountains on the horizon, it's anywhere but Afghanistan,' the gunner says dreamily, although if need be he'll have the grenade launcher pumping out rounds in a moment.

'It reminds me of central California,' says the driver.

'Or the Columbia River Valley,' adds Campbell. 'That's a million-dollar view right there. They've even got horses grazing on the pastures. And insurgents.'

At the first stop the Colonel tells the Akhmadabad district sub-Governor what becomes his mantra throughout the trip: 'I focus on the people, not the enemy. If you do that you create an environment where the Taliban are not welcome.'

Town after village after ANP post recount the same story of clear skies, warm weather and insurgent groups rousing themselves from their winter rest. All local officials ask for more Police to help secure their territory, and Campbell has to tell them there are no more available but that they can have some Hescos

Down time. US troops at FOB Herrera in Paktya province, May
2009. 'You be the top hat, I'll be the gun.' 'No that's Cluedo.'

and concertina wire. As they brace for a new
season's fighting against a recuperated and re-
equipped enemy operating out of Pakistan, the
ANP seem like the little Dutch boy trying to
plug the leaking dyke with his finger.

The pace of events is picking up around
the town of Chamkani located about 15 kilometres from the border. Two days earlier US
Special Forces found an insurgent camp here
with cooking facilities for over a 100 people.
The ensuing fight resulted in 32 confirmed
enemy dead, so several dozen are presumed to
still be out there, moving in groups of 10 to
15 men. The local Afghan NDS intelligence
service chief says his reports indicate large
numbers of enemy will move across from
Waziristan in the next days, and that an anticipated offensive by the Pakistani military on
that side of the border may flush many more
Taliban this way. Now is the time to mount
a show of strength here, he impresses on the
Americans.

'If we appear weak the tribes will say yes to
whatever we say but will not in reality cooper-
ate with us,' he warns.

Having now offered everyone Hescos
and C-wire, Campbell draws on the obvious
remaining resource for the required muscle
flexing, the 263 Afghan Border Police (ABP)
who are stationed in the district along the
frontier. The US drive out to the border point,
which consists of a few small buildings and
guard posts perched on hilltops over a closed
road, and promote the idea that the ABP don't
just sit in their fixed positions but become
mobile assets, providing border protection by
also patrolling deeper in their own territory.
That would mean hooking up with the regular
Police as required. While cooperation between
branches of the Afghan security forces is generally poor, the ABP chief likes the idea.

The Colonel even suggests using his helicopters to move the Border Police on joint
operations. It's a generous offer but the ABP
chief responds by citing a prohibitive obstacle:
his men don't like the US rations. The Americans
exchange bemused glances and then sit back
and listen to a litany of what are otherwise
probably reasonable gripes about the plight
of the ABP here. Their generator is broken so

there is no electricity; they have hardly any fuel for their vehicles and no heavy weapons like mortars .

But since the emphasis these days is on making the Afghans solve their problems through their own chain of command rather than mollycoddling them with handouts, Campbell refrains from making any promises. 'Keep filling in the forms and applications and send them to your higher Command and we will help at the other end and make sure they are being received and that something is being done.'

Back in Chamkani the local ABP commander, a Major, arranges lunch for the US soldiers. He took up his command here two weeks ago and the walls of the meeting room where we eat are covered with three dozen *guligardan* wreaths like Hawaiian leis he was presented by local officials and village heads after his appointment. These congratulatory gifts consist of orange, red and white plastic flowers arranged around clocks and decorated with tinsel, flowers, gaudy bows and clusters of toy rupee banknotes.

Over platters of greasy kebabs, naan bread and spring onions the ABP commander asks Campbell what he gets paid. I wonder if the Colonel will be so bold as to tell him, knowing from my time in post-Soviet Russia and Ukraine that comparisons of salaries between vastly different societies often cause confusion and resentment.

Campbell pauses and then says, 'I get $7,000 a month.'

'I get $320,' the Afghan Major replies. 'How much did your house cost?'

'The Army pays for my accommodation now but my last house cost $175,000.'

The Major says nothing but carries a broad grin of amazement as he grapples with the sum.

'Things cost more in the United States and we have too many material possessions,' Campbell says by way of explanation. As if these two lives weren't different enough already, in money terms the disconnect is huge and unfathomable to the border guards.

The Afghan Captain sitting beside me evidently understands the conversation without the interpreter and I ask him where he learned his English. Zarif lived in London for seven

years and worked at Stanstead Airport. 'I got deported and now I'm stuck in Paktya,' he says resignedly.

Jan the interpreter then tells the story of how Afghanistan's president in the mid-1970s, Daoud Khan, supposedly went to a market and hung a butcher on his own hook for over-charging customers, then for good measure incinerated a dishonest baker in his oven.

'Afghanistan needs a strong ruler like that,' he says, prompting an awkward silence over the table that I venture to fill.

'There is an expression in English "to make the punishment fit the crime", but that's going a bit far…Isn't it better to have working courts and effective judges and humane prisons?'

Campbell smiles but the ABP Major doesn't react at all. He's still thinking about the Colonel's salary.

We set off for the next and last stop, Ahmad Khel, where ten days earlier a large group of insurgents attacked the ANP at the district centre but were bloodily repulsed by a passing US patrol's mortar and .50-cal and a subsequent air strike. More than 20 insurgents died in the clash, after which the American troops and the ANP spent a morning clearing body parts from the hillside and removing corpses from culverts where a few mortally injured fighters had dragged themselves. The leader of the attacking group was shot squarely in the face by the Police Chief through the metal gate panel as he demanded the ANP's surrender, and survivors of the assault who managed to flee relayed threats of brutal reprisals against the ANP.

Some of the insurgent dead were from the outlying settlements, where loyalties these days are split. As the Colonel's column drives through Chamkani, the locals in the bazaar stare blankly at the huge trucks that cause their houses to shake.

'Smile and wave boys, smile and wave,' Campbell urges his men again over the radio and then shakes his head. 'This is wrong, driving through a village in a metal box looking like a robot. That's not how you conduct a counter-insurgency.'

On Monday May 18 in the district centre by FOB Herrera, the US forces and local authorities hold a shura meeting of representatives of six Pashtun tribes and 24 sub tribes that live

Afghan soldier watches a
crowd of children in the village
of Zerok, Paktika province,
December 2006.

in the surrounding Jaji district. There are no
revelations but what happens there is a pretty
good indication that something has to change
fast if ISAF and the government want to avoid
losing the people entirely.

One after the other, a dozen speakers give
the hosts including Campbell a lashing, each
outdoing the last with condemnation of the
failure to look after the locals and provide
essentials.

'Afghanistan received billions of dollars
for reconstruction but teachers here had no
salary in five months and we have no health
care – it's like we are living in a coma,' one
elder complains to the US soldiers, egged on
by *whoahs* of agreement from the villagers.

'Your computers were so busy they ran out
of ink while you wrote down all our problems, and yet nothing was done about them,'
says another, while several cite their fears of
impending tragedy in the summer fighting.

Although located on the other side of the
country, they all know of the US bombing that
month in Farah that killed scores of innocents.
Then a respected veteran of the jihad, an old
man of 84 with an orange henna-dyed beard,
rises and presses home the message that time is
running out for the Americans.

'In the past eight years we had promises of
schools, roads, bridges but only one per cent
of this has materialised. You talk but you don't
act. There's a lot of corruption in the government, which only cares about its own tribes
and people. You hold the government in your
hands but you need to drop them now and
embrace the people, the poor, and the jobless.
You are rich and strong, it was Allah who gave
you this strength, now come and help us.'

Most of it is directed at Campbell as the
senior American and he listens impassively
until he also stands to speak. He's appearing
before these people for the first time and on

the back of countless earlier offers by US troops of reconstruction projects that never materialized. Like the Gurkha Lieutenant in Maiwand he keeps the message short and sweet and hopes some of it sticks.

'I know promises were broken in the past, and all I can talk about is the future. My men will not enter your homes; I will not drop bombs on your houses and will consult with elders before I enter your regions. I believe the focus should be on the people, not the enemy. This is war, mistakes will happen, and when they do you will be the first people we communicate with. And if there is something we cannot do, I will tell you.'

When he finishes there is neither heckling nor applause. After two hours sat in the baking sun the guests stand up and shuffle back to their villages. I get the impression that for many it was simply important to vent their grievances to somebody with power. That in itself was a sign of confidence they wouldn't get dragged off to jail for speaking their minds.

The commanding officer at FOB Herrera, Captain Richard Groen, isn't particularly fazed by the negative response. He also sees the event as a cathartic opportunity for the elders to sound off so he can start to achieve something concrete in his year here. Judging from the chats he has with some guests after the shura it's clear he has a more proactive attitude than his predecessor, who I hear only left the base three times in his year of deployment. As for the more vehement outbursts, he smiles and says, 'You could literally pave the streets in gold and some of the elders would still complain.'

I got the distinct impression in Jaji that ISAF and the Americans have all but exhausted their credit rating and that local confidence has bottomed out. People hadn't turned in large numbers to the Taliban – yet – but nor had they much inclination to believe anything the Americans told them without some proof in the pudding, such as a new road or a clinic.

That week the head of the PRT, Captain Phil Soliz, agrees with the elders on three new construction projects for Ahmad Khel; a madrassa, a girls' school and a retaining wall that are worth a total of $250,000 and will provide much needed employment. Soliz is a reservist from San Diego where he works as a real estate agent. I'm not sure he appreciates the joke when I say to him 'So some of your skills are transferable, like pulling the wool over people's eyes?'

Having attended the shuras, the officer knows or should know that the US has to deliver on these promises at a bare minimum if they are to retain credibility here. But he tells me the projects have to be authorized up an entire chain of command and *still* might be scratched with a stroke of someone's pen.

twenty-one

PIMON

June 3, 2009

I wake at 0630 on the floor of the Estonian sauna. It's the size of a garden shed, neatly done out in pine with a small steam room, two showers, a fridge and a framed map of the republic on the wall. The only military touches are the clothes hooks made of .50-cal shell cases hammered into the wood. A year before I'd sat here with a bunch of sweating soldiers drinking near-beer between forays into the 100-Celsius vapours with the Estonians, who are almost as obsessive about their steam as the Finns.

'In Kosovo, the French and Italians saw our sauna and thought we were crazy,' a neighbour told me as we assumed a lobster hue. 'The French said the sauna is only for rich people and the Italians were afraid their blood would boil at 100 degrees.'

This time it was the only place I figured I could get a few hours of undisturbed sleep, having arrived at Camp Bastion in the middle of the night when the Estonian compound was lifeless.

I emerge that morning to find a middle-aged NCO smoking on the bench outside. His eyebrows arch in puzzlement over his cigarette but he says nothing, so after establishing that Markus speaks Russian I explain that I am expected for a ten-day visit. He shows me into the briefing room where I stretch out for an hour on the sofa until the media officer arrives and takes me to an accommodation tent.

It's a bad day for the Baltic republic's company of troops in Helmand. A couple of hours earlier a 24-year-old soldier lost both of his legs to an IED by the Estonian Patrol Base Pimon, situated in farmland about 12 kilometres west of Lashkar Gah, in Nad-e-Ali district. It's the second serious casualty in three weeks since the deployment of this company of the Scouts Battalion, which is based in the port city of Paldiski. The first man was critically injured on May 18 on the first patrol out of Pimon when an insurgent poured AK fire into him from less than 100 metres away. Four rounds entered his body, as many struck his helmet and rifle. There was also direct fire at the base, to which the Estonians responded by pulling up their APCs to the walls and shredding the enemy positions with heavy machine-guns. Since then the Taliban prefer to wait for the troops to come out on patrol before attacking.

I meet the contingent commander, Major Janno Märk, a tall, friendly, shaven-headed man with very competent, self-taught English. He's just back from visiting the latest casualty at Bastion's field hospital and is understandably sombre.

'It's war,' he says finally, and then informs me that I'll ride out to Pimon with the platoon that is now on its way to Bastion to bring the injured man's brother to see him.

The company doctor, Major Anatoly Semjonov, an ethnic Russian originally from Siberia, is frank about the effect of this latest blow on the company.

'Their motivation is pretty low after taking two casualties in the space of two weeks,' he says. (I later learn that motivation also took a knock when they arrived, with the government responding to the economic crisis by cutting the soldiers' basic pay by eight per cent.)

The only positive aspect of the day is that British doctors at Bastion attributed the victim's survival to his fast and efficient treatment by Estonian medics at the scene. The already heavily sedated man was then anaesthetized into a deep sleep for the long air journey to the UK and follow-up surgery in Selly Oak hospital in Birmingham. Before they put him under, Semjonov assured him he could still have children and was amazed to hear the man say that he wanted to return to Afghanistan as soon as possible despite his injuries. He repeated the wish shortly after he came round in the UK, lucidly and not simply out of post-traumatic shock. It will not happen of course, but the Estonian armed forces generally find administrative work on bases in the republic for badly injured soldiers who wish to continue serving.

I am moved into a huge transit accommodation hut where one half is used for troop briefings. Dozing on a dusty bunk I catch snatches of a British officer's address as one unit hands over to another after spending 172 days on the ground in Helmand.

'The compound walls are two feet thick, you can shoot 7.62mm rounds at them all day long and you might not get through, they've been there for years and are baked hard like concrete…There are plenty of IEDs – we lost eight vehicles to them – and mines, RPGs, small arms, well-set ambushes from two sides if not three…You've got a big tour ahead of you, I'm not trying to scare you, just be aware of what's ahead.'

The Estonian platoon arrives that afternoon from Pimon in their APCs, and the grimy, exhausted soldiers occupy the bunks around me. I notice one man who seems to have lapsed into the sleep of the dead. He turns out to be the platoon leader, Lieutenant Madis Koza. He's had a rough day.

The next evening we leave Bastion in convoy at 1915, straight after supper. The Estonians are known by the British for their canny knack of arriving from the desert just before mealtimes and descending on the cookhouse with such voracious appetites that they were dubbed the 'Bastion Eating Team'.

I am placed in the back of the Finnish-made Sisu Pasi armoured car with three members of the British Fire Support Team (FST) that is attached to the Estonian company. We lurch across the dusky desert for 40 minutes and arrive in the dark at Pimon, where my stay is almost over before it starts. As I pull myself out of the vehicle by the hatch frame the massive steel rear door suddenly slams shut. It is a matter of a split second but I somehow yank my fingers clear before it clangs tight.

Captain Alexander Bourne, a 25-year-old liaison officer from the 1st Battalion of the Welsh Guards, gives me a quick tour. We climb up to the parapet that overlooks the Green Zone to the south and has a rear view north across the desert to the faint lights of Bastion.

'It's spooky; because there are not many civilians here you know there are going to be IEDs and mines everywhere. If you go 300 metres that way there are lots of bad guys. Sometimes they take shots at the base, but usually it's just one or two rounds and they disappear because they know they'll get 100 Estonians appearing at the wall and shooting back.'

I know from my time with the Canadians in Zhari how the posts can be situated flush up against insurgent strongholds and always be on the brink of hostilities. But surely with this amount of troops with massive firepower at their disposal there must be a reasonable belt of control here, maybe a couple of kilometres wide?

It's barely a couple of hundred metres.

★ ★ ★

I am billeted with Bourne and the British signals unit and Fire Support Team, ten soldiers who tie in the Estonians with operations of the UK forces' Battle Group Centre South, covering the area around the provincial capital Lashkar Gah.

So far this summer Sangin, Kajaki and Musa Qala have not exploded with the full force expected, and at the moment this is where it's happening. The Estonians were hastily redeployed from Now Zad to Nad-e-Ali in late 2008 after events that summer revealed a major Taliban threat to the capital from this seemingly calm area of farmland and villages.

A large force of Taliban started moving on Lashkar Gah from the north but was decimated by RAF Apache helicopters. Surveillance drones tracked the wounded insurgents as they were evacuated to hidden field hospitals located right on the Helmand capital's doorstep, overturning previous assumptions about the enemy's placement.

'The Taliban were living not in sanctuaries in the mountains but close to Lashkar Gah and the populated areas,' Major Märk tells me one evening at Pimon. So after holding a fraught yet peripheral position in northern Helmand, his contingent is now in the thick of the fight,

which seems to suit the national agenda for Estonia's Afghan involvement.

'For us it's extremely important to work with the UK and US. Because the US supported us during the Russian occupation we got our independence (from Moscow) in 1991, and it's important to contribute something back and keep those good relations.

'But if we say Afghanistan back home it gets associated with the Russian occupation here and that's really unpopular in Estonia. All news about casualties influence public opinion and a lot of people start shouting 'What are we doing in Afghanistan?' But we can't only consume security, we must provide security, that's the statement the politicians make when the public starts saying we should bring the troops home. It's been hard, those incidents with the casualties happened at the beginning of the deployment, the contingent didn't get time to settle in. On the other hand, maybe the first incident was sobering. It happened during the first patrol, was a shock for the company, but I hope it shook them in a good way, got them on the right track, and demonstrated to them that you have to not let your combat drills down. Everything has two sides.'

The Major is aware he faces a formidable enemy, and not just in their fighting tactics.

'The Taliban also understand that "Hearts and Minds" is important for them to win. The local population is the centre of gravity and whoever wins them over can expect some success. The locals had some hard experiences with the ANP, while the Taliban set up checkpoints, are very polite to the locals, and don't take "taxes" from them. Then a couple of hundred metres away at the ANP checkpoint they take money from people and treat them very badly.'

The Major's candour and frank appraisal is welcome after what has been a slightly uneasy first couple of days at the patrol base. Like their Finnish cousins, Estonians can present a very reserved, gruff exterior, but theirs is tinged with additional guardedness and suspicion.

Opposite from top

Flexing for NATO. Estonian troops work out at Patrol Base Pimon, Nad-e-Ali, Helmand province, June 2009.

Estonian relaxes in mortar pit, Patrol Base Pimon, Nad-e-Ali.

Together with the Latvians and Lithuanians, the Estonians hated Moscow's rule of their little country in the Soviet era. But while they may resent me for this observation, I am also inclined to partly attribute that wary, abrupt streak to the fact of being born in the USSR, with all the social strictures and hang-ups that yields. It takes more than a declaration of independence to erase that legacy.

Soon after I arrive, the commanding officer at Pimon, a short, hairy, barrel-chested Major called Tarvo, appears flanked by his second-in-command and another soldier to remove me from the base's tiny makeshift internet facility.

'It's not my decision, it's Estonian military policy,' the Major tells me, although this hadn't been a problem at the Estonian compound at Bastion. But it's their base so I don't quibble. The following day their media officer says it was a misunderstanding and that it's fine to use the internet. When I try to plug in again the 2IC, a Captain Tiidrus, appears like a genie from a bottle, says it's 'forbidden' and actually tries to yank the cable out of the back of my laptop while I'm writing a mail to ISAF in Kabul about my next embed.

This may just be his manner, but I also take this as a further indication that people are suspicious of my motives for being here. On day two, a cheerful young Estonian radioman says everyone thinks I'm rooting round for dirt on them. So I'm quite content to be put in with the British soldiers, who by contrast seem quite relaxed and unthreatened by my presence.

Their corner of the camp has that familiar end-of-the-line feeling. The Brits live in a small enclosure arranged around two ISO containers, with roller track and wooden boards for a floor, two large benches and some camping chairs. There is a covering of scrim netting overhead that provides precious shade but floods everything with sunny speckles, making it hard to discern between territories on their *Risk* board. The fridge is full of water and sweets, and a PlayStation and TV are cocooned against the dust in a large cardboard box but are still both on the blink. And the element just burned out in the kettle they use to heat the British rations (stuff the packet inside, boil until ready), forcing them to use solid hexi fuel to boil water for cooking until a new kettle can be brought from Bastion.

A notable design feature of the British enclosure is the two-metre square 'pool' made of a tarpaulin and small Hescos that is now covered over, its rancid liquid contents stewing in the savage Helmand heat. There's a London bus snow shaker that someone bought for Bourne at the souvenir stand beside the Ritz Hotel at Green Park.

It is primitive here but relatively cosy, and home to other wildlife too. The newest inhabitants are a scrawny, flea-ridden ginger cat they found and christened Beanhead because of the orange stain on its brow, and its two kittens, Fidel and Castro.

While I'm there, Bourne takes one of the four spent 105mm smoke shell cases they retrieved on patrols (otherwise the Taliban fill them with home-made explosives and use them as IEDs) and using an inverted end of a cut water bottle, creates a kind of lobster pot trap to catch bugs under the floor, for scientific research it transpires.

'I was sitting here watching TV and being attacked by a lot of insects flying round the light. I got a can of insect killer and hosed them down, they fell so densely all over this seat that you could barely see the wood. I was looking at them and thinking I bet no one's been here to study them for a long time.'

An inquiring e-mail to the head of zoology at Oxford University created a stir among Britain's insect fraternity, bringing referrals to the university's chief entomologist, a specialist at Oxford Museum and the keeper of collections at the Natural History Museum in London. Their Afghan specimens and material are no more recent than the 19th century and they ask the Captain to gather insects and try to get ISAF to assist in transporting them to Britain for examination.

The embedded life is now starting to affect my subconscious. On June 6 I wake at dawn from a tense dream about setting an ambush for insurgents but when they appear my finger won't pull the trigger of the rifle I am holding, like the legs-in-treacle feeling when you urgently need to run in your sleep.

The night wind has swept a bucket's worth of desert into my mosquito pod so I get up, shake the dust layer from my body and go for a wander around the slumbering base. Pimon consists entirely of Hescos and tents, meas-ures some 150 by 70 metres and is lined with Mercedes trucks and Sisu APCs. It is bare and besieged and one of the last places I would want to spend six months of my life. But it seems to suit the Estonians for now, even without a sauna.

Later that morning Tarvo comes to the British enclosure to tell me about the next day's patrol south to the Taliban-infested village of Zorabad. The mission will explore the possibility of holding a shura meeting with the elders, and while the village is only about 500 metres away, trouble is expected.

'There will be contact with the enemy, it is your own responsibility if you go,' the Major warns.

That afternoon First Platoon under Lt. Koza visits a village located 200 metres to the east of Pimon. The officer stops to talk to an old man working in a compound with his sons. He is friendly but scared, and urges the Estonians to do their fighting elsewhere.

'Whenever the Taliban fire a few shots you fire back at our village and it's not good,' he says, claiming that there are 'only one or two' Taliban in the area. Koza points out that his troops have seen groups of a dozen insurgents here and have to take firm action.

'When they shoot at us we have to show them we are stronger and that we are not going to leave until we win and Afghanistan is peaceful again,' he tells the man through the interpreter.

Finally the Lieutenant asks them to spread the word that people should not poke their heads over walls during fire fights as they can be taken for the Taliban, and then he raises the possibility of the British PRT building a well or a school here. The old man says they all have working wells in their compounds and that it is premature to build a school.

'The Taliban won't let us have a school. If we do, anyone who uses it will be killed the next day. But we really want one, just not now, only after there is peace again here.'

The next morning the shura recce mission to Zorabad is postponed in favour of some essential landscaping work. Second Platoon under Lieutenant Rauno Vahimets, a fresh-faced, cocky 24-year-old from Tartu, is sent across the canal by Pimon and 200 metres south to cut down a line of willows to improve the base's field of vision.

Here too the Taliban's reach instils a paralysing fear in the locals. The troops previously offered the owners of the land a substantial sum to remove the trees but the farmers refused, saying it would cost them their lives. So the Estonians take saws and axes and go to do it themselves.

We are close to the spot where the company's first casualty was raked with AK fire, while the compound where the machine-gunner stepped on the IED two days earlier is 300 metres to the east. At 0615 most of the platoon assumes defensive positions in the ditches and by compound walls, setting up MG3 machine-guns and a 60mm mortar while a few soldiers start the cutting work. Sitting by his radio operator and monitoring the platoon and base communications, Vahimets nonchalantly explains how it will play out.

'In the first 90 minutes heads will pop up over walls, motorbikes will ride up and down, and my men will fire warning shots. The enemy won't attack until they know exactly where we are. Then they will form a U-shape around us and in two hours or so they will move on us if we are still here. We will call in artillery from Patrol Base Silab seven kilometres away, the base mortars at Pimon, and the Apaches if they are available. Then it usually stops.'

His platoon are already known as the 'shit magnets', having been attacked during four of the six patrols they did since arriving. But it seems peaceful and the doomed row of willows rustles in the morning breeze as the first sawed saplings topple. In front of us flitting swallows dip low over fields of wheat and ragged poppy stems in pursuit of bugs.

'In our country when swallows fly low it means it's going to rain,' Vahimets says. 'But here we say it means there will be contact.'

At 0705 the Estonians get reports of locals leaving the nearest village to the west after the Taliban told them to get out. I-com chatter indicates the insurgents are moving up on the flanks so the soldiers fire sporadic warning shots until 0900 when the last tree is cut and the platoon starts to withdraw.

This is not a mission to engage, the work is done and ration-pack breakfast is waiting. A few parting shots are fired to the south by soldiers positioned at the corner of a compound. Later I learn they spotted a guy with a Kalashnikov working his way up a tree line 200 metres away. The man was promptly felled with shots from a standard-issue Israeli Galil assault rifle before the rearguard pulled out. Today turns out to be pretty quiet, considering what might have happened.

As in many places, the extreme heat demands that missions take place either early in the morning or in the evening. This leaves plenty of time between other duties for the soldiers to eat, sleep, wash, use the internet and read. I am working through Antonio Giustozzi's book on the neo-Taliban, *Koran, Laptop and Kalashnikov*, and note down things that strike a chord:

Says General David Barno, US Commander in Afghanistan from 2003-2005:

> Fourth Generation warfare argues that the enemy's target becomes the political establishment and the policy makers of his adversary, not the adversary's armed forces or tactical formations. The enemy achieves victory by putting intense, unremitting pressure on adversaries' decision makers, causing them to eventually capitulate, independent of military success or failure on the battlefield.[33]

Then, in apparent quotation of the 6th Century Chinese military strategist Sun Tzu, Barno says the Taliban's is a typical 'war of the flea' and similar to the war fought by the Afghan mujahedin against the Soviets in the 1980s.

> Fighting in villages to deliberately provoke air strikes and collateral damage and getting American forces to chase illiterate teenage boys with guns around the countryside like the dog chasing its tail and gnawing at each flea bite until it drops from exhaustion.

The dynamics and scale of the Afghan conflict changed a lot since Barno was here. But as I myself witnessed around the country, it still only requires a handful of guys with rifles to tie down a platoon or company for hours. And the reaction of giving massive suppressing fire in return persists, as noted by a reporter for

The Economist in February 2007: 'In response to a single round fired by the Taliban, British troops responded with dozens of mortar rounds, bursts of red tracers from a .50-calibre machine gun, illumination flares, the flaming rush of a Javelin missile and the juddering explosion of a 1,000lb guided bomb dropped from a Harrier jet.'

The other book I dip into while lying in my mossie pod is a copy of the current US Marine Corps and Army Counter-Insurgency field manual. Amid so much debate about the planned closure of the US detention facility at Guantanamo Bay, these guidelines note: 'Lose moral legitimacy, lose the war,' citing the Algerian war of 1954-62, and the decision of French leaders to permit torture against suspected insurgents. The condoning of such practices 'empowered the moral legitimacy of the opposition, undermined the French moral legitimacy. Illegal and immoral activities made the counterinsurgents extra vulnerable to enemy propaganda inside Algeria among the Muslim population, as well as in the United Nations and the French media.' With Guantanamo on the way out and Bagram emerging as the new hub for detainee operations, it's very topical. Later at a US base an American Sergeant runs up to me and asks me what I think of the Cuban facility's closure, so I cite the excerpt from the handbook.

'So you think Guantanamo loses us moral legitimacy?' he asks triumphantly before showing me a news story about how a former inmate is now leading a Taliban cell in Helmand. In his mind it was point proven and Guantanamo must stay.

There's a lot going on in my head as I try to process daily events and the melee of thoughts and impressions about this conflict and what I'm doing here. I'm noticeably edgier and jump when the scrim netting snaps in the wind or the Estonian mortar men shout '*Tuld!*' as they fire the 81mm.

My mindset isn't helped by recalling how a friend in England glibly wrote to me a few months before that he was convinced 'something horrific' would befall me here. I start to wonder, while at the same time feel I have crossed a threshold to a state of acceptance of patrols, gun fights, rockets and IEDs. But I am also questioning whether anything I am trying

to absorb and convey means much to people thousands of kilometres away, and whether I should say 'enough', get the hell out of here and finish this at home.

Perhaps I am merely going through the motions of weighing it up, because I have no intention of quitting so close to the finish. I just need a graphic equalizer in my head to moderate the vying levels of mental activity, the nervous tension, the analytical musings, the enduring thrill of going out on missions and the logistical demands of coordinating the final embed while I'm out here at Pimon.

Interestingly, while I've not gone down the Howard Hughes path of obsessive-compulsive hygiene, I am now apparently addicted to the use of hand sanitizer after shaking so many sticky, filthy paws. I cleanse with it constantly, whenever I flick through communal books and magazines, touch door handles or examine weapons, and certainly every time I come into hand-to-hand contact with another person. It might just be Virgoan extremes, as I once read somewhere, like crossing a messy room to straighten a crooked picture on the wall. After all, at Pimon and other places I otherwise sleep contentedly in a bed full of dust, brew tea in gritty mess tins, wear the same clothes for many days and shit in a plastic bag. But I still need to clean my hands all the time. Giving myself the benefit of the doubt, it's probably just 'normal abnormality'.

'To Afghan villagers, the ability of NATO and the Coalition to win all battles brought little comfort as the Taliban's ability to roam around the villages was clearly not going to be challenged, nor their mountain strongholds eliminated,' Giustozzi continues.

And here I am with the Estonians and British in the middle of an area the insurgents feel very comfortable in, using rat lines and ditches to move through the surrounding villages with great speed and harassing the patrols as and when they choose.

Pimon is a little fortress that can amply defend itself but has one land route in and out. The sense of being surrounded is a psychological hurdle you have to cross when working in forward positions in Afghanistan. I recall how minutes before flying to Baylough in 2007 an American on the helicopter landing zone told

Estonian soldier watches farmland from Patrol Base Pimon, Nad-e-Ali, Helmand province.

me the base was expecting another big attack that night.

'According to our spies, the Taliban have said they will finally take the FOB today and cut everyone's throats,' he said. I figured he was messing with me for kicks, but remember standing on the roof of the Baylough compound with its Commanding Officer later that afternoon and being told that an attack was probably imminent. I asked him whether they shouldn't be sending reinforcements from Qalat, setting up Claymores around the perimeter and so on?

'We don't use Claymores, if they come that close we're going to smoke 'em anyway,' he replied. To me it was a worrying prospect; to those guys it was just another day of a six-week run of constant attacks and contact with the enemy.

With the absence generally – but not always – of discernible frontlines, it's often possible for the insurgents to encroach on a base from a few or all sides. And the only exit is by helicopter or in vehicles that run the IED and ambush gauntlet every time they go out. As I read, note and ponder, my packet of wine gums from the fridge melts into a sticky roll.

The Brits are busy tidying for the arrival of the Estonian commander Major Märk and Lt. Col. Rupert Thorneloe, who is also of the Welsh Guards and is the commander of Battle Group Centre South. Capt. Bourne sweeps and vacates his small corner of the enclosure and occupies the cot by mine, and the Colonel moves in for a couple of days. A tall, solid, calm man with a rugged face that cracks readily into a smile, Thorneloe is very easy to get on with, approachable, humorous, thoughtful and clearly held in high esteem by his men. Between discussions with the Estonians he hangs out here, sitting on a bench and tapping away with two fingers on his laptop, writing recommendations for valour awards, some of them posthumous, drinking large mugs of tea and generally happy to shoot the breeze with me as I potter around.

We are of similar age and have a mutual friend, Paul Pitchfork of 1RGR. Before the Colonel joins the platoons on a morning patrol to a couple of villages to the east I do the journalist thing, take out my notepad and ask him about the Estonians for a story I'm doing. He is full of praise for the allies, of course, characterizing them as 'well trained, well equipped, well motivated and well led… They've got good experience; have a lot of guys on their second and third tours. Their morale is high, they are very focussed on the task, react well to each incident they've been involved in.'

Nevertheless, during my brief stay at Pimon I get the impression that the British are growing weary of the headstrong impulses of the Estonians and their reluctance to listen to the experience of the British Army, with its long history of fighting Pashtun tribesmen on this soil.

'They are a bit gung-ho,' says one of the officers in the UK support group. 'I was the same when I arrived; I wanted a scrap to see what it was like. But the Estonians are a bit arrogant sometimes, don't see enough of the big picture and don't make full use of the assets available to them.'

Another simply exclaims in a moment of frustration, 'I'm tired of them not listening to what we say but being happy to order us around.'

Thorneloe, however, stresses one of the Baltic contingent's key features: unlike many ISAF contributors, Estonia stepped up to the plate and committed troops to a combat role in a tough place, despite the heavy impact each casualty has on this tiny country of less than 1.4 million people.

'Hats off to them for coming down here and operating in Helmand which is one of the more dangerous parts of Afghanistan. NATO needs members who will sign up and do the full range of tasks,' he says before I put away my notebook and we go on patrol.

Three weeks later I was in Zabul skimming through Yahoo news when I saw the headline 'UK Lt. Col. killed in roadside bomb blast in Afghanistan' and a photo of what appeared to be Rupert in his helmet. As the computer slowly loaded the story, I stared at it with a sinking feeling. Our acquaintance was brief but you know a decent person when you meet one. His death in an IED strike near Lashkar Gah on July 1 shook everyone who knew him.

'After arriving in UK yesterday morning I picked up my car, turned the radio on and heard it on the news. It left me stunned for a few minutes,' Pitchfork later wrote in an e-mail. 'He was a wonderful bloke and a very talented officer. I never really got to know his family but you could tell he was a strong family man. Very sad indeed.'

Another mail I received from Capt. Bourne soon after said, 'We were all devastated by Col. Rupert's death and are still finding it difficult to believe.'

In the places I visited in Afghanistan I drew a variety of reactions from the soldiers around me. Some recognized the effort I made to report with integrity, others didn't want to know me or my trade, fair enough. But perhaps the most valued appraisal I received was relayed to me by Bourne: 'Incidentally, Col. Rupert said to me after you left that it was nice to meet a journalist who was a bit more balanced and not just hunting around for controversy. I also think he enjoyed his chats with you.'

On June 8 the two Estonian platoons set out from Pimon on foot to position an ambush team in a compound overnight. 'It's been a while since we've been this far, let's see what Terry Taliban's got up his sleeve,' one of the Brits says as we get kitted up.

We leave at 1840, pass the compound where the soldier stepped on the IED, moving slowly across the fields and tracks as the engineers clear the route and spray blue paint circles around spots with a suspicious metal reading.

Koza's platoon moves 800 metres east while I go southeast with Vahimets' men and two British JTACs, taking position in a deserted compound and orchard located 500 metres from Zorabad. If anyone is going to be attacked it will be us, being the most southerly element, or so they think. But the Taliban see how the ISAF troops are playing this one and do the unexpected. Everyone is caught unawares when a swift barrage of RPGs and small arms fire hits the position occupied by Koza and Major Märk. It comes across the canal from the north, from the swathe of land and houses that sits on the edge of the desert and in the supposedly protected lee of the base.

No one is hurt and there is no follow-up attack, it's dusk now, the troops have their night vision switched on and the base mortars start dropping illumination rounds. But the enemy's signal to the foreign troops is clear: 'We can and will hit you from any direction.'

By the time I leave Pimon the platoons seem to have regained their confidence after the casualties, but I wonder how deep that confidence runs and how soon it will be shaken again. They've been here long enough to know that they have only a tenuous hold on the area and far from being cowed, their enemy is becoming increasingly bold and adept at exploiting the contingent's mode of operation. And doing what they and their families have done for years, and that's fight.

I watch an evening game of basketball on a makeshift court in the centre of Pimon together with an Estonian with over a decade of service and several tours of both Iraq and Afghanistan. The Afghan soldiers jumping around in front of us are all a head shorter than most of the Scouts but we both know what tough creatures they are.

'They are small but strong,' he says. 'We look OK but are soft by comparison. If we lose a guy it takes us weeks to get over it. That's why it's so hard to fight these people, they expect death, we don't. If we have a casualty, people are shocked, ask how could this happen?'

I ask him if he thinks it's possible to ever fix this place.

'I know it sounds bad but I don't think about it,' he replies. 'I myself can't help these people so I don't worry about it.'

Before I leave the patrol base I say a few goodbyes. In his parting comments and perhaps in an effort to impress the reporter with good morale, an Estonian officer who should know better tells me 'RPGs are fun'.

'Not when they land beside you they aren't,' I reply, surprised by his foolish bravado, and wonder how many RPGs actually came close to him in his short time here.

I return to Bastion in convoy across the desert with Major Märk and a couple of the British. The next evening I join the Estonian officers at the sauna and between bouts of steaming we chat outside, red-faced and wearing only towels as we drink near-beer from the American PX. Dusk falls and a warm, dusty wind rises off the desert, carrying the stink from the Bastion sewage plant to our nostrils while British and Estonian flags flutter on the buildings around us.

On any day helicopters often land opposite the Estonian compound with wounded who are loaded into ambulances and driven to the camp hospital. As we talk, a Chinook dips in close overhead and sets down noisily. Then another lands, and another, until we have seen eight come and go, carrying what we later learn are victims of a car-bomb suicide attack by Gereshk that killed one British soldier and eight Afghans and injured more than 20 people.

The next night I return to Kandahar, travelling with Jaan, a perennially smiling 28-year-old Estonian with bright blue eyes set in a shorn head that's shaped like a pear. He was the crew mate to the machine-gunner who trod on the IED and is himself now on the way to UK and then home for treatment. He suffered concussion and hearing damage in the explosion, as well as a recurrence of an old sporting injury to his shoulder. This will require an operation and exclude him from active duty for a few months, so his Afghanistan tour is over. He is proud of his job here but also mightily relieved to be going home largely intact to his wife and two sons aged five and six.

'I was 1.5 metres behind him and got blown back two metres by the blast, but here I am, in one piece,' he says, still unable to grasp the events.

Jaan keeps seeing the scene in his head, his buddy stepping on the spot and being consumed by the blast that also propels him into brief unconsciousness. The gunner is a big guy and a keen bodybuilder and it was only due to his height and solid frame that the device shattered his legs but left the rest of him virtually unscathed. I then think about the American soldier in Zabul who had his lower legs smashed when his truck ran over an IED. His small stature actually helped him, his friends told me later. A larger man crammed into the rear would have been more badly hurt when the force of the explosion drove the driver's seat into his shins.

'I wasn't prepared for this, if they could show this in training then 60 to 70 per cent of the guys wouldn't come here,' Jaan says of his incident. According to him, a lot of the troops are getting frustrated with the tactics at Pimon, where they always do short missions and return to base rather than staying out and keeping the enemy guessing.

'We clear an area and then give it up straight away by leaving, so the Taliban can then observe patterns, plant IEDs for us.'

But mostly his thoughts are focussed on his friend, who he will visit in hospital in Birmingham in two days and then travel home to Estonia.

'After this I will build a house and be with my family, have a peaceful life, no guns, no insurgents,' he says as we wait for our flight in the PAX tent and watch television with half a dozen British soldiers.

Like Ernie the Dane, Jaan feels he pushed his luck as far as it will go. All the troops I meet in Afghanistan have their own take on whether these tours are a justifiable risk to themselves and strain on their loved ones. The Estonians make almost four times their usual soldiering wage with tours of active duty, so around $3200 per month for a Private

(economic crisis cuts notwithstanding) and the ones I met were enthusiastic and keen to get at their enemy. But at the same time each probably wonders how many patrols and missions he can do before it goes wrong, playing the same numbers game described to me by my Canadian reporter friend.

As we wait in the transit tent, the forces network shows an episode of the CSI forensics show where someone dies in a mysterious parachuting accident. Foul play is suspected, but as one member of the investigating team says, 'If you do enough parachute jumps, something's going to get you.'

Jaan and I spend the next day at KAF where I am offered to sleep in the Estonian quarters until I can move on. He leaves for Britain on a flight that evening. The next morning, Monday June 15, the Estonian press officer tells me one of their men was just killed in an ambush south of Pimon and three more were wounded. This brought the number of Estonian KIA in Afghanistan since 2007 to four, rising to six the next month.

Master Sergeant Allain Tikko, a 30-year-old father of one and a veteran of Kosovo, Iraq and Afghanistan, died as the result of a direct hit to the upper body by an RPG fired from a distance of 400 metres.

In a tribute to Tikko, the chief of the Estonian General Staff, Lieutenant General Ans Laaneots, said the Sergeant had fought for his daughter and in order that the republic's children 'can grow up in a safer and better world and so their children too can grow up in a free Estonia...His comrades in arms will not tire or falter and will continue fighting for Estonian independence.'[34]

Two more Estonians died in an IED blast near Pimon in July.

twenty-two

IED WAR

'IED Valley' in Zabul province is four kilometres long, surrounded by rocky hills and covered in a thick carpet of green thistles in the summer months. It contains a few villages frequented by known IED facilitators who build and plant the devices on routes used by ISAF and the Afghan government forces, but often killing civilians in the process.

Even before British and US troops in trucks enter the valley in June 2007 on a disruption operation, 14 men travelling on seven motorcycles circle their column at a distance, waiting for a chance to plant something in its path. They nearly manage it. As we drive across a wadi a driver spots the threat and skirts round a neat, freshly dug hole in the earth. But two more IEDs will go off before the operation ends two days later.

Having learned that direct assaults on the international forces do not pay off, insurgents in Afghanistan turned like their Iraqi counterparts to the so-called asymmetric tactics of suicide bombings and attacks with IEDs, which are cheap and easy to build but hard to detect and counter.

In the seven years following the 2001 ouster of the Taliban, IEDs accounted for more than a third of deaths among the international forces in Afghanistan.

The occurrence of IED attacks rose steadily until a spike in 2008, when the Pentagon's Joint IED Defeat Organization (JIEDDO) counted 3,611 instances in which improvised explosives were used, representing a 50 per cent increase over the previous year. (By comparison, there were more than 9,000 IED attacks in Iraq in 2008, but that is far below the 2006 level, when there were as many as 2,500 a month.)[35] More than 175 foreign troops were killed by roadside bombs in Afghanistan in 2008, double the number for the previous year. And the devices killed more Afghan civilians.

Buried in the ground, packed into vehicles, hidden in trash cans or animal carcasses, attached to live donkeys and worn on humans in vests, the improvised bombs are made from readily available materials. This can be construction explosives, fertilizer or abandoned military ordnance like artillery shells, mortar rounds or rockets, and also anti-tank mines, of which specialists encounter up to three dozen different types in Afghanistan.

'We've seen Egyptian-made ordnance, Russian, Italian, British – anything they can get their hands on,' said a Petty Officer of the US Navy EOD unit that entered the valley in Zabul.

Generally, an IED consists of a power source in the form of a battery, detonator, container, main charge and a switch. Variants can range from anti-personnel mines placed on top of a buried shells, to complex designs using crude components that defy neutralization apart from in a controlled detonation.

'If I spent a few bucks in Radio Shack I could build a ton of bombs and some of them could never be disarmed,' another American EOD technician said while leafing through a handbook of IEDs made from everyday electrical items and parts.

Another concern and one that is not talked about much publicly is the incidence of explosively formed penetrators (EFPs), sophisticated roadside bombs that must be made with precise machine tools in workshops and can devastate even the most heavily armoured vehicles. These were widely used in Iraq but in 2007 officials first confirmed that two of the devices were found in Afghanistan, one in an arms cache in Kabul, the other close to the Iranian border. Others have been found but not yet in significant numbers, or so one hears.

Most common are victim-operated pressure plates that explode when stepped or driven on. The plates are often made from simple saw blades separated by rubber pads that will crush together under the weight of a person or vehicle and complete the circuit for detonation. Some devices are remotely controlled by a cell phone, although this type became less prevalent as the insurgents became wise to electronic countermeasures being used by troops. Command wire variants are manually fired by a trigger man who waits at a distance and connects wires as a target passes, or just yanks on the trigger cord.

'Bombs hidden in plastic jerry cans and metal pressure cookers have been detonated by kite twine pulled by Taliban, who ironically banned kite flying,' a British newspaper wrote after further IED casualties in Helmand.

Or there might be booby traps disguised as ordinary objects. As the Canadian EOD specialist told the Afghan Police he was training, quoted earlier, 'If you see something attractive, it's probably mined.'

The force of an IED explosion can also detonate any ammunition and grenades soldiers are carrying, while the blast wave whips up secondary fragments like stones and bits of wood at supersonic speed. Suicide vests and car bombs will usually be packed with ball bearings, nails, bolts and other metal to maximize casualties. The hardest variants to counter are the vehicle-borne bombs, which can strike fast out of a flow of traffic.

'The big thing is watching the driver's intent, he could look normal or like he's on drugs; a lot of times they'll drug these guys so they'll go through it,' said another American EOD specialist with 17 years of experience in this field. His prognosis about countering this threat is not good: 'The only way you're going to win against a suicide bomber is to get away from him or shoot him before he can flip his switch.'

Unlike Iraq, where more streets are paved, Afghanistan has a network of undeveloped roads where it is far easier to plant devices. Highway 1 (Ring Road) was also built with thousands of culverts, any of which can conceal explosives. According to the JIEDDO, the military intends to use satellites and Global Positioning System devices to show convoys the exact location of each culvert, and to install monitoring systems that can detect hidden bombs.

A major worry is the appearance of IEDs that contain almost no metal components except perhaps part of a paper clip, and are almost impossible to detect. Utilizing homemade explosives that can be stuffed into plastic containers, these can be dug into roads weeks in advance, needing only to be primed. In the Canadian zone in Kandahar, IEDs were planted during construction of roads and left unused until after the asphalt was laid, ready to be connected and detonated when the route was in service.

'It's evolution, patterns will emerge, they'll get a kill and then we'll adapt and counter it,' British Gurkha Lieutenant Aloysius Connolly said as his foot patrol made a detour round a suspect spot in Kandahar in 2008. 'The Taliban are now using all-plastic IEDs, so ISAF will take a JCB to cut new crossings at wadis, anticipating that the Taliban will notice and to see how they will react.'

Sure enough, incidents were then reported where IEDs were laid at a distance from wadi crossings to hit likely alternate crossing points. Devices are also placed in what's called a daisy chain, spaced apart and linked with each other with the aim of killing and injuring a whole file of troops or vehicles. Others get strung from trees to maximise the blast radius among dismounted personnel.

On roads in Kandahar, ISAF fitted steel grills over the mouths of culverts and sprayed them red so that drivers of security force vehicles could see that they were still in place when approaching. But the method was always expected to yield only a short-term deflection of IED planting techniques against a cunning enemy.

'Everything we put down for them they'll think about it, find a way to defeat our counter-measures, and we then adjust again – they learn from us and we learn from them,' said a Canadian leading the grill spraying in Panjwaii district.

Opposite from top

IED-wrecked Afghan police vehicles at FOB Wilson, Zhari, Kandahar province, July 2008.

Czech Army Humvee on patrol in Logar province.

'We try and work out where they are and where they are going with something and try to beat them to the punch,' adds a member of the US Asymmetric Warfare Team (AWT). 'We've killed all the stupid ones now; it's the smart ones who are left.'

But even without a presumed trend of IED makers bringing know-how from Iraq to Afghanistan, experts say Taliban manufacturers steadily honed their skills in recent years, building devices in workshops in Pakistan and sending over technical emissaries to help cells of fighters plant them to best effect in Afghanistan.

'You'll get a guy come across from Pakistan for three or four months and Khost will get absolutely nasty,' said Steve, a Sergeant with an American EOD team. 'Then he'll get killed or captured and then someone will go to Nangahar or Nuristan and it's the same thing.'

Consequently, counter-insurgency tactics are as much or more about neutralizing these specialized operations as destroying groups of rank-and-file insurgents.

'Finding a big stash of explosives or electrical components or capturing a bomb maker is just as satisfying as a big fight,' said Gurkha Lt. Connolly. 'You've denied the enemy something that's valuable to them. Capturing a bomb maker and taking him out of the equation will have a better effect than killing a few fighters.'

The EOD guys are a peculiar bunch, usually fascinated by the intricacies of the deadly devices they deal with, just like a zoologist might coo at the bared fangs of a viper he holds in his hand.

'Most people don't have a clue when they join EOD what it's about, they think EOD is ordinary ammunition, not IEDs,' said Lt. Petr Tomichek, head of a Czech EOD team in Logar province. 'Once they know that it's about adrenalin they are looking for action. But you spend hours and hours reading intelligence reports about what happened to EOD specialists somewhere else, and sometimes it makes you feel a little crazy.'

Steve the American adds: 'Every EOD technician I've ever met has got some kind of major character flaw; you could write a doctoral thesis about this. You're heart has to be in this job. The Special Forces guys tell us we're

crazy and we say, hell you're the guys running round getting shot at.'

But all the specialists I met were critically aware of the risks of the job, which traditionally has a high casualty rate.

'I'm definitely thankful when I go home from work alive each day,' another American said. He would be injured and his team partner killed when his truck hit an IED two weeks later.

While the IED threat is all around and growing, it usually takes a hit to bring home the reality of this concealed threat to the troops on the ground. For the 2-506th in Khost, the fighting season kicked off with a three successive IED incidents in May, 2008, one of which killed Staff Sergeant Kevin Roberts and two civilians. Close to the Mandozai district centre, soldiers of Third Platoon found one device consisting of two anti-tank and two anti-personnel mines.

'We were tipped off by a farmer,' Humvee driver Alex Maldonado recalled. 'He said there was a bagful of mines there and I thought yeah right, but we went over and sure enough there was. At the time I didn't think about it, just "cool we found some mines". It wasn't until the next day when we were loading flag-covered bodies on stretchers that I realised how badly it could have gone.'

The thought of IEDs is always there when driving in this country. It's not a topic to dwell on when on the road but often someone will put it out there anyway.

'If I lose a leg it's out with the 9mm and through the head because I'm only going home if I've got all four limbs,' a Canadian soldier said as we set off along a notorious IED route in Kandahar in a LAV. A lively discussion started about whether it's better to be blinded or castrated in a blast and it's not fatal for you.

'My greatest fear is losing my eyesight because then I can't read,' said a studious reservist who was engrossed in the book *Corporation, the Pursuit of Profit and Power* in the blue glow of a key light clamped in his lips. 'The coffin is sealed,' someone else intoned darkly as the back ramp clanged shut and the vehicle set off.

In Paktika province some months before I was riding in a Polish Rosomak armoured car that stopped to pick up some Americans who were in this type of transport for the first time.

'How are you supposed to dismount in a hurry, does it go down like a ramp?' asks one, looking at the thick steel rear door.

'If this things runs over an IED you'll find multiple holes to crawl out of if you're still alive,' answers another.

A Polish Captain leaps to the defence of his vehicle and tells them, 'Actually the Rosomak can withstand a very powerful IED.'

Again, it's a matter of evolution. With tough vehicles like these on the roads and the introduction of the American MRAPs with their V-shaped hulls, the insurgents have opted for the obvious counterstrategy – much, much larger explosive charges.

'IEDs have grown dramatically, now they are going for a catastrophic kill,' said Major Chris Adams, the commander of the Canadian tank unit deployed in Kandahar in summer 2008.

The limitations of armour against devices that strike from below was all too apparent when I stood with a platoon of British infantry rehearsing air assault drills in a small graveyard of wrecked tanks and armoured cars at Kandahar Airfield. Some of the hulls were twisted and split wide open by IEDs and we were all thinking the same: No one in the back can have survived. But you still encounter plenty of soldiers with miraculous tales of IED survival. In Paktika in 2007 I chatted to Aaron Cox, a 25-year-old US Humvee driver from Arizona who some weeks before ran over a device on the edge of Dila, a notorious pocket of trouble in the province.

'We were going to check the district centre which was later destroyed. We were just driving along and *boom*, an IED blew off the whole of the front of the truck, the tyres went 50 metres to the left and 75 metres to the right, and pretty much everything under the hood except the engine block was vaporised. We were all concussed and the gunner dislocated his elbow. I still have perpetual migraines and have to constantly medicate. It's funny, I made it through a year and a half in Iraq and come to Afghanistan and get blown up. I don't like being at the front, we were the lead vehicle then.'

Being at the front of a convoy is an unenviable position as you are first in line to be blown up. But a centimetre here or there can mean a pressure-plate IED strikes a vehicle further down the column.

'In Tarin Kowt we were pretty lucky, the ANA not so,' recalled a Lieutenant of the Welsh Fusiliers as we press into IED Valley in Zabul on a sweltering hot day in June 2007. 'Twelve of our vehicles passed the point, and then an ANA motorcycle hit it. One was killed, the other lost his arse and both legs.'

Then two Chinooks land more than 60 Welsh infantrymen who spread out while a detachment is sent to sweep the road with mine detectors. Across the valley a seven-ton truck carrying ANA soldiers runs over a bomb but it's a small charge and no one is injured because of the mass of the vehicle.

The next morning another patrol heads out accompanied by the American EOD team. Minutes after they leave, a powerful blast echoes down the valley and shortly after this they radio in to report that the explosion occurred further down the road, out of sight.

A Predator drone is called in to conduct aerial surveillance and relays grainy images of ten people running to a prone figure on the ground and rushing it to a nearby mud compound. The troops arrive at the site and are told that a local man on a bicycle rode over a pressure-plate. They are shown the mutilated body, which landed 20 metres away from the crater and there are instant suspicions.

'They said he was on a bike and hit it. I think he was either placing or retrieving it,' says the commander of the US team, pointing out discrepancies in the locals' account. The victim lost his right arm and his feet were intact, which would hardly happen if he had been on a bicycle. The weight of a bicycle would scarcely suffice to press together metal plates set on a road for a vehicle, and there's no mangled bicycle to be seen here anyway.

There is a strong suspicion that the man blew himself up while planting the device for the approaching trucks. 'But we'll never know for sure,' says the specialist.

twenty-three

BAYLOUGH PART II

Soldier's Creed

I am an American Soldier.

I am a Warrior and a member of a team.

I serve the people of the United States and live the Army Values.

I will always place the mission first.

I will never accept defeat.

I will never quit.

I will never leave a fallen comrade.

I am disciplined, physically and mentally tough, trained and proficient in my warrior tasks and drills.

I always maintain my arms, my equipment and myself.

I am an expert and I am a professional.

I stand ready to deploy, engage, and destroy the enemies of the United States of America in close combat.

I am a guardian of freedom and the American way of life.

I am an American Soldier.

Baylough has its own draw. I always tell the soldiers who have fought up there that 'There are those who have been *to* Combat and those who have been *in* Combat'. Many soldiers go to war but most never really experience it. Everyone I have ever known to have operated up there, Special Forces included, will say the same thing.

First Sergeant Chris Weiskittel, US 1-4th Infantry.

'It's fucking heavy, it's buried good,' the EOD guy operating the Talon robot tells his team as they try to dislodge the device from the track. The claw of the remote-controlled robot snips a pressure-plate and power pack away from a main charge in a Hessian sack that is buried in the hard-baked earth.

The men of the village sit 100 metres up from us in the shade of a wall and watch the Americans work. It's a large IED that's been well dug into the main track and there's no way they could have not known about it, or they would have detonated it themselves by now on their way to the bazaar.

Acting on a tip-off, the commander at FOB Baylough, Captain Jason Basilides, sends two squads of men and some ANA across the wheat fields to search for the device, amid concerns that it's a trap to lure them into an ambush. Despite the base offering a reward of $200 for every IED reported by the locals, it's only the second one turned in four months. Then again, the cash for the 'Small Rewards Fund' hasn't made it out here yet, so no one actually got paid for the scheme to take off.

After some searching an ANA soldier finds a scuffed-up spot on the track and there it is. This still might have been a set-up. The informant said the device was buried by the stream that runs through the village. But the actual location is way out to the side, on the route everyone knows the EOD and other trucks will use today to drive in.

The specialists give up trying to unearth the bomb and blow it in place with C4 plastic explosives, vomiting a huge pall of black smoke into the sky and leaving a crater the size of a kids' paddling pool.

Exactly two years after my first visit I returned to Baylough on June 21, 2009, after the US 1st Battalion, 4th Infantry Regiment forgave me for unilaterally bailing out of Qalat in 2008. This time I got lucky with transport, flying from KAF to Qalat one morning on an unscheduled Black Hawk flight and straight out to Baylough on another. I arrived with the EOD team and the commander of Bravo Company, Captain Mark Garner.

As soon as we landed, the EOD team went off to destroy another IED consisting of home-made explosives packed into a propane gas cylinder. Five days later they dealt with this one in the village, and also destroyed a few items of scattered ordnance between the calls.

Business has been pretty good of late for EOD in the province, especially after a chief opponent was taken out. Two weeks earlier US forces in the neighbouring Arghandab district killed a known IED maker, Garner tells me. After his funeral a vehicle carrying two dozen mourners hit a pressure plate later confirmed to have been one of his. The blast killed eight family members, including his wife. No one was rejoicing at the collateral damage, but as Garner said, 'There's karma for you.'

Aged 30 and hailing from North Carolina, he is very welcoming from the outset, taking my camera on the helicopter and filming me at the window so I'd have some footage of myself for a change. My reception is up and down in those first days though. Before I left Qalat, the commander of US forces in Zabul, Major Greg Cannata, gives me a briefing and is frank that I'll have free rein at Baylough and if I screw up then they'll review my stay. He's the one who tells me, 'We are still from opposite poles, trying to get on nicely'. But we establish a good rapport and I'm glad to know where I stand. He even relays regards from the Major who blacklisted me the previous year.

But it's still kind of Ground Zero here for me and the media in general. A month earlier the 1-4th hosted another journalist – we'll call him Dan – with a track record of upsetting people with his work in Afghanistan and Iraq, and who I am told was busy ferreting out fresh controversy at Baylough. 'I think he was looking for the golden nugget,' Garner said.

On the one hand a journalist has to get a story, but you have to balance reporting zeal with preserving good relations. Because other-wise your access is limited and they'll tell you nothing. Simple as that. Dan's previous form even resulted in the Special Forces preemptively shunting him back to Qalat before a combined operation in Deh Chopan that ended in a huge fight with an estimated 35 insurgent dead. The reporter had to cover it all from HQ.

Most of the soldiers appear to have been warned to watch what they say to me and that I 'may use it against them', someone tells me. Platoon Sergeant First Class Stephen Carney was in a unit that got bitten by Dan two years earlier in Paktika. Once the ice between us is broken, he tells me he had scant time for the guy during his stay and wanted little to do with me either when I arrived.

Captain Garner recalled the reporter's vociferous demands to be party to every planning session at Baylough, a sure way to antagonize one's hosts. He didn't help matters by publishing a story that cited the failure of Captain Basilides to remove his dark glasses while talking to the locals as an example of the cultural divide.

'Sometimes journalists write without knowing all the facts,' said Garner. 'Captain Basilides wears prescription glasses so I'd rather he kept them on than couldn't see what he's doing if something happened.'

In short, I spent my first ten days at Baylough treading a trail of Dan's droppings. I am the invisible man to a lot of the soldiers, but Garner stops for chats all the time, chewing tobacco through a big grin as he tells me about travelling with his wife Nickayla in Europe, or mulling the fate of Zabul and Afghanistan and what needs to be done here.

I also get some normal interaction with a small group I met here in 2007 who are now back again for another tour. These include Derek Houser, a gun-luvvin, dog-luvvin dude from Tennessee, Sergeant Christian Cisneros, a big jolly Mexican from California and Staff Sergeant Azhar Sher, a big jolly Pakistani from Islamabad who moved to the US ten years ago. Hawaiian mortarman Andrew Toia is amazed I remember his name, and I even get the time of day from Wayne Tibbets, a hardnosed young man who probably saw too much combat for his own good and who scowls to himself while smoking between turns on the weights bench. And finally Chris Weiskittel, a tall wise-cracking 39-year-old from Florida and veteran of both Gulf Wars, who since 2007 became Bravo Company's First Sergeant. On my third day he arrives at Baylough with First Platoon from FOB Lane in the adjacent Arghandab district for two weeks of joint operations in Deh Chopan.

'So you're back again?' Weiskittel says when he sees me, and laughs when I recall how two years ago after the second cancellation of my flight out I heard his voice announce across the FOB through a bullhorn: 'Attention the reporter, you are never leaving Baylough!'

With 'Welcome to Hell' sprayed on the cor-roded metal doors into the inner compound, this is not generally a place people struggle to visit as I have done. Before flying from Qalat I run once more into Major Cannata, who tells me, 'You reporters are nuts going up there without weapons, I wouldn't.'

But the old faces here seem quite OK with being back.

'You've got a better chance of surviving if you know the area,' says Houser, who tells his wife he pulls guard duty all the time and never goes out. Sgt. Sher's father doesn't even know he was here in 2007 and is back again now.

Despite what Baylough represents – IEDs, ambushes and fire fights; footslogging through hills full of fellows with PKMs, mortars and recoilless rifles; spartan conditions and shitting in a plastic bag – I am also genuinely happy to be here again. I have come full circle and am on the home stretch of my project. This is the last stop, the last planned embed, the last time I will invite trouble.

Perhaps as a result of the jittery patch at Pimon, I had to fend off bouts of unease and fascination with unlikely 'omens' on my way here. At Bagram three days earlier I was walking along Disney Drive staring at a pretty bank of white, pink and grey cumulus clouds drifting across the evening sky when a speed-ing sparrow crashed into the side of my head but kept flying. And the name printed on the patrol cap of the American soldier ahead of me was Perdun, 'fartpants' in Russian. What could it all mean?

Later I found written in my notes from pre-cisely this time, 'Am I going to lose my nerve now, so close to the end? No I'm fucking not.

Get to it!' So I suppress worries that I can get hit now after all these months and focus on the job in hand.

★ ★ ★

The mission of the 1-4th Infantry alongside the Romanians in Zabul began in July 2006 after the government in Bucharest committed to an extensive deployment in Afghanistan and asked for US support.

The resultant team comprises a rotating Romanian Infantry Battalion; the US 1-4th, which is based in Hohenfels, Germany; US EOD teams out of Sigonella, Italy; JTACs from US Air Forces Europe; and an intelli-gence team from US Army Europe.

This set-up is unique for the US mili-tary, which typically does not task organize multinationally below the brigade level and does not rotate troops internally in the same place like the 1-4th has done for three years. The result is a regiment with an unparalleled knowledge of its AO and a longstanding part-nership with a foreign Army in ISAF.

Part of the job is to do combined training with the Romanians in preparation for tours in Zabul. It's a running joke how this panned out in practice over two trips to Romania in 2008. On the first, US soldiers were sent to take part in war games by the coastal resort of Constanza. Their accommodation was five minutes from a nudist beach where naked girls would come up and chat to them as they drank beer in cafes after work. To the dismay of wives and girlfriends at home they were let off the leash for those 45 days. By day they would dress as Taliban in *payran tumban* ('manjams', as they call them), sandals, false beards and RPGs for the Romanians to chase, by night they could party, providing they got back to their quarters.

The next trip in late autumn was heavily subscribed to by young bloods eager to have a similar experience. But instead of Constanza, this group spent 45 days living in tents in the middle of nowhere, freezing rather than fraternizing. But things are deadly serious in Zabul, where up to my arrival in 2009 the Romanians had lost six men (and five more in other parts of the country), and the Americans seven, with many more wounded. The number of US KIA would rise by two in Deh Chopan before I left.

Deh Chopan is a very specific environment to work in. Consisting mainly of mountains, rivers and picturesque valleys like the Baylough Bowl, the region lies on main insurgent routes in from Pakistan and is a transit corridor between Ghazni to the north and Kandahar and Helmand provinces to the south and west. There are large areas that are practically uncharted in terms of enemy activity and are thought to hold sanctuaries and training camps.

According to the Americans, Deh Chopan draws foreign fighters including Uzbeks and Chechens. While attacks by local Pashtun Taliban are often poorly executed, these foreign elements have been observed to use conventional infantry tactics like flanking, bounding and fixing targets. Some have uniforms, body armour and chest racks, like the group that got ambushed by Sgt. Sher's platoon on May 28 near Vakil Kur, a village located seven kilometres north of the FOB on an insurgent 'highway' running east to west. As they tried to fight their way through withering fire from the soldiers above they used smoke grenades for the first time anyone could recall, and several even wore helmets. Unfortunately for the intrigued US troops, the area was still so hot they had to withdraw before they could go down and inspect the bodies and gather intelligence. The fight here is all about the high ground and both sides constantly try to outwit each other with feints and manoeuvres that make use of the local relief.

'If you're not on the highest peak they'll come and get you, and there's always a higher peak than yours and there's always someone on it,' says Tibbets.

With their Apaches, jets and bombers, UAVs, 120mm mortars and advanced communication systems, the US should have the clear advantage, but they are still unable to contain the enemy. The insurgents use the land with incredible skill to attack and melt away and attack again, often from concealed positions. The soldiers will swear they have caves with camouflaged doors on them, having in the past surrounded and searched hills with shooters on them but finding no one.

'It's pretty eerie when they can see you but you can't find them,' says Private Anthony Macias, who arrived at Baylough three months after finishing basic training. He's been in plenty of fights now but says his buddies in Iraq were there a year and haven't got their Combat Infantry Badge, whereas he got his in the first month.

As for the FOB itself, I will include a few paragraphs of a description I wrote in 2007 about this highly 'kinetic' place called Baylough that I came to know.

The spent cartridge cases, empty ammunition boxes, and rocket and mortar fragments lying around Forward Operating Base Baylough, not to mention the shrapnel-peppered outdoor toilet cubicles, testify to its reputation as one of the hottest outposts in Afghanistan. Measuring 200 by 200 metres, the base is a ramshackle cluster of tents, metal containers and wooden huts arranged around a central mud-walled compound built by a previous generation of Afghans. The perimeter comprises coils of razor wire and lines of Hescos with sentry posts situated at key points around the battered redoubt.

Most of the fighting occurs early in the day or at dusk, which generally leaves plenty of free time for vehicle and weapon maintenance and 'home improvements' like building defences, or for recreation.

Soldiers retreat from the 40-degree heat into cramped but air-conditioned quarters in the compound to watch DVDs, work out in the weights tent or smoke and chat in a lean-to by the gate.

They can also call home or try to send an e-mail from temperamental internet-connected laptop computers housed in a container. But come the alert they grab their weapons, body armour and helmets and race to sandbagged emplacements on the compound roof, or man the base's 120-millimetre mortar that can strike at up to eight kilometres, often in duels with enemy mortar teams.

When I returned, contractors had built solid accommodation for the soldiers and added fortified watch towers that are manned by guards from the ASG private Afghan security company. The perimeter was built up with

View of 'Mushroom Hill' from FOB Baylough, Zabul province, July 2009.

new walls and a further cordon of concertina wire and fitted with floodlights, closed-circuit TV cameras and a few other hi-tech defensive solutions. The FOB was still taking occasional rockets from the hills but the direct enemy assaults had stopped, now that it was clear that the base would never be captured. The fighting now mainly occurs a few kilometres out and in certain key spots like Vakil Kur. As a final touch of raw comfort since 2007, the FOB's three plastic toilet cubicles were replaced by a wooden toilet block with eight seats. But you still have to use waste bags and throw them in the burns pit.

Meanwhile, the onset of the hot weather not only brings out the insurgents in force, the FOB's reptile population is also waking. The ANA catch and kill a 1.2 metre Oxus cobra near their billet, which Sgt. Bugher from Arkansas cuts open to find a 20-centimetre lizard inside. A greater commotion ensues when the ASG guards see a longer black snake glide across their tower and disappear beneath their feet. The Americans watch with sporting interest as the clamouring Afghans rip out boards and sandbags and fire a Kalashnikov under the floor as they give chase. Eventually someone batters the serpent with a spade and drags it out by its twitching tail and the crowd

looks on and murmurs as Houser exposes its fangs with a stick. Then Bugher removes the skin with his knife, hangs it out to dry, and cuts off the meat which he and a couple of others eat for breakfast the next morning.

I prefer to stick to the FOB food, which considering where we are is pretty good. Two Afghan cooks serve up a cycle of crispy bacon and powdered eggs, enchiladas and other meat dishes with pasta, potatoes and canned vegetables, with grilled steak and shrimp on Thursdays. In a bid to improve the catering, FOB Lagman sends out a US Army cook who initially impresses everyone with his zest.

'I like to come and see what I can do to make the soldiers' lives better,' enthuses John, a skinny little guy from Iowa, a couple of hours before he enrages the platoon by threatening to put everyone on MREs until he gets the right utensils. This probably makes him slightly less popular than the people who just fired two rockets at Baylough from a nearby hilltop.

'We should push him out of the gate and say Kandahar is that way,' suggests one of a group of soldiers who incessantly play Call of Duty 4 (Iraq) in the War Room, a wooden hut where they eat.

'You don't mess around with an infantry-man's food,' another tells me. 'We lay on an OP for 15 hours and all we think about is what's for chow at the end of it.'

Food is a highly emotive issue in any army. I once shared a room at Bagram with an ex-soldier from Luxembourg who worked for the NATO Maintenance and Supply Agency, NAMSA, that does everything from catering to building runways.

'It's only a small part of our work, but there are not many things that can go up the chain to the ISAF commander as fast as the issue of food,' he said. 'A billion-euro operation can hit trouble because the bacon isn't crispy enough.'

But beyond the fiercely protective stance toward their chow, the infantry, or 'grunts', are a special breed, who as one Sergeant at Baylough said, 'basically don't like anyone else'.

All others are POGs, meaning 'people other than grunts'. It's one of those unofficial army acronyms that pepper conversations, like the British REMF (rear-echelon mother fucker), and denote contempt for those who do any other job than frontline fighting. True, as the Dutch Sergeant Dennis notes, everyone plays their part in keeping an army functioning, but I see how the infantry can get aggrieved. Their terms are the same as for those who live on the large bases but the risk is way, way higher, not to mention the psychological effect of what they do day after day.

'I get paid way too little for what I do for my country,' one of the '07 crew at Baylough tells me. 'I get shot at and blown up and these POG-assed motherfuckers on KAF who sit drinking lattes and eating Subway never go near battle-rattle and get paid exactly the same, but they do nothing and get off work at four o'clock.'

Nor are the prospects bright for infantry-men returning to civilian life.

'They'll ask me what have you done in the past six years?' he says. 'Five tours and killed people, got a job for me?'

Sgt. Carney billets me in the 10-man Bunk Room for transit personnel along with Steve, a 53-year-old former Marine drill instructor who now works as a civilian contractor with the PRT in Qalat. On the underside of the berth above my head a previous occupant wrote 'SSGT 'Doc' Williamson slept here, Operation Enduring Freedom 09-08. Nine fire fights, one confirmed kill.'

At 2230 on my first night there is a loud bang outside and Steve and I sit up.

'Incoming?' I ask.

'Sounds like it,' he replies.

I throw on my body armour and helmet and move round to the CPN, the fortified 'Command Post Node' where a couple of technicians run the FOB's computer systems. 'If we take indirect fire get in there and hug a Hesco,' Carney advised me earlier. 'It's about the safest place on the FOB. Unless they drop one right inside, then your time's just up.'

So here I am crouched in the dark with a dry mouth and racing pulse, wondering about the chances of a direct hit. It's all quiet for a few minutes so I make my way back to my quarters, bumping into Steve who tells me it was outgoing mortar fire after armed men were spotted moving on a hill.

The mortar crews are about to get a lot of work with the arrival of First Platoon from Lane for joint operations to Vakil Kur and other trouble spots. These will also involve a large number of Special Forces and Captain Garner warns me there is already talk of flying me out to Qalat during this time. A bit of coolness from the soldiers I can take, but Dan's legacy now looks likely to really screw up my time here.

On June 25 I leave the FOB at 0740 with 18 soldiers in five trucks. We are to drive 12 kilo-metres west to link up with the approaching platoon's Humvees, an ANA truck with heavy rollers that are supposed to detonate any IEDs planted on the track, and three civilian fuel tankers bringing diesel for Baylough. Convoys have been ambushed in this area before and numerous devices were found on the route, so the chances of trouble are high.

'It's a pretty easy spot with IEDs and small arms, the fuel trucks are a pretty easy target and we usually get hit,' Carney tells me just before we go. He is of medium height and build, covered with tattoos, smokes a lot and is constantly bouncing around taking care of business. He seems a decent sort despite his detachment but so far I have stayed out of his way until he gets used to the idea of having me around.

'Someone should probably know my blood group, O pos,' I reply.

'You don't want to go worrying about that, no one needs to know,' he says with a malicious grin. I know he's messing with me now, checking me out.

'Yeah, just throw any old shit into me.'

'Let's not talk about that stuff. Look you've got it written on you here anyway,' he says, pointing to 'O Pos' written in pen on my body armour. 'But thanks for letting us know.'

There are four US in my truck but I am still the invisible man as they chat about home and the growing stand-off with North Korea. At 1305, while we are waiting for the vehicles from Lane, we hear that FOB Baylough is under attack and that 107mm rockets hit near the mortar pit. The new Romanian 82mm mortar team that is attached to the platoon got its first bit of work and did a neat job of plastering the hill the rockets came from. Later intelligence reports say they were fired by Uzbeks who are 'supplied by a man on a white horse'.

It's only a 24-kilometre drive from Lane but First Platoon have been driving for 12 hours by the time their vehicles come into sight mid-afternoon, US flags flapping from the gun turrets and the tankers groaning between them. The two convoys connect and we grind our way back over the chain of hills surrounding the Baylough Bowl, which I see in its entirety for the first time in two years.

About five kilometres wide, this lush valley of green orchards and wheat fields is dotted with villages around the central Baylough bazaar, and dominated by giant conical rock formations, as if some bored god tipped boulders into heaps from his palm like grains of sand. The track takes us past the ANP post where two years earlier I watched Taliban running in the groves before they backed off into the dusk, and past the house of a man I met whose 15-year-old daughter was killed by an IED planted in front of the home.

Curiously there isn't even any enemy i-com chatter today and I start to wonder if my calming influence on Baylough is working once again. When I came in 2007 the platoon had had enemy contact almost every day for about six weeks. Then I arrived and all went quiet, even though they took me to the worst ambush spots they knew. Nothing.

'Before you came it was all action and after you left it was all action – someone up there is looking out for you,' one guy told me later. At this stage in the game I'm quite OK if no one shoots at me any more. But you kind of just want to know if it's coming.

Between missions I wander round the base with my iPod, play with the FOB's six mongrels that lead a pretty carefree life here, stare at the valley and hills, type up my notes and chat to the soldiers. One day I see Houser passing and venture a bit of improvised Baylough humour.

'Hey Derek, what do you get if you drop white phosphorous on those hills over there? Kinetic Fried Chechen, geddit?'

Time passes here with little distinction between weekdays and weekends, but with the internet connection working well now the affairs of the outside world occasionally make a mark on the life of the base.

'Gentlemen, I regret to inform you that the King of Pop, Michael Jackson, is dead,' I announce to the waking occupants of the Bunk House after I check my e-mail on the morning of Friday, June 26, and tell them the media are describing this as a 'JFK moment'. Some of the soldiers do seem shocked but one guy on a tiny top bunk insists he couldn't care less.

'That's as may be, but you will forever remember hearing this news while you were on a shelf in Afghanistan,' I assure him.

Jackson chat and jokes buzz all day but other matters quickly supersede this event, which judging from the sheer amount of related news stories has plunged civilization into pandemonium.

The Vakil Kur operation will start on Monday, June 29. It will be a big deal, incorporating both infantry platoons, 35 members of the ODA (Operational Detachment Alpha) Special Forces and 40 Navy Seals. The last group is so ultra-elite that no one even expects to see them. They will helicopter in and rappel onto peaks by Vakil Kur while the ODA fly from Baylough.

The latter group arrives a day earlier. Wearing their special pattern camouflage, most have tufty beards and while not generally tall are muscle-bound and squat, like supercharged wombats. I stay out of their way as one complaint about an intrusive reporter will not only get me bumped from the operation – if they allow me to go – but sent back to Qalat until it's over. I'm getting paranoid that people around me are getting paranoid and I keep my notebook and cameras well out of sight. But a couple of their men are eating at my table on the veranda and a natural conversation ensues about parts of the country we visited. One had spent time in the west around Herat and was amazed to hear some locals say they preferred the Russians because they gave them more rice and basic products than ISAF.

'I said but didn't they kill you though, and they said yes, but only if you opposed them. They told me they expected the Americans to leave before long and then someone else would come, like the Russians again, or maybe the British.'

I can see him struggle to get his head around this casual lumping of all foreigners, US and Russians alike, in the same pile.

'It's almost as if this country needs to be invaded by someone, that it can't sustain itself otherwise,' he says.

There's a lot of talk on the FOB about an interview with the deputy commander of Zabul's insurgent forces, Qari Saifollah, that was posted on a Taliban website a few days before. He is upbeat and in complete denial of the pasting his group got near Vakil Kur three weeks earlier.

'Jihadi activities in Zabul province seem very successful and strong this year compared to the past, which has caused panic among the enemy,' Saifollah asserts. 'Hardly a day passes when the mujahedin do not attack the enemy along this [Kabul-Kandahar] highway.'

He goes on to say that the whole of Zabul is under mujahedin control and that of its 11 districts, Arghandab and Khak-e Afghan have no 'enemy offices' at all.

'In the provincial capital and other districts the enemy writ does not extend beyond the PRT and the district offices. They have no control beyond these offices, nor would the people accept them. We have our own military and civilian structures in place in every district,' he says, adding that the Taliban have appointed a Governor – or shadow Governor, depending on your standpoint – and deputy in Zabul.

A few weeks ago I was in Deh Chopan where there is a valley called Chenaran. The Americans arrived there during the night and captured a few hilltops. When the mujahedin learned about this they went after them early in the morning and attacked them. More tanks [Humvees] from the district and nearby PRT were dispatched to save the Americans. As the tanks were approaching the area, three of them were blown up by mines and the rest turned back. Then helicopters and aircraft came and carried out heavy bombardment of the area, and the fighting and bombing continued until 1600. The Americans suffered heavy losses but it was due to God Almighty's protection that the mujahedin did not suffer any casualties. I can testify that no mujahedin was martyred or wounded. However, the next day radio stations, quoting spokesmen of the internal and American forces, announced that 35 Taliban had been killed in the Chenaran area of Deh Chopan.[36]

'He says they killed plenty of us, which is funny because we are all alive,' says Private Ryan Delashmit, Sgt. Sher's M240 gunner. 'And that they didn't lose anyone, but I killed two myself.'

One 'tank' did hit an IED on May 28, one of First Platoon's Humvees, causing only minor injuries to occupants in a miraculous escape. The trunk was loaded with 60mm mortar shells and the blast caused one to explode in its cardboard tube while somehow failing to detonate many others packed in around it, which would have blown the truck to smithereens.

During the day Captain Garner informs me that I am good to go on the operation after he assured the SF that I will not film or photograph them. The Sergeant of a squad from Lane that I will accompany gives me a quick briefing.

'What's your name, so I don't have to keep calling you the reporter?' he asks me.

'I'm used to it, only there's usually an adjective before it.'

His CO, Captain Tomberlin, who with jutting jaw and jutting hairline is a close cross of Buzz Lightyear and Biffa Bacon's dad, asks if I have any questions.

'As I understand, I'll be dressed in orange being prodded ahead of the main group, correct?'

'That's right, we'll have your suit ready for you later in the day.'

That night the 120mm mortar starts pounding after a drone spotted 11 men with weapons on a hill in Vakil Kur. The unmanned aircraft takes out four with a missile and as many again fall to rounds from Baylough's tube.

After the lengthy build-up the operation is inglorious but not fruitless for the Americans. We leave at 0420, treading the same trail where one of five IEDs on the road disabled a Humvee on May 28. Everyone gets soaked crossing the river and the Humvees following the dismounts can barely squeeze along the hilltrack winding above the flow. The SF are doing their thing on the high ground and the rest take position in and around Vakil Kur, a cosy village nestled among mulberry and walnut orchards in a stunningly beautiful valley on the main Taliban transit route. We are in the area of last month's battle but today it's quiet, apart from a massive blast as EOD destroy a pick-up truck loaded with more than half a ton of ammonium nitrate, a chemical used to make home-made explosives.

'The Taliban are not going to play today,' says the gunner of the truck I eat lunch in, while someone else sings, 'Here we sit, broken hearted, came to fight and only farted.'

The Special Forces are furious with the infantry from Lane who pushed into the village instead of taking a blocking position, and people are busy apologising for a move that might have scared away the opposition.

In fact, the insurgents are not hiding. On the contrary, the Taliban's top Zabul commander, Mullah Qahar, had arrived to lead the anticipated fight himself together with a posse of extra men. But since Vakil Kur was the target of the last US operation, his forces decided instead to take up position at the other main battle ground in Davudsay, located six kilometres to the west of the FOB.

The mullah is probably also annoyed that his trip may have been in vain, so his men take a swing at the ANP at least. After we get back to Baylough later that afternoon, the Police post above the bazaar takes some RPG and PKM fire. Later the units in Vakil Kur are finally attacked from a distance by about 20 insurgents and again the FOB 120mm mortar frantically thumps rounds north up the valley.

The operation hasn't produced the epic clash that some hoped for but the initial battle damage assessment (BDA) is well received by the Americans: an Apache kills half a dozen armed men on motorcycles following the shots at the ANP post, while 22 enemy were believed killed by Predator strikes and the mortar since the previous evening.

The Seals and ODA leave Deh Chopan but the two infantry platoons decide to make the most of their combined strength and mount another operation four kilometres west to the village of Tangay Kalay. No one has been in here yet but it's a couple of kilometres north of the insurgent stronghold at Davudsay and enemy activity is reportedly high.

At 2200 on July 2 I leave with a squad of twelve under Sergeants Sher and Cisneros. They are to set up an OP on a hill above the village and cover the platoons when they drive in at first light. We are already uncomfortably picked out by an 80 per cent moon but Sher has the Afghan security guards turn off the floodlights as we descend the hill from the FOB. The patrol then wades across the river and cuts into the comparative shelter of the orchards.

Fifteen minutes later Macias badly twists his ankle in a hole and can't walk. His face is contorted with pain but he insists he can keep going. Cisneros crouches down and gives him a sharp talk in Spanish. I can only catch the word 'macho' but it's clear the Sergeant is saying that he shouldn't pretend he's OK and has to go back to base.

I don't have much gear so I help medic Chad Brown to carry the soldier half a kilometre up to Mushroom Hill, a local landmark that's actually shaped like a long wedge of cheese with three humps, where the trucks from Baylough will come for him. The setback threatens the whole mission and Platoon Sergeant Carney is fuming when he arrives. The trucks leave and the silence around us is now disturbed only by canine baying in nearby compounds. Sher gathers us together and as we are simultaneously struck by the smallness and vulnerability of our group he says, 'Well this is it!'

One of the soldiers exclaims 'This is stupid, someone is going to get killed' and is silenced immediately by the Staff Sergeant. But we are

all thinking the same, that the Taliban now know there's a patrol out and may be setting an ambush.

'There was no UAV covering us, we were on our own,' Sher tells me months later. 'After the trucks left I was of course worried that I was one guy down and still had a long way to go. What was going through my head? To make it on top of the hill unnoticed and without getting caught, to kill these guys and go home alive.'

At 0045 we set off again for our destination, spreading out in a staggered single file and trudging onwards into what we don't know. The section stops every fifteen minutes for a breather as some of the men are sucking air like landed fish under the weight of their gear and weapons. Sergeant Eddy Westfield labours past me under a long conical backpack almost the same size as him which contains the mighty .50 calibre Barrett M107 semi-

automatic sniper's rifle and loaded magazines, as well as food and water. The whole pack weighs 77 kilos and juts vertically over the top of his head, creating the disturbing effect of a figure in a Klu Klux Klan hat in the shadows as the moon sinks rapidly over the horizon.

Once again I'm struggling without night vision equipment to discern the contours as we walk. At the same time I occupy myself with thoughts like how to translate into Russian my favourite description of Vladimir Putin as having 'a smile like moonlight dancing off coffin handles'. Each time we take a break all I can see of the others is a couple of dim, panting figures sitting either side of me along the track. Alone in my thoughts I stare up at the sky and count the shooting stars, dedicating each one to someone I care about.

As we get moving again I stop my musing and chide myself for not concentrating on what is happening around me, like where I will take cover if we get hit. Then I realise I already know. Two years after first panting round these valleys as a greenhorn embed, I now feel my environment instinctively, every ten metres subconsciously identifying depressions and boulders that will offer shelter against any incoming fire.

I'm not a member of the military and I agree with the Dutch editor that 'a journalist is a journalist and not sometimes a soldier.' But at least I now know how to maximise my chances of remaining unhurt, and that is a welcome realisation at this moment. And suddenly my apprehension melts away and I am fused with excitement and new energy. We may still get ambushed or wind up in a huge fire fight the next day, but right now I am in the moment and loving it.

By 0130 the last moonlight has gone and I'm working by braille as the squad labours up the target hill and sets up the OP at 0320. A couple of dogs in a Cuchi tent camp below us howl incessantly as we stumble through the Taliban's playground with no support and no drone in the sky to watch over us. Like Houser I am a dog lover but would use a silenced pistol on the animals in a heartbeat if I could.

Once we have reached the shelter of the boulders on the crest, Westfield sets up the Barrett facing west towards Tangay Kalay below us, together with the M240 gunner. No one seems to mind where I go, so I stretch out on the ground a couple of metres behind Staff Sgt. Sher, who is covering the east with Toia and the 60mm mortar. Then we settle down in silence and wait. After the sweating exertion of the march we shiver until the first glimmers appear over the facing hill shortly before four. Twenty minutes later we can hear a distant call to prayer and at 0425 the Sergeant is told that the trucks are leaving Baylough.

They stop at the District Centre and pick up 16 ANP in two Rangers, and at 0600 Sher spots the first vehicles moving up the valley in a cloud of dust. I am lying flat by a rock, hidden from the west but still a little exposed to the east, so I slowly drag some bushy weeds over myself and keep still. Five minutes later the first rays of direct sunlight hit my wet, frozen feet.

Despite the noise and disturbance the previous night, the Taliban are caught sleeping.

It's not until 0700 that a few men are spotted fleeing the village in the direction of Davudsay and a spotter informs the local commander over the airwaves that lots of *amerikayan* are approaching.

'Get close to them and do your job,' comes the reply, then his spotter adds, 'They are just across from you.' Since the trucks haven't yet reached Tangay Kalay this may mean us, but no one is sure.

'Now the Taliban are going to get their friends and when we leave they are going to shoot at us,' Sher predicts.

The NCO has been through countless missions and fights in Deh Chopan and I have great faith in his instincts. We have also established a friendship through our Islamabad connection; he grew up a couple of streets from my house there and we know many of the same places. I remember how in 2007 he told me that a lot of people here don't know what to make of the Pakistani-American.

'Some locals think I'm a traitor because I'm a Muslim, say I'm fighting the wrong war on the wrong side. I think the people don't have enough education, the mullahs come in and manipulate them, say that we are here to take away their land. Some of the people even think we are Russians. I think I'm right though – whatever the Taliban are preaching isn't Islam, not sending girls to school, burning schools down, beheading teachers. But people are illiterate and believe or fear them.'

Today he is more preoccupied with the hill to the east, behind the OP and on the opposite side to the village. As one element of mounted US peels off from the main column and comes round this way they hear more chatter reporting that 'the trucks have stopped and there are half a dozen Americans standing by them.'

These hidden eyes are somewhere in the rocks a kilometre ahead of us and the soldiers keep searching until they spot two guys in dark manjams coming down a draw in the hill. They are unarmed but are moving too suspiciously to be anyone else at this early hour as they carefully work their way down towards the trucks.

'These guys are definitely fighters,' Sher says, peering through binoculars.

Another man drops down between the two facing peaks, having emerged from a stone emplacement in the saddle, and then dips out of sight with a fourth guy. They will be on their way to collect weapons from the rocks before engaging the trucks, but after Baylough drops a mortar round in the vicinity they all vanish from sight.

All this is occurring as US and ANA troops on the Tangay Kalay side of our hill search the village and detain a few suspects. At 0930 we are told to break down the OP position and come down to the trucks to leave. It's not only anti-climactic after all the effort but there aren't enough spare seats and some of us have to ride in the ANP Rangers.

In view of the transport shortage, it was a condition of my coming that I would ride back with the Afghans. It's the first time I have done this, having always previously been in an armoured ISAF vehicle and not a flimsy pick-up that offers sparse protection from bullets and shrapnel. I get in the Ranger's open back with Sgt. Westfield and his giant bag, a cop manning a PKM on the cabin, and two cuffed villagers who were detained after a wooden launch platform for 107mm rockets was found in a house.

The vehicles set off and barely cover a kilometre when it starts. The ridgeline 900 metres to our west suddenly crackles with PKM fire and the first rounds strike around the two overloaded Police jeeps where the passengers are most vulnerable, some zinging close above or between us and kicking up spouts of dust on the track.

I throw myself headfirst over the side of the truck as it jerks to a halt, landing painfully on my left arm and losing my watch. Westfield crashes down beside me together with the two detainees who shelter behind a wheel and hug each other in terror. Sgt. Cisneros tells us later how funny it was to watch our acrobatics from the safety of his Humvee, but there's not much to laugh about outside.

I squirm in the dirt filming two ANP lying behind me as more rounds impact around us, wondering when one of the bullets will strike beneath the Ranger and ricochet into my legs, groin, back or head. It occurs to me that this could in fact be my story, 'Reporter Killed in Afghanistan Ambush,' but I keep rolling around and taking pictures as the Americans unleash a barrage of return fire from the .50-cals and Mark 19s on the Humvees. Some ANP loose off belts of PKM ammo but the Americans with M4 rifles sit it out because these are almost ineffective at this range. Baylough's 120mm mortar starts pounding the ridgeline and eventually the attack stops.

The whole exchange lasts 20 minutes, then we mount up and set off again like nothing happened. As we pull away, a round from an 82mm recoilless rifle ploughs through the air from what appears to be the same hill the OP was on, slams into the ground and explodes 20 metres from the EOD truck. Five minutes later, just as I notice I lost my watch, our attackers open up once more from further along the same ridgeline. We pull up and take cover again and the hills shudder as the mortar barrage resumes. Fifteen minutes later the exchange has petered out. Then after I take some photos of the ANP in action, a young cop from Ghazni comes to me and returns my watch, a princely gesture for someone on his wage.

There is more i-com chatter as we mount up and move off again but no more shooting. An hour later the platoons are back at the FOB and watching the Armed Forces Network and US comedian Jeff Dunham's 'Ahmed the dead terrorist' ventriloquist act (skeleton puppet with bulging eyes threatens 'I keel you, I keel you').

Later on, First Sergeant Weiskittel comes into the Bunk Room looking perplexed.

'I'm a little annoyed with that whole thing. Our job is to close with the enemy and destroy – find, fix and finish – we've got more firepower, more ammunition, more everything, I just don't get it.'

That evening Carney comes up to me and asks: 'You've been here a while now haven't you, about two weeks?

'About ten days, but don't kick me out just yet, I'm just getting into my stride and I think people are getting used to me now.'

'Yes, you're like one of the FOB dogs, every once in a while we stop and pet you.'

I check if today is July 3, because that means tomorrow is American Independence Day.

'I didn't want to mention it,' he replies with a grin.

'It took us 200 years to get over that but it's OK now. So are you going to put me in the stocks and pelt me with rotten fruit?'

Ambush of US troops and Afghan
police in Deh Chopan, Zabul
province, July 2009.

Carney does mention it though. A lot. As does Weiskittel, so for the next day I smile graciously at a steady hale of anti-Colonial digs and gags coming at me. On July 4 an American Christian rock band called Fly Leaf is flown in from Kandahar to do an acoustic set on the veranda while the soldiers each get a boxed take-out from the KAF Pizza Hut. They're cold now of course but it's the thought that counts. As the musicians are shown round the FOB the Redcoat routine of Carney and Weiskittel suddenly resumes, rather like the previous day's ambush. I counter-attack, borrowing a line from the British sketch series 'The Fast Show'.

'Well at least we are punctual for every really big war and don't show up two years late after all the real fighting's been done!'

One of the younger soldiers looks startled but the Sergeants are happy the gloves are off finally and we spend the rest of the day taking the mickey out of each other about our respective history. In the evening I also jibe

that Carney is going bald much faster than me, my 82mm recoilless round fired from the hilltop as he walks away after another passing verbal tussle.

I find out too late that the Sergeants have boobytrapped my accommodation. When I turn in I find pinned over my bunk a large hand-drawn poster of a combat boot with a US flag kicking over a Union Jack cup of tea, and the words 'Happy July 4th Nick!' It's one of my fondest memories of Baylough and I still have the poster.

On July 6 First Platoon set off for FOB Lane at 0500. I heard the group in the Bunk Room moving around me and decided to get up when they were ready to roll and say goodbye, including to Captain Garner who was also leaving. The previous night I could sense the apprehension of the younger soldiers about the drive, during which they could absolutely expect an enemy attack. The Taliban have had days to prepare IEDs and ambush parties, knowing the platoon could only take that route back to Lane. I wanted to push a button and transport them all back safely, and still now would give an arm to do so.

The next I know its 0700, I overslept and they have gone. I go on a foot patrol to the bazaar with Captain Basilides, who has kindly arranged for me to get material I am lacking, like having the ANP locate a shopkeeper I spoke to in 2007, and the father of the girl killed by the IED outside the family home. It wasn't a meeting to look forward to, but for things here to make sense I needed to talk to people like him. Two years ago the man thought it was time for talks with the insurgents; I wondered how he felt now.

But none of my plans come to fruition. Minutes after we hook up with the ANP at the district centre the Captain is informed by radio that the Lane convoy is being attacked. Then we hear there are two US KIA and two WIA but I am not told who and feel awkward asking. At this point more than at any other in my travels I don't want to be seen as the reporter, I just want to know who it is so I can start to process it in my head.

The fight goes on all day until the early evening when the insurgent commander is heard over the radio congratulating his men on a good day's work. The Taliban's website later claimed that five US soldiers and an interpreter were killed that day in Deh Chopan district when their vehicle was hit by a mine, and that the attacking party torched an oil tanker in the convoy.

That afternoon Staff Sgt. Sher and the ANP bring in a woman with severe lacerations to her legs and a sobbing three-year-old boy with clots of blood in his nostrils. The family was riding on a donkey to Baylough on the track we used the other night when the animal stepped on an IED. The woman is evacuated by helicopter for surgery while the boy is judged to be in shock but basically OK after the explosion.

'I'm just waiting for this day to be over,' says the medic, who tells me it was Captain Garner and Petty Officer Tony Randolph of the EOD team who died.

A few weeks later, First Sergeant Chris Weiskittel sent me his account of what happened that day:

On 5th of July Captain Garner and I were discussing him moving to FOB Lane. I told him that since I had ridden with 1st Platoon up to Baylough that I would ride back with them. He said he did not feel comfortable letting the soldiers take all the risk and wanted to also move back by ground.

The 6th of July started with everyone preparing their vehicles for movement back to FOB Lane approximately 24 kilometers away by route and 18 kilometers direct. We had wanted to leave Baylough at 0430, but the Captain's vehicle broke down. The engine had blown. We decided to crossload and leave the truck at Baylough. Captain Garner wanted to take another Soldier's place on another vehicle and leave him at Baylough until the next flight. Myself and Captain Tomberlin talked it over and told Captain Garner that he could ride with the Navy EOD, because they had an extra two seats open.

We started our movement at 0500 and within six kilometres Captain Tomberlin's truck started having power steering problems. So we stopped the patrol to try and fix it. We were at a halt for almost 45 minutes. The Apache support that we had requested was flying and checking the surrounding area and route.

It was established that the Platoon Leader's truck had to be towed, so this changed up the order of movement, placing the EOD truck as the sixth vehicle. We started our movement again and crested the hill for our decent to the valley floor. This is also the area we were most concerned about due to the proximity of a known Taliban safe haven. Contact was expected and everyone was on alert. The nearby village of Marah is where Taliban commanders for Arghandab and Deh Chopan live, and this is also a transit route the enemy uses to move securely between districts.

The route we were using is littered with burned-out jingle trucks from previous attacks. It is very austere and remote, and is the only way into Baylough by ground. As the patrol traversed the switch-back road down the mountain from over 7,000 feet to about 5,500 feet, I heard someone on the radio call out 'IED!' and ask for the medic. The medic and I were all the way back on the top of the mountain because we were the last truck in the patrol. We had been on the opposite crest when the explosion happened and did not immediately hear it. I told the driver to stop and grabbed the medic. We took a quick look at the fastest route down the mountain to the damaged vehicle, chose a spur and ran down it. All the while the urgency of the personnel calling for the medic was increasing. As we neared the bottom I could see the truck gunner in the crater made from the blast. He had been thrown out of the turret and was only visible by his upper torso. Expecting the worse as we approached, I was relieved that he was alive and had already been checked by a Combat Life Savior. His injuries were a broken leg and he was exhibiting signs of shock.

The medic was already at the destroyed truck treating Captain Garner by the time I got there. Captain Tomberlin was trying to call Zabul Base to request a Medevac and I told him that I would find and mark a Landing Zone. We were in a very deep valley and they could not land a helicopter in it so I started climbing back up the mountain to find a suitable place. I found one on another spur that the slope would be difficult but a helicopter could land. We had four casualties and time was of the essence. The medic continued to work on Captain Garner and the gunner was loaded on to a stretcher and carried up the spur to stage for the Medevac.

The Apaches had just gone to re-fuel when we struck the IED. They were now back and securing us from overhead while we conducted Medevac operations. Within ten to fifteen minutes of calling the Medevac they arrived to take the casualties back to the Forward Surgical Team in Lagman, located almost sixty kilometres away. The Medevac pilots were unbelievable, landing on the side of a mountain spur, barely able to get both wheels down before they could medevac our wounded and dead.

I knew the driver Randolph had been killed immediately but was unsure of the condition of Captain Garner at the time. As I watched them place him on the medevac I had a sickening feeling. Once the helicopter had left the area the platoon started reconsolidating and policing up all the sensitive equipment. The wrecked truck was blocking the route and had to be pulled out of the way. We requested Close Air Support to blow the rest of the truck in place since it was not recoverable.

At this point it was decided that we would walk the next 13 kilometres in front of the vehicles with mine detectors. The ANA had their mine roller on but had not activated the IED that had blown up the EOD truck.

As the US and ANA walked out in front of the vehicles we encountered a few suspicious spots but upon investigating nothing was revealed. The empty civilian fuel trucks that had been with us were in the centre of the patrol. About twenty minutes into us continuing our movement the lead fuel truck struck an IED. The IED malfunctioned and only partly exploded and no damage was done. A kilometre or so later that same fuel truck was not so lucky, and was destroyed when it ran over an IED. No one was hurt, so we finished blowing the fuel truck and continued.

The temperature was over a hundred degrees and guys were on edge. There was a patrol moving from Lane toward us to help clear the route, but we still had six kilometres to link up with them. They had found two IEDs and were destroying them on the route.

Our convoy continued on through the narrow valley and found another two IEDs, one that two donkeys had tripped, leaving just carcasses and mangled limbs. The other was a bag of HME (home made explosive) with a pressure plate attached. Once we by-passed it we had the Apache shoot it up to explode it.

We were about a kilometre away from our link up with the US Police Mentoring Team out of Lane when we were ambushed by RPG and PKM fire from the hilltops to the north. The ANA and the lead two gun trucks returned fire, killing one enemy immediately and sending the rest running for the opposite side of the mountain. After a short halt and a quick reconsolidation we continued on until we linked up with the patrol from Lane.

It was almost 1900 when we finally arrived at the FOB. We had maneuvered and fought our way out of the valley finally after almost twelve hours. Within an hour of returning to the FOB, a helicopter was sent to pick up myself and Captain Tomberlin up so that we could pay our respects to our dead at the Rampside ceremony in KAF.

Captain Garner was a unique commander. He was very compassionate and took the soldiers' problems to heart and would worry over them almost as if they were his own. We would have conversations about him being too compassionate and having a hard time saying 'No'. He knew this was a fault of his, but he generally cared and wanted to solve every problem presented that was associated with any of his Soldiers.

No matter what the circumstances he always had a smile on his face. One of my best memories of him is from a few weeks earlier when we were in a fight near the village of Davudsay. The enemy had the pass sealed and the high ground. We were taking extremely accurate fire, but we were manoeuvring on the enemy. Captain Garner, whom we thought was a few hundred metres behind us, showed up next to me and Sergeant First Class Carney with this big smile on his face and snuff all over his face. It was almost hysterical! He placed himself in harm's way and led from the front. He would never ask anyone to do anything he wouldn't or couldn't do himself.

The last thing people needed at Baylough that day was a reporter bugging them about their feelings. There was no visible upset on the FOB but the atmosphere was deeply subdued. Captain Garner was well liked and I know there was plenty of discussion going on behind closed doors.

'He wouldn't want a pity shower, it'll all come out when people start drinking at the end of the tour,' one of the soldiers from '07 told me. 'A lot of stuff gets to you later, I've seen guys you'd never think of just coming apart.'

★ ★ ★

The box of school supplies finally made it to Baylough, having first travelled with me by road from KAF to Qalat, then by air back to KAF and then two more chopper rides in my arms to its destination. But I arrived to find that the tent school had closed down, partly because an ANP officer who taught there had been murdered, but mostly due to lack of funds. Since the teachers were earning maybe $100 a month this school couldn't have cost much more than a $1,000 a month to run, the equivalent cost of one 120mm mortar shell. The FOB had no direct responsibility for the school's function, but for comparison's sake, more than 30 of these shells were expended in that one ambush. So instead I left my box with the Police Chief to distribute among local families, I can only trust he did.

Because of the intensity of fighting around Baylough there is only limited opportunity to do development work. There were steps in the right direction like the new mud brick 'community centre' that was being built beside the bazaar. In reality it was to serve as the new Police HQ and District Centre, situated by the bazaar where it always should have been to help security, as opposed to its then location two kilometres away. But PRT regulations meant no one could approve a second District Centre so the project had to be slipped through under a different name.

I was told there were eventual plans to build a small health clinic to replace the tiny, filthy medical premises located in a dilapidated building among the stores. But for the time being the district's doctor had to make do with a kicker box of medical supplies that was sent from Qalat.

Then there were three bridges that the FOB had built over the river at a cost of $20,000. It's a hefty sum in Zabul, considering the bridges were constructed of logs and mud by a contractor using local labour. But the idea was to spread some cash about and provide work and a sense of pride. The same went for a $5,000

Staff Sergeant Azhar Sher, FOB Baylough, Zabul province, July 2009.

clean-up and basic repair operation planned for the bazaar, which has several dozen stores, only a handful of which were functioning, and resembles a derelict Spaghetti Western set.

One might wonder why more wasn't done in ISAF's three years in Baylough, but it's genuinely problematic to get materials out to Deh Chopan. There isn't enough helicopter transport to move them and civilian road convoys will get ambushed, plundered and destroyed.

'We are doing a lot for them already, we can't do everything,' Captain Basilides said. 'The number one issue is security, without security we can't do a whole lot of development. And change is very slow here. These people live in mud houses, maybe they have a motorcycle, so you can't just revolutionize the place overnight with cars and roads. I could have built these bridges faster. But people have to realise that if I build everything for them right away it gives no incentive to help us out.'

Taking all this into account, to let the school die was still an act of gross negligence on someone's part. (This happened during the previous company's watch.) The task of running the school fell to the provincial administration but nonetheless, someone in the US side let it happen. Which begs the question, what is the point of all this fighting, bloodshed and sacrifice if the rare glimmers of progress in Baylough are allowed to vanish?

I left Deh Chopan on a Chinook on July 9 after doing a final mission to a village three kilometres northwest of the FOB. The soldiers of Second Platoon distributed piles of donated clothes, shoes and toys that the former Baylough commander had collected in the United States and which Captain Garner brought out from Qalat.

It was a chaotic but uplifting scene as the kids received the gifts. Their fathers stood back and watched with smiles as Sergeants Sher and Cisneros bustled and beamed like gentle giants in the centre of the scrum. Ryan Delashmit, the M240 gunner and July 4 poster artist, could be a carefree 22-year-old for a few minutes as he picked out right sizes of clothing and toys from the boxes for the clamouring kids. The smallest ones didn't know what it all meant as they toddled off with full arms, but despite

the frenetic enemy i-com chatter in the background it was a happy day for everyone.

The next morning I knew I would leave for sure because of one of those omens I mentioned earlier. In 2007 the soldiers killed one of the camp dogs, a mangey bitch called Frances. She had snapped once too often at her former abusers in the ANA detachment and the American CO issued orders for her execution. A couple of hours before my helicopter arrived I had heard a commotion and came out to see a few guys standing around her. A 9mm Beretta round through the skull killed the dog instantly but her tail still wagged reflexively for a minute.

Two years later I got up and petted my favourite of the six FOB dogs, a happy, floppy black and white mutt the soldiers called Marshmallow. I wonder how long he and the others would survive, since the FOB dogs get culled eventually when their numbers are too great or top brass is visiting. An hour later I run into Houser and ask him how he's doing.

'It's a black day,' is all he says, motioning at the Gator driving round with two soldiers, one of whom is holding a Beretta. I walk to the trash pit and find the burning remains of Marshmallow and two more dogs. The other three have taken off and are nowhere to be found. It's time for me to leave too.

★ ★ ★

July 2009 was the worst month for casualties among foreign forces in Afghanistan since the start of the conflict in 2001. As the overall number of international troops rose above 100,000, the month saw 74 KIA, including 43 US. Ten soldiers were killed on July 6. As well as the two in Deh Chopan, five more Americans died, as well as a Briton and two Canadians in a helicopter crash in Zabul. The month also broke previous records for IED incidences, with 825 of these recorded, more than twice the amount of the previous July.

A book can never be up-to-date: but things got worse in the summer of 2010. On July 6 an IED blast killed three members of Bravo Company's sister company in Zabul, exactly one year after Captain Garner's death

twenty-four

HURRY UP AND WAIT (AFGHAN STYLE)

I spent a few days in Kabul trying to get an exit visa to leave the country as mine had just expired. Visas ran out before while I was embedded and it was always a matter of a morning to pay the fine and get an exit stamp. This time the Interior Ministry seemed bent on hampering my departure, with meetings, long waits, assurances of help and then snubs and demands for British Embassy letters explaining why I overstayed. Three days of this tested my nerves far more than the hill in Khost or preparing to do the Dallas Dash.

At night I would hang out in the famous Gandamack guest house and its cellar bar with low ceiling and walls adorned with weapons, trinkets and photos. It fills on weekend nights with a rowdy concoction of contractors, NGO workers, journalists and generally, as I wrote to a friend, 'people pushing their balls in wheelbarrows'. But it's a relief to get there, befitting the banner in the garden quoting the words of fictitious British soldier and scoundrel Harry Flashman that 'Kabul might not be Hyde Park but it was safe for now.'

Then I got a call from an Afghan friend negotiating with the ministry, pointing out that my visa actually expires in August, not July. All my life I confused the correllation of the seventh and eight months with July and August and I should probably have felt stupid but didn't, just relieved. I checked out and left on a UN flight to Islamabad on July 14. Afghan border guards examined my visa and vigorously stamped CANCELLED on it three times, saying 'Kandahar no good'. The back-door channel in the south that I used to get my last 12-month visa was now closed.

I arrived in London on Wednesday July 22, my mother's birthday, bought a four-pack of beer at Paddington Station and sat back in a black cab as I drove to see friends in Greenwich, passing Hyde Park, Buckingham Palace, Trafalgar Square and the 'Spendloads-Please Hairdressers' in Bermondsey.

Sandwichboard headlines on the route exclaimed 'Bomb Hero Killed' (EOD specialist Captain Daniel Shepherd died defusing a device in Nad-e-Ali as I was heading home), and 'War on Violence at Pub Closing Time'. But it was a bright, cloudy day in London instead of dust-laden heat, there was no high ground to worry about and the only helmets I saw were worn by cyclists.

My return from Zabul had been in stages over two weeks, first Kabul, then Islamabad and finally London, so the transition was eased. But for the first few days I suffered from sleeplessness, irritability and detachment from people and things around me. A friend in ISAF put me in touch with a British specialist in PTSD and related issues so that if need be I could have an informal chat with him when I got home.

But the symptoms diminished with each step I took away from the badlands and back to normality, and appear to have largely been a bi-product of the relief I felt to finish and not to have to return any time soon. Repeated reimmersion in that environment since 2006 was like plunging into a pool that got icier each time. Before the final nine-week trip I had an old root canal attended to in Islamabad and wrote in my notebook, 'Why am I getting my teeth fixed when I can get my face shot off next week?'

I had no wish to experience the worst horrors of war, and was thankfully spared this. I saw some messy sights and was deeply saddened by deaths of people I met along the way, and also by the thought of those Pashtun families waiting in vain for fallen fathers and sons to return from their jihad. How many thousands of these perished since 2001 will never be known, but by the time this book went to the printers at the end of July 2010, a total of 1,982 foreign troops had been killed, including 1,216 US, and an estimated 6,500 Afghan forces. I still look at the ISAF and coalition forces tallies at http://icasualties.org/oef, wondering when it will come to an end.

All things considered, I was very lucky. But even though my return to western surrounds was basically trauma-free, things could throw me off balance weeks later. I felt slightly shocked after my first shots when resuming my old duty of culling the rabbit population at my parents' home in the country. And ten weeks after leaving Afghanistan I visited a friend who collects deactivated Russian weapons. As I looked at the Kalashnikov, RPK, Dragunov and other models mounted on his workshop wall behind the DShK on a tripod, it occurred to me that most types had been fired in my direction at some time. Then as I studied a body armour plate with some 7.62mm rounds flattened into it, I nearly puked.

After each period spent in that odd bubble of Afghan and Pakistani time and space, plenty had always changed back home. Friends drifted away, girlfriends fell in love, family members had aged, ailed or flown the nest, kids were born. But it is the soldiers who serve successive tours who best know the cost of prolonged and repeated absence from home.

'My son's four years old, he doesn't even know who I am. He was telling people "I don't know my daddy"; that crushed me when I heard that,' one American told me.

I also wrapped up this project at a good time because what I wanted to avoid, apart from death or injury, was to become one of those journalists who covered so much bloodshed and destruction they finally lost themselves in it. I had heard and read enough from reporters saying they could no longer connect with home or that 'pieces of them had died' and I had no intention of letting that happen to me.

I actually find the I'm-so-messed-up reporter a rather self-indulgent cliché, and my feeling is that if this is what your work is doing to you *then stop doing it*. Go home and write 'Heartless Thief Steals Pensioner's Bike' stories for the local paper, spend time with your family and grow daffodils.

But somewhere along the line I seemed to be looking less into the soldiering life in Afghanistan and more out of it. However much parts of it would always make me nervous, sensations like flying through mountains at night, checking paths for IEDs or tucking my body out of the line of fire had become very familiar and, dare I say it, natural.

Goodbyes at home and the break-up of relationships because of Afghanistan were not just things I wrote about but accepted myself. And while going back into the embedded existence was often hard, being inside it was generally not. Despite the exertion, stress and danger it was a straightforward life in many ways, far removed from the bothersome minutiae of living in the West, 'refreshingly simple' as Lt. Col. Bourne of 1RGR liked to say.

Before I returned to civilization I got an e-mail from Lt. Col. Andris Sneiders, the former commander of the Latvian contingent I'd befriended in Mazar-e-Sharif who was now back home and engrossed in daily Army business. Quoting an old adage, he gave me the wry piece of advice to 'enjoy the war because the peace will be terrible.'

I often heard how after the enormity of war the trivia of homelife can be exasperating. I'd seen it in myself, notably after a heavy three-month summer haul in 2008, so I gave myself a good talking to then about how the trivia are in fact part of what pegs down a stable life. The best you can do is to recognize which are worth getting bothered about. As that Canadian Military Policeman said one night in the tower over no-man's land at Spin Pir, what's a dented fender in the grand scheme of things?

I'm still in touch with a lot of the soldiers I got to know. Some I will see again for sure, some I already did, and others I will stay in distant contact with. And these experiences will stay with me for the remainder of my days, some of them great, some not, but all enduringly **memorable**. Here is part of an e-mail I sent to some of the Americans I met in Khost.

Afghan police officer,
Maiwand, Kandahar
province. February 2008.

I know, having embedded a lot and at times having been as welcome as a 'fart in a Humvee', as a Marine Colonel jokingly put it, that you guys might be a bit wary about what I wanted to extract from this as a writer and reporter. I can only say that I have written up our few days as honestly as I could. It was a moment of truth for me as well, as we got through Oct 2/3 all right, and I am so happy to hear of many of you going on to make careers in other areas. Of all my embeds, the one with 2-506th was the most real and the most lasting in its associations, because I could live the regular platoon life for a few weeks and found myself in a situation where all of us thought 'OK, we may well be screwed but in this moment we are all here and alive and ready.' I had many embedding experiences, bumpy and boring, but OP5, Qalandar, Narisah COP and just Mandozai life was special. I really appreciated how you all looked out for me and how fortune smiled on us.

Occasionally I get urges to return at length to Afghanistan and may still do so. One thought that entered my head once home was, *What if nothing is that good ever again?* Perhaps you really do have to have been there and come out OK apart from fluffy hearing to appreciate where that came from. My fortune is to leave and have that choice to go back. I feel bad for the millions who don't, who live day for day, keeping their heads down and saying nothing that can bring them harm, hoping and praying their family remains unscathed by the violence.

Then again, I've seen farmers calmly walking between the conflicting sides as if the shooting and shelling has nothing to do with them, presumably sustained by the belief that if Allah wants you, he'll take you. Religious fatalism aside, what terrible damage must have happened to people's lives and minds that they will send their kids trotting off to school during a fire fight, as I witnessed in the Korengal Valley?

Every step back from the war brings distance and a change in perspective. It starts with you rising in a helicopter over hills or fields that hours before boiled with shellbursts and machine-gun fire, and then you hit that magi-cal height where the huge, gaunt beauty of the landscape swallows everything.

This was brought home to me in conversation with two Russian civil aviation pilots who delivered cargo to bases across Helmand, their helicopter being rerouted if there was any trouble in their drop zone.

'How is it down there, are there fire fights and ambushes and things? It all looks so peaceful from above,' one asked, oblivious to the slaughter below.

That shift in perception grows severalfold by the time you get back to the West, where events pass through the media filter for domestic consumption. The day's top Afghanistan story becomes 'Taliban shoots at Ant and Dec and misses', when a visit to Kandahar Airfield by the two British television presenters was incidentally punctuated by rockets that landed far away ('We couldn't believe how close we were to being hit').

ISAF becomes NATO for the home audience, or the fact that this is a broad, multinational effort is in danger of getting lost altogether, in Britain at least. The conflict is sucked through a Ross Kemp-tinted prism of battle footage of 'our boys', and the endless scandals and political bickering about the (mis)management of the Afghan campaign.

But some people still ask me intelligently about the differences between national contingents. It's nothing I can ever answer in a neat, authoritative sound bite after paying only fleeting visits to many of them, but there are discernible traits.

Some countries are on the ISAF ticket out of solidarity, while their leaders at home stress that this is a reconstruction or peacekeeping mission rather than a fighting one. Some smaller NATO members eagerly seek to demonstrate their allegiance to the United States but at the same time must be highly cautious how and where they operate, and not get out of their depth – every KIA for them is a serious shock to the system. Some countries also cannot sustain the expense of an open-ended involvement so they review their Afghan mission year by year, while others sign up for longer periods and might extend annually thereafter.

You get the impression that ISAF Command doesn't know what to do with small contingents that arrive with numerous caveats limiting their use, so they get packed off to quieter parts of the country to play a supporting role to the lead nations. The effect of others is negligible and they basically just bolster the number of ISAF members on paper and help prevent this from being perceived as a primarily American and British war, thus fanning flames of jihad in the tribal lands. At the time of writing, Ireland's contribution was seven soldiers and an armoured car based at Kabul International Airport. And there were said to be more Austrian flags in ISAF HQ than the number of Vienna's military personnel serving in Afghanistan (two).

Larger troop contributors are cornerstones in an undertaking that showed more and more cracks with each fighting season since 2006. Even dedicated and battle-hardened countries like Britain were suffering heavy Afghanistan fatigue in the summer of 2009 as the death toll ratcheted its way past 200, and the Labour government was accused of scrimping on payouts to wounded troops and undersupplying helicopters and blast-proof vehicles.

In late July, when 22 British soldiers had already died that month, a snap poll by the *Independent* newspaper found that 52 per cent of respondents thought the troops should be withdrawn immediately.[37] According to a September poll conducted for *The Times,* 40 per cent of Britons wanted a timetable for the withdrawal of troops over the next year or longer, 29 wanted an immediate withdrawal, and only 28 per cent favoured staying 'until the job is done', whatever that means these days.[38] The government reacted by reiterating Britain's commitment to the fight despite the hardships, and drawing up plans to send hundreds more soldiers, bringing the total to around 9,500 by the end of 2009.

In a message marking the end of the Muslim holy month of Ramadan that September, Taliban leader Mullah Omar seized on the tensions and predicted another defeat of British forces in Afghanistan.

'We would like to point out that we fought against the British invaders for 80 years, from 1839 to 1919, and ultimately got independence,' Omar said in widely reported comments.[39] 'Today we have strong determination, military training and effective weapons. Furthermore,

we have preparedness for a long war, and the regional situation is in our favour.'

Whatever other tactics they use, the Taliban and their allies are banking on cumulative fatigue taking its toll on western societies as the casualties mount. It's all in line with the Pashtun saying that 'The West has all the watches and we have all the time.'

Or in military jargon, it's the 'Fourth Generation Warfare' cited by US General Barno, where the enemy seeks to win by bringing unbearable pressure on decision makers in foreign capitals, regardless of developments on the battlefield. In other words, there is a growing likelihood that this vast international effort will be defeated by our own political systems and values, economic crises and just public exhaustion at the sight of flag-draped coffins arriving from Afghanistan.

The sense of urgency was growing in US circles in the summer and autumn of 2009, even after thousands of extra troops became available for Afghanistan during the drawdown in Iraq.

In a report to President Obama, details of which were leaked to media in September, ISAF commander General Stanley McChrystal warned that without even more troops and a new strategy NATO would fail to defeat the Taliban. The western forces were too concerned with their own safety and too detached from the Afghan people, wrote the General, who was asking for up to 40,000 extra troops (he got 30,000 in the end) for the last big push of this war.

'Failure to gain the initiative and reverse insurgent momentum in the near-term (next 12 months) – while Afghan security capacity matures – risks an outcome where defeating the insurgency is no longer possible,' the report said. Not least of all, McChrystal deemed corruption in the Afghan government as big a threat as the Taliban, and said an observed 'crisis of confidence' among Afghans could attract many to the side of the insurgents. (President Obama dismissed McChrystal as ISAF chief in July 2010 after he and his staff made disparaging remarks about senior civilian officials in *Rolling Stone* magazine.)

The Hearts and Minds mantra is certainly sounding tired these days. More and more

Afghans are disillusioned with the notion of a Western-backed, supposedly democratic Afghan state that is in reality propped up by crooked officials who stuff their pockets and conspicuously favour their own tribes and factions. Mired in allegations of vote-rigging, Karzai's claimed first-round victory in the August 2009 elections can only have cemented this in the minds of millions, while weeks of wrangling over the validity of the result did nothing to help.

'The election is not only boring now but disgusting too,' an Afghan friend wrote from Kabul in September 2009. 'They are just wasting time so that the people finally say OK, fine, just tell us who the president is and leave us alone.'

Things only got worse the following April when Karzai accused Western officials and their embassies in Kabul of tampering with the elections results in a bid to weaken his government. But in the post-Cold War era the conflict is, as the 'politicians' in the *Kamp Holland* play noted, also about NATO's future.

'Defeat in Afghanistan could mean the end of NATO as an effective military alliance,' *The Times* wrote after it conducted its poll that autumn. The paper added that the general consensus among experts was that 'the Western mission probably has two to three years to get it right before the battle is lost'.[40]

While no doubt having watched NATO's growing hardships since 2006 with a good measure of schadenfreude, Russia became more cooperative, notably after the establishment in 2009 of new, lucrative US supply routes through its air space when the Taliban choked routes through Pakistan. Suddenly the Kremlin acquired serious leverage regarding its objections to Washington about NATO's inclusion of Georgia and Ukraine, or a US missile shield in Europe, plans for which were subsequently canned by Obama's administration. But apart from immediate gains, there was always the basic worry that a resurgent Islamic movement spearheaded by the Taliban could start digging into Russia's underbelly from Afghanistan after any hasty NATO departure.

'I can responsibly say that in the event of NATO's defeat in Afghanistan, fundamentalists who are inspired by this victory will set their eyes on the north,' Moscow's ambassador to the alliance, Dmitry Rogozin, said in 2009.

'First they will hit Tajikistan, then they will try to break into Uzbekistan … If things turn out badly, in about 10 years our boys will have to fight well-armed and well-organized Islamists somewhere in Kazakhstan,' he predicted.[41]

While addressing the Russia-NATO council in Brussels, Moscow's ambassador to Afghanistan until 2009, Zamir Kabulov, also urged the alliance to alter its tactics and strategy if it wanted to avoid disaster. Kabulov, who had always darkly maintained that NATO was making the same mistakes as the Soviets, finally warned in clear terms that continued negligence of the Afghans' national, religious and cultural traditions was the fatal error.

'If things carry on like this, it will be a complete defeat, military and political, and when this will happen is only a question of time,' he concluded.[42]

I personally believe the history books will one day observe that NATO's fortunes took a disastrous blow with Obama's announcement in late 2009 that a gradual drawdown of US forces in Afghanistan would start in mid-2011. While meant to placate objectors at home and furnish some sort of timetable, this can only have been hailed as a stride towards victory by Taliban minds, and, crucially, by many Afghans still sitting on the fence.

'This is all a war of perceptions,' General McChrystal said during a February 2010 visit to Istanbul with Secretary of Defense Gates. 'This is not a physical war in terms of how many people you kill or how much ground you capture, how many bridges you blow up. This is all in the minds of the participants.'[43]

That same month, the huge Operation Moshtarak launched by ISAF and Afghan forces against the insurgent stronghold of Marjah in Helmand showed that the Taliban were now embracing Sun Tzu's 'war of the flea'.

Despite the media's breathless pre-op billing of 'the largest battle since 2001', insurgent forces wisely avoided a head-on fight and instead saturated the area with IEDs, threw cells of fighters into the fray but mostly melted away and waited. They filtered back within a month, successfully intimidating locals under the noses of US forces and effectively undermining the much trumpeted Marjah reconstruction drive.

As this book was heading to print, ISAF and Afghan forces were mounting even bigger operations around Kandahar City in the summer of 2010. The likelihood was that the insurgent leadership would employ the same tactics to achieve the same result: vast sums of western money spent on massively publicised NATO drives that brought no big battles and rout of the enemy, followed by the Taliban's creeping return to 'cleared' areas once the commotion abated.

'Not a physical war in terms of how many people you kill,' notes the former ISAF chief. Eight years into the conflict, it had at least been widely recognized that killing farmboys only creates more fighters and sympathizers, confusing the war's origins (to catch bin Laden and destroy al-Qaeda after 9/11, remember?) while nudging the situation farther down a calamitous path if not to jihad, then to a broad-based Pashtun resistance movement.

Accordingly, the Pentagon and NATO state a key task as separating rank-and-file insurgents who can hear sense from the irreconcilable ideological hard core. It's a difference that is perhaps lost on many in the West who think 'surely a terrorist is a terrorist?'

'Some local Taliban are seen as bad boys, like for us old schoolmates who joined motorcycle gangs or became shoplifters,' said the Pashtu-language trained Danish intelligence officer Michael. 'People grew up with some of the guys, know they are doing nasty things like planting mines but think they are not so bad and just need to calm down a bit.'

Steve, the US civil affairs worker with the Zabul PRT with whom I shared the Baylough Bunk Room, added: 'To us he's a Taliban, and he is one, but to his family he is a breadwinner, goes out and earns $300 per month, it doesn't matter to them that he's fighting us – who are we to them anyway?'

That's where the cash incentive comes in. There is a strong case for continued efforts to eliminate top insurgent leaders with the concurrent use of 'economic levers'. Given the high level of cronyism and corruption in Afghanistan, this means winning over – buying off, if you like – key people and communities with projects, jobs and money, splitting the opposition and using the traditional local double-dealing to inch trouble spots away from the Taliban and towards a new thinking.

This doesn't have to mean an assault on people's faith or basic way of life, but certainly an uncompromising stance on issues that should be sacred to Christians and Muslims alike, that throwing acid on the faces of schoolgirls isn't on, and that providing education, employment, healthcare and nutrition for all should be our common duty. Then again, amid talk of economic levers, there is a local saying that 'You can't buy an Afghan, you can only rent him.'

As indicated by McChrystal's leaked report to Obama, a winning strategy remained vexingly elusive eight years into the conflict. Or maybe effective approaches were becoming clear, but as with a moving oil tanker it is impossible to quickly switch the course of ISAF and all the institutions behind it. Alternately, the international undertaking that was assembled in Afghanistan since 2001 is like an immense engine trying to engage with the local environment and population through a faulty clutch plate, and some smart mechanical intervention can still fix it.

Like everyone else, the ISAF commander stressed that the training of the Afghan National Army was paramount and that the target of expanding it to 134,000 troops by late 2011 should be brought forward a year. And the onus on providing security should gradually be passed to the ANA and Police.

But it's plain to anyone who has seen these in action that while they want to do a good job, they need several years yet to become a viable force – time the international community and the government in Kabul doesn't have. So if the United States, Britain and partners from 2011 start to say 'we helped create the Army and Police forces, now it's their responsibility', pack up and leave, it's nothing but a craven cop-out from the original pledges to assist post-Taliban Afghanistan. And the world should prepare to see the Afghan government forces be ground down as they were after the Soviets withdrew in 1989, and once more witness the country sink into horrific civil war that destabilizes the entire region.

Also in September 2009, McChrystal told his commanders to pull forces out of sparsely populated areas of high conflict with the

Left to right: US Army Staff Sgt. Aaron Bunting, U.S. Army Capt. Thomas Glynn, and US Naval Cmdr. Raymond Benedict meet with elders of Bar Kut Shomali village, May 11, 2010. Benedict was commander of the Nuristan Provincial Reconstruction Team, and Glynn and Bunting were assigned to the PRT. *US Air Force photo by Staff Sgt. Steven Doty*

Taliban and focus them on protecting major Afghan population centres. The Korengal Valley was just such a place. But while logical in the face of manpower shortages, the step sounded alarm bells.

'The changes, which amount to a retreat from some areas, have already begun to draw resistance from senior Afghan officials who worry that any pullback from Taliban-held territory will make the weak Afghan government appear even more powerless in the eyes of its people,' the *Washington Post* wrote.[44]

One friend in the US military also wrote to me voicing concerns at the developments.

'I think they are fighting the war wrong and soon it will be like Vietnam was, where the enemy controlled the countryside and we had the cities,' he said. 'Officers have not studied the history books well – we must take the fight to the enemy.'

So too continues the debate about the balance of 'kinetic and non-kinetic' means, of fighting and development. Generally it's recognized that the answer lies in a combination of combat forces and the builders and educators who come behind them, according to the much touted 'Clear-Hold-Build' strategy. However, judging from the US PRTs at least, which were half of the two dozen operating in Afghanistan in 2009, these too are still groping around for a clearly defined mode of operation.

One American who did 18 months with the PRT in two highly volatile southern provinces described the overall PRT structure as 'disfunctional'. American teams first train in the US and the ones he met there still finished their preparations with scant idea of what they had to do. The commander of a PRT is always a Navy or Air Force officer and its leadership will include representatives of USAID and the departments of State and Defence. It sounds a powerful line-up but the head of the table is still the commander and the results of that PRT will depend on his quality and the level of continuity: 'If the next commander decides he wants bicycle shops in each village, that's what happens,' he said.

At the same time, there are probably plenty of people who don't particularly want the war to end as they are doing very well out of it, from the military-industrial manufacturers and suppliers to contracted firms and drug traffickers.

What will become of Afghanistan's narcotics industry was scarcely clearer during writing. In view of vast revenues it brings to insurgents and by all accounts to bent government and security force officials, the poppies will keep being cultivated, regardless of the efforts of some NATO members to eradicate them or displace them with alternative crops. Some food for thought: Western countries decry the flood of Afghan hard drugs onto their markets. But rot in government and lack of a single international vision since 2001 meant vast fresh tracts of poppy were allowed to spring up across Afghanistan when they should have been instantly eradicated, before they became pillars of local economies.

A Canadian wrote on an internet discussion forum: 'Of course, they are all "Taliban" these days – which is kind of ironic: we paint a false picture of a single enemy "bad guy", but the "good guys", including NATO, have almost as many different agendas as the insurgents. Where's Hollywood when you need things simplified into black and white?'

Another pivotal reality is that without order in nuclear-armed Pakistan nothing much will get resolved in Afghanistan. But that country is still too internally fractured, troubled and corrupt, its tribal areas too wild, and its ruling class too absorbed by infighting and intrigues to count on any lasting stability there.

Attempts by Pakistan's US-backed government to forge truces and agreements with the Taliban in recent years failed every time. These were used by the insurgents as breathing spaces to consolidate and prepare new offences, either across the border into Afghanistan or within Pakistan.

This was best demonstrated in the Swat Valley in 2009, where Islamabad acceded to demands for Sharia law in exchange for guarantees that the militants would disarm. The Taliban consolidated their hold on Swat and then marched into the next district, just 100 kilometres from the capital. Eventually the Pakistani authorities quit dawdling and launched a major offensive to counter the threat.

While the frequently heard idea of talking to Taliban leaders might sound reasonable, it only is if you are dealing with reasonable people. It made an impression on me when during my first visit to Afghanistan in 2001 an Afghan intelligence officer said, 'What you in the West fail to realise is that the spirit of compromise is regarded as a weakness here.'

The more Karzai's government publicly favoured talks with the Taliban in recent times, the more victory must have beckoned to the insurgent leadership. No one should be surprised when they scoff at these overtures. Among many of the contingents I visited or whose troops I encountered, the 'Who's losing Afghanistan' debate often translated into anti-American sentiment, with frequent accusations that US troops are heavy handed and culturally insensitive.

'My opinion is that the Americans are not so interested in reconstruction as attention-grabbing headlines back home that they killed so many Taliban,' a Danish officer in Helmand said. 'They measure a good operation in how much ammunition they fired.'

On December 24, 2007, I attended a large Christmas gathering of Polish soldiers in a tent in Paktika to which a few US soldiers were invited to sample national delicacies like *kabanosy* smoked meat, pickled herrings and *borshcz* cabbage soup. When a pimply Pole called Marcin came up to me I braced for another of our baffling pidgin English-Polish exchanges. But this time he just nodded towards the allies and said, 'I don't like American soldiers – Iraq, Somalia, Iran, Afghanistan. I must go, Happy Christmas.'

But a lot of Americans feel they are bending over backwards to accommodate their more cautious partners, above all in the actual prosecution of the combat. And the rigorous 'fair play' dictates of ISAF only breed resentment among US troops under its command. (In 2010 there were also 20,000 troops under separate US command, mainly in eastern Afghanistan.)

'We could actually go out and fight the war in Iraq and we didn't have NATO breathing over our shoulder with all its rules,' an American infantryman in Khost complained to me. 'All we're doing here is waiting around to get killed, that's all this shit is.'

Beyond the fact that something must change fast and cardinally to stem the decline,

I saw no homogenous view across the ISAF armies of the outcome of this conflict, or even what it has to do with soldiers who get sent so far from home. Eventually you hear the full gamut, from the disillusioned to the unbendingly principled.

'Millions of people died so that I could enjoy the rights I have,' said Private James Chitwood, a 21-year-old SAW gunner from Vermont I met in Zabul in 2007. 'I see a lot of my friends living off what other people have done for them. I'm kind of buying my own freedom by being out here.'

'This is unwinnable. I know I should believe in victory but when I look at the problems here…What it will take is a new generation, time and money – this is also all extremely expensive,' a Lithuanian Major told me at KAF.

During a visit to Kabul in March 2010, I heard the best definition yet of the bleakest scenario from a German involved in his country's work in the north: 'We are rearranging the deckchairs on a sinking ship.'

Amid the incessant discussion of 'whither Afghanistan', how much the goal should be to change or modernise the Afghans themselves is a topic that crops up constantly.

'We should drop whisky and televisions all over the country, and computers so they can have the internet,' suggested one American, soldier, while commanders reassure locals that no one is trying to take over their lives.

'We have no interest in disrupting your village and will show as much respect toward you and your people as we can, forgive us if we make mistakes, we are learning about your culture all the time,' Lt. Col. Bourne told a village mullah in Maiwand. As he spoke, two villagers restrained and lashed to a tree a dribbling madman who was shuffling towards us brandishing a pickaxe.

Sometimes it seems the best that can be done is to lend a hand, shed a little light where there was once darkness and see what people do with it. And to try not to expect too much.

'Whether they like it or not, we are going to drag the Afghans kicking and screaming into the 17th century,' Captain Garner said to me on the eve of his death.

★ ★ ★

May 28, 2009. Helicopter landing zone, FOB Gardez, Paktya. While a soldier drives golf balls across the HLZ, a US Lieutenant, Private and a civilian contractor who served in the Vietnam war sit in the shade discussing Afghanistan.

'I don't think we can create a democracy here.'

'Maybe they don't need democracy.'

'This country's caught in a 15th or 16th century feudal system, you're not going to change that in 10 years. We're trying to set standards for people who have no standards.

'They do have standards, just not like ours.'

'What does freedom mean anyway – the right to make your own choice. Often they don't have that here. Most people aren't free, they'll grow up, live where they live, do what their fathers did, not move away from their village and live according to the rules of that small community. They don't hoard stuff for next year because they don't necessarily believe there is going to be a next year, they live day to day, week to week. And freedom is a slippery word anyway, freedom the way we live isn't free either, there are also boundaries and rules.'

'This thing is going to last decades, you'll see your own son enlist and come here. Most of these guys we are fighting have to die, retire or be bought off. We don't win wars by killing everybody. The Russians were much more brutal than us and they still couldn't pull it off. What we need to do is send these kids to college in the States by the thousands, let them come back and modernize.'

'We're just setting ourselves up to be frustrated, we're trying to make them like us – but do they even need to be like us?'

'Americans like victory, victory parades, final outcomes, but life here doesn't work like that. Most of their guys are fighting for tomorrow, when we leave someone's going to be in charge and they want to be on the right side. The thing is everybody's got a departure date here and everyone knows it. These guys are just going to wait it out.'

POSTSCRIPT

Dr Nina

Copenhagen, August 2009

It struck me that I was back in civilization when I stood in line at the register at the local food market and everyone was annoyed that they had to wait. I was just real happy to know that I would still be alive when I reached the end of the line. Being on a mission and facing danger makes it crystal clear what really matters in life. It isn't money but people, your kids, you friends, your loved ones. While I was laying down during attacks, not knowing if I was going to survive those next few minutes, I would reflect on my life and it wasn't at all the things I had done that frustrated me but all the things that I would still like to do before I kick the bucket, the unfulfilled dreams and the quests that are still to pursue.

I think that certain sounds will now always make me duck. Once I was walking along a busy road and a car backfired. Logically I knew I wasn't in danger but the sound made my reflexes kick in and I found myself on the ground. Needless to say, people look at you funnily when you get up.

I know that a lot of couples where children are involved have a hard time adjusting when the deployment ends. Often the mother has been the sole caregiver while the father is away so she has to provide both physical and emotional support to the kids in spite of her own fears. Then the soldier comes back tired from the deployment and she is ready to hand over everything to him and that is real hard and often a cause of tension between couples. Or just the fact that some girlfriends or boyfriends don't want to wait around. I know one platoon had a 'Wall of Shame' where they hung pictures of their loved ones when they got the 'Dear John' letter.

I myself had lived in an unhappy marriage for more years than I care to remember, but being on deployment made me realise that there was still a life worth living. It was a very hard decision but one that I am very happy to have taken. So it is not just us that get the Dear John letters, many of us who are deployed take such measures too. I was by no means the only one in that situation.

It is also a very easy way of life out there. All you have to do is your job, you get fed so no figuring out what you have to cook for tonight, and your clothes get washed. You spend less and earn more so financially you are also better off. It is a lifestyle that can become quite addictive and you do see soldiers who go on tour after tour after tour.

And it can actually feel quite lonely to be back. You have lived many months so close to so many people and many of them became

very close friends. The bond that you form is quite unique and very hard to describe to an outsider. You can tell family or friends something and they listen very interestedly the first time but you lose them on the second or third time around. What they don't understand is that you are reliving the things that you have experienced and it is a way for you to deal with it.

That is where the bond with the others comes in, because they will listen because they are reliving it too. Always.

Sergeant Major Dennis

Lelystad, Netherlands, October 2009

April 2006; 30 eighteen-year-old faces full of questions are staring at me. So there they are. The men that I go to Afghanistan with. I remember thinking that this was Mission Impossible, to create warriors out of these teenagers. But, after a year of basic infantry-training, I gained confidence it was possible to carry out missions with these boys. I promised myself I would bring them back alive, all of them. Some of their mothers knew me and I quietly promised them the same thing.

Then in March 2008 we deployed and our first task was to act as a QRF (Quick Reaction Force) and recover a vehicle that exploded on an IED. My boys had to recover some of the wounded guys' equipment with blood and puke on it. In just a couple of minutes the boys became men. Their faces didn't carry any questions any more. One month later, two guys from another platoon died in an IED attack. A Lieutenant and his driver. The driver was the best friend of my .50-cal gunner, they went to kindergarten together. That same evening we held a wake next to the bodies of our fallen mates. I looked my gunner in the eye for two hours as he stood like a statue next to the body of his dead friend. I will remember that face for the rest of my life.

Then, after five months of experiences like these, I landed on the airfield back home, kissed my wife, hugged my kids and stepped into the car. As we gained speed on the highway, I started to sweat a bit. We drove at 140km/h. During the mission, our maximum speed was 20km/h. I almost pissed my pants.

We went straight to our vacation address, a camping site where we own a small caravan. 'Did you kill anyone?' people asked. 'My beer is warm,' people complained. And as I passed them in the bar I saw them talking about me. Was it out of respect? Or was it something else? I didn't know, and I didn't care. The only thing I cared about was my men, and how they would reintegrate back into their old lives. At the medal parade, a couple of weeks later, some of their mothers came to me. 'Thank you for keeping your promise,' they said. It was one of the best feelings I ever had.

Now, a year later, when I see my guys I have chats with them about our tour in Afghanistan. Despite all the bad things they experienced they all want to go back. Why? Because it's the real deal. Because of the adrenalin. Because of the companionship. Because life is simple over there. Because they cannot explain it to their family and friends when they're back home. Because.

And me? I will go with them.

'Be Careful What You Wish For', Lt.Col. Paul Pitchfork

London, October 2009

I've been back from Afghanistan for 18 months now. Life has moved on, as it always does in the Army; I am now living in London, working as a staff officer in the Ministry of Defence. The distant 'boom' of the IED that nearly killed Major Leigh Roberts and his crew on 21st January 2008, or the bitter cold that nearly claimed the life of one of my soldiers in the mountains east of Lam, now seem a world away.

But I remember those days, and indeed most of the others during my seven months in southern Afghanistan, as if they were yesterday. I remember the heat and the cold, the exhaustion and the exhilaration, the fears and the camaraderie, the harsh enchanting beauty of the country and the sense of absolute purpose each day held. And I miss it. When my time came to leave Kandahar and return home, I said to several people that I would have willingly stayed in Afghanistan for another six months and I meant it. My tour had been a hugely enriching experience. I saw the best of soldiering and was incredibly lucky to avoid the worst; all my men came home and the

Battalion lost only one of its own – Major Lex Roberts, a fellow company commander, whose coffin I bore on my shoulder.

I have watched a bloody and tragic summer unfold in Helmand over the last four months. The scale of the British casualties has shocked even those of us who know the dangers of Afghanistan first hand. Amongst the dead have been a friend and a Gurkha soldier I formally commanded – both true gentlemen, husbands and fathers. Anyone who has served in Afghanistan will feel some connection to every casualty: a friend of a friend; a soldier from a colleague's regiment; a familiarity with the place where the incident occurred; or simply being about to picture – to feel – the circumstances around the contact or the IED. But despite this familiarity and empathy, what I have observed this summer has felt very much like someone else's fight, a different war to that which I took part in. My tour was an adventure; theirs seems to me to be a hopeless lottery. For me, leading my men out on patrol, it was a matter of 'if' we took casualties. For those doing so now, it must be a case of 'when'.

My battalion will be returning to Afghanistan next spring without me and there is no reason to assume that their tour will be any less bloody than this summer. I fear for them – I have known many of them since I was a young officer 15 years ago and consider them dear friends – but I am jealous of them too. Despite the unprecedented tragedy that this summer's fighting has visited upon the Army and the country, the draw of Afghanistan is as strong for me as it was when I left Kandahar 18 months ago. Is it the soldiering that appeals, or the country and its people, or sharp definition that such endeavours give to life? I don't really know. Would it be worth the risk? Probably not. But this is the emotional paradox that has faced me since the day I left and I expect will remain with me for some time yet.

'Be careful what you wish for.' If there is one phase that captures the essence of a tour in Afghanistan, it is this. I heard it a hundred times, the veteran's response to our eagerness to get into the fight. I guess after seven months I should have graduated to being one of those sage veterans, offering this warning to those who followed. But instead, for now, I keep wishing.

'A formidable enemy', Captain Shane Oravsky

United States, January 2010

This was my first deployment and I had the fortune to be a platoon leader for its entirety. With this, I experienced a number of encounters with the enemy and each encounter was unique in its own way.

The terms and conditions for engagement always seemed to be up to the Taliban. They were patient as well as experienced in their tactics. My platoon was in Khost Province, home to the infamous Haqqani network. On July 20, 2008 I experienced the largest engagement of my 12 months in Afghanistan.

Once again, the Taliban waited until they had the distinct advantage. Approximately 150 of them massed and wreaked havoc on our 17-man platoon on a small mountain pass leading into one of our districts we were responsible for. The complex ambush stretched approximately six kilometres and the enemy held key terrain above our convoy on both sides of the mountain pass. The RPG, recoilless rifle, PKM, and small arms fire were incredibly overwhelming, raining down on my convoy.

I was especially surprised at the accuracy of the fire hitting the same areas on all four of our trucks. They seemed to favor RPGs through the back hatch of the Humvees and the wheel wells. Furthermore, they looked to dismantle our lead vehicle at a natural choke point in the pass, leaving us nowhere to go when they initiated the contact, also demonstrating their tactical soundness.

On this day, the enemy was waiting for us. They had scouts to notify them of our location through the various towns, wadis, and check points of our three-hour journey to the location. There was also a suspected leak in the interpreter network, since locals said the enemy cleared the area of women and children and test-fired their weapons the day before while they were waiting for us. Unfortunately we were unable to bring everyone back from this patrol, however I had great experienced NCOs, Staff Sgt. David McNeil and Sergeant John Yeager, whose bravery and expertise minimized our casualties.

A few weeks after this incident we conducted an air assault mission to dismantle the

training camp that conducted this ambush. To be honest, it would be extremely hard to positively identify this as a training camp from an aerial view. There was a bunch of lean-tos, tents, and trash scattered throughout the mountainside. At one of the sites there was an especially large tent with a huge homemade antenna. Alongside that was a crater from one of the 2,000-pound bombs dropped in support of us while we were waiting for reinforcements during the night after the ambush. It looked as though it had fallen on a cave complex of some sort.

Everything from these camps to the Taliban's fighting positions blended perfectly into the side of the steep slopes, nestled under trees and dug stealthily into the mountain. I remember thinking to myself the damned trees were shooting back at me because I had a hard time at first seeing the enemy.

It occurred to me during various moments in Khost that a majority of the positions we were attacked from were also probably utilized by Jalaluddin Haqqani himself against the Soviets. I have to reiterate that the enemy never attacked us unless they had the clear advantage from the high ground. Every ambush or attack, some larger than others, either occurred from another ridge line if we were dismounted in the mountains on multi-day missions, or from the high ground. The enemy also favored having men on both sides of the high ground shooting down at you from key terrain.

I remember trying to prepare for this whole experience of combat prior to deploying with my unit. However, nothing can truly prepare you for being the prey.

My memory of fighting the Taliban consists of our Platoon's biggest engagements in Qalandar and along the Pakistani border, and the friends I networked throughout Khost along the way. I miss my dear friend Arafat, and his crew of Afghan Police from the Shembowat Check Point, who essentially became a member of my platoon during the deployment.

I am now a Captain and training to become a Green Beret. The prospect of returning to Afghanistan gives me hope of working with people like Arafat in Special Forces. Moreover, my deployment to Khost better prepared me to understand the Taliban and the culture of the Pashtun people in eastern Afghanistan. I respect the enemy's tactical ability and I will never underestimate their combat power after our harshest encounters and my hardest lessons to date in life.

Jaan, machine-gunner's assistant, Estonian Contingent

Estonia, October 2009

It was a regular day in June 2009, we were out doing a patrol a few hundred metres from base and, as usual, Second Platoon got into contact with the enemy and our platoon was sent to help them. After the enemy were pushed back we started to move back to Pimon, the fields were burning and you could still hear small arms fire in the background. Then suddenly a British fighter plane flew by and destroyed an enemy compound. We all shouted a satisfied 'yehaaaaa' and things like 'get some you motherf★★★s', just happy that we stayed alive and they didn't.

Our patrol then took regular formation and continued to move back to Pimon. I was second from last and my friend the gunner was the last man. When we next stopped we started to argue, I wanted to put him last in

case we took enemy fire from behind but he wanted to take my place and he won the argument. And off we moved again, everyone covering their own direction, he and I talking about food and what we'd cook up when we got back. Approximately 300 metres from base half of our section turned into a compound and I was thinking 'OK, almost done for today' when my friend turned around and said 'Jaan …', only to be cut short by a big explosion and a load of flying stones and dust and a massive blast wave that swept me off my feet.

I remember clenching my teeth with a whistling in my ears, unable to breathe, and when I stood up and tried to run I fainted; this happened a few times before someone dragged me into the nearby bushes. I sat and pointed my rifle all around me until I remembered that my friend was somewhere in front so I stood up and ran back to where we'd been. Halfway there I started to hear screaming, it was him, he had been badly injured by the IED blast and needed to be taken to hospital fast. Thank God the medical chopper arrived as soon as it did.

That same evening we were both lying in Camp Bastion Hospital, my head full of thoughts about how close I had come to death or getting wounded, what if I hadn't changed places with him, why I let him take my place in the formation, what if it had happened to me, what if ,what if..? I didn`t know what to think or do, I was backed into a corner by all these thoughts with no way out, it was horrible. In the evening I asked the nurse to see my friend and drove my wheelchair to his ward. Another nurse standing by his bed asked me to speak to him although right at that moment I had no idea what to say, all I wanted was for him to stay alive. So I told him, 'Hey, it`s me, Jaan, we survived, I don't know if you can hear me but we will come through this, together, I promise. We survived and nothing will change this, I will meet you back in England, we promised each other we'd stay alive, so stay alive, please stay alive.'

I remember this British officer who helped roll me out in my wheelchair for a smoke. He told me that he had a family back in England and he missed them a lot, but here in Afghanistan we have a duty and a soldier never knows what will happen the next day,

so we have to be strong because of our comrades and because of our family back home. He really gave me strength, that officer, I will never forget him. About a month or six weeks later I heard that he and another British soldier had been killed in an IED blast. R.I.P. fellows.

That evening in the Camp Bastion hospital I understood that there is a reason for everything, always a sense to it, and for me it was my family. After two days my friend was flown to England for treatment, and I followed two weeks later and went from there back to Estonia. Halfway on that journey I got a call from Estonia saying that my section commander Allain Tikko had been killed in an RPG attack and some more guys were wounded, so they were minus five in our section already. He was the best section commander I ever knew, the best in our company. R.I.P. my friend.

When I got that call I was queuing at check-in at Heathrow airport in England. I put my bag on the ground and looked around me; people were going about their business and it was just too noisy, too much, I wanted to stop everything and rewind the tape to before all this happened. It was a turning point in my life, feeling so alone among so many people, like

I was from another world, unable to understand what was going on around me. So I just stood there, hung my head and looked at the ground, aware of people looking at me as they passed by. I don`t know why they did it but I felt it nonetheless, and I felt like a specimen, an example of the war. I never thought something like that could happen to me, I always thought I was strong and could take anything but in that moment I found I couldn't. Then I remembered that I have a family waiting for me at home and I'm alive, and that this was the main thing.

When I go to shopping malls and other crowded places now in Estonia or just walk in the streets I still can't understand why people are so busy or get so agitated. There's no need, no chance of you being blown up by an IED or shot by enemy fire, so just calm down and enjoy your life. But I still jump if the door slams or one of my mates punches me on the shoulder. Once I was having a smoke with a group of friends and some fireworks went off outside. I leapt from my chair and asked 'Who's shooting?' They all looked at me, some laughed, others seemed to understand. And sometimes when I walk outside and the road isn't paved I avoid spots that seem different from the surrounding ground, still afraid to step on an IED. I find myself getting very nervous very quickly in different situations, then I remember that there is a reason for me being alive and being here with my family and friends, and I should never forget it.

I feel most comfortable when I'm with guys I served with or others who have been to Afghanistan or Iraq; we always find our own theme of conversation straight away. We call each other every week and are really concerned if any of us have any problems. We are like family, even now. And when I'm looking at the guys who are missing legs or were more badly wounded than I was it always helps me to go further and carry on with my life, for they are the really strong soldiers. And even if we don`t wear a uniform or carry a weapon we are still brothers, brothers in arms.

Sometimes people ask me if I want to go back to Afghanistan and I answer yes. I think about it every day but I can never be sure if I will be so lucky next time, whether my guardian angel will be so close to me. You never know. But I still visit Afghanistan in my dreams. The guys who don't have legs any more or who are dead are with me, we are still all moving in formation and we are happy like brothers should be. This is my dream, no-one can take it away from me, and I will keep it with me as long as I live, my little secret.

Corporal Genevieve Dureau, 1 Field Ambulance, Canadian Armed Forces

Quebec, May 2010

Upon my return from Afghanistan in May 2010 I visited my parents in Gatineau, Quebec and took time to reflect on my experience. I deployed for this second tour after having been home for only one year following my previous deployment. As many other veterans have said, you usually get bombarded with questions about your time there. I find that I get asked the same questions, which are usually pretty fitting in my case, considering that I am a medic.

The most asked questions go a little like this: 'Have you seen lots of things over there?', 'Have you lost any friends?'. I find that people don't come out and say exactly what they want to ask; maybe that's because they are a little afraid of the answer that you are going to give them. Even though they really want to know, some people, especially the ones that have never experienced anything like it, are afraid of making you re-live your experiences. With everything I have seen, I still consider myself as one of the lucky few medics that have not had to work on any of their comrades.

During my two deployments, I worked in two completely different environments. My first, in 2008, was spent patrolling with a platoon from the Provincial Reconstruction Team, and the other was spent working with the Commander of the Battle Group. But on both occasions my experiences were similar. When on patrol, the reaction of the population was always the same. The men would just stare at me and the kids would crowd around me wanting to shake my hand over and over again. Being the kind of person I am, I would go out of my way to shake the hands of the young girls too timid to come forward. It was very rewarding to see their smiling faces when

I walked away. When I shook the hands of the young boys, I would always wonder about whether these boys were going to grow up to become part of the Taliban, or if their fathers or uncles were the ones who planted the Improvised Explosive Devices that we found on previous patrols.

Even though you ask yourself these questions, you can't help but think that these kids are unbelievable. They have next to nothing, compared to our standards, but they still seem happy, they just seem like regular kids, running around playing with each other, big smiles on their faces. On the other hand, I found it hard to see these same kids, who are barely old enough to take care of themselves, carrying huge bundles of provisions or caring for their baby brother or sister without any difficulty. Every time I walked away from them, I always wondered if they were going to grow up and be able to live their lives without constant war. I just wish for them to have the chance to grow up and have a better life.

As most soldiers who have served in a war-torn country, I have also lost friends in Afghanistan. This is not an easy thing to live through, especially while you are still over there and have a job to do. From my experience, you somewhat deal with it when it happens, but you have to push it to the back of your mind, otherwise you might not be able to

keep going. Only when you come home can you really start to come to terms with the loss and deal with it; and if you are lucky, you will be surrounded by family and friends to help you through it.

When I return to my unit in Edmonton, I will continue medical training both on base and in the field to ensure my medical skills are kept at a high standard so that if re-deployment is necessary I will be ready. Even if the thought of returning to Afghanistan so soon is not my first option, it is not to say I would not return, to serve my country, in the future.

Nickayla Myers-Garner,
Widow of Captain Mark Garner

Hohenfels, Germany, December 2009

Mark and I had discussed the possibility of his being killed in combat. Besides, given his line of duty, death was something that needed to be discussed. Deployments were normal in our lives – this was going to be his third. I am a planner and list maker, so as we relaxed in bed, I encouraged him to talk about his wishes for his funeral. My thoughts were that we all are going to die some time. I hoped to use the info in fifty years, not in a few months. And besides, if we were prepared, of course it wouldn't happen to us. We were both twenty-nine. He felt uncomfortable with the conversation, but there was some playful, witty humor to lighten the tension. We laughed. I cried …

This strong, healthy, intelligent, attractive man, who had so much energy and zest for life, planned his funeral. He wanted Bist Du Bei Mir and Pie Jesu sung; the 2-508th PIR that he served with on two tours in Iraq to be his honor guard; a scholarship established in his name to help students be more educated and see the world like he had (Mark visited 52 countries, most of which he drove to); he wanted me to wear a black hat like I had at his West Point graduation and officer commissioning; he wanted to be buried at home in Elkin, not at West Point or the National Cemetery, so it would be easier for his family to visit him; he wanted a closed casket regardless of his injuries – the list went on and on. I asked, 'What will the Army do to help me? What will I do…?' I had shaped my life and career around his career to support what we both felt was important; the ideals of a free nation and the protection of our families and citizens. Mark assured me that the US Army would take care of me. He wanted me to take a year to stay in our community in Germany where I could be surrounded by friends and have a stable environment to help me rebuild my life and develop new goals without him.

I hid notes of love and encouragement in every crevice of his bag for him to find later. I fixed dinner and waited for him to get home. He ate and went to bed for a nap. We woke up at midnight. Mark was exhausted from predeployment training and responsibilities of a commander who was only days before getting new soldiers as well as dealing with exorbitant amounts of paperwork and pressure from his commanders, the lack of resources such as motormen, and soldiers needing eyeglasses. Many thoughts were going through his head. He was not himself. I was sensitive to the stress he felt. We cuddled. We talked. We made love. He got ready. The time was ticking. I drove him to post. We had a photo taken together. We said goodbye in the bitter Bavarian cold of January. I handed him letters and told him what songs to play on his iPod as he read them. He smiled at me and held me tight. We let go. I wept the entire drive home and the entire night.

The handwritten letters began to come again, like the hundreds I had gotten from his two previous deployments. His letters talked about food he wanted me to mail him, trips we were going to take, frustrations of war, cultural differences and respect for the Afghans, how proud he was of the men he was serving with, places to see, his love for me, and then, what to do with my life if he were to be killed. In typical Mark fashion, he expressed his wishes that I continue traveling to new and exciting places as we loved to do together, start dating and experience life to the fullest, do the things I had always dreamed of. These were very difficult letters to read, but written with so much selflessness, passion, and humor…they were just like him.

I thought we were as prepared as we could be. I knew his wishes. Our affairs were in order. I played the scenario over in my head. We had a plan. Everything would be OK.

He deployed as the sole company commander from his battalion. There were about 180 soldiers spread between four different bases. He constantly moved from place to place. He enjoyed being with the soldiers. He lived in fear that he would make a decision that would get one of his soldiers or innocent civilians killed. He stated that he would rather die than to lose one of his guys. He lost sleep over his concerns. His wish became reality.

Around 0415 on July 6, 2009, I woke up with a pounding headache and an upset stomach. I decided to stay home from work. I would learn later that at the same moment I was sick, Mark was being killed by a Taliban placed Improvised Explosive Device in the Deh Chopan district of Zabul Province, Afghanistan. His blood was spilled upon the Afghan soil in service of his nation. Twelve hours later there was a knock on my door. Two of Mark's fellow officers were standing at my doorway. I quickly said hello in a 'surprised to see you' kind of way, and then I realised they were wearing the dreaded Army Class A uniform (a sign of trouble and pain to any Army spouse when it is at his or her front door). Being a hospitable Southern gal, I invited them into my living room. I was told of the loss of the person whom I adored and loved more than anything, my husband, CPT Mark A. Garner. It is at this time that my life began to spin and tumble … but we had a plan.

I have had many titles in life: Daughter, sister, friend, wife, war bride, student, farm girl, teacher, writer, traveler, but it is that moment on the sixth of July that I assumed my newest and most difficult title of all: war widow.

The questions began. Should I call Mark's family or let the notification team tell them in person hours later? Would they learn from someone online or the news media? What to do? How do I tell his mother that her only son was killed? I called Mark's parents' home. I got his mother. I told her Mark was killed. She whispered, 'No, no, not my baby.' That was the hardest thing I have ever done. I was alone. I started calling family and friends. My house began to fill with people. The phone and doorbell rang and rang and rang. My parents and oldest brother flew from NC and Singapore and were with me in less than 24 hours. My middle brother stayed home to run the farm.

I didn't sleep for days. I wailed and cried. My eyes were swollen and burning. I wasn't hungry. No one would give me answers. I kept having vivid images of Mark hurt and suffering in my head. There were so many possibilities and no answers. No one could definitively tell me if he was killed instantly or not…all speculation. Was he in pain? Did he know what had happened? What were his injuries? There were no details until over a month later when I got a letter from a commander of his downrange. I am sitting asking, where are the people who Mark said would come from the Army to help me?

I went into 'business mode' on my own. I started implementing the funeral Mark had planned. The paperwork started and has not stopped. People were in my personal space and business. This was hard for me as a strong independent person. Then I was given news that came like a smack in the face. I was told that I had to leave my Army accommodation in 90 short days. To leave my community, my friends, my job, my support network, my home, everything I know, to find a new home, new community, new friends, new support group, and a new life without my best friend, lover and husband all the while developing new life goals that no longer involve Mark and his career. I felt as if I had been stabbed in the back. Mark trusted that the Army and our nation would help me have stability to transition into a new life, but all in 90 days? Grief counselors are saying not to make a major life decision within a year of a tragedy. I am being told by the Army to make almost all life decisions within three short months, of which three weeks were devoted to acquiring my husband's remains, burying him and returning to my home. Unrealistic and unethical!

I now feel that I have a scarlet letter on me that is a 'W' for widow. Many people avoid me as if I am contagious. I have always been friendly and happy, and now because I have a dead husband, all of a sudden I am to be avoided. Soldiers and people who were friends avoid me. I think they are uncomfortable and feel guilty. They shouldn't be. I am still friendly and accepting Nickayla. The pain continues and gets deeper. It feels as if being a War Widow is a disease and many people are scared that if they talk to me they will catch it. This is their cross to bear, not mine. Why should I be pushed out because other people are not handling their fears?

My life was a gorgeous design in the bottom of a kaleidoscope tube. Just one turn made all the pieces spin. Our plans are what helped me through this spinning kaleidoscope as a War Widow. I know there will be a pretty design at the end of the kaleidoscope tube some day, but it is just difficult getting through the turns as the pieces of my life jumble and fall. They will begin to fall into place; however one major piece is missing, called Mark Garner. My life will be beautiful again. Mark wanted it to be and knew it would be. I know it will be.

I have been asked, 'Do you harbor anger towards the Taliban for what they have done to your husband?' My answer: I am angry and sad about the loss of the man I adored more than anything, but I also respect other beliefs. They are fighting for something in which they believe, much like Mark was fighting for that in which he believed. I respect that. Does it make what they are doing right? No.

[Since the loss of her husband, Nickayla Myers-Garner has travelled extensively, and been volunteering and running classes for military couples to prepare for a casualty.]

I just hope people can be informed and can prepare the way Mark and I did. The preparation helped initially and especially as I transition into a new life without Mark.

Captain Alexander Bourne, 1st Battalion Welsh Guards

London, October 2009

March 2009 – I knew where Estonia was on the map, I knew Estonians were not very religious and I knew that the Russians had turned off Estonia's internet for three days in protest at the removal of a Red Army war memorial a few years back, but that was about it. Estonia seemed a distant and far off land, one that I had never considered visiting and one that I never thought I would have a lot to do with. That was until my Commanding Officer at the time, the late Lt. Col. Rupert Thorneloe MBE, called me back from an attachment with the Household Cavalry and told me that I was to be his liaison officer to an Estonian mechanized infantry company attached to the Welsh Guards Battle Group.

The prospect was an exciting one: six months in Afghanistan with a band of foreign soldiers who I had heard were not particularly interested in withdrawing from a fight and had built up something of a fearsome reputation with previous British battle groups that they had served in. I set to work. Straight down to Waterstones on Piccadilly to pick up a Baltic phrasebook (no Estonian ones – too obscure) and then cosied up to a lap top for an evening of Wikipedia to learn something about the

people I was soon to join on operations in Helmand Province.

Fast forward a month and I am now in the familiar surroundings of Camp Bastion, Helmand Province. I had gone ahead of the Estonian Company to get my operational bearings and help prepare some in-theatre training. I remember wandering the grid system of roads in Bastion musing over the prospect of being with the Eesti boys for six months. I had only spent ten days with them in Estonia and most of that time was at a distance, I still spoke very little of the language after an abortive attempt at learning it (completely impenetrable, by the way) and Nad-e-Ali where we were to be based had really hotted up – that day a good friend and brother officer had been brought into Bastion from his patrol base with a gun shot wound which he would not survive. I was apprehensive.

It's all over now. I'm back and the Company has got less than a month to go in Afghanistan. Three Estonians won't be coming home and several more have life-changing injuries. Looking back I still find it all hard to understand. I remember the first casualty we took suffered five gun shot wounds to the body and head. I remember ANA warriors covering the move of an Estonian platoon with their casualty back to their patrol base, whilst British signalers called for an American helicopter to get him back to Bastion field hospital, a British, Danish and American venture. I remember Estonian medics keeping us informed of his progress in hospital after he had been moved back to the UK for treatment. I remember the look of horror on his platoon commander's face when he came back in and the fear for his well-being that we all shared, regardless of nationality or creed. A fellow soldier had been hurt badly and we did not know whether he would survive.

In the aftermath that evening I reflected on what had gone on. People had risked their lives to give someone the chance to continue his. They didn't know him: the warrior from Herat, the signaler from Bridgend, the pilot from Kentucky or the doctor from Copenhagen. However, they were brought together in adversity by something that international boundaries and treaties can't describe: the duty and honor that leads a man to help his comrade in trouble.

I think it is something our enemies understand as well as we do. When the chips are down we forget our differences and help each other, potentially leading to one giving his life for another to have a chance to lead his own. Mankind has that ability – that is why I can't understand why we are there in the first place.

Qari Abdul Razaq Hanifi, Mid-level Taliban commander

Afghanistan, July 2010

I studied the Holy Koran in the Akora Khattak area of Pakistan in 1994 and then joined the Taliban's ranks because the jihadi commanders were oppressing the people of Afghanistan. There was no power to stop them and the common people's dignity, lives and property were all lost to war. When the Taliban rose up to eliminate these corrupt people and their regime and bring Islamic order, I joined them. I served in the movement as a foot soldier and as a field commander after that.

When the Americans invaded Afghanistan (in 2001) I was working as a mullah for my village mosque and I continued there for three years. Then I contacted my leaders and after consulting with them I began jihad and I have been serving ever since. Since the US invasion I have fought in Logar, Wardak, Ghazni, Uruzgan, Helmand, Zabul and Paktika provinces. I now command 60 fighters but when needed I am given responsibility for between 100 to 200 fighters.

I serve with the Taliban now because my country is occupied by Christians and Jews. I fight for Allah to safeguard the independence of my country and to bring Islamic order here and to implement the orders of Allah as written in the Holy Koran. Like my forefathers I will force the enemies of my country to their knees and will revive the history of the Afghans.

The Taliban's tactics are not exactly the same as the tactics of the mujahedin in the fight against the Soviet forces. Some are the same but others are different, although no one tells anyone about their military tactics, this would be an act of great stupidity. But some of our tactics are known, such as roadside bombs and attacks on main targets and bases with suicide bombers. We fight ISAF forces with our foot-soldiers and the bombs that we make. We have killed a lot of foreigners with these roadside bombs, or they were burned inside their tanks. When ISAF forces come to our area we are very happy - we can fight them much better than we can fight with Afghan forces. ISAF have everything but we have Allah, and that is why we are always the victors.

The foreigners are cowards. They don't have any motivation to fight. They rely heavily on the use of air strikes and heavy artillery. If they don't have this power they can't stand against Taliban fighters on the ground. They are such cowards that when we fight them and they are under pressure they open fire on civilians and kill them. The foreigners have been completely defeated in ground fighting. When they come on foot or in their tanks we plant whole roads with IEDs and turn the daylight into dark night for them. Nor are they any better at air strikes, not even these harm us. Their bombing only kills civilians and when this happens the residents of that area all begin supporting the Taliban and take up the jihad against the Americans. We have all the necessary support and equipment and are not lacking in anything. Whatever we want we can get wherever we are, from weapons to more fighters. We now have so many fighters that we don't know how to organize them all.

My life is full of memories but my best memory of this nine-year war is how some three and a half years ago the Taliban from Wardak, Logar and Ghazni held a meeting and decided to close down the Kabul-Kandahar highway in Wardak and Ghazni provinces so that our enemies were not able to transport their logistics supplies on the road for one week. Then we torched 60 trucks that were carrying supplies and food to the Americans and seized 15 other trucks and that really solved our problems. We were very happy to see the scene of the attack on TV that night and felt this to be a great victory. We could not fit in our clothes from happiness when we saw the report.

Both the Russians and the US forces came to occupy Afghanistan with their own objectives. The Russians wanted to reach warm waters via Afghanistan's soil and bring the region's countries under their control. But with the help of Allah, the Afghan people gave them such a lesson that they would no longer look at any other country with bad eyes. The Western and American forces of today have also invaded our country. As you see, they disrespect the Afghans' sacred values. This invasion is even more shameful than the invasion of the Russians, because they eliminate human beings in the name of humanity. They kill women, men, and children and then identify them as Taliban. They occupy free countries and loot their mines in the name of assisting that country. But they will face the same fate as the Russians faced.

We are successful in our struggle and success will ultimately fall to the Taliban and the Afghan people, because the Taliban have motivation for this war, which is to wage jihad and free the country. We also know the terrain here while the foreign forces do not. They have invaded our country; they strip our mines and kill our Islamic scholars. They bomb our wedding parties, they bomb our funerals and they don't leave us to have happiness. Therefore we call them invaders and regard jihad against them our obligation.

We do jihad to gain the consent of Allah, and our main objective is to have an Islamic government in Afghanistan and put Allah's orders in practice. We want to implement the orders of Allah's holy book. We want to force the Christians and Jews out of our country, and free it from the infidels' dirty hands. We will continue our jihad until the foreigners have left Afghanistan, and when they are gone we will finish other criminals like Dostum, Mohaqiq, Fahim and other so-called leaders who are now in Kabul. They are the enemies of Afghanistan and their hands are stained with the blood of the people.

We want an independent, Islamic Afghanistan that stands on its own feet. We don't have problem with the Western world. During the Taliban government we had a representative in the United States and had good relations with the West. And if this time with the help of Allah we throw these Jews out of our country, we will not only have good relations with the West but we will also have good political and economic relations with the rest of the world too.

Muslims are not aggressors. We do not oppose anyone's belief, we do not have problems with any country's freedom and we want the Westerners to learn this humanity, because we don't have any peculiar animosity towards them. 99 per cent of our people are Muslim. We have the same faith as Muslims in Palestine, Iraq or other parts of the world like Pakistan and Uzbekistan. Muslims, wherever they are, have one united idea. They have sympathies with each other based on Islamic principles. This unity will be there forever. Whenever the infidels invade an (Islamic) country and oppress its people, it is the obligation of all Muslims to go and help them, and this unity will be there forever.

I have four daughters and three sons who are engaged in Islamic studies. But I don't miss my family members. The whole of Afghanistan is my home and all Afghans are my family. If they are killed, detained or oppressed by foreigners, it means that it is my own family members who are in trouble. I sacrifice my life for the holy system of Allah and will continue my jihad until my last breath. We are very grateful to Allah because we are given the power to turn our enemies' lives into dark night. We can hear their crying all too well; sometimes they make a jirga for bringing peace, sometimes they talk about the extremist and moderate Taliban and sometimes they talk about removing names from the blacklist. All these things show that they are desperate and have lost their way. The fact is that they do not have the power to stand up against the forces of the Taliban and have already been defeated.

The Latest Figures

Almost $300 billion were spent on the Afghan war by the United States alone since 2001, and by the beginning of August 2010, the foreign forces had lost 1982 killed in action. Civilian deaths in the first half of 2010 (Afghanistan Rights Monitor counted 1,074 dead) caused by NATO action appeared to decrease, a drop attributed to the 'courageous restraint' policy towards use of force in populated areas instigated under former ISAF chief McChrystal. But increased IEDs still pushed the level of innocents killed above the 2009 tally.

In the information war, western officials must maintain that gains are being made despite the escalating violence; that Afghan security forces are steadily 'reaching maturity' and that however lamentable, human losses should not be allowed to obscure the bigger picture. Meanwhile, insurgent spokesmen cite rising public resentment of the misery, NATO casualties and closure of small bases in remote areas as harbingers of their enemy's looming defeat.

Notable events included the August 1 withdrawal of the last 250 Dutch soldiers of 1,950 deployed to Afghanistan. Despite the loss of 24 troops since 2006, Dutch military chief General Van Uhm said they 'achieved tangible results that the Netherlands can be proud of' and have trained 3,000 Afghan soldiers who he said were now able to independently carry out operations. A Taliban spokesman said the group wanted to 'wholeheartedly congratulate the citizens and government of the Netherlands' for pulling out and urged others to follow suit. NATO officials in Brussels insisted the rest of the military alliance remained solid and that the Dutch withdrawal had not spawned a chain reaction of other announcements about pull-outs. But Canada was still expected to withdraw its forces in 2011; Poland's 2,500 troops will leave in 2012, and the UK forces in 2014 or 2015.

NATO managed to squeeze some additional forces from its members, although always fewer than the generals wanted. Despite growing public opposition to the war at home, Germany's contingent grew by more than a third since 2008 to 4,660 troops, yet was struggling to contain the insurgency, notably in the province of Kunduz, as the notion of a 'stable north' continued to teeter. And even Austria boosted its presence by 50 per cent (to three people).

New kids on the ISAF block were soon to include an Armenian contribution, bringing the number of former Soviet republics with forces in Afghanistan to seven. The largest foreign presence naturally remained the United States, with more than 60,000 ISAF troops plus the separately commanded force of 20,000. Altogether, the number of international troops exceeded 140,000.

By province, Helmand and Kandahar were easily the most severely inflamed, and together accounted for more than 40 per cent of the international casualties since 2001. With a massive injection of US Marines into Helmand, control there was transferred from the British, but progress remained painfully slow.

As for the sliding authority and appeal of the Kabul government and their international backers, media stories proliferated about how locals in many areas are afraid to interact with ISAF for fear of retribution or just distaste, and often openly voiced a preference for the Taliban over the Afghan security forces and their government's writ.

Amid ongoing operations to clear trouble spots in Nad-e-Ali and around Kandahar City, the messy innards of the Afghanistan involvement were starkly revealed in July 2010 with the release by WikiLeaks and media publication of thousands of leaked US military reports. While mostly unsensational in their content, some of the so-called war logs suggest that many civilian casualties caused by both Taliban roadside bombs and NATO missions have gone unreported; that there is ever more evidence of Pakistani ISI support of the Taliban, and that the insurgents have had access to portable heat-seeking missiles to shoot at aircraft.

If nothing else, the reports seemed to confirm fears around the globe that the international effort in Afghanistan had lost its way in recent years. Put on the spot by the security breach, US officials noted that the logs only span until the end of 2009, to the start of President Obama's 'new strategy' in Afghanistan. But the leaks also made it more difficult for the Obama administration to persuade sceptics that changes to strategy can now make a difference.

At one end of the timeframe for achievement of results, as perceived by US officials after the disclosures, judgement of the Afghan mission should apparently be withheld until new initiatives have had time to work. At the other end, beyond the woeful inadequacies of the ANSF and like a vice being wound shut, came the decision reached by an international conference held in Kabul in July 2010 that Afghan government forces should take charge of all provinces by the end of 2014. This left just over four years, time that barely suffices for hosts of the World Cup to organize that event, let alone to achieve a turnaround in a country

that seems to evolve with only glacial speed and is mired in surging violence.

Those who wish to see how its desired development looks on paper should consult the 2008-2013 Afghan National Development Strategy (ANDS). Originally described by President Karzai as 'an Afghan-owned blueprint for the development of Afghanistan in all spheres of human endeavour', the document projects a vision for security, governance, economic growth and poverty reduction, and envisages that by 2020, 'Afghanistan will be a stable Islamic constitutional democracy at peace with itself and its neighbours'. Once pointed to by ISAF and Afghan officials as proof that everything will be OK, it's doubtful nowadays that the ANDS, much like the Buddha laser project for Bamyan, is even remotely in tune with realities. With Kabul itself approaching a state of effective lock-down, is it possible to achieve aims like providing '98 per cent of villages with access to safe drinking water by 2013'? Or in the light of the inability to build a few kilometres of road through the Korengal Valley, building – and preserving – in the same period a railway line linking Kabul, Kandahar and Herat?

Not that vast sums of money won't theoretically be available for such commendable projects: in addition to international donations received by the Afghan government, it was revealed in June 2010 that according to latest geological surveys, Afghanistan's soil holds roughly $1 trillion in mineral resources like iron, copper, cobalt, gold and lithium. The US Department of Defense promptly began to advise the Afghan government on how to formulate bids for companies to develop the deposits, and it seems NATO may place hopes on these mineral resources favourably determining the country's future. But given the level of rot in local government, even if that entire mineral wealth were cashed in tomorrow it's probably safe to say that plenty of Afghan villages will only be able to dream of safe drinking water in a decade.

After all, it could be like a British infantry major said to me in 2009: 'Maybe there is no solution, maybe with all the factors like corruption, Pakistan, the tribal areas, the border and so on, it's like three jigsaws shaken together in one bag and you'll never put it all together.'

END NOTES

Chapter Three – Southern Scorpion

1. http://www.mod.uk/DefenceInternet/
   DefenceNews/MilitaryOperations/
   MajorAlexisRobertsOfRgrKilledInAfghanistan.htm

Chapter Four – Nothing Personal

2. Remarks of Secretary of Defense Donald H. Rumsfeld at
   US National Press Club Luncheon, September 10, 2003.
3. 'Controlling the media in Iraq', Lindner, Andrew M.,
   Contexts, Volume 7, Number 2, April 2008, University of
   California Press.
4. 'Embedded = Censorship', NRC Handelsblad, January
   6, 2009.
5. http://www.globalsecurity.org/military/library/
   report/2008/
6. 'For Media After Iraq, A Case of Shell Shock', *Washington
   Post*, April 28 2003.
7. 'AP and Death of a Marine', http://www.ap.org/fallen_
   marine/ The Associated Press, September 4 2009.
8. http://afghanquest.com/ September 4 2009.
9. http://lens.blogs.nytimes.com/tag/don-mccullin/
   September 29 2009.

Chapter Five – Action And Reaction

10. http://www.mod.uk/DefenceInternet/
    DefenceNews/MilitaryOperations/
    MajorAlexisRobertsOfRgrKilledInAfghanistan.htm

Chapter Ten – Kamp Holland

11. Progress toward Security and Stability in Afghanistan,
    report to US Congress, January 2009.
12. NRC Handelsblad July 4 2008.
13. This and successive Defence Ministry polls are from
    http://www.defensie.nl/missies/afghanistan/actueel/
    monitor_publieke_opinie
14. de Volkskrant/Review/Arts & Culture/November 8 2008.

Chapter Fifteen – Khost and Pakistan

15. http://islamabad.usembassy.gov/pr-08091701.html
16. *Counterinsurgency in Afghanistan*, Seth G. Jones, Rand
    Corporation, 2008.
17. http://www.defense.gov/news/newsarticle.
    aspx?id=54393 May 18 2009.
18. http://news.bbc.co.uk/2/hi/south_asia/7636845.stm
19. http://democrats.senate.gov/newsroom/record.
    cfm?id=303496&
20. 'President Asif Ali Zardari: friendship with America is
    a blessing' http://www.timesonline.co.uk/tol/news/
    world/asia/article4833890.ece
21. 'We can't defeat Taleban, says Brigadier Mark Carleton-
    Smith', http://www.timesonline.co.uk/tol/news/
    world/asia/article4887927.ece

Chapter Sixteen – Buddha Bing

22. 'Afghanistan Makes Haste Slowly', Williams, Maynard
    Owen. *National Geographic* Magazine, December 1933.

Chapter Eighteen – Northern Lights to
Ghowrmach

23. *Limited Contingent*, Boris Gromov, Progress, 1994.
24. 'Minister Jung soll dicke Soldaten fit trimmen' *Der Spiegel*,
    March 4 2008.
25. The *Daily Telegraph*, December 3 2008.

Chapter Nineteen – Among the Afghans

26. Munich Security Conference, February 8, 2009, http://
    www.securityconference.de/General-David-H-
    Petraeus.211.0.html?&L=1
27. *The Hidden War: A Russian Journalist's Account of the Soviet
    War in Afghanistan*, Artem Borovik, Grove/Atlantic, 2001.
28. http://unama.unmissions.org/ July 31, 2009
29. http://www.mcclatchydc.com/2009/07/01/71134/
    troops-told-to-stop-taliban-pursuit.html July 1 2009.
30 Directive shown to author.
31 'Civilian deaths deeply shame US' http://news.bbc.
    co.uk/2/hi/south_asia/6636343.stm, May 8 2007.
32. Smierc pieknej armii, Gazeta Wyborcza, December 29
    2007.

Chapter Twenty-One – Pimon

33 *Koran, Kalashnikov and Laptop: The Neo-Taliban Insurgency
   in Afghanistan 2002-2007*, Antonio Giustozzi, Columbia
   University Press, 2008.
34 'Eesti saatis veebel Allain Tikko viimsele teekonnale'
   http://www.epl.ee/artikkel/471823, Eesti Päevaleht,
   June 20 2009.

Chapter Twenty-Two – IED War

35. www.jieddo.dod.mil

Chapter Twenty-Three – Baylough II

36. Provided by US 1-4th Infantry, Zabul.

Chapter Twenty-Four – Hurry Up and Wait

37. *The Independent*, July 28 2009.
38 *The Times*, September 10 2009.
39 CNN, September 21 2009.
40 'Vision of victory in Afghanistan - but time is on the
   Taleban's side', *The Times* September 21 2009.
41. 'Afghanistan Help Restores NATO-Russia Ties', *Time
    Magazine* Jan 27 2009.
42. http://en.afghanistan.ru/doc/91.html June 28 2008.
43. 'Top U.S. Commander Sees Progress in Afghanistan's
    side', The *New York Times*, February 4 2010.
44. 'U.S. Commanders Told to Shift Focus to More Populated
    Areas', *Washington Post*, September 21, 2009.

INDEX